METAL

DESIGN & TECHNIQUE

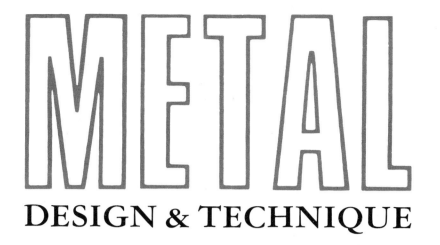

METAL
DESIGN & TECHNIQUE

Wilhelm Braun-Feldweg

Translated by
F. Bradley, F.R.P.S., A.I.I.P.

VAN NOSTRAND REINHOLD COMPANY
New York   Cincinnati   Toronto   London   Melbourne

Van Nostrand Reinhold Company Regional Offices:
New York Cincinnati Chicago Millbrae Dallas

Van Nostrand Reinhold Company International Offices:
London Toronto Melbourne

This book was originally published in German
under the title Metall—Werkformen und Arbeitsweisen
by Otto Maier Verlag, Ravensburg, 1968

Translated from the German by Fred Bradley, F.R.P.S., A.I.I.P.

Library of Congress Catalog Card Number: 74-14001
ISBN: 0–442–21039–6

This book is set in Garamond and
printed in Great Britain by
Jolly & Barber Ltd., Rugby, Warwickshire

Published in 1975 by Van Nostrand Reinhold Company Inc.,
450 West 33rd Street, New York N.Y. 10001

Library of Congress Cataloging in Publication Data

Braun-Feldweg, Wilhelm.
  Metal; design and technique.

  Translation of Metall; Werkformen und Arbeitsweisen.
  1. Art metal-work.   I. Title.
NK6404.B7213   739   74-14001
ISBN 0-442-21039-6

16 15 14 13 12 11 10 9 8 7 6 5 4 3 2 1

Contents

Preface

The first edition of this book was published shortly after the end of World War II, at a time when it was hardly possible in Germany to overcome the cultural isolation of that country. The title of the book was the same; it was, considering the general standards prevailing at the time, sumptuously produced; and, in spite of all the restrictions on communications and information, it contained many illustrations, mostly good ones. Some of these, above all of course those of historical examples, proved resistant to the passage of time and its criticism. They survived, untouched by the increasing violence and even greater frequency of the fluctuations of fashion. Others, because all too ephemeral, had to give way to something more up-to-date and—occasionally—better.

When the frequent demands for a new edition made new planning necessary, it had long been evident that the intellectual climate had radically changed. Not only had Scandinavian, British, and American designers and workshops entered upon the scene, but as protagonists of new ideas they had come to exert an influence even on developments on the continent of Europe—an influence that could no longer be ignored. This caused a shift of emphasis from the national to the international sphere, which constitutes the main difference between the new and the old version of the book.

For, strangely enough, only a few sections of the text were found to be out-of-date. The inexorable decay of the old crafts, the possible conservation and rediscovery of their potentialities through individual initiative, and lastly the emergence of new artistic activity in the industrial field—all these trends were already evident then in a way that has not called for any revision. This proof of a realistic assessment of the future opportunities of the crafts poses this question: What purpose can a book of practical instruction serve today?

Any answer to this question can only be personal; nevertheless, it can rally supporters of its claim that the achievements and quality of craftsmanship constitute an inestimable reservoir of creative forces even in this industrial day and age. This is what Jean Cocteau means when he says: "Not to support the crafts is a serious mistake" and "The crafts are France's last weapon". He calls the tapestry weavers of the Gobelin manufactures of Aubusson "The silent harpists playing to our eyes with the woollen yarn, with the shuttles, with the alertness of their spirit, with their glances, and with their fingers". Max Bill, obviously, expresses similar thoughts: ". . . do not let us forget that it is this unbroken tradition of craftsmanship which is an important guarantor of an unbroken development of the essence of our environment." Many an anaemic designer may smile at such opinions, regarding them as anachronistic and romantic into the bargain, and swear by the drawing board (and soon the drawing computer) as the only true interpreter of art. Like everybody else, he is entitled to his views.

Finally, a word about what not to expect of this book: It is not intended to serve the modern vandals who unscrupulously loot any treasure-house of historical design to market it in fashionable boutiques.

It is, lastly, my pleasant duty to thank all those who supported this book with contributions of articles and illustrations, by giving permission for reproduction, and by offering technical advice and co-operation. Their number is large, and it is not possible to mention all the artists, archaeologists, photographers, and craft practitioners by name. My thanks go out to all of them, not least to the staff of my own studio.

WILHELM BRAUN-FELDWEG

Introduction

A technical book cannot take the place of practical experience, many years of expertise, a craft apprenticeship—and even less that of talent, dexterity, and every gift the good craftsman and anybody who takes a pride in his work must be born with. But it can help such persons: It can increase their specialized knowledge, offer them suggestions and, above all, sharpen their eye and improve their judgement.

A revival of the "arts and crafts" was attempted in Europe in the nineteen-twenties. "What is lacking is continuity of development, the passing on of skills from father to son." "Many a technique is in danger of dying out unless artists champion their survival." Such were the diagnoses and warnings at that time.

The critics turned reformers. What Hermann Muthesius, cofounder in those days of the League of German Craftsmen, demanded in a few fundamental pronouncements, others have confirmed in speeches and articles, but above all, and most meaningfully, by sound work. The points they made have lost none of their force even today.

This is what he thought the attitude and the standard of skill of the individual should be: "It is said that the aspiring artist should first learn a craft. This was completely accepted in the past and should again be accepted today. That a designer of jewelry should fully master the goldsmith's craft, gemmology, the art of enameling and related fields is quite obvious. Those who attempt design without practical knowledge of the relevant craft will only too easily lose the ground from under their feet. They will produce 'commercial art' divorced from any meaning, in other words they will create form unrelated to the object".

About the training of a craftsman he has this to say: "Far more important than practical exercise is the spirit a college inculcates in its students."

However, if we look at the work of the craftsmen practicing then, which has been handed down to us in collections and photographs, we can find few designs that justify the adjective "immortal". We can only agree with what critical reviewers noted in those days: "All those objects that bear a personal stamp appear studiedly peculiar and are no longer of any interest."

There were periods in which dexterity, technical knowledge, and skill were highly developed without achieving valid and in the long run satisfying results. A book on this specialized subject presumably must and can show why industry, dexterity, and skill, no matter how consummate, cannot by themselves reach the ultimate goal in those crafts which, concerned as they are with design and form rather than the construction of machinery, demand of their practitioners further, more important qualities than those just mentioned. This constitutes the primary task of a book whose purpose is to educate, not merely to instruct, and it is the main difference between this book and others of its kind.

The old handbooks, large and small, describing metalcraft in general or the working techniques of various special crafts (of the silversmith, engraver, chaser, etc.), offered collections of expert knowledge of varying quality and usefulness. They were full of advice on technical matters and recipes for the treatment of raw materials, and described methods of production. They hardly touched upon the burning questions of creative effort.

It is not the aim of this book to give a complete list and description of all the techniques and working methods that fall under the heading of "metalwork". Only what can serve dynamic creative achievement, and prove useful to contemporary ideas, to our conception of style, and to our needs is worthy of description. But not as a technique in limbo; it must be related to an example, and if at all possible demonstrated with the aid of a representative object, a masterpiece.

The plan of this book transcends the framework of conventional classification into crafts, and deals with the field of metalwork as a whole. There are good reasons for this. Firstly, the progressive specialization and splitting up of formerly connected craft occupations is only a necessary evil and has produced anything but outstanding results. Secondly, metallic raw materials still have very much in common today, at any rate when compared with glass, stone, wood, and other materials; they are also subject to laws of treatment different from those of nonmetallic materials. To demonstrate their common characteristics along with the specific ones of gold, silver, or iron is one of the main objects of this book. The choice of illustrations and their interpretation have been guided by this intention.

The shape of an object has its roots in the kind of raw material and its properties on the one hand, and in the purpose and function of the finished product on the other. Language, which always expresses itself with precision, appears, in the case of metalworkers, to have focused attention from the very beginning on the typical properties of their raw material. It classes the various activities according to the raw material, and thus distinguishes between gold-, silver-, and coppersmiths, the pewterers, steel- and copperplate engravers; whereas with cabinet makers, bookbinders, and bootmakers it describes the purpose of their work.

Precious and base metals? An ancient classification loses significance in an age that is adopting a new attitude to metals as a whole. Copper and tin, together with their alloys, previously cheap and used in the manufacture of utensils of all kinds, have become rarer and more expensive. Iron, which—apart from wrought-iron work—no longer appeals to us as a raw material for beautiful craftsman's work, was formerly considered a common raw material for creative work in the hands of the iron engraver. Now our "Iron Age" is imperceptibly giving way to the age of synthetic and plastic materials. The light metals and their alloys, which so rapidly displaced the nonferrous metals in the home and in vehicle building, are themselves in danger of being ousted by these cheaper materials.

This development has made the boundaries between the various metalworking craft occupations, which have never been rigid, even less important. Those working in these crafts must therefore become conscious of their parallel aims.

Studios are already established which not only produce ornaments in gold but also work on a larger scale, even buildings, in copper, bronze, or aluminum. If to some such versatility appears too daring, they should remember the much greater versatility of the goldsmiths in fifteenth-century Germany and Italy. The goldsmith in those days was often a copperplate engraver, bronze founder, even a painter and a builder all at once. In the present century, on the other hand, occupational limitations have led to a specialization which—not only in the jewelry trade—is rather sad and often unable to escape the narrow rut of workshop convention.

The craftsman, whose privilege it is to create a unique, individual, custom-built product, has now been joined as a creative force by the industrial designer. He is more than the designer of the past, or the pattern maker, for his task is to create practical and attractive utensils for stylized mass production.

It has long been accepted that both the craftsman and the designer have their place in the scheme of things, and that they achieve their best results where they do not work in wasteful competition but are clearly aware of their different tasks: Individual and original form, attraction, and uniqueness of handiwork on the one hand, deliberate use of all the potentialities of the machine, the development of inspiring functional designs on the other.

When one looks at the situation from this angle, it becomes clear why products of individual craftsmanship are shown in this book side by side with mass-produced objects as examples of good metalwork.

1. Metalcrafts in the Past and Present

Before the evolution of economy, technology, and industry—those factors in modern life which are unthinkable without metallic raw materials—there were long periods of human existence during which all tools and implements were made of stone and earth. A subsequent, very much shorter period was dominated by the discovery that metal, especially the alloy of two metals, in other words bronze, was a better raw material for weapons and tools than stone. Lastly, the steadily advancing utilization of iron as a raw material has brought us to our present level of technological development. In the changing course of economic progress, in abundance and shortage, we have come to appreciate the value of the metal and its immense influence on our way of life.

The production and use of metals have today reached such an enormous volume that it is difficult to find the right viewpoint from which to assess the importance of individual metalcrafts which are generally regarded as having established themselves on the fringe of these developments. Since heavy industries and crises in them now have such a direct bearing on the existence of both the individual and society as a whole, we are only too ready to see in "artisan" metalcraft occupations trades which tack onto useful, necessary, and functional implements superfluous accessories, a little "art"—a luxury appropriate perhaps to the fat years of prosperity, but otherwise easy to do without. Builders or constructors are considered to provide the necessities of life, whereas the creative hand is merely dabbling in inessentials.

It would be self-deception, romantic notions gone astray, if we countered these voices by citing the achievements of the past. Those achievements are not ours. But we must nevertheless study the outlook on life and the creative urge which were responsible for them—even if only to receive fresh impulses.

Man's nature, fundamentally restless and insecure, demands a firm basis, seeking it in the "timeless" form. It wants to escape from fashion with its short-lived exaggerations and follies. The eighteenth century is evidence that a really "timeless" form does not and cannot exist; only consistent development which respects the heritage of form amassed during many centuries keeps it alive.

Metalwork in Ancient Times

Bronze Age: Egypt and Crete about 2500–1100 B.C.
            Italy about 1800–800 B.C.
            North Germany about 1600–600 B.C.

Metalwork proper originated in the Eastern Mediterranean about 2500 B.C. with the discovery of a new raw material, bronze, harder than copper which was already known to man. Tools fashioned of this alloy made it possible to work the much softer gold, occurring in the pure state on the surface. Tools of this period have been found in Egypt. But centuries later the hammer used for chasing and embossing was still an oval stone without a handle.

Metalwork of several early civilizations and production periods is compared on page 14. Both place of origin and raw materials are different. On the left are tools, weapons, ornaments, and utensils made of bronze, on the right gold vessels. Together they represent work in the two most important initial metallic raw materials: The casting material of bronze and the softer gold, in which, with the aid of the harder bronze tools, it was possible to develop forging and ornamental techniques. If we look at the objects from a functional point of view, we recognize a third contrast: It is the dual aim which even today dominates the metal craftsman's work: Usefully shaped utensils on the one hand, and on the other hand objects designed for religious rites or to satisfy the urge of adornment, in whose creation aesthetic factors were more dominant than the—not totally absent—aspect of usefulness.

It is between these two extremes that the creative metal craftsman has always moved. If wealth and power, opulence and love of pleasure fashion the spirit of an age, the pendulum swings in the direction of ostentatious display in material, execution, and subject of the products. If poverty and a modest way of life predominate, simple, utilitarian designs are preferred. Seen from this angle it appears arbitrary to regard gold ornaments as an expression of a highly developed civilization, and the others as primitive. What appears to be good, indeed exemplary, measured by today's yardstick of the most advanced technological development, cannot be primitive. Our point of view needs to be changed.

The creative activities of our age have their roots in both worlds. Since we are influenced by the technological character of industrial designs, we are more closely attuned to the simple shapes, the unrestrained application of the principles of usefulness. We recognize and admire the spirit of a work fashioned by the craftsman's hands, especially when its creator shuns the method of persuasive representation, but appeals to us through the harmony of proportion and a convincing use of the medium without neglecting the other aspect. For we cannot base our judgement on functional form on the one hand, and artistic form on the other. Some functional forms are bad, and works of art can be good, excellent, or very poor. What we look for today in kitchen utensils is utmost usefulness; and in decorative pieces a select and well-matured character.

Thus we see products of the ancient metalcrafts handed down to us in a different light from that of the immediately preceding era. We no longer root around for useful objects to be copied, but seek to recognize the forces motivating them in order to reestablish contact and to reenter the stream of creative craftsmanship that has been flowing for thousands of years. These forces had to prove themselves in the face of the triple demands of functional shape, raw material, and technical treatment. These three foundations of the craftsman's product are thus the constant factor that our modern work, too, must seek to incorporate.

From the early periods of these Mediterranean civilizations (whose importance in the development of the metalcrafts in the West cannot be overestimated) objects have come down to us from excavations at Mycenae, showing that metalcrafts were developed equally highly both in technique and in artistic conception. Luxury and refined enjoyment of life, a court society and the popularity of adornment were expressed in the ingenious treatment of gold as a raw material. Masterpieces of chasing such as the gold cup richly adorned with figures of astonishingly realistic representation *(Fig. 1-8)* were the result. The obvious question asked by the craftsman interested in the technical aspect of whether they are cast pieces subsequently chased, or the work of a goldsmith, could be answered only by investigation of the originals, not of the galvanoplastic copies. At present it cannot be answered with any certainty, although there is little evidence to suggest casting. Other, similar objects display primeval ornaments of a rhythmical character (it would be wrong to call them geometrical), or a simple grooved design *(Figs. 1-6* and *1-7)*.

We do not know whether the craftsmen who, according to our present-day notions, were also artists, were esteemed and rewarded adequately. It was rather unlikely, considering that the Greeks used a word synonymous with "philistine" to imply "craftsman". Perhaps they were slaves, or at any rate members of the lower classes. This makes their evident achievements all the more puzzling to us, to be explained only on the basis of a confidence in original creative forces which modern man, trained conceptually and intellectually, has lost.

Vessels of superb formal simplicity, smooth, and probably hammer-finished, were found *(Fig. 3-1* left). But there were also sumptuous cup-shaped vessels, perhaps used by the nobles at table, in which ornamental or figurative relief design is the dominating feature. Pieces from other Middle Eastern civilizations, for instance the gold vessel *(Fig. 3-1* right), are punched. Punching is a method of expression that imparts a characteristic beauty to the material because it is appropriate to the luster of the metallic surface. Its discovery and practice in widely separated regions of the world would suggest its natural evolution.

To the examples of the mastery of casting, embossing and forging discussed so far, we must add those of extremely delicate engraving (metal cutting) found on signet rings *(Fig. 2-53)*. Apart from the artistic achievement of drawing, the enormous technical skill demands admiration, especially when the smallness of these representations is taken into consideration. This skill had its origin in the lapidary art (glyptics) of the Mesopotamian civilizations. A large collection of signet cylinders cut from semiprecious stones, evidence of incredible accomplishments in handling extremely small objects, is displayed in the Museum of the History of Art, Vienna. From here it was obviously only a small step to the minting dies of the Greeks in the seventh century B.C. The development of these techniques is described in the relevant chapters, as are the ancient ornamental techniques of niello, inlay, and enameling.

Fig. 1-1. Egyptian chariot, XVIIIth Dynasty. An early wooden construction of great elegance.

Fig. 1-2. A more recent "chariot", but just as elegant. Evidence that design and creative work are closely linked in the industrial product. Mercedes "Silver Arrow" racing car (1954).

1-3

1-6

1-4

1-7

1-5

1-8

The Middle Ages

Alemannic-Frankish metalwork about fourth to end of eighth century
Carolingian-Ottonian metalwork about 800–1000
Romanesque metalwork about 1000–1250
Gothic metalwork about 1250–1500

The illustrations of medieval metalwork, too, reveal a clear contrast. This time it is based on a division, characteristic in retrospect, into two fields of patronage: The wide range of secular demands on the one hand, and the Church with its many kinds of commissions on the other. Only two of the most important among the many objects of ritual purpose are shown here: Reliquary and cross *(Figs. 1-9* and *1-10)*. Work of this kind belonged to the domain of the goldsmith, who, however, was very fond of using copper and bronze, particularly for sacred vessels, right up to the thirteenth century. The division of crafts according to the raw material was not as yet as rigid as it was later to become. Thus a German chronicler from Ulm has this to say about medieval organization of the various guilds: "The fourth guild is that of the smiths: It comprises goldsmiths, farriers, locksmiths, cutlers, armorers and weapon grinders, spurriers, artists in copper and brass, braziers, in short all those working with an iron hammer, like masons and gold beaters".

Discrimination between "precious" and "base" metals had not yet begun, so that copper was considered a worthy material even for a chalice; in the skilled hands of the sword cutler and armorer even iron became a pliant raw material, made precious by the application of superb craftsmanship. Its perfect fashioning led to a subdivision into various trades. The toolmakers separated from the blacksmiths, and the armorers split up into specialists making the various parts of a knight's armor, such as helmets, spurs, breastplates, etc. There were also hammersmiths, who worked in pig iron.

The nonferrous metals—copper, bronze, and brass—were very popular raw materials for household appliances, and cast or wrought by red casters and basin makers, coppersmiths and braziers. The former cast the heavy cooking pots and braziers, mortars, candlesticks, and measures; the latter beat brass sheets into basins and bowls *(Fig. 3-41)*. It is well known that gold and silver were also used for altar vessels. Some of the gold- and silversmiths, who might spend decades on a single task, for example the making of a great shrine, were monks or persons of equal devotion to their work. The cast or embossed miniature figures they incorporated in their masterpieces are equal in quality to the monumental sculptures; sometimes they were epoch-making. The sculptures of the Hildesheim font, the reliefs on the door panels of Hildesheim Cathedral, and those of Augsburg Cathedral, have quite rightly long been regarded as equals in artistic merit of the outstanding monumental sculptures. A line dividing the craftsman from the artist had not yet been drawn.

The medieval achievements in seal cutting and stamp cutting and therefore minting are described in separate chapters *(Fig. 5-10)*. Others deal with the techniques of cloisonné and champlevé enameling, niello, and other processes almost unknown today, which transformed the metal workpiece into a medium of artistic representation, now relegated to the more ephemeral paper and canvas.

It is not the purpose of this comparison of ancient and modern crafts to explain why medieval artistic production—which includes metalcrafts—could be so excellent and uniform and reveal such compelling creative forces in spite of the seemingly primitive technical aids and tools available. To do this would require detailed investigation of

Fig. 1-3. Tools: Cast axes, Bronze Age.

Fig. 1-4. Decoration: Bracket fibula with oblong buckle plate and chip-carved ornaments. Coat buckle from Alemannic-Frankish Merovingian burial places (fifth to eighth century A.D.)

Fig. 1-5. Utensil: Wine strainer, Roman, bronze cast, about the time of the Birth of Christ.

Fig. 1-6. Mycenean gold cup, diameter about 5·8 ins. (14cm).

Fig. 1-7. Mycenean gold cup, with nine grooves, forged from sheet gold.

Fig. 1-8. Late Mycenean gold cup, found near Vaphio. Chased representations: Capture and taming of wild bulls.

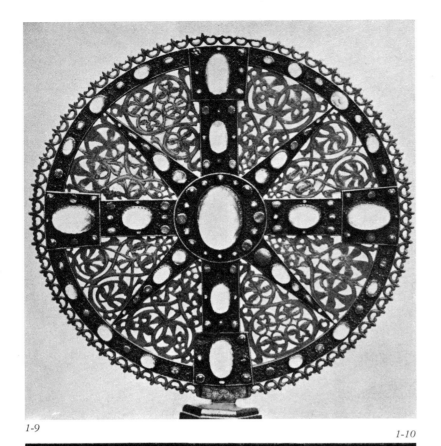

the different intellectual and spiritual situations in the Middle Ages and in our own time. They will be found in other books. But the young craftsman, to whom these explanations are mainly addressed, should nevertheless be given some idea of how the use of techniques and even the choice of raw materials can be understood from the intellectual intentions of the masters.

Bronze, for instance, was the favorite material for casting during the early Middle Ages—the Romanesque Period—not least because its physical as well as its artistic weight was attuned to the solemn, austere, creative mood of that age *(Fig. 4-39)*. In the luminous colors of enameling, completely divorced from any realistic representation, the goldsmith found the same symbolic value as he experienced in the mysterious color atmosphere of stained-glass windows. He therefore had an utterly different, more disciplined, and more intimate relationship to his rare and precious raw materials than the modern enameler, who chooses them from the hundreds of different samples industry provides him with, in every conceivable hue and shade, to suit his purpose and personal taste. It was the period when people painted on gold size, which was then a symbol of infinity, and when the same artistic perfection was expected in the engraving of figures in a copper reliquary or a silver cross as in a picture painted on wood. In the face of this uncompromising rejection of anything but the best, the claims of our modern practitioners of these crafts appear to us rather presumptous.

It is the hallmark of medieval arts and crafts that they were practiced for their own sakes or for the glory of the Church. The master remained anonymous; the work was everything.

Fig. 1-9. Processional cross, Hildesheim, twelfth century. Scrolls and palmettes copper; on the arms of the cross: Filigree, precious stones, and large rock crystals; diameter 14 ins. (33·4cm).

Fig. 1-10. Romanesque reliquary. Limoges, twelfth century, blue champlevé enamel on gold base.

From the Renaissance to the Eighteenth Century

Renaissance about 1500–1650
Baroque about 1650–1780
(Rococo about 1730–1780)

In the North, a rebirth of antique art forms was not possible. Here, the new spirit of the Renaissance emanating from Italy never advanced beyond the transformation of decorative features, and of ornamental accessories. As far as metalwork is concerned, the change of subjects is more important than that of style. Metals that had hitherto served mainly the needs of the Church now became popular among the well-to-do middle class, too.

In Italy and Germany the urban middle classes became more influential, and soon opposed the might of the nobles and the princes. They aspired to power and status. Such forces also affected the work of the metal craftsmen. The arms the self-confident burgher now bore were expensively finished. Richly ornamented daggers became the fashion among members of the upper and middle classes. Iron engravers shaped scrolls and arabesques on the hilt and quillon of a sword *(Fig. 1-11)*. The blade was etched, and so were table knives and other iron implements. The prestige of a town council demanded "council plate", and the upper class table required silver plate. Showpieces pure and simple such as the centerpiece, huge goblets, and cups to offer a draft of welcome were evidence of the increased demand for ostentation. Long-standing traditions of the guilds were expressed in ornamental pieces, and in the contents of a guild's chest.

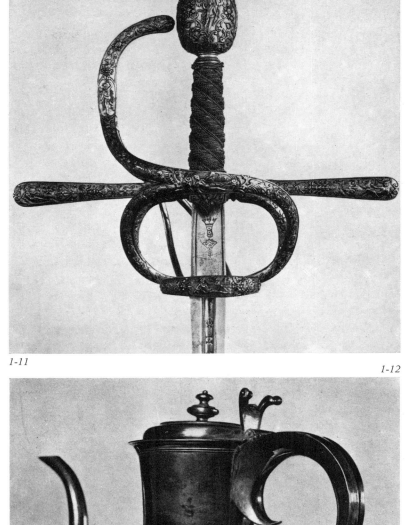

1-11

1-12

Fig. 1-11. Precious side arms as fashionable adornment, Renaissance: Sword hilt, iron engraving by Daniel Sadeler. Figures from Greek mythology, partly after French engravings. Spanish blade of 1605.

Fig. 1-12. Silver wine flagon with engraved arms, about 1685. Rotund, somewhat uninspiring form, similar to that of communion flagons after the Thirty Years' War (1618–1648).

"Artificial" objects in particular—automatic mechanisms and mechanical toys in boxes fashioned by goldsmiths, oddities and rarities of exotic origin, ostrich eggs mounted in precious metals, and similar curios were acquired by the princes to fill their show cases. Utensils were cast in pewter in large quantities for the middle class household, too, and even the pewter plate, hitherto simple and functional, became the vehicle of pretentious figure representations, not altogether to its advantage. This "precious pewter", although much sought after by museums during the last century, has lost much of its attraction today.

The portly silver flagon (Fig. 1-12) radiates strength. It is a beautiful example of Renaissance work, representing the essential spirit of the age in which it was made. The same cannot be said of everything that has come down to us from that period. Much of it is ostentatious and contrived; for the unity of the medieval conception of the universe has been destroyed. The individual artist has emerged from the guild of his particular craft. The designer drawing patterns and inventing ornaments already existed. Copperplate engraving as a medium of reproduction permitted the printing of originals, and thus their wide distribution. Trends, fashion movements, and limitations began to make themselves felt.

On the simple form of the Italian cup (Fig. 5-45) is overlaid a filigree scroll pattern which does not clash with it and therefore appears as restrained and refined as Romanesque scrolls, although its design is clearly Renaissance. Thus the arabesque, particularly where it assists the craftsman's technique, is often much more pleasing than the figure representations in relief smothering the simple form. This is where metal engraving comes into its own. The dynamic, decorative, heraldic designs of engraved armorial bearings—leafwork, luxuriating acanthus leaves as helm mantles—have, because of their superb effect in metal engraving, maintained their undisputed position right up to the present. Even today, most people commissioning a heraldic engraving still think in terms of a Renaissance coat of arms.

The collections in museums of arts and crafts for a long time presented a distorted picture of metalwork in the eighteenth century. It became known only as the the medium of dynamic, ostentatious, Baroque and Rococo ornamentalism. There is no doubt that the curving lines and flutes of a Baroque silver flagon with its reflecting lights show up the metallic raw material from a new angle, doing full justice to its character. Not only during the nineteenth century was this effective treatment of metal held in high esteem; even today, most buyers of silverware, genuine and otherwise, find the tableware designs of that period superior to the simpler and more austere contemporary ones.

In the eighteenth century, work was not, however, confined to pretentious objects for the treasure chambers of rich princely courts, the religious treasures of the monasteries, and the interior furnishing of splendid churches. Simple, functional utensils, too, were made of copper and brass, bronze, tin, lead, and iron for the less ostentatious middle class household.

The beauty of the wrought-iron garden gates of the Würzburg Residenz in Germany is out of this world; it expresses perfectly the spirit of opulent leisure and love of life of a feudal age; but for this very reason it is utterly divorced from us and our entirely different way of life. Those unpretentious objects fashioned in copper, brass, tin, and iron (Fig. 4-65) can on the other hand serve us as perfect examples of formal design—even in the narrower sense that we are guided by them in our own work. This does not mean that we should copy them. But the very best contemporary work reveals in the natural development of old and well-tried designs for everyday use the influence of that functionally inspired craftsmanship. These ideas will be discussed in greater detail elsewhere in this book. Here we are merely recommending a look at the eighteenth century from a less conventional angle.

For during that century craftsmanship in every field, in the quantity as well as the quality of its products, reached its zenith. Nuremberg and Augsburg silverware flooded South Germany. The technical skill of the smiths, casters, medalists, copperplate engravers, silversmiths, and chasers had attained a level never since reached, and its whole character, which simultaneously embraced refined artificiality and natural naïve sensitivity, was as many-sided as the Age of Baroque itself. Even the smallest towns boasted masters of metalcrafts, creating on the basis of a sure fund of tradition, but at the same time responsive to the currents of the age. The beginning of industrialization was already revealing itself in the working methods. But the age was so certain of its strength that even the mass-produced article was still of graceful design despite its cheapness (Fig. 3-40).

There was probably no period of artistic style that gave a freer rein to its own exuberance than the Age of Baroque, without ever abandoning, deliberately or by default, its essential connection with the past. This is the secret of the last great creative period of craftsmanship, which was followed by total collapse, the catastrophic decay of form that took place during the nineteenth century.

Fig. 1-13. Tea caddy, eighteenth century: Popular, primitive style. The broken-up surface of the Baroque silver intensifies the highlights. Cast lid. Body of a single piece (with soldering joint), bottom and neck also soldered. Example of artisan mass production of great carelessness (uneven edges, flooded joints, coarse grooving).

Fig. 1-14. A contrasting example: Silver bowl with lid, early eighteenth century (Régence: 1715–1723) from the Dresden Court Silver Collection. Gilt inside, but restrained decorations. For less than a decade, quiet, rounded forms and refined styles were preferred; effects were shunned.

Fig. 1-15. Silver as casting metal: Neoclassical wine flagon, 1820. Its austere surfaces originate in the casting pattern produced on the lathe.

The Nineteenth Century

The century of industrialization not only destroyed the organization of the metalcraft occupations; it also deprived most of them of the very reason for their existence.

There was no longer any need for the coppersmith; the tin founder and basin maker had already succumbed to the competition of new raw materials (china in the eighteenth century, enameled tinplate and other materials in the nineteenth), and to cheaper mechanical production. The smith and the locksmith still enjoyed, for the time being, full order books as long as increasing affluence and the popularity of ornate fittings and lattice work offered plenty of scope. Nevertheless, in spite of ingenious technical achievements, the skill of the craftsman and the feeling for what was genuine and what did justice to the nature of the raw material steadily declined, and casting and tinplate often replaced and simulated wrought iron. But it was later generations who were first able to realize this. At the turn of the century, awareness of it produced a reaction and, together with the demands of realism in the years after World War I, quickly and completely put an end to this deplorable situation—as well as to most of the craft occupations.

The development took a similar course in those crafts that had originally been only branches of the all-embracing craft of artistic metalwork: Chasing, engraving, enameling, etc.; a splendid, spurious heyday during the decades of economic and political prosperity, a severe setback during the periods of crisis, which are more familiar to us. The vast majority of the affected craftsmen gave up their independence and became skilled workers, in great demand in the precious-metal industries, which enjoyed a great boom before the economic crises began. This had the result of subjecting their work to methods of industrial rationalization, which in the course of the last hundred years has led to the splitting up of hitherto related skills and employments. This phenomenon created innumerable specialist occupations, previously unknown.

This is a mere record of facts, not meant to imply any criticism, which would in any case be pointless because we could not, even if we wanted to, reverse such developments. But to understand the present situation of these crafts, we must be aware of what caused this development. A few examples will demonstrate the typical trend.

The eighteenth-century silversmith at Augsburg, Nuremberg, and elsewhere really "forged" a jug, which meant that he raised the body with the hammer, perhaps presinking the spout and handle with a die, but forming them mainly in pure hammer and manual work. On the other hand the skilled worker—likewise known as a silversmith—in an industrial silversmith's workshop, now received these parts ready-made from the press room. His function was confined to fitting and soldering the work together. At best (or worst, whichever way we look at it), he had to finish the pressed parts with the hammer or to bend large plates which did require considerable skill and much experience. However, the only occasions when he was able to practice his craft in the accepted sense were those when he had to fashion purely by hand "one-off" models or short-run orders, since the provision of stamping dies would not in this case be economical.

The gradual transformation of the goldsmith into the jewelry worker illuminates even more harshly the decline and disappearance of craft methods and the consequences of the division of labor.

Progressive specialization in the engraver's workshop is, however, an essential part of our investigation. The engraver and the iron (relief) engraver had established independent branches of the same craft as far back as the Baroque period. The iron engraver became the steel engraver, because of the pressure-shaping technique, which calls for the use of the hardenable die. This highly skilled craft, perhaps the most important in the metalware industry, immediately underwent a quite extraordinary degree of specialization because of the enormous spread of molding and stamping in all fields of metal processing. The "hollow-ware" steel engraver often used to spend months of concentrated work on chiseling, scraping, fluting, and grinding the embossing dies with which the various parts of silver or base-metal cutlery and other "hollow" metalware were pressed. This happened for a few decades. With the modern copy milling machine having relieved him of much of his work, he, too, seems no longer irreplaceable. The cutlery-steel engraver uses the same technique—if possible, with even greater precision—to engrave the stamping dies used in the pressing of spoons, forks, knives, and other pieces of cutlery. Steelware and instruments of all kinds, buttons, trinkets for the jewelry trade, pens, and innumerable other everyday mass consumer goods are stamped and pressed in presses of various designs. They all owe their shape to the steel engraver's craftsmanship, adapted to the requirements of production and specialized for a closely defined purpose. Not only three-dimensional metal products, but stamps and embossed printing, indeed the molds in which type for printed texts is cast, also bear witness to manual skill with the graver. Other skilled occupations have developed purely from the potentialities of the machine tool. They often straddle the dividing line between the craftsman and the skilled factory worker. One of these is the job of spinning lathe operator. The special features of his work are described in the section on the operating processes of this machine. Combining the skills of the wood turner with those of the sheet-metalworker, he raises on his machine (the spinning lathe, which resembles an ordinary lathe) sheets of various metals, using wooden or iron chucks. This takes a fraction of the time needed in the past by the coppersmith or brazier wielding his hammer. The members of most of the modern metal trades mentioned so far find employment in industrial plants large or small. But the same occupations still exist in purely artisan enterprises, too: In engraving works, tin and copper foundries, silversmiths', goldsmiths', and locksmiths' workshops and forges, because the hand-made metal workpiece retains its place alongside the industrial mass product. Thus individual highly skilled industrial workers have reverted to crafts, and set up workshops of their own. Conversely, in industry, too, many an idea is due to the influence of individual creativeness among craftsmen, not only in the fields of ceramics and textiles, but also in metalwork.

In this context, it is interesting to note that quite a large number of leading contemporary craftsmen, artists, teachers, and industrial designers have begun their careers in industrial workshops. It was precisely their personal experience of the division of labor which often made them prominent in the fight for liberalization of the all too specialized working methods; in the rediscovery and practice of old techniques and means of expression; and in the reestablishment of contact with the great traditions of craftsmanship and their combination with today's technological requirements and potentialities.

1-16

1-17

Fig. 1-16. Silver vegetable spoons, first half of the nineteenth century. Practical and beautiful, evidence of a tradition of solid craftsmanship, continuing in the old Imperial Cities and practiced by the cutlers still established mostly at Augsburg and Nuremberg.

Fig. 1-17. Silver mocha pot. Carl Weisshaupt, Munich, about 1850. Body: Developed cylinder (soldered piece), bottom also soldered, lid with hinge and holder. Knob of lid and handle, polished wood. The design, evolved from French and English examples, follows tradition. Simple, unaffected style is evidence of confident technical skill.

The Present

In the light of all that has been said so far about the changes within the creative metalcrafts, changes that are rooted in the economic and technological revolution of the nineteenth century, the ambiguous situation in which these crafts are caught up is easy to understand. The division between skilled worker and craftsman is one of the characteristics of recent development, and it is not easy to draw a clear line of demarcation. Large industrial establishments employ workers who, by the nature of their occupation, are clearly grouped as craftsmen, whereas workshops in the category of small artisan establishments also accept unskilled workers for work which differs not at all from mechanized factory methods.

Not only is the division between the craftsman's and the factory worker's methods in a state of flux; it becomes even more obscure when we base our judgement on the quality of the products and their cultural standard. Some craftsmen take their creative efforts very seriously, while others make their living by producing trashy and worthless articles. The same applies to industrial enterprises: Badly designed but money-spinning goods appear on the market side by side with mass products of excellent design; the good products are rare, however, and the lightweight, fashionable ones the rule; the term "artistic" is misused mostly for trivial rubbish.

The powerful impulses that at the turn of the century induced creative craftsmen to take stock of themselves after a period of meaningless imitation of earlier original styles came from the world of artists, sculptors, painters, architects, art teachers, and other experts. As far as the craftsmen themselves were concerned, only the succeeding generation was able to advance in the adopted direction on the strength of its own resources. But the number of the leading exponents in industry and in the crafts whose creative activities are convincing is still small. They need support and successors.

Individual pieces of contemporary jewelry and other products of creative craftsmanship now reveal the same fundamental approach as industrial products. Their designers respect all the technological and artistic traditions and seek to take advantage of them, but above all strive to be true to the function of the article.

We can advance along the path chosen for this work only when the education of the following generation is rooted in ideas that are called artistic, but could with equal justification be called ideas of solid craftsmanship. They have little to do with precision work in the technological sense. If you examine gold- and silversmiths' work with measuring instruments and evaluating charts, whose true place is in precision engineering, you fail to grasp the essentials.

A fresh breeze in the workshops could be of more value to the practical training of apprentices than one in the technical colleges. For young workers quickly replace their elders and within a few years take over the positions of superannuated teachers and model designers who have got themselves into a deep rut. If we persist in channeling apprentices in a workshop into one-sided specialization, preventing them from looking beyond common production methods in the technological processes of manufacture, the standard of their work will remain unsatisfactory. The same applies to the teaching in technical colleges. To train apprentices in a creative craft, to stimulate the creative forces and ideas existing in the young, and to guide them towards their own original conceptions we need talented teachers who are themselves engaged in creative work, not technicians and engineers who are part-time instructors in arts and crafts. Even during the nineteenth century this was thought to be a task for the artistically gifted; the fact that

imitation then became the order of the day does not disprove the soundness of the view that cultivation of the creative forces should take precedence over conceptual and intellectual training. As long as schools for craftsmen and specialist workers see their task mainly in the passing on of knowledge, the training of the eye and of the hand will remain stagnant.

Craftsmanship in the past was an end in itself. We lack achievements of a similar quality. We can expect them only from a rising generation creating intuitively, to whom the value and form of their work is of vital importance.

The Character of the Raw Material—Theories and a Caution

Every visit to a museum is an act of humility. It is easy to understand why the young Cézanne demanded that the Louvre should be burnt down. The past and its achievements weigh all too heavily on the courage of those alive today. If this applies to painters and sculptors, how much more must it affect craftsmen, who are hampered at every turn by industrial technology and the social structures totally changed by it.

What then is the purpose of confronting the "original framework of a car" with modern technological form? Not because of the wheel, one of the most ingenious inventions of man. It was in general use during the Hyksos dynasty, and indeed a thousand years before among the Sumerians. Even the wooden wheel does not astonish us: The peasant cart, indeed the early motor car still used it. But the light Egyptian war chariot shown on page 13 is made entirely of wood: The shaft, harnessing gear, and even the prow-shaped chassis. And if we did not have examples of superbly curved Thonet chairs, the spirals on the rocking chair by the inventor of that name, and did not know that luxuriously rounded seats found on Greek tombstones of the fifth and fourth centuries B.C. were also made of wood, nobody would doubt from the impression conveyed by *Fig. 1-1* that the chariot is made of metal. Compare with it the Mercedes racing car (*Fig. 1-2*): You might think the softly flowing shapes were turned in solid wood— if you did not know about sheet steel and streamline. There are no obvious lines of force here as in the Egyptian war chariot. Only a look underneath the bonnet, backed up by your knowledge, creates the functional image in conjunction with the external appearance.

The comparison suggests that we should approach with caution all theories concerning the character of raw materials, the suitability of a given object for them, and the laws of design derived from them. These laws are frequently mentioned in this book. But their validity is only relative, and they demand that a creative person should look at them sceptically from time to time.

1-18

Fig. 1-18. *Biscuit tin and tobacco tin, chased sheet brass, inside silver-plated. Max Fröhlich, SWB Zurich.*

Fig. 1-19. *Small 925/1000 silver boxes. Andreas Moritz, Nuremberg.*

Fig. 1-20. *Cruet, hand-forged silver. Allan Adler, USA.*

1-19

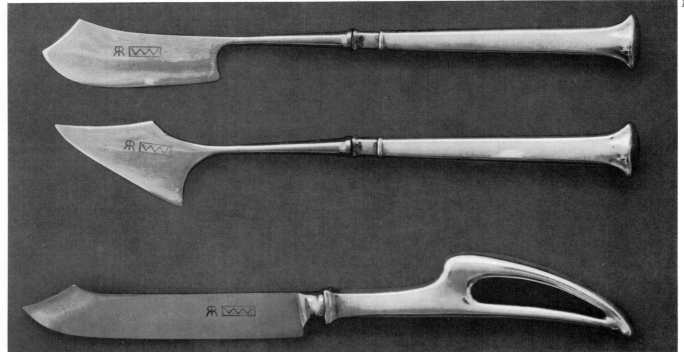

Fig. 1-21. *Table knife with double handle, butter- and cheese knives. Design: Richard Riemerschmid. Manufacturers: Deutsche Werkstätten, about 1900.*

Fig. 1-22. *Parts of a modern silver set, USA. Manufacturers: The International Silver Company.*

2. Objects

"A utensil is created first and foremost for a practical purpose. Artistic design and ornamentation must be adapted to its practical function if the utensil is not to become useless and pointless. Design and ornaments should above all never destroy nor even restrict its usefulness, and furthermore should not conceal its practical purpose; indeed, they should emphasize it.—The most beautiful utensils are almost always the best, too—and they appear to be the best precisely because they are the most beautiful."

Otto Kuemmel

This chapter deals with the question of the suitability and esteem of the various metals compared with other raw materials.

When we try to study this question, a large number of related problems of similar importance arises. They all revolve round the question of what is required, in other words what is really necessary? Where is the line dividing the implements in daily use, whose possession is considered essential even today, from those regarded as luxuries? What is luxury? Do we perhaps still produce, out of sheer ingrained habit, objects nobody wants any more today, objects which have lost their *raison d'être*?

Without doubt, the preference for metallic raw materials and their use depends on the changing spirit of the ages and the people living in them. This question will be discussed in greater detail in the chapter entitled *Raw Materials*. The decisive factor is at any rate the suitability of a raw material for the intended purpose. An examination of objects made of metal must therefore be concerned mainly with their practical function. This immediately shows that many purposes served by metals in the past are today served as efficiently by other materials. However, the realization that many functions have been made redundant by developments is even more important. This applies particularly to those objects whose precious and durable material, or whose craftsmanship, worthwhile only in durable material, was the real reason for their high esteem. Here are some examples: The inn or craft sign expensively wrought in iron was justified on a house owned by the customer and intended for occupation by generations to come, but not on buildings rented only for a short period. Those who are about to acquire a set of valuable tableware piece by piece must believe in continuity.

Here, too, replacement and exchange of objects are the result of a change in life style and customs. The advent of technology and mechanization in the household plays a part in this. Light fittings, for instance, were subject within a short period to extreme changes of function and therefore also form, because of the rapid succession of kerosene, gas, and electricity, after a period of many centuries during which these fittings had been able to remain unchanged, at least as far as their function was concerned. The number and range of sacred objects,

formerly a main subject of creative metalwork, are reduced. Old uses in this field lapse, and new ones arise infrequently. The situation is similar or even more pronounced in the negative sense where the reproductive capacity of the machine has merely had the effect of reducing the demand: Only a fraction of the former number of coins and seals is required today; as a consequence, the skill in making these articles has diminished—not to speak of the superb craftsmanship in metal which is the hallmark only of the artist who has reached the pinnacle of perfection demanded by copperplate and other metal engraving. The demand for such work, once urgently felt, has become confined to luxury items and the collector's hobby.

Even fashion influences this development: Some types of jewelry become oldfashioned and are gradually forgotten. Our laboriously evolved functionalism, on the other hand, together with a steadily decreasing creative ability, has the effect of making any use of technical skill for decorative purposes *a priori* suspect.

The present situation thus supplies no answers at all to those who want to know what work can rightly be considered dynamic and appropriate to the needs of our age, and what is produced only from backward-looking sentiment, from romantic muddleheadedness.

Our comparisons of old articles with those fashioned in modern workshops are intended above all to offer ideas, to make objects we still produce and use today better understood by being suddenly presented in a form they acquired in a different age—especially when this form strongly appeals to our present taste. Others arouse interest in spite of the fact that their function has by now become extinct, because they impose a distinct obligation on the creative activities of our time. This applies to some old household utensils and tableware which are beyond revival and whose raw material (usually pewter) can no longer serve the real purpose today. They are good examples because of the unity of purpose, raw material, and design they represent *(Fig. 3-53)*. Others again, seemingly utterly oldfashioned, are meant merely to encourage luxury and lightheartedness. They represent another feeling, no less justified than the only acknowledged one—the practical one. This applies to jewelry and articles of decoration *(Fig. 4-1)*. Few people will contest that love of adornment is a fundamental expression of the human spirit. It is a pleasure that is not confined to jewelry proper worn on the body or the dress.

Lastly, our choice and arrangement of the objects is also intended to explain, briefly and objectively, their purpose and how they have developed. If you want to make or to design a spoon or engrave the stamping dies for its production, to design a brooch or an altar candlestick, or to create a coin, you should know at least the outline of their historical development. Otherwise the resulting designs will be arbitrary. The intention in this book, then, is not to offer a complete

2-1

2-2

Fig. 2-1. Wrought mountings hold the heavy planks together. Rich ornamentation consisting of nail heads, bands, and accessories. Door mounting, Vetlanda Church, Sweden.

Fig. 2-2. Early Gothic door mountings: Part of the left-hand leaf of the West Portal of St. Elisabeth's Church, Marburg, West Germany, about 1270–1280.

2-3

2-4

Fig. 2-3. *Gable cross, chapel at Vence, French Riviera, built in collaboration with Henri Matisse.*

Fig. 2-4. *Brass weathervane, height 69 ins. (165cm). Ewald Mataré.*

Fig. 2-5. *Weathercock of an old village church, cut from iron, partly wrought.*

enumeration, a historical picture, or a scientific evaluation, but to reveal how much living form is hidden in old products of craftsmanship, and how purpose and beauty of design can and should combine in old utensils as well as in new ones.

2-5

Iron and steel, copper, bronze, brass, even lead and the light alloys, have all been used at one time or other as raw materials for outdoor work.

The necessary weather resistance can be achieved with surface treatment and coats of paint. Alloys, too, are suitable as protective substances. Some sculptures, for instance, are made of stainless steel. Tin, on the other hand, cannot meet this demand. Lead, in spite of its high chemical resistance, is rather soft and can therefore be used—as cladding for instance—only in combination with sturdier materials. During the Age of the Baroque it occasionally served as material for figure casting.

We accept today, as we did in the past, that metals can replace wood and stone, but should not imitate them. How far the new building methods will adopt metals for house building it is not yet possible to foresee. But cast-iron pavilions, railings, fountains, pillars supporting railroad station platform roofs in the shape of antique stone architecture, and seats made of "rustic" branches which were such favorites in the nineteenth century, will perhaps never again be perpetrated.

Whereas at present interest is focused on metals as building materials, beautiful metalwork on buildings or outdoors is not fashionable. Yet it is the most natural ornament for masonry and walls, and its costly use on the restful background of modern architecture could perhaps have a stronger and more meaningful decorative effect than ever before.

Doors, gates, and grilles

Metalwork on wooden doors was at first confined to mountings, hinges and locks, door handles, and knockers. Heavy oak door boards needed horizontal iron brackets which also afforded protection against burglars. All the smiths' and locksmiths' products in a solidly built house—heavy locks with complicated mechanisms, iron grilles on windows and openings—served the purpose of security. But people living in those ages found it impossible to design any object in such a way that it was merely functional and nothing else. It also had to be beautiful and to bear witness to the craftsmanship of its creator or to the wealth and good taste of the patron who ordered and paid for it. Thus if old wrought iron and locksmiths' work was good, it was also artistic. This claim covers not only the elaborate wrought iron in churches and palaces of the Age of the Baroque, but especially those simple grilles and mountings of an earlier age in which beautiful proportions alone produce the effect. A rhombic grille made of square bars, strongly forged in good proportions and attractively pierced, can have as much decorative effect on the front of a building as the bold curves of window grilles and graceful lattices of the Rococo.

This should be appreciated especially today, when we neither feel the urge permanently to settle in a home, nor can we afford expensive wrought iron. If such work is commissioned today, the guiding principle should be to achieve a good effect with the greatest economy of means.

Memorial crosses and slabs

The craftsman's form of the metal memorial is the wrought-iron cross. The cast slab calls for a wall, for inclusion in an architectural entity; today, since burials in churches are no longer the custom, this is possible only on a cemetery wall or inside specially built monuments. (The monument composed of sculpted figures is beyond the craftsman's scope and is therefore ignored here.) There remains only the memorial cross, which is most attuned to our feeling as a symbol, wrought of iron bars and devoid of all adornments.

Although we may find the wrought-iron crosses with luxuriant scrolls and hung with tablets in rural cemeteries in Sweden and the Tyrol original, their naïveté and local roots are alien to us. It is not enough to copy, in a proper and craftsmanlike medium, forms which, though old and representative, were the products of a different way of life. Memorials made of durable material and intended for posterity should also convey something of the spirit of our age: Of its striving for lucid and unsentimental expression. This does not exclude a survival in them of ancient symbolism and old craft methods. But tradition must not be merely copied without understanding, when it might be compared to an oldfashioned, ill-fitting garment.

Those technically and artistically inferior sheet-metal or cast-iron memorial crosses in nineteenth century churchyards are a genuine, although disagreeable expression of their age. Decorative metalwork is absent from the tombs of today, or it is ineffective. It is true that Alfred Lörcher's distinguished work has done much to make the stone memorials of the last few decades more beautiful and dignified, but apart from a few beautiful examples by the sculptor Ewald Mataré, we can find no memorial made of metal by any leading artist–craftsman. And what industry has marketed in this field—mass-produced cast or galvano-plastic articles, realistically modeled flower garlands, and lettering that can be assembled—is so poor that it is not even worth mentioning. Here and there we still find village churchyards that have not yet been completely turned into rows of stone. Between the modern, boring, polished stone blocks we still see a few old, original wooden or iron memorials. Certainly the peaceful uniformity of some military cemeteries would be appropriate to those who after their widely different fates have at long last become equal. Shall we ever achieve this ultimate simplicity? The vanity and ostentation of famous *campi santi* in Southern Europe offer as little hope as the mindless "simplicity" of northern countries.

Plaques and inscriptions, house signs, weathercocks and vanes

It is the outline which determines the character of those metal signs that attract the eye in the street or on roofs and spires. They are isolated, and designed to be viewed from a distance, often from below. Even if they are made of plastic, it is the effect of their silhouette that is decisive. A vane on the roof of a farmhouse can, by its original outline, accentuate the whole neighborhood. Bold treatment is quite appropriate here *(Fig. 2-4)*.

House and inn signs contribute much to the friendly, spirited gaiety of the streets of a South German, Austrian, or Swiss country town or village. The gracefulness and exuberance of the eighteenth century is revealed in these wrought-iron products of craftsmanship.

Because they can be used for advertising and therefore have commercial value, more and more metal plates and inscriptions are found on buildings as sheet-metal frames of neon advertising, as company names made up of separately cast letters, or more rarely in the form of chased or cast plaques. The suitable raw materials are bronze for cast lettering, brass and copper for embossed letters, and the electroplated light alloys for large mounted casings for lettering. The architect may

Figs. 2-6 and 2-7. *Angel as weathervane. Copper chased, fifteenth century, about 62·5 ins. (150cm) high, spire of St. Mary's Church, Reutlingen, West Germany. The figure rotates around a vertical axis, the wing serving as weathervane. Newly fire-gilt, amount of gold used 9 oz (260g). (Fire gilding, see page 137).*

Fig. 2-8. *Bronze doors, Cologne Cathedral. Ewald Mataré, 1948. The cast was chased by the artist. For details see Figs. 4-41 (figure of St. Ursula on the left-hand leaf) and 4-42 (handle of the right-hand leaf).*

2-6   2-7

use fancy types for the front of a modern business block, foundries may supply individual letters of various sizes in ordinary Roman type; this is no reason why the craftsman should not fix less austere or classical lettering between the windows of an old gabled house. A treasure trove of examples of the harmonious combination of old and new in the street scene can be seen in the old city streets and Rhine embankments at Basle in Switzerland, where architects and conservators collaborate successfully.

2-8

Kitchen and Household Utensils Old and New

Over the course of time, metals and ceramic materials often took turns and replaced each other as raw materials for utensils in household and kitchen. In some periods it was the metals that dominated; more recent developments have for various reasons favored ceramics, which include all earthenware, porcelain, and china. The suitability of the various metals for service in household and kitchen was not always assessed at the same level. With the steady encroachment of technology even into the domestic scene, most strikingly shown in the transition from the open fireplace to the stove and finally to the hotplate, the judgement of their usefulness also had to undergo changes. The heavy cast bronze cooking pots of the Middle Ages had to give way to the lighter copper bowls wrought in sheet metal, and to brass implements *(Fig. 2-10)*. Pewter plates and bowls *(Fig. 2-9)*, for centuries the pride of the burgher's table, were replaced by china in the eighteenth century.

But the new products were not always better than the ones they replaced. A few alloys were introduced by industrial manufacturers in the late nineteenth century as raw materials for cheap tableware and cutlery. They proved unsatisfactory and of doubtful value, and they have now either been improved or are about to disappear.

Old, well-known raw materials turned up with new properties: Glass, for instance, became fireproof. New materials acquired additional advantages: Light alloys became stronger and more corrosion-resistant. At long last, types of steel could be refined so that their most objectionable characteristic, rust, was eliminated. Rust formation had hitherto imposed limitations on the use of iron and steel for household and kitchenware *(Fig. 4-23)*. All the other properties: Hardness, solidity, toughness, and therefore resistance to mechanical damage would long ago have made steel, especially, a desirable raw material not only for cutting tools, but also for table- and kitchenware of all kinds. The invention of stainless steel was largely achieved by alloying it with semiprecious metals, above all with chromium and nickel *(Figs. 2-12–2-13)*.

Even before that time, a suitable material had been found in German silver, which had come to Europe from China during the eighteenth century; its hardness and relatively high resistance made it a useful base for silver-plated tableware and strong cutlery. But without the insulating coat of silver, this quite attractive metal suffers from the disadvantage of all copper alloys—the formation of verdigris. In addition, it has a peculiar taste and smell. Thus metals—since the more precious tin had by then become scarce and too expensive (besides, it was too soft and brittle to be suitable for heavy-duty use in large modern kitchens and catering establishments)—were giving way in kitchen and household to the competing ceramic materials. None of the known metals completely satisfied the housewife's or the kitchen and restaurant staff's demands for saving time and labor. The weak points were known, and continuous efforts were made to eliminate them. Plates, pots, tureens, and bowls were nickel-, chromium-, and silver-plated. But these methods, too, had their obvious disadvantages. A practical objection was that the necessarily thin electroplating was subject to gradual wear. Another objection was more aesthetical: The idea of genuine material could not easily be reconciled with such superficial improvement.

The demands made of a metallic raw material from this aspect aimed at the following qualities: Complete absence of smell and taste, resistance to acids and lyes, the least possible tendency to oxidation, which in practice means polished, non-tarnishing surfaces that are easy to clean, and finally hardness and toughness as conditions of robustness and durability.

Striving to fulfill most of these wishes, the laboratories of the steel industry developed a chromium–nickel steel several decades ago; in Germany, Krupp produced it under the technical code V2A. Its resistance to acids, sulfur- and albumin-containing substances, and lyes most closely approximates that of platinum. This steel is almost twice as strong and tough as German silver, and its melting point is 350°C higher, in other words above 1400°C. These advantages, on the other hand, obviously make the forming and machining of the raw material more difficult. The drawing press, die stamping, and electric spot welding are the technical aids used in mass production of items subjected to heavy wear.

These conditions present the designer of metalware with an interesting task. When he plans and designs his pots, plates, dishes, and other utensils he must also consider the resistance his raw material offers to forming. His approach resembles that of the engineer. Sheet steel of resistant toughness and hardness must be subjected to noncutting cold-shaping under tensile and compressive stress. This calls for types of design of great simplicity and lucidity. All unnecessary frills are quite out of the question. The only design this raw material permits must be austere and strictly functional. Grinding and polishing of large areas, achieved on steel with great difficulty compared with the easily polished softer metals is the only "improvement" appropriate to the products *(Figs. 2-30–2-31)*.

Detailed remarks on the items illustrated are unnecessary. Their purely functional design, their carefully chosen dimensions, as well as the technically sober and naturally shaped handles, knobs, and handgrips have all been very well tried, generally confirmed by traditional forms. Their usefulness is self-evident, as is the integration of character, the specific industrial raw material, and the appearance of the openly displayed machine finish. Compared with so many superfluous and ugly articles, simulating craftsmanship, produced by the metalware industry, these completely functional but nevertheless (or perhaps precisely for this reason) beautiful utensils seem to encourage the great hope for reconciliation of functional technical design and the need for creative form *(Fig. 3-59)*.

2-9

2-10

2-11

Fig. 2-9. Pewter cake plate, diameter 14·5 ins. (35cm), with popular decorative openwork patterns. Pomerania, eighteenth century.

Fig. 2-10. Brass bucket for washing lettuce (salad shaker); therefore pierced. Height about 10 ins. (24·5cm) without carrying handle. From the Berg Country, Germany, beginning of nineteenth century.

Fig. 2-11. Waffle iron, sixteenth century. Host irons were of similar design, but were decorated with Eucharistic motifs. The line patterns can be traced, cut, or etched.

Figs. 2-12 and 2-13. *Stainless steel kitchen utensils: Cooking pots and pans with plastic handles and sandwich bottoms. Mass products for automated manufacture. Design: Braun-Feldweg. Manufacturers: Prinz A.G., Solingen-Wald, West Germany.*

Cutlery

Silver spoons, polished before the guests arrived and carefully counted after the last had said goodbye, were not only designed "to convey in their cavity liquid food from the plate to the mouth" (as defined by an expert lecturer). Their true purpose was to advertise, in a refined way, the host's wealth.

But during the early nineteenth century, when such spoons were made amazingly thin, silver was almost five times as expensive as today. This would suggest that nowadays, when the raw material has become so much cheaper, and the manual labor of the cutler (capacity from six to eight pieces per day) has been replaced by the stamping machine, silver cutlery would be found on every table. But this is not so, for the simple reason that cheaper, more robust, and more easily cleaned materials have appeared as rivals of the precious white metal. It is true that genuine silver cutlery has been able to maintain its prestige value. It is still the hallmark of a refined table and is likely to remain so. But it requires the care of a sensitive hand. It would be a pity to entrust it to a dishwasher *(Fig. 3-36)*. This mechanical aid, welcomed by every housewife as a release from daily drudgery, unfortunately leaves its mark even on the so much harder silver-plated alpaca cutlery; but it can do little damage to solid stainless steelware. And steel cutlery, available in different qualities, has proved robust and easy to keep clean in daily use: It does not become discolored, its surface retains its mat sheen, it is not affected by chemical attack, and does not have to be polished. Added to this is its great hardness and resistance, compared with that of silver or the steel alloys. If you want to save yourself extra work you will appreciate these advantages.

So much for the raw material. Its choice depends on considerations of practicality and on the purse, and therefore on pure commonsense. Conflict arises as soon as the design is discussed. We are reminded of a tie: Does it go with the suit, the time of day, indeed the wearer? The selfservice shop can make you uncertain—and cutlery catalogues even more so. They contain everything: Brand-new Baroque designs, almost eighteenth century, only more modern; asymmetrical oddities; simple spoons and forks snugly fitting the hand; knives with which one can really cut without effort; but also arty-crafty and pretentious structures obviously designed only to create an impression.

Let us disregard the mass of "colored" cutlery flooding every exhibition, and look at the well-designed products shown at a special display. Quite a number of them exist, they are well known, illustrated, and discussed—but unfortunately not always bought as widely as they deserve.

To begin with, we can ignore the often overemphasized arguments of functionalism; in this context they are not essential. One can eat with almost any type of cutlery. Nor are the demands of production technology of any interest here. There remains the question: Is tableware developing towards some standard to be reached sooner or later, after which—because it will be perfect—it will be incapable of any further development? Or is there a continually and dynamically changing human imagination at work to modify even these small utensils of everyday use?

Style and custom, in short a form which only appears to agree with the fundamental aspect and in reality is completely natural, at any rate transform cutlery into something more than a mere set of tools. At the same time, the narrowly circumscribed definition of purpose prohibits any free variation of this form. When we compare a few types of the eighteenth century, of Art Nouveau, and of the present period we shall see only slightly different variations of the same basic form. Yet these differences, negligible if measured, leave enough latitude to express a very different spirit. The essential feature, the change of style, therefore does not require any violent swing of the pendulum.

Cutlery could not and should not be short-lived. And the occasional recent criticism of the similarity of new models has perhaps been voiced too summarily; because the better the average, the more difficult it is to recognize the top quality. Those who deplore the uniformity of design overlook the fact that current Baroque imitations vary far less. There will therefore be no return to the flourish simply for the sake of variation. Nevertheless, when we buy cutlery our taste is more conservative than when we buy armchairs or settees.

Cutlery has a long history, with which those about to change its shape or dimensions must be familiar. They must also be acquainted with the manufacturing methods of modern all-metal cutlery, the engraving of steel blanking tools, and the rolling and stamping of the strong sheet-metal blanks, so that they can judge what models represent a happy compromise between the various requirements of function and of engraving and stamping techniques.

Spoon, knife, and fork, the three main constituents, had separate existences long before they combined to form a set of cutlery, which after use was put into a container or quiver carried by the owner on his belt.

All this is useful knowledge when we look at a modern case of cutlery and examine the representatives of the wide range of its specialized forms, from the cheese knife to the grape scissors and sugar tongs. It makes it easier to discriminate between what is necessary, functional, beautiful, and, at the opposite end of the scale, merely fashionable and decadent.

While we are speaking of fashion and decadence: "The introduction of the tablefork by the Italian nobility and the French court was not only the occasion for satirical poems, but also led to protests by the Church, which saw in such luxury something to be condemned." (H. Gretsch.)

The spoon

The handle and bowl of the spoon were originally carved in wood. The English *spoon* is derived from the Old English *spon* (chip). The antiquity of its form is borne out by an Egyptian stone spoon (about 300 B.C.) with a round bowl and a snake-shaped handle. The early tablespoon was held in the fist. Its handle, made of metal quite early, often with figures as ornaments, was therefore straight with thin edges, the bowl was circular, and later round-oval *(Figs. 1-16, 4-83)*. The flat spoon handle to be held between three fingers seems to have developed as late as the second half of the seventeenth century. Strangely enough, however, there are some designs by Dürer of spoon handles decorated with figures, anticipating the later outline by two hundred years. The spoon whose bowl and handle were wrought in one piece thus initiated the development of the present all-metal cutlery, whereas knife and fork were affected by this trend only gradually, and long retained their separate handles. The hand-beaten designs of the eighteenth century, especially the thread patterns, lent themselves readily and without difficulty to the stamping technique which was soon to be adopted.

To begin with, only the bowl was embossed with a die. The handle was still hand-decorated with bead patterns, but soon outline, curve, and decoration were stamped in a hardened steel die in a single operation. This was the beginning of modern mass production of silver

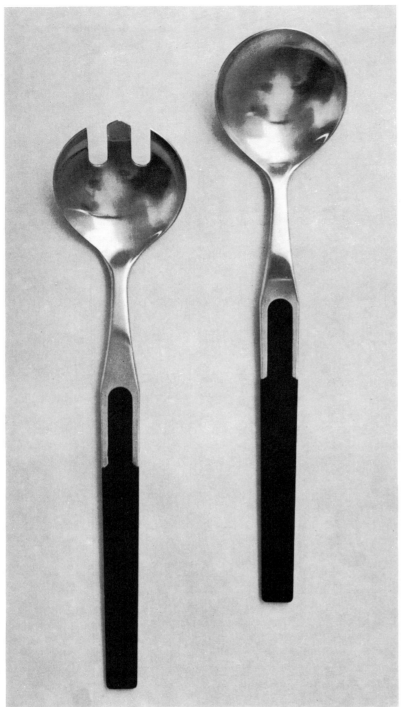

2-14

2-15

Fig. 2-14. *Salad servers: Steel, with plastic handles. Design by Bertel Gardberg. Manufacturers: Hackmann & Co., Helsinki, Finland.*

Fig. 2-15. *Salad servers. Normal use of raw material reversed: The bowls are plastic, the handles are metal shells. Design: Henning Koppel.*

Fig. 2-16. *From left to right: Egyptian stone anointing spoon, Roman silver spoon, decorative spoon of the Italian Renaissance.*

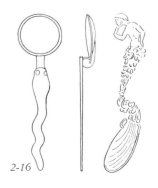

2-16

cutlery. The core metal of the cheaper—nowadays harder and more robust, too—electroplated silver cutlery, first brass, later exclusively German silver, was stamped in the same way. The second half of the nineteenth century also has much to answer for in the production of cutlery. Whereas "good" silver cutlery luxuriated in a horrible exuberance of pretentious ornamental patterns of a latterday rococo, cheap "everyday" cutlery was roughly stamped in Britannia metal and aluminum, with practical, clear line patterns brutally maltreated. Alongside this trash, however, good designs, simple Regency-style patterns of the solid middle-class household managed to hold their ground. A pointed egg-shaped bowl and an exaggerated length of all parts is a characteristic they all share. The end of the handle is slightly thicker and curves downwards, which makes their manipulation appear a little affected, yet competent.

These were the well-tried designs of good tradition which, almost submerged during the decades of a proliferating imitation of styles, inspire the work of craftsmen and industrial designers today. Like the manufacturers, designers still find it difficult to convince a public obsessed with bogus ostentation that their newer cutlery designs are superior, although they can rightly point out that the modern version is more practical than the highly polished or pretentious showpieces of a bygone age, complete with nooks and crannies (also called decorations) in which dirt collects. Our best contemporary cutlery is shorter than those older models, in length about halfway between the earlier main course and dessert sets, and the pointed-oval bowl is reverting more and more to the round shape.

The hand-wrought cutlery designs of today, especially Scandinavian ones, have initiated this return to stylistic awareness, and the well-tried traditional functional form has been adopted for industrially mass-produced cutlery, too, with fortunate results—further confirmation of the claim repeatedly made here that even in our time leading craftsmen are well able to influence the design of industrial products.

Cheap alloys in the class of Britannia metal, which were rather impractical, have now been replaced by various types of stainless steel, a raw material which is as corrosion-resistant as precious metals, even harder, and of better service value. Designed to suit practical needs as well as streamlined industrial production methods, many quite satisfying patterns have already been created (Fig. 2-14), whose style, too, appeals to our taste and meets important functional demands. They are inert to chemical attack by food and cleaning agents (compare the objectionable smell of nonplated alpaca), lie snugly in the hand, and are easy to keep clean. It no longer has to be emphasized that decorations hankering after the past have disappeared. It is much more appropriate to point out, in the face of architects' ideas that are both excessively functional and doctrinaire, that perfect smoothness does not exhaust the technical possibilities of metal stamping. Metal, after all, is not a synthetic material for the press. And a hammer-forged smooth surface looks different from a pressed and ground one—it looks alive. An old example, the thread pattern, owes its natural appearance precisely to this fine feeling for the stamped form.

The knife

For a long time, eating and table use was only a subsidiary role of the knife; its main purpose was that of cutting. Besides large carving and broad-bladed serving knives, pointed knives with handles of various raw materials were used for picking up large chunks of food and meat before forks came into use in the sixteenth century. The outlines of both blade and handle changed repeatedly, at the same time offering a

suitable surface to the childlike pleasure in decoration and representation as well as to the craftsmanship of the age. Examples of this can be seen in iron handles engraved with patient artistry, and with etched linear decorative patterns on the blades. Centuries ago, Solingen, Steyr, and Schmalkalden manufactured the best blades in Europe, which were bought by the cutlers of Nuremberg and Augsburg and set in handles.

Three different shapes of blade have recently developed in the table knife:
1. The so-called English blade: Back and edge are parallel, its rigid, straight shape permits the use of the edge at one point only. It is suitable for spreading butter, etc., and until recently was the conventional shape used in hotels (Fig. 4-79).
2. The German blade is a little less uncompromisingly straight, curved slightly backwards, but also has a broad sweeping front.
3. The French blade is the most elegant and probably also the most practical: More strongly curved backwards, with a tapering, slightly rounded tip. Although eminently suitable for cutting food on the plate, it wears down in time and becomes excessively slim.

Today, the rigid, straight English and German blades still used in restaurants, as well as the more elegant French blade, are rightly regarded as obsolete and impractical. During the last decade or so a very short, very functionally curved blade, influenced by Scandinavian designers, has become popular; its extreme versions resemble the scalpel, and sometimes the penknife. Although blades of this kind are less suitable for spreading butter on bread, they are more convenient to use on the table than any of the previous designs because they are matched to the cross section of the plates.

In cutlery with handles, the continuation of the blade—the tang—is surrounded by the two halves of a wooden, horn, tortoiseshell, mother-of-pearl, plastic, or other handle, and riveted to them. In all-metal cutlery, it is a screwlike pin cemented into a metal handle matching the design of the blade. Stamped out of tinplate, usually 0·8mm thick (approx. 20 gauge) with die and upper die (matrix and patrix) and soldered together or, with steel cutlery, welded, this metal handle does not yet represent a fully satisfactory solution even today. Blades that wobble sooner or later and handles that buckle clearly indicate that the inventiveness of the craftsman–technician still has some scope in this weak point in cutlery.

A few attempts to make handle and knife-blade of a single piece (monoblock knife) have not yet produced completely acceptable results in steel. The difficulty is that the very hard steel offers far too much resistance to the plastic deformation during upsetting and pressing (to obtain body in the handle, and a thin blade). The monoblock knife does, however, represent the first attempt to depart from the old Baroque form of the hollow knife handle.

The fork

This is the most recent of the three parts of the table set. It started its career as a long, two-tined steel fork, initially only used as an implement for cooking and carving, and was first used for eating in sixteenth-century Italy. Before its introduction, people ate with their fingers. Two-, three-, and four-tined forks have always existed. In the newer models, the tines are shorter, but the "boat" (the part between tines and handle) is wider and longer (Fig. 3-39).

Silver has long been the favorite raw material for eating implements, not only because of its favorable chemical behavior, but even more on

Fig. 2-17. *Whether the swages are made by the steel engraver using precision craftsmanship, or by the milling machine controlled by the pattern, the dimensions and sections entered in the structural drawing must always be strictly adhered to. Note: The dimensions in the drawing on the right are all in millimeters (Drawings: K. Dittert.)*

Fig. 2-18. *The basic shape of a table fork is evolved by the designer-craftsman.*
1. *Length and curvature of a piece of wire is determined by the results of the procedure illustrated below.*
2. *The same wire straightened, i.e. development of the profile.*
3. *The spatular broadening as basic shape develops spontaneously when a rod is forged.*
4. *Side view of the result.*
5. *The solid rod is the starting material for the forging process.*
6. *First flattened, then—as the arrows show—laterally upset.*
7. *Thus a spatula is formed as a rough shape for shank and tines; a second spatula provides the handle.*
8. *The outline of the forged shape is tidied up with a file.*
9. *Bent according to profile 1 and filed to gradually changing thickness.*

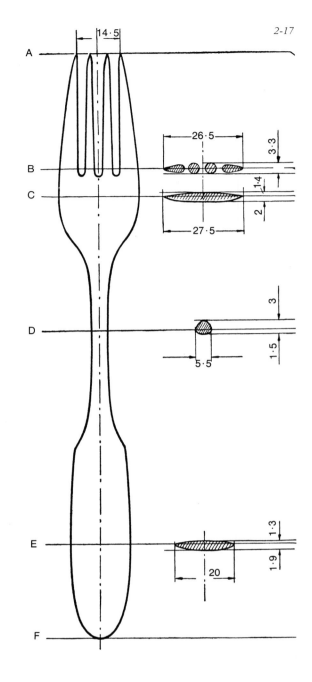

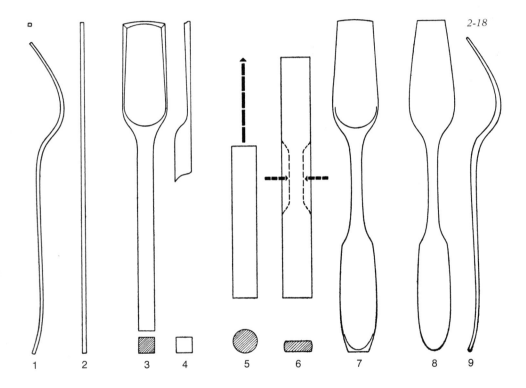

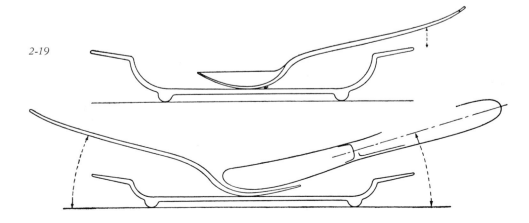

Fig. 2-19. *The curvatures of the various pieces of cutlery are determined by experiment. Top: Cross section of a normal soup plate. Bottom: Cross section of a shallow vegetable plate. It can be seen that the longitudinal profiles of the articles of cutlery and the curvature of the knife edge have been adapted to the cross sections of the plates for convenient handling. (Drawing: K. Dittert.)*

account of its appearance. The preference for all silver cutlery is based on the table laid for festive occasions, where the luster of china, glass, linen, and flowers is further enhanced by the mat sheen of the silver. But it should not be forgotten that the older and more modest cutlery with handles, less festive and ostentatious, may often look more casual and intimate. The breakfast and tea table, the small country inn, and the kitchen/diner are more suitable for less expensive cutlery with handles, or corrosion-resistant steel cutlery, than for the silver-plated variety.

Table Implements

There are tables and tables. In times past, the style of life, of certain classes at least, was more discriminating and sumptuous than in our age. We sit at a round or oblong table, perhaps Formica-topped, at any rate inconspicuous, relatively small. The large, sumptuous dinner table at which we sit down to a festive meal has become rare. Even when we ask guests, we usually eat in an intimate and casual circle, without fuss, service, or ostentation. The functional value of the table implements has become more important to us than superficial appearance. We do want to see stylish design around us, but simple things of convincing quality in material and design—things we can live with. The opulence, the ostentation, the blatant showy vulgarity of the end of the nineteenth century, the salons, antimacassars, and monstrous imitation-metal tableware are really a thing of the past. The fact that it is still difficult for the designer to find his way back to a noble style of metal cutlery is simply due to the scrapheap of antiquated ideas still occasionally disfiguring our homes.

Tableware reflects table manners. The creative craftsman must be aware of this if he wants to work in the true style of his age. Huge bowls and heavy plates are no longer appropriate in an age that knows of boars' heads and whole venison only from old fairy tales.

Hermann Gretsch, the successful designer of tableware, eminent practitioner, and well-known museum expert, relates in an essay on eating utensils some amusing details which lucidly illustrate the change in manners only briefly touched upon here:

"The pictures showing laid tables give us accurate information about the kind and number of eating utensils used in the late Middle Ages. It is well known that people in the Middle Ages were very fond of good eating and drinking. The expense sometimes lavished, especially on family occasions such as christenings and weddings, was beyond our comprehension. Thus a chronicler notes that in 1496, at the wedding of an Augsburg baker's daughter, 20 oxen, 49 kids, 500 birds of various kinds, 1006 geese, 25 peacocks, 46 fattened calves, 95 fattened pigs, and 15 turkeys were slaughtered to feed the members of the family and distant relations."

Gretsch, after describing ceramics production, has this to say about the ostentation of precious utensils common among Roman patricians: "In addition, eating utensils made of metal were in great demand among the well-to-do. The luxury they indulged in is evident from the fact that at times it was forbidden by law to lay more than a hundredweight of silverware for a meal. Thus, for instance, Rufinus was expelled from the Senate because he owned ten hundredweight of silver. In view of the high standards of craftsmanship, it is obvious that in antiquity implements of other metals than pure silver were made and used. Bronze and copperware, too, were often in evidence; sometimes to prevent the formation of verdigris they were covered with a thin sheet of silver, or tin-plated. The spoon, usually bronze cast, played an important part on the table, since neither knives nor forks were used. The meat was carved in the kitchen and served ready for the plate; liquid food was taken with a spoon, meat and similar dishes with the fingers. The hands were cleaned with bread or washed between courses."

Museum studies and interesting historical findings can only stimulate us to adapt the old raw materials to our own needs. The size and capacity of utensils of modern style must be well thought out and adapted to our requirements (Fig. 3-30).

To do this, it would be necessary gradually to identify those items that are essential to the general notion of the laid table as those which are in fact more useful in metal than in glass or china. This is of course quite obvious in the case of eating utensils. But in dishes and plates, coffeepots, teapots, wine jugs, and all other drinking vessels, metals have long given way to ceramic materials, which are cheaper if not always more practical. Only the very lucky ones could boast of a wine barrel in the cellar; therefore the bottle, instead of the jug or pitcher, appeared on the table, creating a new habit. The wine glass, too, is not likely to be displaced by the metal cup. The silver or pewter cup, where it is found at all, roughly takes the place occupied until recently by the tankard. Designed for prestige, it is brought out on rare occasions and to drink from it is regarded as an obligation rather than a pleasure. The once highly esteemed tankard is regarded with the strongest possible distaste nowadays, and for a good reason: like the pointless centerpiece, it has become a mere showpiece: False in material, execution, and sentiment, for nobody likes to drink from the common trough—and it is no longer done to advertise one's capacity for liquor. As a sports award or other trophy it is no longer fashionable. And the roles it played in guild traditions and drinking habits of a bygone age, no matter how splendid, cannot revive it.

This brief survey may be enough to show why we may well ponder about what place metal utensils can still rightly claim on the modern table. This applies particularly to the craftsman who is frustrated with producing knickknacks and filling show cases and exhibition shelves with his work.

A revival would have to begin with those metal objects whose role is still unquestioned, for example the teapot. Today, teapots are made of ceramics, but also of silver, copper, brass, even of tin. The housewife, who, in spite of its bright pattern, soon consigns her earthenware pot to the cupboard because it does not pour properly, and therefore needs an ugly drip catcher to prevent stains on the tablecloth, will prefer the equally well-designed metal pot, which pours cleanly. Sugar basin, salt cellar and cruet, biscuit tins and fruit bowls, coffee and tea services can be easily shaped of metal in a way that will make them practical enough to hold their own against tableware of other materials. The highly advanced table of the eighteenth century with its silver and pewter tureens, gravy boat, cream jug, and little vessels of all kinds, perfectly designed for handiness, can teach us much in this respect—but only when the superficial and materialistic imitation of the old forms gives way to an intellectually independent interpretation of these examples (Fig. 3-23).

Form is a strange magic, capable of changing many a seemingly final decision. Should it become possible to fashion objects as systematically in metal as they have been fashioned for years in glass and china by leading and gifted designers, there is little doubt that here, too, the tables will be turned—provided that a certain amount of standardization is practiced. Obviously, dimensions and forms of suitable

2-20

2-21

metal utensils should not be standardized, but they should be improved according to consistent ideas derived from the functional aspect.

Clear, simple designs that are in no way conspicuous have been purposely chosen for this book. The implement whose usefulness and quality are almost taken for granted is without doubt the best. Its sole purpose is to satisfy the user, to fit in, stand securely, handle well, and avoid irritation. Because it is so unpretentious, content to carry out its function, its form is easy to criticize.

Such simple objects are more difficult to design than others whose decorations detract the user from their shortcomings. The dimensional discrepancy between the rim of the lid and the height and diameter of the bowl shows how much more effort and skill are necessary to make even a small and inconspicuous object appear perfect and wholly convincing *(Figs. 3-24, 3-35)*.

Naturally, a work fashioned entirely by the craftsman cannot compete in price with the machine-made article. It is a luxury insofar as every hand-made article is a luxury today. Its justification cannot be measured by economic yardsticks alone. This problem, too, must be considered in the context of similar questions of our times. The works of the plastic arts, in fact all artistic achievements, are a luxury. But the original hand-made object is the strongest antidote to the pressures of the day, which are concerned only with superficialities and can be judged only by superficial standards. By satisfying its creator, and providing the beholder or user with the pure pleasure of enjoyment, it is something that can truly help to educate the mind. Seen in this light, craftsmanship and the forms it creates are derived from the "love of play" which to the dramatist Friedrich Schiller was the only road to freedom. For "only when he plays will man be wholly man".

Fig. 2-20. Cup, beaten, and executed in brass as a practice piece. Staatliche Werkkunstschule (State School of Arts and Crafts), Schwäbisch Gmünd, 1948.

Fig. 2-21. Cup-and-ball, 925/1000 silver, profiled rim filed. Ball feet, profiled rim, and bottom of cup fire-gilt. Andreas Moritz, Berlin, 1941.

2-22

Figs 2-22 and 2-23. Two silver tea strainers. Fig. 2-22: Design: Walter Lochmüller, Schwäbisch Gmünd. Fig. 2-23: Design: Franz Rickert, Munich. Whereas the first, smoothly rounded design follows the German tradition, Rickert's design has been influenced by the more austere English style.

2-23

2-24

2-25

Fig. 2-25. *Teapot, beaten tombac, with ivory knob on lid, and ivory as handle insulator. Designed and produced by Sieglinde Maurer.*

2-26

Fig. 2-26. *Phoenician silver pot, design from Asia Minor, fluted, height 7·5 ins. (18cm).*

Fig. 2-27. Side view of the silver teapot shown in Fig. 2-24. Note the lid with hinge and small handle, pinned ivory inserts for insulation, reinforced rim of spout.

Fig. 2-28. Cast teapot, pewter. Design: Karl Leutner. Manufacturers: Zinngiesserei Schreiners, Nabburg, Bavaria.

Fig. 2-29. Copper kettle, inside tin-plated. Without separate bottom section, with handle, therefore suitable for use on the hearth or on an open fire. North German, about 1800.

Fig. 2-30. *Coffeepot, cream jug, and sugar bowl, stainless steel, black plastic handles. Design: Magnus Stephenson, 1954. Manufacturers: Georg Jensen, Copenhagen.*

Fig. 2-31. *Teapot and water kettle, stainless steel, black plastic handles. Design: Magnus Stephensen, 1957. Manufacturers: Georg Jensen, Copenhagen.*

Fig. 2-32. Silver fruit bowl, hammered, with soldered, partly twisted wires. Workshops of the City of Halle, Burg Giebichenstein, about 1936.

2-32

Fig. 2-33. Copper, brass, or aluminum ladle and bowl, traditional design with riveted handles.

2-33

Mass Production and Imitation

Up to the middle of the nineteenth century, craft and technical traditions, and the adherence to functional forms evolved and well-tried through centuries, still produced astonishingly good results. We thus have little silver, copper, and brass jugs of the French cylindrical style with wooden handles *(Figs. 1-17, 2-30)* as products of reputable workshops, side by side with industrial mass production already completely obsessed with the imitation of ostentatious historical forms and oddities. But even inside the factories the modest functional shape survived unnoticed. Thus the soup tureen designed in 1873 by the Plaquée Works, as they were then called (now the Württemberg Metal Works) and still produced almost unchanged as a Cromargan tureen, is evidence that utensils for everyday use which were too far removed from "commercial art" proper, were, so to speak, below the level that was considered worthy of "artistic" interest, and thus they escaped its obnoxious influence. The same applies to many types of cutlery (thread pattern, smooth servers, vegetable spoons, etc.), which remained unaffected by the pompous imitation of styles. While it is these objects (not deemed modern in those days) which we value and look for today, it was the dominant mass products, the imitations of overvalued ostentatious designs of the past, that in fact shaped the character of the period.

It is revealing to compare the real functions of these objects with those their pretended origin suggests. Let us say we have what is supposed to be a table service: Teapot, coffeepot, milk jug, and sugar basin, but the latter an imitation of an antique cantharus, and the other items "recreated"in pure classical outline. The large vase, a cross between lecythos and amphora, owes its solemn, monumental effect to an outline which our imagination rightly associates with Greek tombs. Everybody knows that it is neither ceramics nor a thick-walled casting, but made of thin sheet brass. The components were mass-produced on the spinning lathe, often enough stuck together only with a soldering iron and tin, the thin sheet metal not even reinforced along the edges. Awkward but pretentiously antique handle-shapes betray the semi-craftsmanship. Lastly, electroplating silver to make a superficial finish hides the base metal and all the sins—at least from the eyes of mindless buyers.

The so-called décor consists of unimaginative "ornaments" imposed on the shape of the body. It is immaterial for the marriage of body shape and ornament (neither successful nor ever attempted) whether these strips were mass-produced and stuck onto the object like wallpaper, or stamped from the body itself as an edged border. It would be wrong to hold the mechanical methods of production responsible for the lack of imagination in the decoration. The old braziers merely used a technologically more primitive method—hand stamps—to impress their charming ornamental patterns; the process was basically similar *(Fig. 3-41)*.

Nor were production by machines and industrial manufacture alone responsible for the decay. The craftsmen, proud of their manual skill, only rarely produced something better during this period of the worst excesses. And if we still see some of this junk in shop windows, one excuse should at any rate never be accepted: The claim that it is what the customer wants.

Candlesticks and Lamps

In the modern household, candles are only used decoratively, and where there is no permanently fixed light source (a shed or an attic), the electric pocket torch is more convenient and practical than an open light. Yet the burning candle still retains a place here and there. The most important use is in churches. The various types of lamp and lampholder employed in church ritual, from the large paschal lamp, the apostle lamp, and the altar lamp to the sanctuary lamp offer rich opportunities for good metalwork.

It is true that the silver table candlestick is still being mass-produced in the more or less closely copied or "modernized" styles of its flowering period, the Baroque, but as decorative candles are favored more by the young, who cannot usually afford expensive silver candleholders, the evolution of a new style cannot be expected.

The situation is completely different with everyday utensils, and electric lamps for living rooms. It is a long way from the electric lamps with proliferating floral and leaf decorations and Art Nouveau figures that won awards at the 1907 Paris World Exhibition, to the functional, mature work of the Swiss and Scandinavian designers—but it only covers a few decades. We now appreciate the profound influence the work of the Bauhaus had, especially on the design of new lamps. But the style of the great mass of such lamps is not keeping pace with these consistent designs, and still suffers from all kinds of concession. If we look into a shop window displaying a large selection of bedside, table, and ceiling lamps we will find little that satisfies us. But it is not so much the practical aspect of these conventional lamps that is so unsatisfactory (practicality is not usually disputed) as their poor form.

The organic connection of the diaphanous materials glass, fabric, parchment, and paper with the metal frame poses interesting problems. As to the suitability of metals, however, there can be hardly any doubt that the light metals aluminum and magnesium and their alloys are eminently adaptable to the practical and technical requirements. It can easily be seen that beside these materials, suitable mainly for mass production, the craftsman's individual output in brass, bronze, and iron could provide good specimens to satisfy a personal taste. Here is a field which could be more rewarding both in the artistic and in the material sense than the imitation of old designs of silver table candlesticks.

2-34

Fig. 2-34. Romanesque altar candlesticks, cast in bronze.

Ritual Metalware

At all times and in all civilizations, the requirements of religious rituals have provided the craftsman with his most important outlet. This applies as much to Egyptian and oriental metalcraft and its development of decorative techniques, as to American and Far Eastern metalcraft, whose bronze ritual vessels are among the finest artistic creations ever produced *(Fig. 3-52)*, and to Early Christian Byzantine and Western medieval metalcraft. Nevertheless, the description of purely artistic metalcraft in a book of this scope can take up no more than a few pages. Illustrations of metal objects of religious and ecclesiastical significance are also found in other chapters *(Fig. 3-62, etc)*.

The following notes explaining the purpose of the various objects have been kept as brief as possible, and do not claim to be exhaustive; but they provide the creative designer with a survey of some kind. They do not trace the historical development of the various articles, but hint at possibilities of design determined by liturgical tradition, church rules, suitability of the raw materials, techniques related to function and

Fig. 2-35. Design of the monstrance in Fig. 2-36 by Wolfgang Tümpel, who made the following comment ". . . the art of drawing has degenerated with many goldsmiths to such an extent that their designs lack any graphic appeal. These people envisage precision machine work, which is utterly alien to the design of a goldsmith's work."

Fig. 2-36. Monstrance, silver-gilt, and silver-plated and gilt brass, with rose quartz. Wolfgang Tümpel, Hamburg, 1947.

purpose, and present-day ideas of style. The happy blending of these demands in the finished product, of which low cost is usually one of the harshest (a consideration playing hardly any part during the great creative periods), is the aim of all planning.

Altar candlesticks

Candlesticks have stood on altars since the eleventh century. Made of silver, bronze, brass, and later also of pewter and iron, usually cast and turned, their design is a reliable indication of their date of origin.

Altar plate

In present-day Roman Catholic ritual we distinguish between sacred vessels and other liturgical articles. Sacred vessels consist of the chalice, paten, ciborium, pyx, monstrance, custodia, and communion plate. They are described individually below, as are all the other liturgical requisites.

Protestant altar furnishings comprise, in addition to communion and baptismal requisites, only the altar cross (Fig. 2-46) and the altar candlesticks; in Reformed churches, even these are absent.

Ampullae

Small vessels for various purposes: Small jugs for wine and water for the sacrifice of the mass, flagons for holy oils, ceramic or metal containers for essences (silver gilt, lead, pewter with silver, etc.). Even Early Christian pieces had stamped relief representations made with stamping dies, (the Church Treasure at Monza, Italy, about 600 A.D.). Recently, cylindrical vessels made of silver or other metals, with lid, to contain the three holy oils.

Antependium

This is the decorated altar cloth, which, as its name implies, hangs down the front of the mensa. Frequently the metal-chased panel, the front attachment of the altar or frontal, is also called an antependium. Main examples of old altar panels: At San Ambrogio, Milan (middle of ninth century), the Gold Frontal from Basle Minster (around 1020, now Paris, Cluny Museum), the Pala d'Oro at St. Mark's, Venice (enamel-work from Constantinople, 1005), and the frontal of Gross Komburg near Schwäbisch Hall, Germany (Fig. 5-23), third quarter of the twelfth century, copper gilt with champlevé enamel. Silver-embossed Baroque antependia are found at Fulda and Hildesheim, Germany; Gothic painted wood panels date from the thirteenth century onwards.

Apostle candlesticks

Metal sconces (wrought-iron, brass, bronze), mounted above twelve crosses painted on, inlaid in, or attached to the walls inside the church (crosses for anointing the inside walls of the church).

Apostle spoons

Mostly silver, more rarely pewter or brass spoons with little apostle figures at the end of the handle. Especially English goldsmiths' work. Also engraved figure of an apostle or of the Virgin Mary in the bowl.

Aspergillum

Holy-water sprinkler. More recent designs: Pierced metal globe, on a handle.

Baptismal font

Baptismal bowl, baptismal ewer: Copper, bronze, brass, or silver, hammer-finished, or cast. The possibilities of expressing simple proportions and restful surfaces are more important than the usually inadequate figure ornaments. Engraving more appropriate than embossing.

Bells

These were cast in bronze, and have been precisely tuned according to key and pitch in more recent periods, and therefore permit little change in form. Ornamental features and inscriptions can no longer extend to the bottom rim, for the same reason. Relief ornaments are integrally cast and must therefore be cut in plaster and molded. The fact that bell ornaments are no longer designed by the founder but have become an artistic addition has generally been detrimental. Sacristy bells announce the beginning, altar bells the main part of the Service.

Candelabra

Candelabra of bronze, brass, copper, or iron, consisting of foot, stand, and two to seven branches supporting candles. Unlike those of the chandelier, which radiate in all directions, the branches are all in one plane. Seven-branched candelabra are very numerous and were important in the Middle Ages (the number symbolizes the number of lights in the Temple).

Censer

With swinging chain, pronounced openwork, or pierced to release the clouds of frankincense. Romanesque and Gothic censers were cast in strong-walled bronze (Fig. 4-40). Later designs were spherical with foot. The censer includes incense boat and spoon.

Chalice

As mass chalice the most important liturgical implement of the Roman Catholic Church, and, as communion chalice, of the Protestant Church. Its parts are the bowl, the stem, interrupted by the knop, and the foot. Figs. 2-38–2-43 show the development of the chalice design diagrammatically. In the Early Christian chalice, the antique cantharos form was adopted, which accounts for the two handles. The influence of early chalice forms of the West on present-day designs is unmistakable. Like the Tassilo Chalice (777 A.D., Kremsmünster) and the Ludgerus Chalice (Werden–Ruhr), they have no real stem (Fig. 2-37), and the knop, designed for easier holding, and on early examples only a thickening of the stem, has also disappeared from Protestant chalices. The Roman Catholic chalice must have the knop and a maximum diameter in this part because of liturgical rules. Whereas in the Romanesque chalice the knop is directly below the cup, separated from it only by a ring-shaped constriction, it moved lower down along the narrow, high stem of the Gothic chalice, and became an independent intermediate feature assuming many forms. The shape of the bowl, too, changed repeatedly in the course of stylistic development. In early periods parabolic, in the Romanesque hemispherical and slightly tulip-shaped with a narrowed rim, the bowl again became half egg-shaped in the Gothic period. After a temporary broadening during the Renaissance, this shape returned in the Baroque Age. The main change

2-37

Fig. 2-37. Chalice with niello inscription (Niello, see page 200). Elisabeth Treskow, 1949.

Fig. 2-38. Tassilo Chalice (about 777), an early occidental design. The Ludgerus Chalice is similar, but its outline is more pronounced.

Fig. 2-39. Wilton Chalice: Influence of the double-handled Early Christian chalice. Niello figures in the panels.

Fig. 2-40. Typical Romanesque chalice, twelfth to thirteenth century.

Fig. 2-41. Late Gothic chalice from a village church. The clear separation of bowl, stem, and knop is typical.

Fig. 2-42. Renaissance and the Schism: Various forms of chalice. Pewter chalice, hence lathe profile (Lutheran).

Fig. 2-43. Mass chalice, Prague, typical Rococo design: Small bowl, broad foot, knop much reduced.

2-38

2-39

2-40

2-41

2-42

2-43

2-44

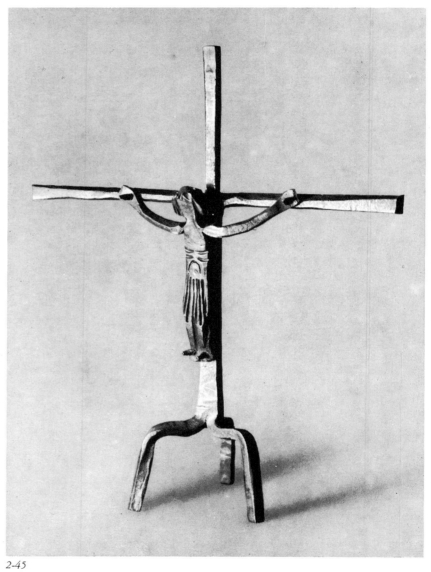

2-45

Fig. 2-44. Altar cross by Henri Matisse, cast bronze, chapel of Vence, Côte d'Azur, France.

Fig. 2-45. Altar cross, wrought iron. Ferdinand Hasler, Altstätten, Switzerland.

2-46

2-47

2-48

Fig. 2-46. Altar cross, 925/1000 silver, soldered with 900/1000 gold, ball fire-gilt, height 26 ins. (55cm). In an old country church, Sussex, England. Andreas Moritz, 1935.

Fig. 2-47. Pectoral cross, gold, soldered with silver wire. Elisabeth Treskow, 1936.

Fig. 2-48. Pectoral cross, gold, with ruby and moonstones, height 2·4 ins. (6cm). Andreas Moritz, 1936.

wrought in the general form of the chalice in the eighteenth century consisted in the reunification of the various parts, sharply distinguished and separated from one another in the Gothic style, in an outline richly overgrown with riotous ornaments. The division into stem—knop—foot became blurred; instead, the foot assumed proportions too large for the bowl; its stability was strongly emphasized. Foot and stem, divided into two parts during the Gothic period, were one again. This reunification has become even more pronounced in the most recent designs. The rule lays down that the inside of chalice-bowl and paten must be gold-plated.

Ciborium

Round or polygonal vessel (pyx) with lid and chalice foot; contains the wafers to be distributed during communion. The ciborium for administering the last rites is smaller, and is used on the same occasion as the paten for the sick (small container with plate). Commonly used materials are copper, gilt, or silver, during the Gothic period often with superbly engraved figures on the surfaces of the vessels. Subjects from the Old and the New Testament: The Gathering of Manna, Feeding of the Five Thousand, etc. *(Figs. 5-16–5-17).*

Communion bowl

Better: Communion paten: A silver plate or shallow bowl: It is held below the ciborium during communion to prevent the host from dropping to the floor.

Communion plate

In Protestant churches, this consists of chalice, wine flagon, paten, and pyx for unconsecrated hosts, and sometimes a strainer spoon. Chalice, flagon, and pyx are described separately. The communion plate in the Lutheran Church is small and shallow, as host plate like the Roman Catholic paten; in the Reformed Church it is a larger, deep, bowl-shaped paten. There are no binding rules prescribing raw material and shape. Besides baptismal and altar plate, communion plate constitutes the only valuable artistic metalwork in Protestant churches. Silver is the rule; in poor rural communities the flagon may be made of pewter. Original and beautiful pieces usually date from the generous period of reestablishment and reequipment after the Thirty Years' War (1618–1648).

Cross and crucifix

Originally without a figure representation of the crucifix, which did not begin until the eleventh century, and was often absent in more recent periods because of a lack of artistic force of expression. As an altar cross it is the symbol of Calvary. Compared with other raw materials, metals have been particularly favored from early times. Cast and wrought gold, silver, copper, bronze, brass, and iron were used in every kind of ornamental technique. Figure representations on the surface in cloisonné and champlevé (new) enamel, niello, and engraving; bands of letters as ornaments etched in copper; monumental and extremely slender forms, effective only because of their proportions and dimensions, as creations of our own period without crucifix. Recent examples of pendant and processional crosses sometimes also without crucifix, otherwise as crucifix only. Steeple cross *(Fig. 2-3)*, processional cross *(Fig. 1-9)*, crucifix *(Fig. 2-44)*.

Custodia

A vessel for the host, with support (lunula) from the monstrance.

Flagons

As mass flagons (Roman Catholic), communion flagons (Protestant), baptismal ewers, and aquamaniles cast in bronze, pewter, and silver, or wrought in copper, brass, and silver. Contemporary mass flagons contain wine and water for use during mass. Material: Glass, gold, silver, or pewter. A plate or bowl for washing the hands forms part of them. The Protestant communion flagon of about 2 pints (just over 1 liter) capacity (reason: Communion cup) is larger than the small mass flagons. As they did not appear before the Renaissance, they are usually silver or pewter jugs with lids, with engraved symbols or representations. Secular drinking mug and quart jug designs gave place to the double-curved body shapes of the eighteenth century, and the neoclassical outline (similar to *Fig. 1-12*). The spout was absent at first, but appeared in later designs. (Baptismal ewer, see *Baptismal font.*) The medieval ewers in animal shape (lion, etc.) were cast in bronze or brass. Their name, aquamanile, first referred to the washbasin associated with them, and was transferred to the ewers only later.

Frontal

An altar front of metal or wood corresponding to the antependium (linen) (see *Antependium*).

Holy-water font

Cast bronze or wrought copper and brass bowls, true or modified hemispheres, with bracket and carrying arm for wall-mounting. Portable vessels with aspergillum for sprinkling; symbols (lamb, cross, palm) and inscriptions as decoration.

Incense boat

Silver container for frankincense grains, with hinged lid, tapering towards both ends, hence the name. With incense spoon for pouring the grains into the censer.

Lighting fixtures

Arrangement of electric light in churches is often unsatisfactory. Indirect light from wall-mounted lamps (screened from below by metal bowls) or suspended lamps, whose austere metal bodies spread diffuse light only downwards, appear suitable. Model designs by C. Holsmeister, Vienna (St. George's, Cologne, destroyed) and by the studio Licht im Raum (H. Dinnebier, Düsseldorf).

Lunula

Crescent-shaped metal support, device for setting up the consecrated bread in the monstrance.

Medals

Common for centuries as pilgrims' badges and souvenirs of centers of pilgrimage, cast and stamped. Raw materials formerly lead and pewter

(Fig. 2-98), bronze, more recently silver, brass, and silver-plated German silver. Recent designs usually indifferent.

Missal

Stronger association with metalwork in earlier periods, weaker in the present; chased metal covers, locks, mountings, metal letters as ornaments.

Monstrance

Used since the introduction of Corpus Christi Day (1264) to display the consecrated host. Name derived from Latin *monstrare* (to show). Developed from the form of the old vessels for the display of relics (ostensories) by the addition of the foot of a chalice. Special types: Tower monstrance of the Gothic period, glory monstrance as an ostentatious Baroque design (*cf.* pages 280–281). Beginnings in 1930–1933 of an austere, monumental new design, very recently displaced again by imitation of past styles.

Offertory box, alms box, poor box

Stationary or mobile collecting devices for money offerings.

Paschal candlestick

Very tall candlesticks on both sides of the main altar for the paschal candle, burning during mass until Ascension Day.

Paten

Plate for the priest's host, flat, designed as a lid for the chalice. Symbolic or figure representations, therefore only engraved. (Old representations: Saviour, Madonna, Apostle, Lamb.) Theophilus described the manufacture of a paten.

Pectoral

Pectoral cross, also vestment clasp, generally pectoral ornament.

Pectoral cross

General pectoral ornaments; pectoral also means the clasp of the cope. We distinguish between the liturgical pectoral cross worn only by high Roman Catholic Church dignitaries as a badge of their office, and the older pectoral cross used for private devotions. Early examples niello and cloisonné enamel, later engraved (representation of the crucifix); on the pectoral cross by E. Treskow *(Fig. 2-47)* wire soldering and granulation (competition of the German Society for the Goldsmith's Art, 1937). The crucified Christ is represented on the front of the pectoral cross earlier than on large crosses; displaced by precious stones and pearls during the Renaissance and the Baroque. (New: *Fig. 2-48.*) Height of the pectoral cross 2–4 ins. (5–10cm), of the liturgical cross up to 5·2 ins. (13cm). Dimensions of two fifteenth-century pectoral crosses in the Prague Cathedral Treasure:
1. Silver, 2·8 × 2·2 ins. (7·1 × 5·4cm). 2. Silver gilt, 5·5 × 4·7 ins. (13·7 × 11·8cm).
Pectoral cross by A. Moritz: Gold, height 2·4 ins. (6cm).

Portable lamp

Candle lantern with little bells for use during the last rites, square or round (glass cylinder), with metal mount and metal handle.

Pyx for unconsecrated hosts

Usually round, sometimes oval container for unconsecrated bread in Protestant and Roman Catholic churches, made of metal (rarely wood). Engraved or chased symbols, sometimes figure representations.

Reliquary

Case (shrine), box, container of any kind for keeping the relics of saints. In the Middle Ages, large numbers were made of metal, depending on the type of relic, as head-, arm-, foot-, finger-, etc. reliquary. Main products of artistic metalwork are the large reliquaries (metal sarcophagi designed as houses or basilicas, decorated with sculptured effigies). *Fig. 1-10* shows a small, simple Romanesque reliquary of austere design.

Ring

Common even in early Christian times as insignia of the episcopal office. Gold, with one or more precious stones, more rarely silver gilt or bronze. Also used as signet ring (See *Ornaments: Early Christian rings,* page 55). Signet in place of the precious stone, sometimes inscriptions on the shank or surrounding the stone. (Mainz, Germany, Cathedral Museum: ring of Archbishop Arigo, before 1031.) New episcopal rings: E. Treskow (granulated gold with Siberian amethyst), F. Schwerdt (gold with cut amethyst).

Rosary

The beads may be of metal or semiprecious stone instead of wood. Pendants cross- or medallion-shaped, cast, chased, engraved, inlaid, nielloed, enameled.

Sanctuary light

Part of the tabernacle as symbol of Christ's presence. It can be suspended or supported by a stand. Red glass is not prescribed. Compared with the richly-ornamented Baroque lamps, new designs, in copper and other metals, often with hammerwork, are more austere.

Seal

Not only wax seals as in the past, but also modern rubber stamps for the authentication of documents, product of metal engraving (the matrix for the manufacture of the rubber stamp must be cut). Importance and durability require top-quality graphic design.

Tabernacle

In modern usage: A small cabinet to house the monstrance and hosts on the High Altar, in the Middle Ages kept in a pyx (this design has been revived in some recent instances). According to Church rules it should have a strong lock and be of artistic design. Sculptured (cast, embossed) or flat ornamental (enamel, inlaid, niello) representations of eucharistic symbolism are therefore appropriate.

Tombs

Since burial in church is no longer usual, made of metal only in the form of plaques (remembrance of the fallen), embossed or cast. Embossing is less suitable, since the cast plaque looks more solemn and monumental.

Vases

More recently in both Roman Catholic and Protestant churches, especially in Northern Europe, used for flowers on the altar. Beside ceramic materials also silver, pewter, and sheet brass.

Ornaments and Their Shapes

Shapes of ornaments have been closely associated with fashion since prehistory. When in Egypt the short garment gave way to long, flowing robes, decorating the feet became pointless and superfluous. Such direct dependence of decorations on the type of clothes can be traced through all civilizations and periods of style right up to the present. There is therefore hardly a class of adornments which in the course of historical development was not completely mature in design, and which was not brought in past periods of metalcraft to the highest level of technical and artistic quality.

Almost all the adornments worn on body and clothing to the present day were invented during one of the oldest and most important early historic periods of metalcraft, the Egyptian. Necklaces and brooches, pendants, buttons, clasps, amulets, bracelets, and anklets of the most varied designs, finger rings, earbuttons, eardisks, and earrings, head-bands and diadems, metal flower wreaths, hair slides and back combs—all these things were evolved during the last four thousand years B.C. in gold, silver, and other metals; almost all the techniques of decoration known to us were used. It must be emphasized here that some of the achievements of that period are impossible to equal today artistically, and often technically too. It is not the aim of the explanations which follow to offer a historical survey, but to examine the attitude of the present age towards traditional forms.

The ring

It has had different meanings throughout history, as an adornment, signet ring, and token of love and affection. We distinguish, according to how they were made, between cast and wrought rings. To these must be added the pressed ring of the costume jewelry trade. The ring as a pure adornment, to enhance the beauty of the wearer's hand, seems to be older than the signet ring. It is found in the tombs of the Early Egyptian period, smooth and undecorated. By the time the Egyptian goldsmith's art faltered, it was already richly designed (after it had been temporarily forgotten); in the Late Roman and Early Christian civilizations it was cast and became the bearer of symbols and inscriptions; it was made of bronze, silver, or gold depending on its owner's wealth. During the Renaissance, it graced the fingers of nobles of either sex in refined and widely varying designs. A ring finger proper was not yet established in those days. Several rings on one hand, even on the same finger, were quite usual, and they were sometimes even worn on the thumb. The brilliant as a ring stone is comparatively recent; although it

Fig. 2-49. Egyptian gold bangle with cornelian Ment Hawk from the tomb of Tutankhamun, about 1350 B.C.

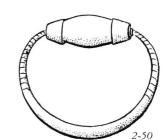

Fig. 2-50. Egyptian gold bangle with large roller-shaped lapis lazuli, from the tomb of Tutankhamun.

Fig. 2-51. Gold bangle with iron udjat eye from the tomb of Tutankhamun. (Iron was rare and precious.)

Fig. 2-52. Assyrian bracelet (upper arm), bronze, with animal heads, ninth to eighth century B.C.

2-53

2-55

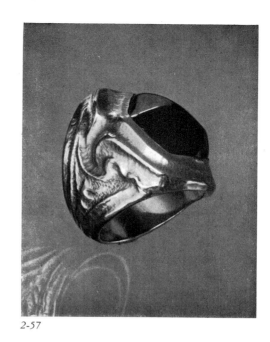

2-57

2-54

2-56

2-58

Fig. 2-53. Gold ring, Mycenae, with cut bezel (ritual theme). Diameter of the shank so small that it could probably be worn only on the top joint of the finger. Sixteenth century B.C.

Fig. 2-54. Gold ring with moonstone, twisted wires soldered onto shank. Richard Steck, Nenningen, 1938.

Fig. 2-55. Gold ring, double shank, boldly chased. Richard Steck, Nenningen, 1937.

Fig. 2-56. Ring with cloisonné: Pattern light blue, base black. Staatliche Werkkunstschule (State School of Arts and Crafts), Schwäbisch Gmünd, about 1948.

Fig. 2-57. Gold ring with amethyst en cabochon and chased relief. Richard Steck, Nenningen.

Fig. 2-58. Silver ring with large red cornelian (cut en cabochon, backed with gold leaf). Recess of the rosette oxidized dark. Braun-Feldweg and Karl Rau, Geislingen-Steige, 1938.

2-59

2-63

Fig. 2-59. Gold signet ring, with monogram and bead border popular in the Merovingian period.

Fig. 2-60. Gold signet ring, period of the Barbarian Invasions, with engraved cruciform monogram (presumably the initials of the owner's names, combined with an indication of his membership of the Christian community).

Fig. 2-61. Cast signet ring, gold with silver inlay in the arms. Italy, about 1500.

Fig. 2-62. Ring, 750/1000 gold wire, with a pearl. Brigitte Braun-Feldweg, Berlin, 1958.

Fig. 2-63. Greek silver coin with stamped figure, known as an obolus, is set in a solid gold ring. The stamped figure is probably an owl, the symbol of Athens. (Obolus: Very small coin, originally iron, placed into the mouths of the dead as payment for Charon who ferried them across the Styx.)

Fig. 2-64. Ring with star sapphire, white gold, Elisabeth Treskow, Cologne, 1938.

Fig. 2-65. 750/1000 gold ring, with sapphires set in pure gold. The arched peripheral leaves are delicately engraved and bent. Emma Schempp, Schwäbisch Gmünd.

Fig. 2-66. Platinum ring with undrilled pearl. Elisabeth Treskow, Cologne, 1930.

2-60

2-64

2-61

2-65

2-62

2-66

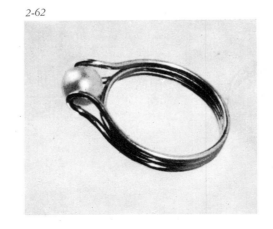

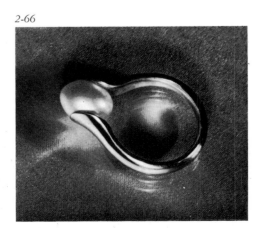

2-67

2-68

2-69

demands the utmost precision in cutting and polishing, it rarely contributes to artistic achievement. The signet ring of gold, silver, electrum (a natural gold–silver alloy), copper, bronze, and tin has probably developed from the stone signet, which the Egyptians attached to the finger with wire or a thread in the form of a scarab. The wire became a bracket, then a band with socket, and finally the cut stone was replaced as a signet by the engraved metal bezel. Cretan–Mycenean metal craftsmen probably developed the all-metal signet ring, which was already of some importance in Egypt, very common among the Greeks, and also popular with the Romans.

When names, dedications, and symbols were engraved on the bezel, replacing the typical seal, the ring became a token of love and through Early Christian symbolism (fish, sacred Monogram, dove with olive branch, etc.) a badge of the community, but also a symbol of the union of husband and wife. Inscriptions of splendid simplicity of old and more recent origins are known: *vitativi (tibi)* (late Roman); *immer und immer* (for ever and ever) (fifteenth century); *ne veut autre* (fifteenth century); *myt wyllen dyn eygen* (Frangipani's Ring 1515). The modern craft-fashioned ring is more often wrought and soldered than cast, in other words it is "assembled". *Fig. 2-61* shows a cast signet ring.

Fig. 2-67. Brooch, 900/1000 gold, partly granulated, opal set in pure gold. Emma Schempp, Schwäbisch Gmünd.

Fig. 2-68. Brooch, 900/1000 gold, orient pearl and tourmalines, set in pure gold. Chased, filed, and granulated parts, as well as some filigree work. Emma Schempp, Schwäbisch Gmünd.

Fig. 2-69. Brooch, 750/1000 gold, pink tourmaline set in pure gold. Soldered wires, leaf patterns mounted on wire base, chased and filed. Emma Schempp, Schwäbisch Gmünd.

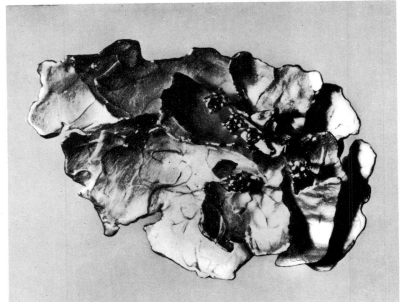

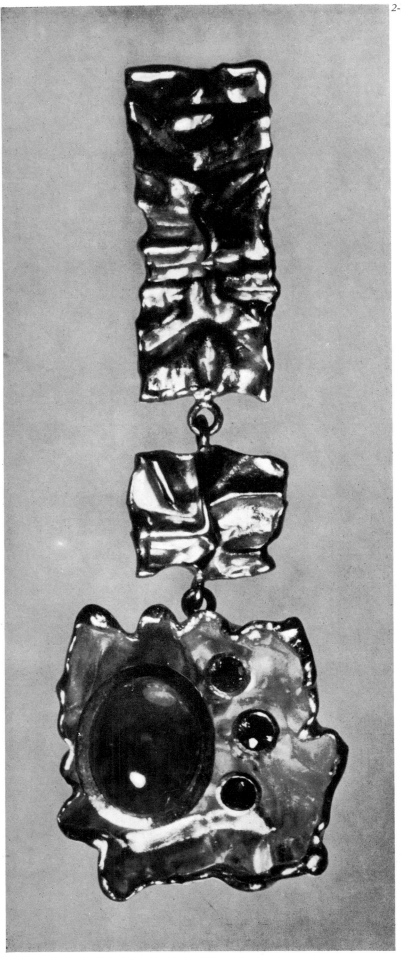

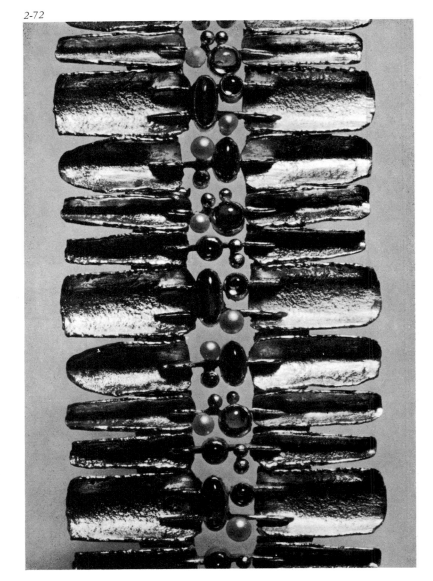

The brooch

Under this name (French *broche* = spear, needle) it first became widely used at the beginning of the nineteenth century, when it was needed to hold together the many little collars, scarves, and fichus worn at that time. In this function, it continued the development of the old fibula (*Fig. 5-66*) and of the clasp. Unfortunately, the imitation of earlier styles in the nineteenth century, the ostentatious, pretentious ornamental designs and indiscipline of the "Second Rococo" really ran riot and played havoc with its shape. On the other hand, it became the favorite article of the cheapest and nastiest type of mass production. Evidence is provided by many paste-filled tinsel brooches still found in rural districts.

Brooch and pendant have been close rivals. Depending on fashions of dress and the stylistic preference of the age, one type of adornment occupied pride of place at the expense of the other. During the Renaissance the pendant was preferred, and during the Rococo period with its playful and voluble sentimental notions the brooch, which was better suited to this mood, came into its own. Beside the taste influenced by fashion, other forces, too, altered the shape of adornments: Working methods changed, jeweler's work increasingly replaced the pure metal-oriented goldsmith's work: This trend began in the seventeenth century, entering and spreading from France. Cut and polished gems, pearls, and brilliant-cut diamonds are particularly suitable for creating the intimate appeal of color and design in a brooch of simple, restrained outline. Motifs of plants, grapes, bows, and little pendants which had formed a lively outline in the eighteenth century were replaced by the more austere oval or round basic shapes of the neoclassical period. These shapes readily accepted small enamel paintings, allegorical representations, symbols, flowers, and portraits in the form of cameos and silhouettes. Precisely because of these sentimental, romantic frills and their popularity during our grandmothers' time, the brooch today carries with it a persistent reputation of oldfashioned frippery. We associate it in our imagination with frilly, high-necked blouses. This by no means precludes it from regaining all its popularity overnight—but with our all-too-rapidly changing taste hardly for long enough to give it time to develop a good, new design, nonimitative and not deliberately oldfashioned.

The bracelet

The bangle, armband, or armlet, in Antiquity worn in pairs on the upper and lower arm, developed very early into various designs: A closed ring, consisting of two semicircles with hinge and lock; composed of loosely connected plate-shaped parts; finally taking the form of a completely flexible chain (*Figs. 2-75, 2-77, 2-79, 5-44*). As an ornament of the man and the warrior, the bracelet was well known both in the Greco-Roman and the Early Germanic periods. It was a badge of honor, a precious gift, wages, and thus also a means of payment, especially if it was made of gold. The bracelet, too, displays early decorative techniques: Niello, almandite and glass paste inlays, and enamel. Very early abstract ornamental designs, developed from the possibilities of metalworking, gave way with the advent of Christian symbolism to engraved and chased figure representations. After the twelfth century, the bracelet disappeared as a male ornament, nor did ladies' fashions in the Middle Ages offer it much scope. Long sleeves were bound to discourage the wearing of ornaments whose purpose was to enhance the beauty of a shapely bare arm. During the Age of the Baroque, too, the broad, strong metal bracelet was out of favor; the more delicate, intimate pearl necklace was preferred. Only after the Napoleonic Wars did a new kind of metal bracelet temporarily come into vogue, succeeding romantic-looking headbands with very little metalwork: It was a graceful, black, cast-iron bracelet composed of links, and made in foundries in Berlin, Paris, and London. Jewelry fashions of the present time have been strongly influenced by the splendid bracelets, clasps, and bands of Egyptian metalcraft, especially after the discovery of Tutankhamun's tomb. The originality of the yellow brasses of African tribes, too (*Fig. 2-78*), provides excellent examples.

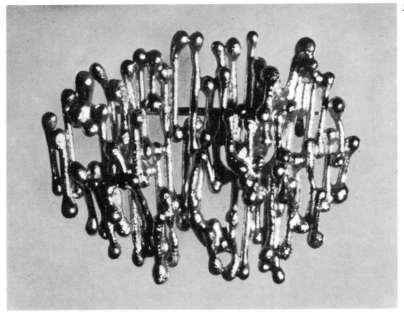

Fig. 2-73. *Brooch, 750/1000 gold, round wire, plastically shaped (thickened ends) by means of welding. Barbara and Rudolf Kratz, Munich, 1966.*

Fig. 2-74. *Detail of the bracelet in Fig. 2-75.*

2-74

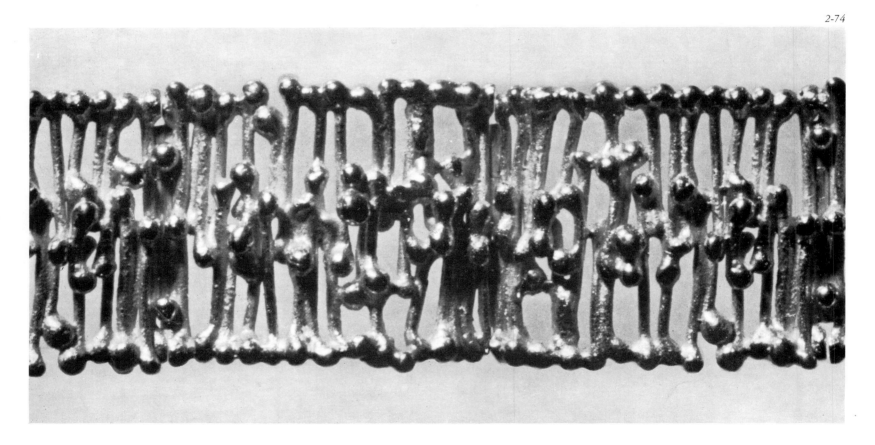

2-75

Fig. 2-75. *Bracelet, full length, 750/1000 gold. Barbara and Rudolf Kratz, Munich, 1966.*

2-76

2-77

2-78

2-79

Fig. 2-76. Solid silver armlet, with amazonites.
Sonja Mataré, Büderich-Neuss, 1951.

Fig. 2-77. Armlet, 750/1000 gold, with pearls,
sapphires, and moonstones. Irregular contours, surface
pattern enlivened with welding. Reinhold Reiling,
Pforzheim, 1966.

Fig. 2-78. Armlets from the Cameroons, yellow brass,
diameter 4·6 ins. (11cm).

Fig. 2-79. Bracelet, 750/1000 gold, ruby beads on
gold wire, soldered twisted wire, and a brilliant on
the lock. Emma Schempp, Schwäbisch Gmünd, 1963.

2-80

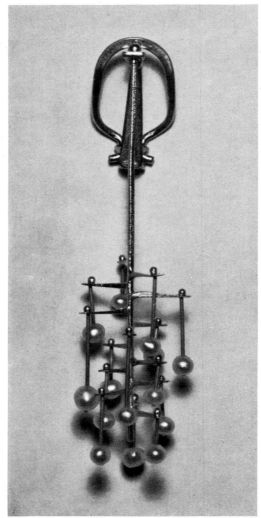

2-81

2-82

Fig. 2-80. Ear pendant, 750/1000 gold: Wrought wire with sheet gold and turquoise insets (triangular plates), brilliants and pearls. Reversed on the other side, so that both sides are equally decorative. Gisela Philippen, Berlin, 1966.

Fig. 2-81. White gold ear pendant, 750/1000, plastically wrought square wire and pearls. Klaus Neubauer, Hamburg, 1965.

Fig. 2-82. Ear pendant of plastically shaped gold plates and orient pearls on loosely suspended wires. Klaus Neubauer, Hamburg, 1966.

Fig. 2-83. Earrings with tourmaline and orient pearls. Erna Zarges-Dürr, Murnau.

2-83

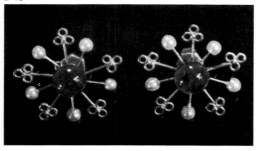

The pendant

In the earlier and more comprehensive meaning of the word, this ornament takes many forms, and is worn by both men and women on the most varied parts of their dress: From a cross on the chest to a trinket on a watch chain, on ornamental belt buckles, marksmen's trinkets on the hat, baptismal coins, pendants as talismans and amulets on the rosary, as pomanders (scent bottles in metal), in the form of a medallion, or as a locket for small souvenirs. Today, a pendant is only a piece of jewelry in the narrowest sense; it is of various shapes, worn on a chain or ribbon round the neck. Coins with holes in the center, and later bracteates specially struck for this purpose, represent the simplest form of pendant. Every ornamental technique ever attempted was tried on this type of jewel, from cast or stamped pieces and openwork, sometimes silver-plated, and ornamental bronze disks, to the highly elaborate pendants designed by famous ornament engravers of the sixteenth century. Openwork, almandite and colored-glass inlays are found in the earlier examples, then filigree and granulation, metal cutting, engraving, and chasing, and, finally, enamel of every description from cloisonné to painters' enamel, jewelry work, gem cutting, and ivory carving set in metal. Raw materials and techniques, outline, size, and popularity of the articles changed with the fashions of the time. The pendant, much worn during the Renaissance, played the most prominent role in middle-class jewelry of the fifteenth and sixteenth cen-

2-84

2-85

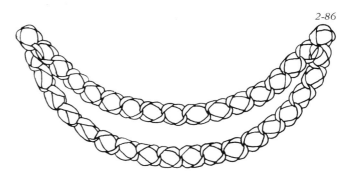

2-86

Fig. 2-84. *Decorative bracteates (ornamental gold disks) and irregularly cut stones from an Alemannic tomb in the simplest regular sequence (a:b:a:b).*

Fig. 2-85. *Bronze Age necklace. String of identical ornaments (a:a) as original arrangment. A translation of the more ancient arrangement of amulet-like objects (animal teeth, bones), associated with ideas of magic, into the language of the metallic raw material.*

Fig. 2-86. *Another string of identical shapes, but with technical variations: Renaissance necklace, sheet copper gilt.*

Fig. 2-87. *Another variant of this type: Silver necklace and pectoral (collar) from Indo-China.*

2-87

turies, often in pretentious, luxuriant figure representations. Scholarly interest in mythology combined with rationalized methods of production at Augsburg and Dresden, and lastly, when the cut diamond came into fashion, there developed the artificial ornamental and figure constructions of the Renaissance, which appeared so worthy of imitation during the nineteenth century. In contrast to this, the present style favors simple outlines which emphasize suspension from a chain or ribbon. Whether the pendant is to be worn on the bare skin or on the dress is an important factor determining its color and shape.

The necklace

When we look at the innumerable, flexible, but often decadent and inane designs of chains marketed by the costume jewelry trade under this name, we forget too easily that this, probably the oldest type of adornment, had its origin in magic and evolved from a collection of charm-like objects on a string *(Fig. 3-2)*. Even when, later, adornment became the main purpose, the element of stringing-up remained. This is the reason why we find the "primitive" necklaces of small threaded metal plates of identical shape so convincing *(Figs. 2-85, 3-14)*. Egyptian necklaces deviate from this law of deliberate serial arrangement no more than later examples from the period of the Barbarian Invasions, with their ornamental bracteates and identical stones *(Fig. 2-84)*. Thus the best examples of the necklace are rows of identical, clear, and integral members of distinctive shape. This definition also applies to the pearl necklace. Even during the Renaissance it was adhered to in

Fig. 2-88. Necklace, chased 750/1000 gold plates and wire structured by beating, gray and white cultured pearls, together with small brilliants. Georg Seibert, Berlin, 1965.

necklaces of gold wire with amethysts suspended from it. And the best of the more recent work confirms this where the effect of the wire approaches that of the ribbon *(Figs. 2-93, 3-13)*. When the row, in other words the repetition of the same basic shapes, is interrupted, the necklace has lost its strongest and most direct appeal.

Broad necklaces became the fashion in the fifteenth century when the plunging neckline returned. But the broadest necklaces ever were the Horus collars, consisting of dozens of small gold plates, of Egyptian metal craftsmanship of the New Kingdom. Their cloisonné work was filled with colored inlay, the back engraved. Nowadays, we distinguish between the "collar" resting on shoulders and chest *(Fig. 5-86)*, and the "choker" tightly enclosing the neck.

Since any adornment of the neck can develop its color appeal only against the background of skin- and hair-tones, composition is also concerned with the many colors of the material (see *Egypt*).

Fig. 2-89. Bottom part of the necklace in Fig. 2-88, showing details of the embossed work, the wire structure, pearl- and brilliant settings, and indicating the relative thicknesses of the materials.

2-90

2-91

2-92

Fig. 2-90. *Detail of Fig. 2-91, showing the position of the pearls, disks, and beads, and their loose connection, whose stiff links, as well as the casual finish, are reminiscent of Alexander Calder's technique. Seibert, too, is a sculptor.*

Fig. 2-91. *Necklace, 750/1000 gold in the shape of wire, disks, and beads, with orient pearls. Georg Seibert, Berlin, 1965.*

Fig. 2-92. *Pectoral, 750/1000 gold with rubies and brilliants. The plastic formation of the sheet metal parts (pendant) is beaten and, like the structure of the wire, produced with the peen. Georg Seibert, Berlin.*

2-93

Fig. 2-93. Necklace, white gold wire, genuine gray pearl drops (with brilliants above), and black star sapphires. Elisabeth Treskow, Cologne, 1963.

2-94

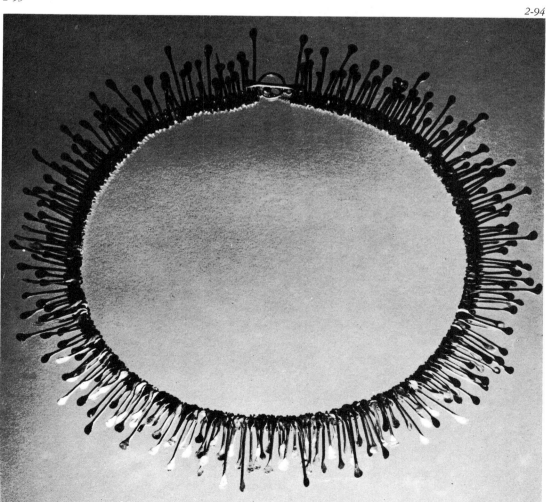

Fig. 2-94. Necklace of stringed pure gold rods beaten out at both ends. Each rod has double eyes soldered onto it, which connect them with two independent chains of the inner circle. The halo-like effect is based on the radial and regular arrangement of elements of different length. Brigitte Braun-Feldweg, Berlin, 1959.

Fig. 2-95. Clasp, silver gilt, thirteenth to fourteenth century (left), and a buckle resembling a round fibula (right).

The clasp

Unlike the brooch, which on the whole remains a pure adornment, the clasp has a better-defined functional role: It clasps or gathers the fabric and holds it together. For this purpose, one side of it is sewn to the material and both sides are fitted with hooks and eyes. A strong buckle fastening, too, is possible. Clearly, modern, closely-fitting garments with only the very occasional loose, flapping attachment have little need for this type of fastening. The most suitable place for the clasp today is on a cloak. Ecclesiastical vestments of the Middle Ages offered a vantage place to strong, cast clasps of vigorous relief effect. Later, the clasp mostly held plumes on hats and, when jewel-studded, similar adornments on the shoulders of very low-cut dresses. In many respects the clip can be regarded as a modern, simplified fibula. The breast pin is a similar diminutive form, derived from the clasp and not related to the decorative brooch.

Seals, Stamps, and Coins

Seals and stamps

From the time of the Assyrian and Babylonian seal cylinders, there has been a constant interrelationship between the engraving of seals and stamps on the one hand, and coinage on the other. We are interested in their engraving only insofar as it was executed in metal, that is, without glyptics or gem carving. Apart from a few exceptions, they used bas-relief engraving: Symbols, figures, or letters were always cut into the material, and not cut in high relief. The technical skill as well as the artistic power of the early seals and stamps are far too little known even among craftsmen and experts working today. This was not always so. The stamp engravers and medalists of the Baroque age and even during the age of neoclassicism knew their antique models very well indeed. Their own achievements were very largely based on the study of these ancient examples. Contemporary masters, too, have trained their artistic approach and engraving techniques by learning from the work of earlier stamp engravers, whose delicacy and elegance were due to the superb mastery of the graver. Only when we compare the mindlessly designed and casually engraved monograms of most of the modern seals with the old masterpieces, will we fully realize the low level of craftsmanship, from which only a few good examples stand out. At the same time we should understand that only by a very thorough study of the forms and the development of our letters can we overcome this situation.

Seals are no longer as important today as they were up to the end of the eighteenth century. This should be no reason why authorities and private individuals using them should not take a special interest in their design. It is immaterial to the quality of the design whether the seal is engraved in a gold ring or executed in the form of a rubber stamp. (See *Development of the signet ring,* pages 52–55.) Negative engravings can be made of seals in plaster of Paris, wood, or soapstone, and then cast. More beautiful and more satisfying as a piece of craftsmanship is the seal directly cut in metal, that is, engraved—provided, of course, that design and execution are of equally high quality. Here, too, specialization has had a detrimental effect. The designing artist rarely has the craftsman's skill to execute the engraving in the hard metal himself; the technically experienced engraver, on the other hand, often slavishly follows the original, which prevents him from freely and impulsively developing his own creative ideas. The seals of the past are both excellent in execution, and of sensitive design. They are completely satisfying only because the same master was responsible for both design and execution.

Embossing dies are needed in large numbers even today by the paper industry. The containers of the most varied brand articles, letterheads, and book titles intended for gilding, all present challenging fields to the die sinker. Such dies are engraved mostly in brass. The letters, drawn in reverse, are left in relief, and the surroundings are slightly cut away or scooped out with the graver depending on size and intended depth; the letters are cut conically.

Blindings are engravings for letterpress printing, in which no ink is applied to the relieflike, almost always raised, letters or symbols. Here, too, the engraving is reversed and negative in metal. For embossing requires a soft and fibrous type of paper, preferably handmade or India paper. Rag paper is eminently suitable, but art paper is not. Good notepaper takes embossing perfectly; for its refined effect as a letterhead, this method is superior to all other techniques. A strip of leather as counterpunch is usually adequate for clean embossing.

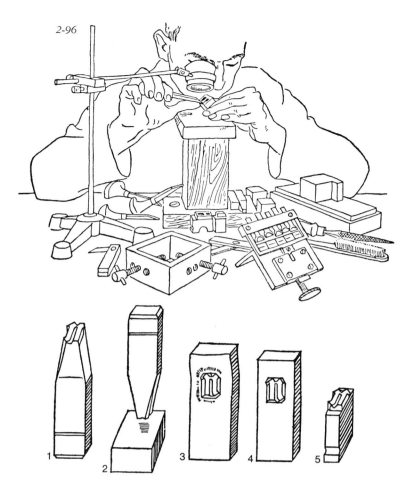

Fig. 2-96. Above: The type cutter with cutting tool and magnifying glass, and in the foreground a clamping device for angle-true filing. Below, from left to right: Finished steel type. Steel type imprinted on a polished piece of copper or iron. Piece of copper distorted by imprinting. Justified finished matrix. The type cast from it. [From "Schönheit von Schrift und Drück" (Beauty of handwriting and printing) by H. Klingspor].

Dies for type casting

A type, for instance Garamond, in which this particular book was set and printed, consists of individual metal letters cast in type metal (lead–tin–antimony alloy) in a type foundry. But first a pattern must be available which can be molded, and this pattern is the die engraved in steel. The engraver who cuts each single letter and all symbols of a type in all sizes (size of type in this case: 10 point; there are 72 points to the inch, and one point equals $0 \cdot 376$mm) is called a punch cutter (see Fig. 2-96). With the engraved and hardened steel die (1) the copper or iron matrix is hobbed (2); after the lateral buckling (3) caused by the hobbing, it must be "justified"(4). The type (5) is cast from it. A cheaper method than hand engraving is the direct production of matrices with a machine working to templates.

Medals, medallions, plaques, badges

The medal, a coin not designed as a means of payment, was first cast, and since the Early Italian Renaissance struck to mark special occasions (memorable events, awards, etc.); at the beginning of the nineteenth century it became a collector's item as a miniature work of art. Originally the medallion was larger, round or oval, and bore or enclosed mainly portraits. Plaques are representations in relief of small size. They can be cast, embossed, or stamped; galvanoplastic copies, too, are called plaques. Unlike the medallion, the plaque is angular.

If you are bored by the modern often tasteless souvenirs, sports plaques, and club badges made of tinplate and enamel, you will be only too ready to seek the cause of this lack of artistic quality in mass production. That this need not be so is shown by an account describing the mass production of medieval pilgrims' badges, whose methods and volume are fully comparable with the manufacture of modern badges. According to this account, no fewer than 130,000 such badges were sold within a fortnight in 1422 at the pilgrimage center of Einsiedeln in Germany, at 2 pfennigs a piece. They were souvenir plaques, usually cast in lead in negatively engraved slate molds; they had eyelets soldered onto them so that they could be worn as pendants on rosaries, hats, walking sticks, or dresses (see Fig. 2-98). Unfortunately, these miniature works of art, of most attractive design, are known only to the experts, and, tucked away in museum show cases, have little chance to influence modern design. To realize our remoteness and decline, we must compare their compactness and force of expression with modern plaques.

Coins

Coins were minted because of the need to strike, in the cast gold and silver pieces of the earliest legal tender, a symbol guaranteeing their weight and fineness. For weight and alloy (weight and fineness) determine the value of a coin. The old engraved seal provided the technical and artistic example for the engraving of metal dies for coinage. The round, precast metal piece—the blank—was stamped into the bas-relief-engraved die—a little matrix—with a counterpunch. Soon the upper die, too, was engraved, thus producing the coin struck on both faces. The restriction of the punch cutter to the small circle, the shallow depth, and the prescribed symbol did not, as in our age, lead to mental poverty, but to superb achievements. And the fact that the dies, which were not hardened and were originally probably engraved in bronze, wore away quickly and had to be replaced often, promoted a lively style and force of expression of the most resourceful figure designs.

Whereas the engraving of these early coining dies was of equal technical and artistic perfection, the coin itself was struck in the simplest and most casual manner as regards neatness and uniformity of the coining. This at least is present-day opinion, which is spoiled by the precision of mechanical production. The edges were bent and torn by the process of coining, and top and bottom match only rarely (Fig. 5-12).

The Romans took over the engraving of coining dies and the technique of coining from the mints of the Greeks (Fig. 5-12) in Southern Italy. Their great achievement was—in agreement with the basic trend of the other arts—the portrait of the individual ruler. The primitive Celtic cup-shaped coins (popularly called "rainbow cups") developed into Carolingian coinage and the medieval bracteate whose splendid originality, especially during the Hohenstaufen era (Fig. 5-10), could teach us much today and well overthrow our unspeakably degraded ideas of coins and medals.

Although these bracteates may appear crude and primitive at first glance, close inspection reveals a superb, competent, and forceful flair for form, forcing inscription, building, animal and human portrait into

Fig. 2-98. Pilgrim's badge, lead, cast in stone mold, fifteenth century.

Fig. 2-97. Mainz penny of Charlemagne (carolus).

an integrated symbol, and into the round shape. These so-called bracteates are struck on one side, in thin silver foil *(Fig. 5-11)*. It appears that the foil was placed between the coining die and a lead or buckskin counter, and struck with a hammer. The use of hand die and hammer for striking continued for centuries. A woodcut by Jost Amann dated 1568, shows us the mint master, still with the die in his left hand, wielding the hammer with his right hand. Soon afterwards the hammer was replaced with the screw press. Today, the minting of coins is dominated by precision tools, automatic balances, and special machines, so that the rate of production and the uniformity of the coins is surpassed only by the utter boredom of the engraving and the poverty of the pictorial design.

This lack of expression of the product (not of the design) is due to the engraving machine. This is a complicated milling machine, guided by a tracer in contact with the projections of the enlarged master. Because the master is executed in a different raw material (plaster of Paris), and in the wrong scale, the immediacy of craftsmanship is lost. Reducing the dimensions by means of a pantograph the machine "engraves" the stamping tools. Obviously, intuition during the making of the coin or the intelligent use of tools is out of the question here.

The question is still open, in an age in which previously unknown results are achieved in the imitation of even the most accidental stimuli, whether, in the reproduction of historically interesting objects, we are really incapable of harmonizing our technical potentialities with the demands of art when we undertake to create our own designs.

Metal Printing Plates

Copper engraving (Fig. 4-47)

After the woodcut, the cutting of pictures into copper plates is the second oldest method of reproducing a drawing by means of printing. Today only a very few artists who do their own engraving still use it as a medium of expression. The reason for this is the unusually high standard of technique and craftsmanship it demands. To use the graver with confidence, years of training are necessary, and the skill of our ancestors in engraving was based on a life of effort and perseverance. It must be remembered that the statutes of the goldsmith's guild reserved a whole year of the apprenticeship exclusively for the learning and practice of line engraving. Thus the technically more convenient skill of etching, in which chance and picturesque effect often go hand in hand (both alien to the exact art of engraving) has taken the place of the most difficult of the graphic arts.

Copper engraving originated in the goldsmith's workshop, and those painters who achieved greatness in it (Dürer, Schongauer) were sons of goldsmiths and had received a thorough grounding in engraving in their youth.

Unlike the woodcut and the equivalent metal cuts, copper engraving is an intaglio printing process. The printing ink is not applied to the raised surface, but received by the groove of the engraved lines.

On the smoothly polished plate, blackened with soot or some other darkening agent, the copper engraver traces the lines of the drawing with the burin, which is today more frequently called a single-point tool. The slight burr produced along the edges is scraped off with the triangular scraper. During printing, the plate must first be inked on its entire surface. This is done with a fabric pad. The surface is cleaned again with rags, and finally with the palm of the hand, and then rubbed until it is shiny, so that the printing ink remains only in the grooved lines. Damp paper, covered by a felt-like cloth, is pulled through below the brayer of the copper plate printing press, together with the engraved plate under heavy pressure. During the process, the paper is pressed into the finest lines and takes up the residual printing ink.

Copper engraving has served the purpose of the graphic arts as much as that of reproducing designs, working drawings, and patterns of ornaments. We know of more than three thousand fifteenth-century engravers, most of whom, however, were by occupation pewterers, goldsmiths, or workers in other metals. During the eighteenth century, when the copper engravers constituted numerically one of the strongest crafts in Nuremberg and Augsburg, most engravers worked only to the painters' originals, in other words their trade was merely imitative. The abbreviations engraved in the plate—*inv* and *name* (author of the representation), *del.* (draftsman) and *sculpsit* (engraver)—give us some information about an already highly developed specialist trend.

Metal engraving

As a relief printing method identical with the woodcut in execution and similar in effect, metal engraving was already occasionally practiced as early as the fifteenth century, but has never gained the importance of the woodcut or of copper engraving. Lead engraving is still used today in book and newspaper printing, if simple linear or two-dimensional black-and-white representations, for instance of a trademark or a signet, are desired in small runs when blockmaking would be uneconomical. The demands made of it are thus small, and as a branch of the graphic arts it has declined rather steeply. Execution requires only little experience in the handling of single-point tool and flat scorper, as the soft lead can be worked easily. But great caution is necessary because of the constant danger of lead poisoning, avoided by cleanliness and washing the hands immediately the work is finished.

Etching

Drypoint etching requires no previous craft skill at all. With a pointed needle, which may be mounted in wood, thin or thick lines and hatched areas are drawn on the unprepared copper or zinc plate. The printing method is the same as in copper engraving. The velvety tone which immediately reveals drypoint work is caused by the metal burr, which is not removed, along the scratched lines; it takes up the ink very readily and gives the individual line a soft-flowing edge during printing (Liebermann and Slevogt etchings: Usually drypoint). To produce a beautiful burr, the needle must have a very fine point.

Compared with drypoint, etching has a harsher line effect. Its picturesque appeal cannot be created spontaneously, but must be achieved through experience and thoughtful consideration during the process. First the polished copper or zinc plate (copper for a finer line effect, zinc for a stronger one) is heated on a hot plate to a little more than body heat, so that it just begins to hiss when it is touched with a moist finger. Solid asphalt varnish is now melted on in as many places as possible to form an evenly thin film. The molten asphalt varnish is now distributed with a small leather-covered roller so that it becomes a thin, uniform layer covering the entire surface. Application of asphalt varnish and rolling must be repeated if the varnish coat shows pores and cracks. Any small remaining gaps can be covered with liquid varnish, but this is only a makeshift method. After the varnish has cooled, it is possible to draw on the surface quite easily with the etching needle. The tip of the needle removes part of the protective varnish coat, and the acid can attack the blank metal during the subsequent etching process. Although the corrosive action of the acid does most of the work, the lighter or heavier pressure used for the individual line nevertheless determines the character of the work. Before the metal plate is immersed in the diluted acid bath, its back and edges, too, must be protected against the acid with a coat of varnish. The etching is carried out in stages, that is, the more delicate parts of the drawing are etched for a shorter period, and the heavier parts for a longer one. So that those parts of the etching already deep enough can be inspected, and, if necessary, protected from further etching by a coat of liquid varnish, the plate is removed from the bath from time to time. Do not use bare fingers. (For further instructions on the handling of acids, their suitability for the various metals, and how best to dilute them, see Etching, page 208.)

A description of other techniques of etching (aquatint, mezzotint, stipple engraving) is outside the scope of this book.

Clocks and Watches

If you buy a wristwatch in a stylish steel casing, selfwinding, waterproof, and with other features, you will look first and foremost for a perfect product of precision engineering. But very few will neglect to judge this little magic gadget critically for its design, and its appearance on the wrist. For even the most functional, austere wristwatch, designed to meet the exacting demands of the sportsman, still plays a decorative role. It is thus a piece of work which, although very largely the product of structural design, owes much to the creative element of design. In the past, when that proportion of effort that went into beautiful appearance was expressed mainly in rich decoration, the division of labor was obvious: The watchmaker built the mechanism, the goldsmith, engraver, chaser, etc. "created" and decorated the casing. This was probably true as long ago as the time of Peter Henlein's first "Nuremberg Eggs": An existing casing wrought in gold—the openwork pomander—was found suitable and therefore used.

Today the watch has long been a showpiece of mechanical mass production, and its components are punched and assembled at a breathtaking rate. This is perhaps most clearly seen in the wristwatch, which is a product of our time, and, because practical considerations are decisive, has also been given the most convincing form.

A watch or clock is basically a measuring instrument, and therefore a piece of technical apparatus like any other. In fact, the clock on the facia panel of an automobile very closely resembles the speedometer next to it. We have only tradition to thank for the fact that it has not yet descended to the level of a measuring instrument in our homes, too. Since the times of the water-, candle-, sand-, and oil clocks and sundials, this appliance has been closely connected with the human world of experience and feeling. This is why so much loving craftsmanship, so much thoughtfulness and charm, but at the same time an excess of sentimentality and allegory have become associated with timepieces. But today we are none too fond of sentimentality, and modern designs are simple and uncluttered. The grandfather clock in a heavy oak cabinet, which adorned many drawing rooms at the turn of the century, is now also out of favor in the smaller homes of today. Practical considerations are paramount, which explains the popularity of the traveling alarm clock. Is the living room clock also beginning to be no more than a sober measuring instrument?

The time has passed when the craft-produced individual item, attractively engraved, chased, filed, or otherwise decorated, could enter into a personal relationship with its owner and his way of life. With the replacement of the spindle escapement about the middle of the nineteenth century, all the attractive details which were a part of craftsmanship also disappeared. We judge the achievement of the creative industrial designer by the clarity and beauty of its proportions. Here a great deal still remains to be done. It is by no means necessary for clock- or watchface and hands to consist only of lines, as in a tower clock; they should be as expressive as a good modern typeface. It is worthwhile to look at an old timepiece which is by no means pretentious but restrained in raw material and execution (Fig. 3-44), and to observe its careful finish. It is not an impersonal piece of machinery, because even its smallest figures still express the stylistic spirit of its age.

Although artistic craftsmanship in the watch ended with the replacement of the spindle block by cylinder and lever escapement, and design passed exclusively into the hands of the industrial designer, the individual craftsman nevertheless was occasionally interested in the watch. Goldsmith's work is still found sometimes, but usually only to increase the value of the watch through jewel setting instead of achieving something outstanding through the use of artistic decorative techniques. The monogram of the owner of a pocket watch, too, could be such an achievement if we had engravers of the caliber of the English silver engravers of the eighteenth century. Even guilloching, tastefully executed, can produce attractive designs on a watch casing. The principal need here is for industry and craftsmanship to join forces.

Craft Ornaments

Fig. 4-1 shows a nonfunctional, frivolous, but not pointless product, cut in iron, of a craftsmanship that has now died out.

The medalist or worker in iron engraved not only seals, stamps, or dies, but also ornamental designs in high relief, and even iron pieces of various sizes in the round. The obvious opportunity to use such work as decoration was provided by the custom of bearing arms. The Renaissance habit of carrying a dagger gave rise to ornaments in engraved iron, which were no less popular later on swords and firearms. The ambitious seal engravers, engrossed in their work, aimed at showing their skill even on the handle of the seal. Much figure work was thus created that with our sober and matter-of-fact approach we regard only as frivolity. But modern creative craftsmanship would perhaps have remained more solid had we not completely lost the capacity to enjoy beautiful luxury articles.

3. Raw Materials

Fig. 3-1. Gold as sheet metal. Left: Gold vessel from the third shaft grave, Mycenae, about 1600 B.C., with wire handle locating the lid. Right: Gold vessel found at Zagazig (Lower Egypt), dated about 1250 B.C. The embossing on the bulge is punch work from outside. The cast figure of a resting calf becomes a fitting for the ring used to hang the vessel up. The rim is hemmed. The contrast between the depth effect of the embossed bulging lower part and the flat chasing of the cylindrical neck is interesting: Both were worked from outside with punches.

Gold

The metallographic chapter (page 237) contains the basic information about the chemical element gold (aurum, Au) and about the raw material of the goldsmith, his alloys and solders, possibilities of treatment and properties. This section is confined to demonstrating the artistic treatment of this material and its creative possibilities by illustrating selected examples of the goldsmith's art.

The popularity of gold has at all times been great, but its high material cost has always inhibited its unrestrained application and use. This explains why gold jewels have degenerated from the strong castings of ancient times to the putty-filled tinsel brooch and pressed, paper-thin foil. Naturally, the demand of a large section of the public for gold jewelry at prices they can afford is completely justified. But the concept of genuineness includes solid strength. If you appreciate more than just the material value of an object, you will prefer a good silver-gilt design to the genuine, but absurdly thin and mean common-or-garden article of mediocre appearance. The high price of gold should at least have the effect of making the mental effort and craftsmanship expended on it commensurate with its cash value.

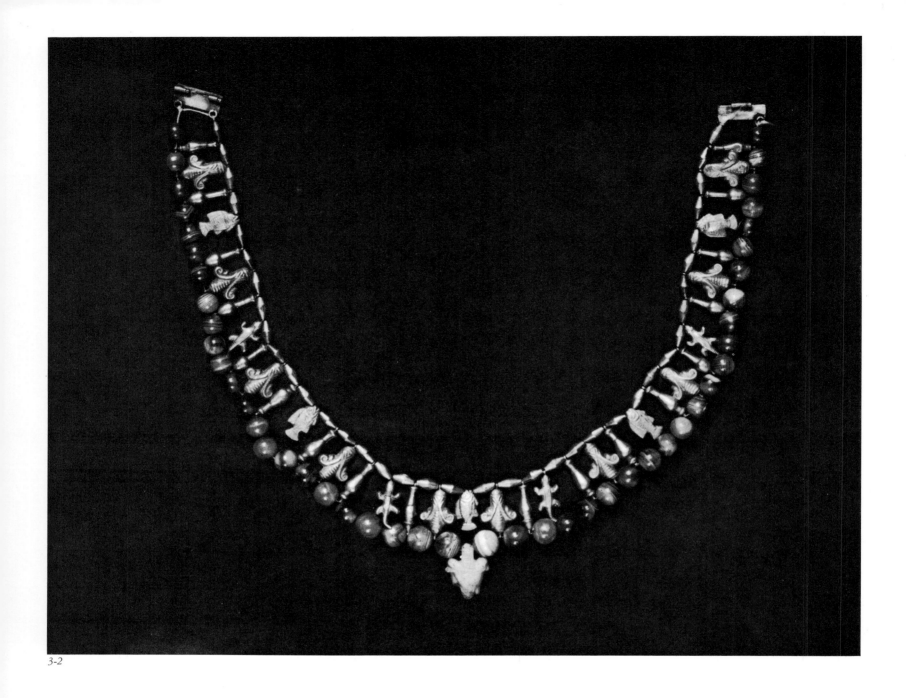

3-2

Man's first artistic activity was to adorn, and mainly to adorn his own body. In jewelry, the first-born of the arts, we find the germ of all the others. . . .

This work of art consisted simply in the combination of two works of nature that nature had not combined. Man fixed a bird's feather on his head, wore a string of wild animals' teeth on his chest, or a bracelet of sparkling stones round his wrist. These are the first expressions of the multiform and divine language of art. (Ortega y Gasset.)

Fig. 3-2. Necklace: Gold and agate beads. Strung amulets in the form of fishes, lizards, lilies, and the larger ram's head as the centerpiece. Egyptian Department, Louvre, Paris.

Fig. 3-3. Necklace of alternating smooth and grooved gold beads. Probably Middle Kingdom, but collected and strung more recently. Egyptian Department, Louvre, Paris.

The metal craftsmen of antiquity reserved gold for religious ritual and for persons wielding power. It was the metal of the Egyptians' worship of the dead: The funerary mask of the dead king, his jewels, and the arms and badges of his office were wrought in pure gold, and the utensils were at least gold-plated. This religion-oriented outlook and the extreme delicacy of the work, which was obligatory for everybody working in gold, are in the strongest possible contrast to today's materialistic valuation of this metal—witness the hoarding of huge unformed masses of gold in the vaults of state banks and forts. The aristocratic quality of the Etruscan work in gold is evidence of a different world, and the solemn austerity of the gold cups of the Eberswalde treasure *(Figs. 5-30–5-31)* proves the mystical veneration of gold by the Teutons, too. They were votive offerings to some god. The same applies to gold work from Columbia *(Fig. 5-71)*.

Gold can be cast easily and beautifully. Nevertheless the goldsmith today does not see casting as the only technique appropriate to gold. As a creative artist he wants his raw material initially in the form of foil, wire, and granule. He considers casting to be a method of reproduction

3-4   3-5

Fig. 3-4. Gold chain of rings beaten flat. Pendant of two contrasting parts. The compact shape of an opal set in pure gold is offset by the exuberance of a sprig of leaves and flowers. Its numerous forms are either sawn, filed, or granulated. Emma Schempp, Schwäbisch Gmünd.

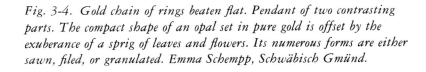

Fig. 3-5. Wire and sheet: The two decorative elements alternately forming the chain consist of superimposed pieces of gold wire; the centers of the rosettes are embossed sheet gold squares joined to a wire ring. Emma Schempp, Schwäbisch Gmünd.

in which the original form was fashioned in an alien material such as wax, and where the product always betrays the the alien character of the material. Casting is also more expensive, because it uses more gold. He therefore consistently refuses any further treatment of the casting and finds it quite in order that a bronze bowl, untouched since it left the mold, should be gold-plated. The execution of a detailed design in alien material will also run counter to such a concept of the nature of the raw material; small sketches will be quite adequate.

The gold alloy intended for creative work is used by the goldsmith in three basic forms: As sheet gold, as solid or hollow-drawn wire, and as granules. This division goes back to the very first beginnings of metalcraft, and determines the various working methods: Bending, which does not change the even consistency of foil and wire—this is how rolls, ribbons, chains are made *(Fig. 3-13)*. Sawing and cutting (snips) are essential to bending in foil *(Fig. 3-10)*. The second group includes cutting methods: Cutting (graver), drilling, turning, filing, and grinding. The third group consists of the highly deforming methods of forging, embossing, and pressing *(Fig. 5-76)*.

3-6

Fig. 3-6. Compact and luxuriating forms in reverse arrangement (cf. Fig. 3-4): Sapphire in pure gold setting as a pendant, above it a composition of bent, embossed, and filed sheet gold shapes of plants. Emma Schempp, Schwäbisch Gmünd.

3-7

Fig. 3-7. Necklaces, 750/1000 gold, the inner one of bent wire and embossed, engraved rosettes; the outer one, also of bent wire, regular sequence rhythmically broken up by round, lightly chased disks. Emma Schempp, Schwäbisch Gmünd.

Fig. 3-8. Gold as grain: Plain face and grain are contrasting means of composition. Ring of the Deutsche Gesellschaft für Goldschmiedekunst (German Society of Goldsmith's Art). Dragon and letters granulated. Elisabeth Treskow, Cologne.

Fig. 3-9. Grain and plain face: Gold ring with emerald and granulated animal figures on the shank. A. Stengele, SWB, Lucerne, Switzerland.

Fig. 3-10. Gold in sheet strips. Pendant with smoky quartz. A. Stengele, SWB, Lucerne, Switzerland.

Fig. 3-11. Pendant, representing galleys, gold with inlays (paste). Egypt, XXVI Dynasty (663–525 B.C.).

Fig. 3-12. Gold pendant, perhaps an ear pendant, of wire and sheet metal, about 0·8 ins. (2cm) high. Egyptian Department, Louvre, Paris.

Fig. 3-13. Gold in the form of wire: Necklace in which wire has been used both as a structural and as a decorative element. The contours of flying swans on the lock (soldered wire) provide the decoration. Scattered granulation of the essential forms. A yellow sapphire in the center. Elisabeth Treskow, Cologne.

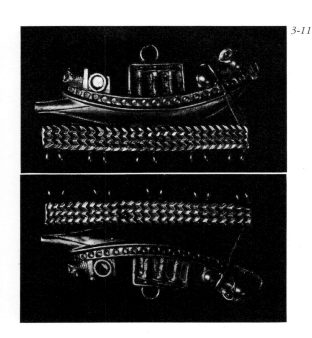 

3-11

Fig. 3-14. Necklace of beaten, very fine pure gold plates. Brigitte Braun-Feldweg, Berlin, 1960.

3-12

Fig. 3-15. Necklace: Triple row of gold wire rings. The outer, more widely spaced fourth row consists of pearls. Brigitte Braun-Feldweg, Berlin, 1964.

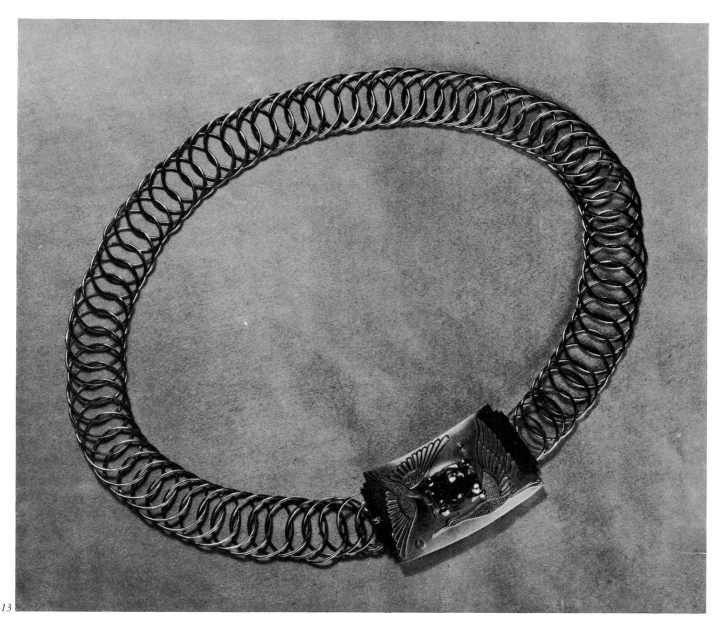

3-13

3-14

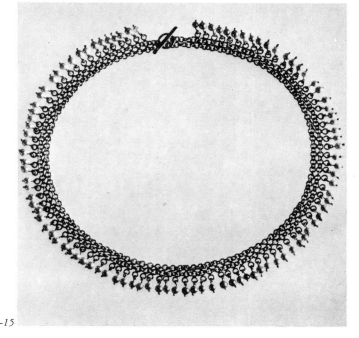

3-15

Fig. 3-16. *Gold as sheet metal. Diadem, 900/1000, wrought. Andreas Moritz, London, 1935.*

Fig. 3-17. *Gold and colored stones: Arrangement of colored stones (star- and Burma sapphires), pearls and brilliants, fashioned according to ancient goldsmiths' art. Distribution of sizes and colors to rich multicolored effect, enhanced by soldered wires, granulation, and various techniques of setting. Elisabeth Treskow, Cologne.*

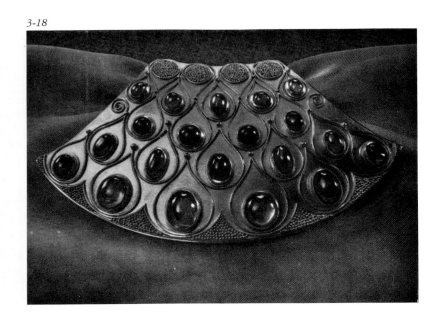

Fig. 3-18. *Gold clip with colored stones cut en cabochon (sapphires and rubies), soldered wires and infilling granulation. Elisabeth Treskow, Cologne.*

Sheet gold

During the melting and alloying of gold as raw material, which he usually does himself in graphite crucibles or in his melting furnace, the goldsmith determines the fineness and the color of the alloy. He pours the liquid metal into molds (sheet and laid molds) which favor whatever further fashioning he has in mind—thin, flat bars, for instance, if he wants to roll them into sheets, and rods if he wants to draw them into wire. After the pouring he must calk the bar. With his sheet and wire roll (see *Figs. 4-85–4-87*), he rolls the foil down to the desired thickness, and then draws out the solid and hollow-drawn wire on the draw bench. From the foil he cuts or saws, bends, embosses, files, and solders the various components of his work, and assembles them. Unity and force of expression will be achieved by carefully maintaining in the foil the characteristics of whichever techniques have been used, and by avoiding the indiscriminate use of too many techniques. The structure of the piece, even in a photograph, must reveal whether a form was created with the hammer from thin foil on wood, or whether it is solid. Old masks and head reliquaries, and the best of the new ones, clearly show their technical origin. They do not conceal that they are made of sheet gold.

Wire

Wire can be strong or thin, round or square. The drawing of solid and hollow-drawn wires is described on page 162. Smooth, twisted (or knurled) wires can be bent with roundnosed or flat pliers: Round and angular, wavy, or in spirals, into bows and scrolls, and worked in their own right or soldered onto sheet gold. The Egyptian bracelet of Meroë (first century A.D.) *(Fig. 5-44)* is an early example of such gold filigree work, which was in evidence in Asia Minor from 2000 B.C., and in Italy from 850 B.C. Etruscan pieces show the finest rhythm. Gold and silver wire are quite distinct; likewise, the two metals differ considerably not only in their color, but also in their whole nature. Their use in the basic forms of wire and granule must therefore also differ. Marc Rosenberg pointed out that filigree techniques are associated with silver, not with gold. He contrasts the popular filigree with the once courtly, elegant, delicate, and painstaking granulation, which is "appreciated only by the connoisseur". A wire work like that shown in *Fig. 3-13*, however, is by no means popular in this sense, but very refined. But it is not filigree work either, because the wire has been used in a structural role rather than as a decorative accessory.

Granules

Several items from the treasures of Tutankhamun's tomb, (discovered 1923–1926) and especially the handle of a gold dagger, show, in addition to soldered wire ornaments, other patterns formed by granules which were thought to be soldered on (see *Granulation* page 202). Attempts by Italian goldsmiths at the turn of the century to rediscover the use of this forgotten artistic method failed. It was a non-Italian who found that a chemical transformation of the surface of these granules is essential to attachment without solder, that is, to welding. It has thus become possible to achieve once again the technical cleanness and clarity of Etruscan granulation *(Fig. 5-41)*.

This most delicate of all decorative techniques, granulation, is indeed feasible and beautiful only in gold, although technically it can also be executed in silver, and even in brass. Its dependence on the raw material is so great that naturalistic forms can never be imposed on it. It is difficult to use it in a mediocre manner. The success with which recent goldsmiths have employed the rediscovery of granulation is evident in the work of Elisabeth Treskow and J. M. Wilm *(Figs. 3-8, 3-13, 5-40)*.

Fig. 3-19. Silver vegetable dish. Design: Magnus Stephensen, 1954. Executed by Georg Jensen, Silversmiths, Copenhagen.

Silver

The esteem in which silver tableware is held seems unshaken. The demand for the true article in cutlery and other utensils favors the appropriate design in a metal whose precious character is so obvious that it needs only a well laid table to convince everybody of its worth (*Fig. 3-37*).

Work in silver has always been clearly distinct from that in gold. The true silversmith works mainly with the hammer. The natural product of his working method is therefore the rounded rather than the angular shape. This is described in greater detail in the section on *Cold forging*, pages 138–144. The freshness and manual dexterity of the silversmiths of the eighteenth century are amazing, especially when they worked on large pieces, for instance the silver altarpieces so popular in the Rococo period. Portrait sculpture, rocaille work, fruit, and flowers were hammered and embossed with as much abandon as technical skill. The angel—part of the silver altar candlestick shown in *Fig. 5-25*—is

evidence of this power of craftsmanship, although here it is expressed in chased rather than wrought silver work.

When metalcraft began to develop, silver was presumably rarer and therefore more highly prized than gold. Since then, steadily increasing production has tended to reduce its value. A reason for this decline is not only the quantity of silver that accrues when copper, zinc, and lead ores are smelted; the role of silver as a coinage metal is no longer important, which has made considerable quantities formerly used for coinage available on the market. Nevertheless a reversal of this tendency has recently been noted, because of technological consumption.

Fine silver is not suitable for everyday utensils, because it is too soft. Nor does it lend itself to satisfactory casting. Silver and silver alloys must be hallmarked. Silver alloys in common use are available in the proportions of 800/1000, 835/1000, 900/1000, 925/1000 (sterling silver), and 935/1000.

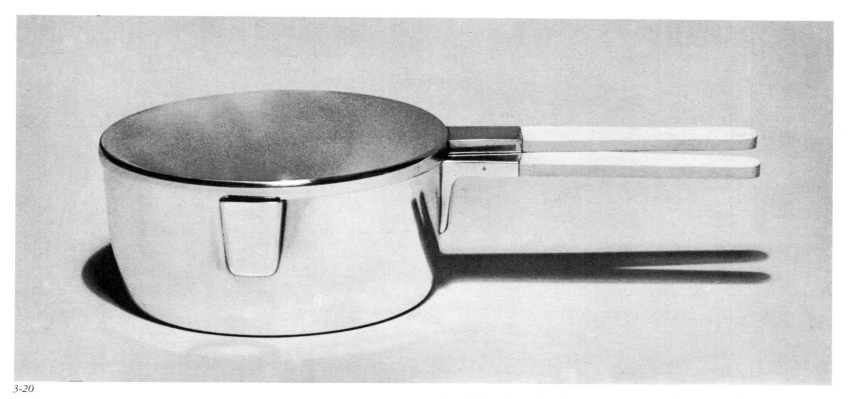

3-20

Fig. 3-20. Casserole, silver with ivory handles. Design: Magnus Stephensen, 1953. Executed by Georg Jensen, Silversmiths, Copenhagen.

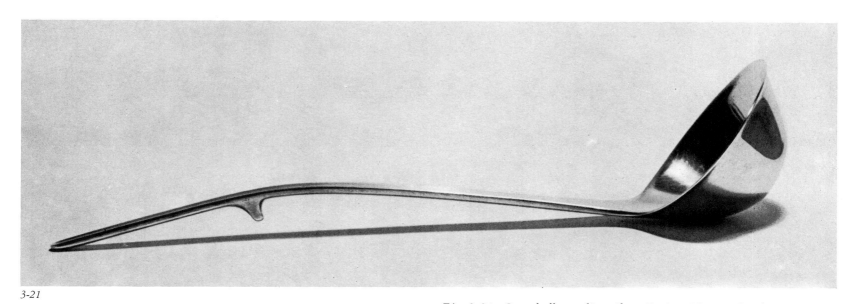

3-21

Fig. 3-21. Soup ladle, sterling silver. Design: Magnus Stephensen. Executed by Georg Jensen, Silversmiths, Copenhagen.

The history of the gold- and silversmiths' craft through the centuries abounds with rules and regulations about the fineness of the material, formerly expressed in "lot" (16 lot = 24 carat). Sworn heads of the guild had to smash, in accordance with their statute, silverware that did not conform to current fineness regulations. The standard of silver for everyday use in the seventeenth century can be accepted as 14 lot. Since pure silver was 16 lot, this corresponds to the modern standard of 875/1000. In times of lax supervision, however, 8–10 lot silver, too, was used; today, such an alloy could no longer be legally called silver. Silverware "fashioned with hammer, or bending pliers, or cast" had to have the maker's mark impressed on it before it was blanched, and after it had been sampled by members of a jury it received the municipal inspector's mark, which guaranteed the fineness of the metal. For the flame test on the cupel (pages 245–246), a little metal was removed from the product with the wriggling tool; silverware therefore often displays the wavy pattern produced by this tool, in an inconspicuous spot such as the underside of the bowl of a spoon. After it is alloyed, the silver is cast in intermediate molds for further treatment. Before it enters the plate roll, the cast silver bar must be calked in a hot state with a mallet. Large silverware factories and refineries employ heavy steam-, compressed-air-, or spring hammers at temperatures of up to 700°C. The changes wrought in the crystalline structure of the metal by casting, annealing, rolling, etc., and the dangers these present to craftsmanship will be discussed in detail on pages 245–248. All the other methods of sheet-metal working are the same as for other metals. This obviously does not mean that experts in working copper and brass can handle silver easily, and that there is no difference between the soldering of sheet brass and sheet silver. Every metal has its unwritten rules, and the experience of working with them is a matter of intuition rather than knowledge. Thus the engravers distinguish between gold and silver damascening for good reasons; each demands its own conditions.

Uses and characteristics

Silver is the raw material of refined utensils, among which tableware takes the pride of place. Its suitability for cutlery, jugs, candlesticks, and bowls is described in the chapter *Objects*. Its use for jewelry is less easy to outline. Compared with the splendid hue of gold, silver jewels always display a thin, cool pallor which, although it will show up in noble contrast against the background of dark or strongly colored fabric, will never be able to equal the harmony between gold and the color of skin. This coolness is very little reduced by colored gems, but can be considerably increased by an unhappy choice of them. Not because of their lower value, but because of the restrained hue of their surfaces, which makes them better suited to silver than the precious stones proper, colored semiprecious stones such as cornelian, rose quartz, and coral go well with silver in jewelry. Silver jewels are austere. It would be wrong to conceal this with an expression of form whose liberal use of solder, granulation, and stones is derived from goldsmith's work. It is better to enhance characteristic features. Silver yields the full and restrained appeal of its metallic beauty only in forms with large surfaces, and really only when the hammer is used *(Fig. 3-22)*. This means that a pressed or stamped form, no matter how well designed, can never produce the best and most delicate surface effects of this highly distinctive raw material. Even photographic reproduction reveals the perfect finish and delicate effects which silver, in this case pure silver, is capable of transmitting *(Fig. 3-28)*. The illustrations of silver objects demonstrate the various possibilities of silver work in thin and thicker sheet form

(Figs. 3-20, 3-27), in coarse filigree *(Fig. 3-29)* and in casting *(Fig. 1-15)*. At the same time, the various pieces reflect the very divergent concepts about silver and its treatment, current at their times of origin. An example is the Age of Baroque with its love of reflection and refraction of light; the tea caddy *(Fig. 1-13)*, series-produced in the eighteenth century, with clear indications of semi-industrial manufacture, is a modest representative. Fluting and bossing to make the metal sparkle are usually much more pronounced in the Gothic and the Baroque style. The coarse surface of the Burg Giebichenstein box *(Fig. 3-24)*, rough-finished with the beading hammer, represents the strongest contrast with this quest for the effect of surface lights. It shows clear emphasis on the hammer and sheet metal effect. The severity of neo-classicism, lastly, is apparent not only in the outline of the Kassel wine jug, but equally clearly in the austere but mat sheen of extensive areas unbroken by any ornaments. Modern taste, too, prefers extensive undisturbed areas on silverware, seeing in this emphasis on surface in silver *(Figs. 3-34–3-35)* a contrast with the delicate technique of the goldsmith. It has been found that silver demands a treatment different from that of gold.

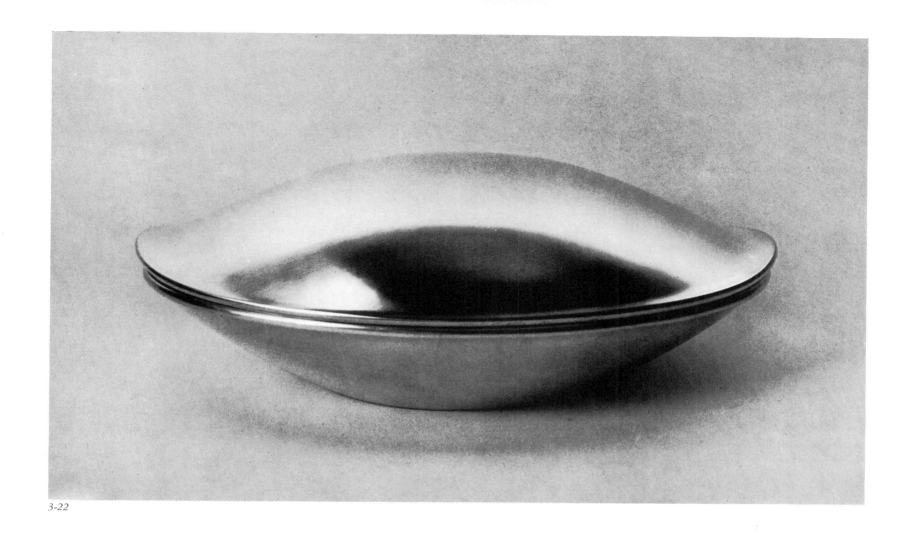

3-22

3-23

Fig. 3-22. *Dish with lid, beaten sterling silver, designed by Henning Koppel, 1960. Executed by Georg Jensen, Silversmiths, Copenhagen.*

Fig. 3-23. *Coffeepot, sterling silver. Design: Henning Koppel, 1956. Executed by Georg Jensen, Silversmiths, Copenhagen.*

3-24

Fig. 3-24. Silver bonbonnière, oval cross section 7:4·7 ins.
(16·7:10·5cm), coarsely beaten from 24 gauge (0·5mm) sheet with the
swaging hammer, handle lightly rough-planed and soldered to the lid.
Workshops of the City of Halle, Burg Giebichenstein, about 1937.

Fig. 3-25. Drinking bowl ("eye bowl"), for wine, 925/1000 silver,
soldered gold, diameter 6·3 ins. (15cm). Andreas Moritz, 1927.

Fig. 3-26. Interior of the eye bowl by Andreas Moritz. The pattern is
executed in soldered gold.

3-25

3-26

3-27

Fig. 3-27. Wine bowl with handles, 925/1000 silver, sheet thickness 21 gauge (0·7mm), soldered green-alloyed gold, bottom of bowl fire-gilt. Andreas Moritz, 1931.

Fig. 3-28. Silver in the form of sheet: Laurel wreath in pure silver, whose softness demands very careful, delicate working. Egon Ehrath and Andreas Moritz, 1927.

Fig. 3-29. Silver in the form of wire: Bread- or fruit basket. Wolfgang Tümpel, Hamburg.

3-28

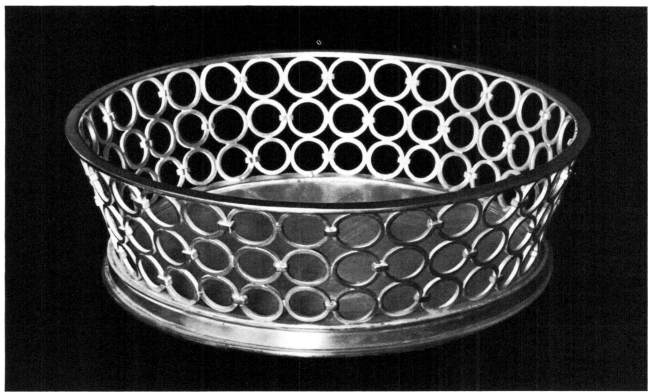

3-29

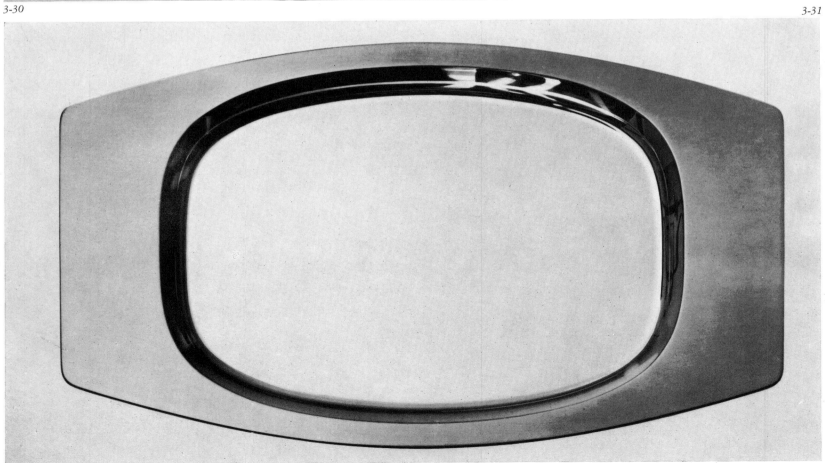

3-32

Fig. 3-30. *Machine-formed silver. Teapot on its heating element, with strainer insert and drip catcher. Design: Karl Dittert. Manufacturers: Gebrüder Kühn, Schwäbisch Gmünd.*

Fig. 3-31. *Pressed meat dish, silver, made in two different sizes. Design: Karl Dittert. Manufacturers: Württembergische Metallwarenfabrik, Geislingen.*

Fig. 3-32. *Coffeepot, sugar bowl, and cream jug, silver, body mass-produced on the spinning lathe. Design: Karl Dittert. Manufacturers: Gebrüder Kühn, Schwäbisch Gmünd.*

Fig. 3-33. *Silver bread bowl, also designed as an industrial mass product. Design: Karl Dittert. Manufacturers: Württembergische Metallwarenfabrik, Geislingen.*

3-33

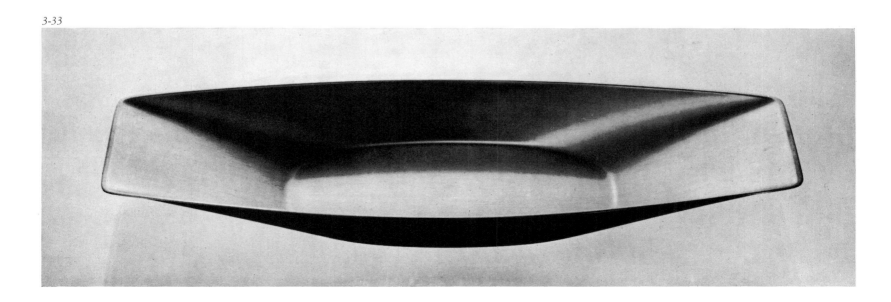

3-34

Fig. 3-34. *Tea set M.41. Design: Leo Sabatini. Manufacturers: Argenteria Christofle, Milan.*

Fig. 3-35. *Vegetable dish, silver with ivory handles. Design: Henning Koppel, 1961. Executed in the Workshops of Georg Jensen, Silversmiths, Copenhagen.*

3-35

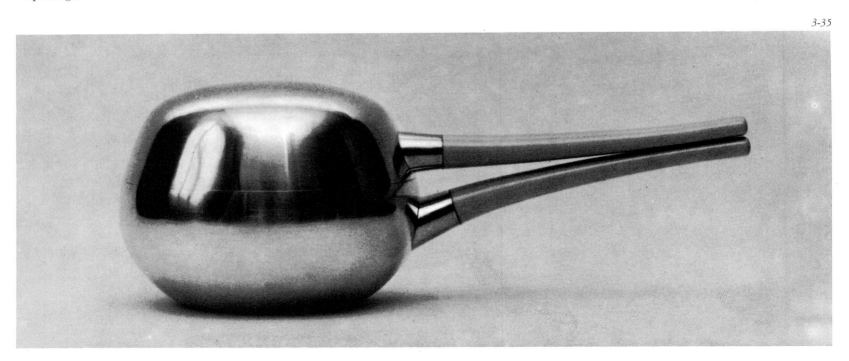

Fig. 3-36. *Place setting, sterling silver, for use in British embassies. Designed for the British Government and executed by David Mellor RDI, DesRCA, FSIA. Made in Sheffield.*

Fig. 3-37. *Soup spoon, plate, fork, and knife. Part of the set for British embassies in Fig. 3-36.*

3-38

3-39

Fig. 3-38. *Knife, fork, and spoon, silver, designed in about 1927, by the Berlin gold- and silversmith Lettré, for P. Bruckmann & Söhne, silverware manufacturers, Heilbronn. Still part of the firm's production range.*

Fig. 3-39. *Knife, fork, and spoon, designed by Magnus Stephensen, 1962. Executed by Georg Jensen, Silversmiths, Copenhagen. Radical change of general appearance.*

Copper

Since bronze is an alloy of copper, copper must have been discovered and worked first. Presumably this occurred during the middle of the fifth millenium B.C. And not until the beginning of the second millenium B.C. did the alloy with tin—bronze—make its debut. It is astonishing that it was possible, as long ago as the beginning of the Metal Age, to produce sufficient heat for melting. Egyptian murals in tombs at Thebes, dated at about 1450 B.C., show us early stages of the techniques of melting and casting, and even the use of bellows. Yet copper is not a suitable metal for casting. It is soft, tensile, and elastic, and can therefore be cold forged, embossed, rolled, pressed, and drawn, offering little resistance to noncutting shaping. Its casting properties, however, are poor, which is why its alloy with tin, bronze, was initially so much more important than copper.

But as soon as the cold working of metals had been learned, copper came to play a prominent role again. Not the most important role—it was never suitable for this—but a very respectable role nonetheless: quite often it deputized for gold and silver. The Tassilo Chalice *(Fig. 2-38)*, for instance, is made of copper, covered with nielloed silver plates and parcel gilt; the antependium of Gross Komburg is embossed in gold-plated sheet copper *(Fig. 5-23)*; and many an ecclesiastical metal object, even during the Late Middle Ages, was made of copper. The fact that enamel takes well on copper (see page 12) greatly favors the aims of ecclesiastical design.

But household materials old and new also testify to the usefulness of this metal in spite of its tendency to form poisonous verdigris, which is countered by tin plating the inner vessel walls. Coppersmiths produced not only brewing vats and similar large vessels, but also copper basins, cans, vessels, and cake tins. In Southern European countries, splendid copper vessels can be seen at the village well even today.

Its high conductivity of electric current, and the enormous consumption of copper and brass shells, cartridge cases, and driving bands have had a catastrophic effect on copper as a raw material for the creative artist. Countless copper implements, works of art, and designs have been swallowed up by scrap metal collections during the two World Wars.

The properties of copper as a raw material determine the way in which it is worked even more drastically than already described. Whereas bottoms, feet, handles, and other parts of silver vessels can be soldered on without difficulty, this method has its disadvantages when making copper vessels. The red heat unavoidable with hard soldering destroys the spring temper of sheet copper produced by hammering. Another method of joining is therefore more appropriate here: Riveting, and hemming or folding. The rims of sheet silver and brass vessels are bent double or reinforced with solder to make them stronger and feel more solid, and less paper-like and tinny. The reinforcement of rims of copper vessels should in addition include a wire, which can be of iron if very high rigidity is required.

A characteristic attraction of copper, rare among metals, is its richly glowing color. It is extremely variable. There are many steps from the bright red of the metallically pure, shiny surface to the chestnut-brown of natural patina. Chemical treatment, too, offers further possibilities of beautiful and durable coloring.

The coloring of copper and copper alloys

Chemical compounds into which copper enters can be used for color-ing. Oxygen compounds produce the colors brown to red (cuprous oxide Cu_2O) and black (cupric oxide CuO). Sulfur compounds (copper sulfide) also result in brown to black. The use of Schlippe's Salt (sodium sulfantimoniate), too, comes under this heading. Liver of sulfur (impure potassium sulfide), sodium sulfide, barium sulfide, and calcium sulfide also serve for coloring. Basic copper chlorides and carbonates produce brownish or green tones (resembling malachite, copper blue).

A few directions and formulae are given below. The relevant literature contains many agents and solutions of varying concentration. Chloride-rich solutions act rapidly, but their colors darken after a while. Acetates, too, are comparatively quick-acting, resulting in a yellowish-green patina, but are more difficult to use, since during a second application they often dissolve the film of patina already produced.

Preliminary treatment and procedure

Perfect coloring is possible only when the surfaces are clean and free from grease. Remove grease with a paste of French chalk, and rinse with water. Brush with a steel- or brass-wire brush. Grind and polish by hand or on the wheel stand with the usual abrasives. Castings should not be polished, so as to preserve the casting skin. The method by which the work is made metallically pure depends on its character.

The solution can be applied with a brush, rag, sponge, etc.; spraying is not recommended. Apply as evenly and thinly as possible, and rub the first coat into the surface. Let the second application wait until the first is dry. Pools of solution produce poorly adherent crusts of salt. Solutions of weaker concentration are safer than stronger ones containing free acid; these cause a roughening of the surface. The patina loses its metallic character, and the impression of a coat of paint is created. Less strongly acting solutions, and frequent rubbing down with a soft piece of rag or leather between the various applications, result in the glossy colors appropriate to natural patina. Mercury salts in some solutions make the metal surface more reactive. Correctly applied, the colors are durable. This demands frequent applications with intermediate treatment, in other words much manual work. Patinating fluids are not expensive, and can be stored for long periods.

Brown coloring

Schlippe's Salt in solution is suitable for coloring large pieces that cannot be immersed. Cold or hot application (brushing) produces copper sulfide, whose color can be intensified from the lightest brown-yellow to black-brown hues by concentration of the solution, and duration of the treatment. The solution has good keeping qualities if stored in a closed vessel.

Reddish-brown color (cast bronze): 3 parts antimony pentasulfide and 1 part ferric oxide stirred to a paste. Reddish-brown copper hue: 2 parts verdigris, 2 parts cinnabar, 5 parts sal volatile (ammonium carbonate), 5 parts alum and vinegar.

Brown coloring of bronze: Stir antimony pentasulfide with water and a little liquid ammonia to a paste. Apply with a brush. Rub off the red deposit with a soft brush after allowing it to dry.

Alternatively: Dissolve 0·8 oz (25g) Schlippe's Salt in 1·8 pints (1000cc) water. Stir in antimony pentasulfide until a thin paste is obtained. Mix with a little liquid ammonia. Use fine steel wool for

3-40

Fig. 3-40. *Example of traditional coppersmith's craft: Eighteenth-century kettle, copper, internally tin-plated. Knob of lid turned brass, hinges of the handle soldered, hand guard turned wood. Diameter of body 4·4 ins. (10·5cm), height without lid 2·8 ins. (6·8cm), thickness of sheet metal about 21 gauge (0·7mm). Body shaped from a soldered sheet and superficially beaten. Spout wrought in two parts and soldered together, handle beaten and filed, bottom and rims hemmed (joined by folded seam).*

vigorously rubbing the surface to be colored, and a dry rag for removing the substance after some time. Aftertreatment is with steel wool or a soft brass-wire brush. The color can be intensified by repetition of the treatment, or a larger quantity of liquid ammonia.

Steel-gray–black

Arsenic pickling, applied electrolytically or by the dipping process, produces a steel-gray to black color on copper and copper alloys (structural bronze). Formula: Dissolve 2·8 oz (80g) powdered arsenic together with 3·2 oz (90g) ferric chloride or iron sulfate in 1·8 pints (1000cc) concentrated commercial hydrochloric acid. Heating accelerates dissolution (caution—poison). Ready for use after 1–2 days. Immerse the dry work or apply the solution with a brush. Allow to dry between repeated immersions. After coloring, rinse with water, neutralize in a solution of sodium carbonate, thoroughly rinse and dry. Coat with neutral varnish. Prepare and apply the pickle in a well-ventilated room or in the open, using an earthenware vessel. Dip for up to 30sec., temperature of the solution not above 45°C.

Green coloring

The natural malachite-green color of old pieces of copper or bronze is called patina. Exposure to air or damp soil produces a dirty gray tone, yellowish to greenish-brown, brown, and finally a black color. Different chemical effects account for the different colors produced in the soil or in air (climatic differences). The atmosphere of big cities, which is rich in sulfur compounds from industry, produces "city patina".

Artificial patination is obtained by brushing, stippling, spraying, etc. the coloring solution on the work. Alloys containing zinc are easier to patinate than copper; tin bronze is the most difficult. Solutions: 0·7–7 oz (20–200g) ammonium chloride, 0·4–7 oz (10–200g) verdigris, 1·8 pints (1000cc) vinegar. Bronze without zinc: 0·4 oz (10g) copper nitrate, 0·4 oz (10g) copper chloride, 1·1 oz (30g) zinc sulfate, 0·5 oz (15g) mercuric chloride, 1·8 pints (1000cc) water.

Brass

Copper alloyed with zinc, a metal which on its own is useless as a raw material for the metal craftsman, is eminently suitable for treatment of every kind. Brass can be cast, rolled, drawn, embossed, cut, and lends itself equally well to noncutting and cutting shaping. It can be polished, is sufficiently elastic, not too hard, and has a beautiful color, which with chemical treatment is capable of wide variations. The two most important alloys, consisting mainly of copper, brass, and bronze, are not always easy to distinguish. Thus the sculptures on the Emperor Maximilian's Tomb at Innsbruck in Austria are generally considered bronze castings. But according to recent investigations by technical experts they are now thought to be brass. Many Gothic momumental slabs, cast and engraved, are made of brass. Old records are not always reliable in their descriptions. Thus much cast brass is found outside and inside old houses: On the doorknob or doorknocker, in the scullery and the kitchen. Even today, many rural water faucets are brass castings.

Brass as a raw material occurs more frequently in the form of sheet metal, wire, and tubes than as casting. *Fig. 3-41* shows an ancient use of sheet brass, extremely widespread up to the eighteenth century: Water bowls—those for daily use and ornamental ones to be displayed on the shelf—were beaten from it. The somewhat obscure process used to produce such bowls in large quantities suggests that the favorable forming properties of brass as a raw material led, even in those days, to a mechanization of production approaching that of the modern method of pressing. We cannot say with any certainty how the hollow shapes were embossed from the brass sheet, whether with lead hubbing dies in iron dies, or in wooden patterns. But the thickness of the sheet, increasing from 0·3mm (approx. 30 gauge) in the bottom of the bowl, which was often torn, to 1·8mm (approx. 16 gauge) at the rim, clearly indicates that these vessels were all somehow embossed, and not raised with the hammer. That they were turned on the lathe after embossing, as has also been claimed, is most doubtful. They could not be centered accurately enough for this method. It is more likely that an early method of spinning was used; it is not known precisely when this was invented. At any rate all the ornamental forms, figures, and inscriptions were struck with stamps. This explains both the use of Gothic types of lettering and ornaments as late as the eighteenth century, since workshop equipment was inherited, and the often random sequence of letters struck by assistants who could not read.

Old and new brass utensils fashioned by craftsmen are made of the alloy in its natural color, mat-brushed as well as polished, and occasionally coated with clear varnish. In the factory process, on the other hand, brassware, especially household, kitchen, and table utensils, is often plated with some other metal such as chromium, nickel, or silver, depending on the intended purpose. For, like all copper alloys, brass develops an unpleasant smell of its own; in addition it forms a poisonous chemical compound, verdigris. There are innumerable brass implements which no longer betray their raw material: The shiny nickel-plated machines in a coffee bar, silver-plated tea glass holders, lighting fixtures, and many other objects which by metal plating have acquired a different appearance.

In addition to these machine-made, mainly spun, drawn, and pressed brass products, whose shaping demands technical and creative skill, craftsmen create individual works, such as teapots and water jugs *(Figs. 3-45–3-46)*, in which traditional manual skill and original forms evolved with the forging hammer survive. Vessels such as these must be tin-plated inside to keep them clean and to eliminate health-damaging

3-41

Fig. 3-41. *Fourteenth-century brass bowl: An interesting example of early, semi-industrial mass production. Clear indications of what is probably mechanical embossing: Uneven sheet thickness, maximum 15 gauge (1·5mm), very thin at the bottom, cracked in some places. The palmettes on the flat rim are clearly hand punched. However, the figure representation (Caleb's cluster of grapes), with its surrounding inscription, may well have been roughstamped in a die, and subsequently chased. Wear and tear makes an accurate assessment difficult, but the fact that similar, and therefore stylistically obsolete, representations are found as late as the seventeenth and eighteenth centuries indicates that tools and dies were passed from generation to generation and continued to be used in the workshops. Bowls of this kind were used both in the medieval household and in the church. The inscription consists of three words repeated to make a full circle "Geluk alzeite wart" (everlasting good fortune), and of decorative fillers in the style of the lettering.*

effects. It is also advisable to clean household utensils made of brass, like silverware, regularly and frequently.

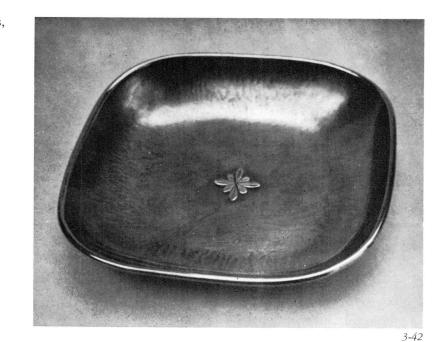

3-42

Fig. 3-42. Ashtray, brass burnished, about 3·3 × 3·3 ins. (8 × 8cm). Rolf Koolman, Lübeck.

3-43

Fig. 3-43. Biscuit tin, brass, internally tin-plated. Oval diameters 7·7 and 6·5 ins. (18·6 and 15·5cm). Beaten, raised from 20 gauge (0·8mm) sheet metal, inner rim reinforced with soldered 0.125 ins. (3mm) square wire. Feet worked from the solid and filed. Lid handle made of wire, riveted inside. Workshops of the City of Halle, Burg Giebichenstein, 1936.

3-44

Fig. 3-44. *Brass casing of an alarm clock, eighteenth century, engraved and punched. Tin clock face, figures engraved, heavy bars of the Roman numerals recessed in wrigglework. The ornamental curves of the case were traced with punches, the little circles in the quadrangular panels punched with ring punches.*

3-45

Fig. 3-45. *Tea set, brass, hammer-forged, internally tin-plated. Zinnschmiede Raichle, Meersburg, Lake Constance.*

Fig. 3-46. *Kettle, brass. Body formed of a single sheet. After the inside walls were tin-plated, the bottom was soldered on with tin, and the rim is therefore hemmed. Handle cut from a strip and bent, the fittings for it riveted. Franz Rickert, Munich.*

Fig. 3-47. Tombac as base metal for enameled bowl. Walter Lochmüller, Schwäbisch Gmünd.

Red Brass (Tombac)

Red brass differs from brass only in its higher copper content. Its color approximates that of red gold, and it is therefore occasionally misused to imitate gold; more appropriately it is used as a base for gold-plating in rolled-gold manufacture. Red brass objects without precious metal plating are rare. A beautiful example of this kind is shown in *Fig. 2-25*, a teapot by Sieglinde Maurer. This alloy is normally used almost exclusively in the jewelry trade and in the enameler's workshop *(Fig. 3-47)*.

Fig. 3-48. *Side view of baptismal font by Andreas Moritz, cast bronze, diameter 25 ins. (60cm), height 7·5 ins. (18cm); executed 1930.*

Fig. 3-49. *The eye in the bottom of the font is silver champlevé (niello), inlaid with gold. Stages of inlaying: First, the large almond shape was chiseled out of the bronze in the bottom of the bowl. Then the silver plate to be inlaid was prepared as follows: The pupil was inlaid with pure gold, and the delicate lines indicating the eyelids were inlaid in green gold. Finally, the entire figure was force-fitted into the chiseled recess. Only then was the ring of the iris chiseled out as a recess and its entire width filled with niello (hence the description as champlevé).*

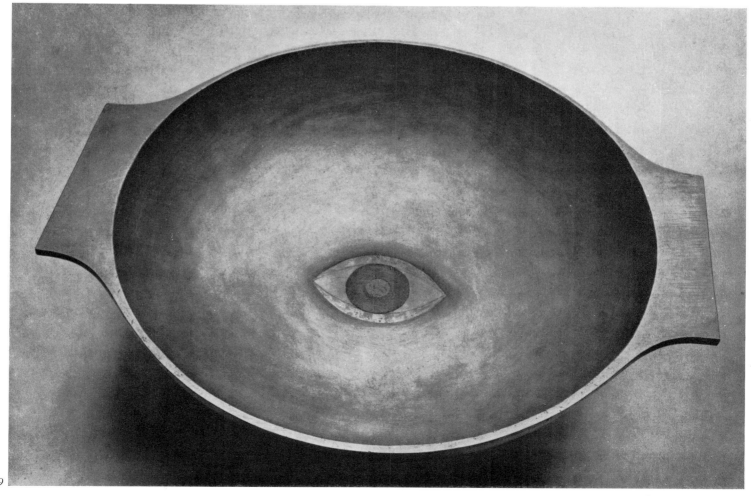

Bronze

Apart from its importance as a bearing metal in the engineering and automobile industries, the old, precious casting metal—in the past called bell metal, and gunmetal by the guildsman—seems to have fallen into almost complete disuse today. It is restricted to a very few applications, such as bell founding and the casting of sculptures of all sizes. Utensils are very rarely made of bronze now. A survey of its use and significance can therefore be little more than a historical review. This alloy of copper and tin (brass, in contrast, consists of copper and zinc), which has given its name to a period of man's development, has receded into the background more and more in spite of its excellent qualities, because both the top-grade material and the casting of it are expensive.

Its excellent formability favored creative shaping: Perfect castability on the one hand, and the possibility of the most delicate finishing of the casting with cutting and embossing tools on the other. Bronze implements range from prehistoric weapons, tools, and ornaments to tripods, candelabra, candlesticks, lamps, mirrors, antique heating and cooking utensils, medieval lattices, door leaves, mountings, and handles, baptismal fonts, engraved slabs, bells, ewers, mortars, basins, weights and measures, and the last utensils made during the eighteenth century, such as the inkpot shown in *Fig. 3-50*. The properties of bronze can be graded and predetermined with the ratios of the alloy. Even old alloys therefore vary in their tin content from 1 part to 3–9 parts of copper, in Egypt 12–14% tin, 85% copper. A frequent ratio is 1 part tin, 4 parts copper. This 20% tin content is usual in bell metal today. Small admixtures of zinc and silver, and lead as a constituent of impure copper, also occur. Knowledge of the alloying of the casting metal and the technical mastery of the molding and casting methods were at all times greatly esteemed, often more so than the achievement of the designing artist, who did not always do his own casting. Where these skills were highly developed, the establishment of the artistically prominent casting houses soon followed—for instance Vischer's workshop at Nuremberg, which existed for more than a hundred years—and bronze casting spread. There probably never existed a sharp distinction between the guild of braziers producing everday utensils, and the casting houses engaged in the production of great works of art. The low esteem in which the bronze cast is held, and the lack of appreciation from which it largely suffers today, are perhaps due to the fact that bronze is regarded as a material only for reproduction, and no longer as a raw material whose beauty demands thoughtful treatment. Only those who are aware of the possibilities of expression inherent in this metal, and the attraction of the color of its natural or artificial patina, will be able to appreciate the perfect casting of the sacred bronzes of East Asia, which refute the unfortunate European distinction between "pure" and "applied" art, which was unknown during the Middle Ages *(Fig. 3-52)*.

The technique of bronze casting is described in detail under *Casting,* pages 115–137.

The yellow color of metallically pure bronze is strongly varied by natural and artificial patina. Chinese bronzes of the earliest periods display gorgeous colors: Bright-green, gray-green, olive-green, and dark-green hues occur side by side with earth-colored, turquoise, red-brown, and purple patina. Shiny-smooth and mat surfaces can sometimes be found on the same piece. It is difficult to determine with any certainty which of these colors were produced by natural influences in the course of time, and which are the result of deliberate action.

German Silver

German silver is even less suitable than red brass to stand on its own as a raw material without silver plating. Its constituents are copper, zinc, and nickel. And even more than the other copper alloys, German silver has a smell of its own. Furthermore, its yellowish-white color is not very attractive, and polished surfaces soon become dull and plain. The metal craftsmen of the Bauhaus used unplated German silver for tableware, regardless of the fact that it is unsuitable for this purpose. The attempt has never been repeated. But the very hard and resistant alloy is eminently suitable for the manufacture of silver-plated cutlery, instruments, and other metalware intended for silver-, chromium-, or nickel-plating. German silver can be pressed, stamped, spun, and drawn; it is, however, less suitable for shaping by hand. Because of its hardness it is not easy to engrave, and neither its appearance nor its behavior encourage embossing and hammering. Nevertheless, plastic embossing is occasionally carried out in German silver.

3-50

3-51

3-52

Fig. 3-50. *Ink stand, cast in bronze, with three recesses inside for ink wells and sand boxes. Fitting mark on the lid. Diameter about 5 ins. (11·7cm), height 2·4 ins. (5·8cm) with feet, dated 1773.*

Fig. 3-51. *Lübeck herring measure, cast in bronze, dated 1469.*

Fig. 3-52. *East Asian cast bronze: Ritual vessel (for sacrificial wine), height 14·4 ins. (34·5cm). China, about 500 B.C.*

Tin

Since the discovery and exploitation of tin ore deposits in the Erzgebirge ("Ore Mountains") in the Middle Ages, this soft, silvery metal, of low melting point (234°C), has become increasingly common as a raw material for household appliances and tableware. It was used especially by the pewterers for jugs, beakers, measures, plates, bowls, spoons, and salt cellars, and in times of economic depression for ritual objects, candlesticks, chalices, and basins. Nuremberg, which in the Middle Ages was the center for pewterers, counted in 1363 thirty-three masters of the craft, who were joined in a guild with brass forgers, braziers, and plumbers. The export of engraved or etched pewterware was considerable. Whereas during the sixteenth and seventeenth centuries luxury and ornamental objects, too, were cast, in the eighteenth century there was a return to functional forms such as coffeepots and teapots, cups and bowls, which are appropriate to the nature of the material. The raw material of practical everyday utensils, still cheap at the beginning of the nineteenth century (it was known as "the little man's silver"), has now become a luxury metal because of its scarcity and the requirements of technology to use it for other purposes. Although the increasing appreciation of good traditional design has brought with it a renewed esteem of this material, so despised at the beginning of industrialization, there is little likelihood that tin will once again be of interest to a wider public than to collectors and connoisseurs, and that it will meet a genuine demand instead of being confined to showpieces and luxury articles. Thus pewter has become the sphere of the art historian, antique pieces are sought by collectors, and the number of surviving pewterers' workshops is steadily decreasing. New raw materials and industrial progress make it very difficult for the few stalwarts to revive craftsmanship in pewter *(Figs. 2-28, 3-55)*.

Some table utensils made of pewter, such as teapots, may perhaps return to favor. Tea and coffee caddies, tobacco tins, or boxes could be inexpensively and functionally designed.

Tin is a casting metal. Although like copper and brass it has recently been forged with the hammer, this is not the appropriate treatment, quite apart from the fact that this method makes the work very much more expensive. The restful, austere surface, and the clear roundness produced on the lathe, are more in tune with its unobtrusive nature than the freely forged shapes and the glittering vagueness of their hammer finish. Where the shape requires organic composition, this should be produced on the lathe. Here, antique work can point the way in which the carefully chosen proportions can be enhanced with delicate grooves and bosses. A casting demands cutting tools. With the cutter, handled forcefully and dynamically on the soft material, the mat surface can be enriched most beautifully. The swift and effective wrigglework or tremolo should again be practiced for original, ornamental ideas in engraving. Punching and embossing, on the other hand, and even simple chiseling, are really alien to tin and its coarse crystalline structure. We should be glad that there is at least one metal that does not lend itself to common-or-garden shaping in sheet form, and demands its own characteristic solid design. Any sheet metal that appeared on a tin casting was a strip of brass or copper to add a touch of color to it.

Tin, when alloyed with other metals, improves their casting properties. When alloyed with copper, it produces bronze, the ideal casting material. Tin itself requires small additions of copper or lead (5–10%) to become a real casting metal.

The "standard" tin of the nineteenth century contained 10% lead; today household tin is completely free of lead, because lead is poisonous. The Württemberg "Pewterers' Ordinance" of 1554 prescribed the lead content of pewter: "Beaten or raised articles of pure pewter without any addition of lead" should be stamped with the Württemberg hallmark. The Imperial (German) assay, on the other hand, permitted a lead admixture of 10% for jugs, bottles, bowls, plates, beakers, etc.

Tin is cast in iron or brass molds, which are first lined with a little clay. In the sixteenth century, brass, copper, or stone molds were etched for the casting of pewter. More recent molds for tin figures were cut in the negative in slate slabs. The tin ashes, a layer of oxide forming during melting, must be skimmed off. Theophilus Presbyter (eleventh century) described in his *Schedula diversarum artium* the medieval method of casting pewter flagons.

The finished pewter article, too, will in the course of time get covered with a gray oxide film, and must therefore be looked after similarly to silver to preserve its mild, bright sheen. Warm water and granular tin or dried horsetail are suitable for its care. Two further characteristics of the metal must be mentioned: Tin cry, a creaking sound caused when the metal is bent and the crystals change their position; and a mysterious "disease"—the so-called tin plague—that can attack tin and dissolve its metallic structure. It is transmitted at temperatures below 14°C by tin articles already affected. Articles in unheated rooms and in the neighborhood of tin objects already infected are therefore at risk. In other words: The element "tin" (stannum, Sn) exists in two morphologically completely different forms—as a metal of crystalline structure, and as an amorphous powder into which it suddenly disintegrates from the metallic structure after it has become infected, and low temperature and shock intervene.

Because of its low melting point, easy flow, and readiness to form alloys, tin is used as solder, but only for work that does not have to satisfy stringent demands of finish or use. Since it is completely nonpoisonous and does not react chemically with food, it continues to be used for the internal plating of copper and brass vessels, which without this treatment would develop verdigris and a characteristic smell and taste. Today it is used mainly for the manufacture of hot-dipped tinplate (for cans), foil, tubes, and similar packing material.

3-53

Fig. 3-53. *Pewter vessel with handle, about natural size. Delicate turned grooves, a little bolder round the knob of the lid, enliven the design. The handle has a vigorous profile. Ulm, probably eighteenth century.*

3-54

Fig. 3-54. Tea and coffee caddies, cast in pewter, plain or with turned grooves. From the workshops of Eugen Wiedamann, Regensburg.

Fig. 3-55. Pewter box, Lindau, Lake Constance, about 1700.

Iron and Steel

We must distinguish between iron and steel as raw materials in their own right for creative purposes, and as materials for tools used in the making of metal articles. In both cases it can be the object of a craftsman's shaping as distinct from a structural operation. With this differentiation from the purely technical use in engineering, we do not wish to detract from the stylistic composition the designer achieves, often unintentionally and as a mere by-product. On the contrary, it can serve as a very necessary counterpoint to some craftsmen's often specious traditionalism. What was formerly called wrought iron now bears the name of structural (nonhardenable) steel. In this sense the term "iron", too, is applied mainly, but not exclusively, to the carbon-rich, nonforgeable cast iron. The raw materials "iron" and "steel" are therefore divided into the following main groups.

Tool steels

This group comprises a multitude of alloys, high-speed steels, and other special types. They are worked in all shapes and sizes, even as wire and sheet metal, both cold and hot. In addition to the carbon content $(0 \cdot 4 - 1 \cdot 5\%)$, alloying with manganese, chromium, silicon, tungsten, vanadium, etc. is important for the properties of the various types of steel.

The properties of the steel used for tools and their processing differ radically from those of wrought iron. Dies, cutting and stamping tools, stamps, and matrices are almost exclusively cold worked. Planing, turning, milling, chiseling, cutting, filing, and grinding can all be used to shape the tool. The property of the tool steels of becoming as hard as glass as a result of forced chilling from red heat (water-, oil-, or air-hardening), and the possibility of adjusting this hardness to the desired degree by the process of "annealing", makes them suitable for the machining of other metals. This is the basis of their great importance in the whole metalworking field. Hammers and chisels, punches, gravers, and files, and a thousand other manual and machine tools, are made of tool steel. Knowledge of the properties of the various types of steel, and of the hardening and annealing processes, is therefore of fundamental importance to every metalworker. The chapter on metallography contains information about types of steel and their most important properties (page 255).

Structural steel (nonhardenable steel)

Steel of a carbon content below $0 \cdot 6\%$ used to be called wrought iron. It is the proper raw material for artistic wrought-iron work, for gates and doors, grilles, mountings, and utensils. The material comes from the rolling mill in rod bars or faggots, as sectional steel (rounds, square bars, rods, and flat bars). The metal is forged at red heat; this is followed at the finishing stages by a few processes of cold treatment, such as riveting, filing, and, with sheet metal parts, embossing and punching as well. The shaping proper is reserved for the hot treatment. *Working in wrought iron*, page 118, includes further details on the subject.

Iron (formerly cast iron)

Carbon content about $2 \cdot 8 - 4 \cdot 5\%$. Its use as a raw material by the creative craftsman is very limited today, not least because of the misuse it had to suffer during the nineteenth century. Cast iron was the cheap material in which the architectural designs of past periods were copied extensively. Cast-iron pavilions boasting Greek capitals and ornaments, bridge railings and balustrades, even paraffin lamps and candelabra aspiring to Renaissance ornaments were cast. This abuse has long ceased. *Fig. 3-58*, on the other hand, shows a cast-iron stove panel, which is a true example of relief representations adapted both to the purpose of the article and to the difficult material. Here, a love of ornamentation which was naïve yet sure of its effects expressed the outlook of the period. To be able to appreciate these panels properly, we must remember that the reliefs of huge stoves were often the only ornaments in the bare, whitewashed peasants' parlor—inviting leisurely contemplation during long winter evenings before the days of television and radio. Even though such stoves and their ornaments are no longer fashionable, the use of cast iron for related purposes is still fully justified. Memorial plaques of similar design on buildings would appear more dignified than many a pretentious, ostentatious sculpture. That at one time cast iron was used as a raw material for jewelry—delicate bracelets of the neoclassical period—has long been forgotten.

Cast iron is not the only material which in our age has gone out of favor with the creative artist; his attitude towards wrought iron (nonhardenable steel) is not clearcut either. Wrought-iron work, where it is found on public and private buildings, is rarely good. It would be easy to select old examples of good wrought-iron design and to show that even a simple piece can be durable, functional, as well as distinguished at the same time. Several publications exist on this subject. The main point here is to find the few achievements of craftsmanship in which the exacting, severe characteristics of the raw material and of the forging technique submit to the slight demands of our time. We do not need the massive coffers of the medieval kind; today the use of wrought iron extends to lamp supports, fire sets, and delicate, stylish building ornaments (for examples see *Figs. 4-20, 4-22, 4-26–4-30*). Study of *Working in wrought iron,* page 118, will reveal what is meant by "design appropriate to the nature of the raw material", because no other work in metal depends as much on craft methods and the characteristics of the raw material as working in wrought iron.

For use indoors, wrought iron should be tarnished black and coated with transparent varnish; outdoors, it should have a coat of weatherproof paint. But in the past this material was finished black or blue, in other words a tempering color, for special purposes. This happened whenever the artist-smith worked on the material, and used all the techniques of his art such as cutting and engraving, inlay, embossing, and etching, for weapons, armor, and ornamental pieces (*Figs. 1-11, 5-32, 5-38–5-39*).

3-57

3-58

Fig. 3-56. Tabernacle grille, fifteenth century, height 14·6 ins. (35cm), width 12·5 ins. (30cm). Example of combination, popular at the time, of a rhomboid bar screen and punched-out sheet. The square bars are not punched, but notched in a swage.

Fig. 3-57. Iron bar screen, Freising, 1620. Symmetrically arranged spirals, punched intersections, with parts welded on or held by strong collars.

Fig. 3-58. Württemberg coat of arms, Baroque, 1687. Cast-iron stove panel, Schwäbische Hüttenwerke, Wasseralfingen.

3-59

3-60

Fig. 3-59. *Casserole: Industrial product, stainless steel, with plastic handles. The elongated-oval cross section of the handle prevents accidental tilting, its conical longitudinal shape permits production without ugly die-casting seams. Design: Misha Black and Ronald Armstrong, Design Research Unit, London. Manufacturers: Ernest Stevens Ltd. (UK).*

Fig. 3-60. *The comparison of steel- and silverware on this page is relevant not only to the style of the designer, but also because the same technological processes of industrial production lead to analogous forms even where the raw materials differ. Coffee service, silver and lignum vitae. Design: Misha Black. Executed by T. J. Boucher, Royal College of Art, London.*

Fig. 3-61. *Aluminum as material for vessels: Coffeepot and water kettle with lid and handle insulation of black plastic or teak. Design: Eero Rislakki, 1962. Manufacturers: Ammus-Sytytin Oy, Rauma, Finland.*

The Light Alloys

Aluminum and magnesium, the two most important elements of the light metal group, together with their technologically important alloys, will be described in greater detail in the chapter on metallography (pages 257–258). Properties and behavior, possibilities of working and shaping, of hardening and surface finishing through anodizing and coloring, are discussed at length. This emphasis is justified, because these most recent metallic raw materials are typical of our age—not so much for the craftsman, but more for the kind of mass production that depends on the latest technological methods of casting and hot and cold shaping *(Figs. 3-63–3-71)*.

The reader might well ask why a discussion of these metals has been included in this book, which, after all, is in no way concerned with purely technological areas of metalworking. The answer becomes obvious as soon as you consider the range of applications of the light metals, enormously expanded of late: Display window frames, doors, staircases, railings, mountings and fixtures of buildings and vehicles, clothes hooks and lamps—the list could be extended at will. These new raw materials are taking the place of wrought iron and of the nonferrous metals (production 1876–1900: 0·02 million tons; 1926–1950: 17·2 million tons). In public transport vehicles, private automobiles, and in the home they are handled and used every day. But our interest in the shape of a light alloy door handle differs from that in the shape of an electrum metal piston of an engine. Whereas normally the technologist has adopted for his purposes metals long fashioned by hand and tools, the development proceeded in the opposite way with the light alloy raw materials. Tested, improved, and refined in aircraft construction, these alloys are increasingly entering the craftsman's preserves.

In architectural design, aluminum and magnesium are accepted materials. The architect relies on their potentialities, their light weight, and their very much increased rigidity and corrosion resistance. Perhaps he values even more highly the ease with which these metallic raw materials can be adapted to every creative idea. There are no disturbing reminiscences and canons of style that interfere, no inconvenient craft traditions that condemn gas welding of wrought-iron grilles as running counter to time-honored practices. Work proceeds in the functional atmosphere of the factory floor, where the metal is cast and planed, milled, drilled, and ground—strictly according to the constructional drawing. In Canada, a freight car was recently built entirely of light alloy sheets and sections.

Whereas pure aluminum is used for household utensils, which require a certain quality, aluminum alloys are specially suited for other purposes. Hydronalium, a corrosion resistant, copper-free aluminum alloy suitable also for chill casting, is available in a quality capable of being engraved.

3-62

Fig. 3-62. Cast aluminum used for a religious symbol: Dove and glory.
Wing span of dove: 35·4 ins. (85cm). Cast, chased and polished by the
artist. Church of the Epiphany, Berlin. Alexander Gonda, Berlin.

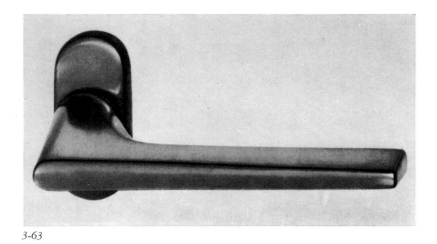

3-63

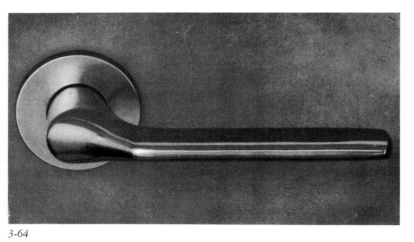

3-64

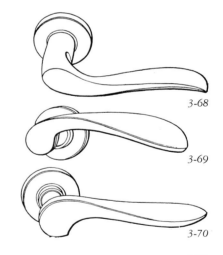

3-66

3-67

Figs. 3-66 and 3-67. Door handles of about 1928. Sharp edges were fashionable then.

Figs. 3-68–3-70. Light alloy door handles, 1930–1948. Manufacturers: Wehag-Wilh. Engstfeld, Heiligenhaus.

3-68

3-69

3-70

Figs. 3-63 and 3-64. Symmetrical door handles, light alloy. Automatic chill-casting, swaged and mechanically ground. Modern industrial mass product. Design: Braun-Feldweg. Manufacturers: Wehag-Wilh. Engstfeld, Heiligenhaus.

Figs. 3-65 and 3-71. Aluminum door handles. Design: Braun-Feldweg. Manufacturers: Wehag-Wilh. Engstfeld, Heiligenhaus.

3-65

3-71

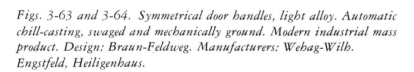

4. Techniques of Forming

Several methods exist for the forming of hollow bodies from metal. The first question to be decided is whether the work is to be cast or fashioned from sheet metal. In the first case, the way to the final form is short and direct; in the second, processing into the semifinished product of sheet metal, whose use is not predetermined, and which is therefore made in different well-tried thicknesses and sizes, intervenes.

Various methods are also available for the processing of sheet metal into hollow forms. Apart from the old techniques of manual work, many new possibilities of forming have been created by the advent of machine tools. The significance of the most important working methods is explained briefly below. Individual descriptions of these methods follow, illustrated by characteristic examples.

Casting

The oldest method of forming is casting. It is based on the discovery that metals can be made liquid by heating, and solid again by cooling them. Like any other liquid substance, the melt fills the hollow spaces of the mold; the hollow spaces to be filled must not, however, be too narrow because of the high viscosity and rapid cooling and solidification of molten metals. This explains the fairly massive appearance of the castings and the thickness of their walls. The absence of resistance during the forming of molten metal has led to the casting especially of those components of a work produced with other techniques which could be forged or embossed only with great difficulty or waste of time, such as handles, spouts, lids, feet, and similar parts. Where casting can be used as the proper reproduction method of a sculpture modeled in soft material (clay, wax), the results are very beautiful indeed and superior to other techniques. This applies to medals and plaques, where cast relief appears more rounded and softer than stamped relief; the latter method is characterized by the sharp cut in the hard material.

Casting is the proper method of forming tin and bronze. It greatly favored the orientation of early medieval metalcraft towards its magnificent and solemn style. For sacred implements (candlesticks, censers) casting was therefore the method used for centuries *(Figs. 4-39–4-40)*. A mass-produced article of the eighteenth century may serve as an example of cast components fitted to noncast utensils where this saved labor *(Fig. 1-13)*. The lid of this tea caddy is cast, and the body is in embossed sheet metal. The process of casting has become too cumbersome and expensive for modern mass production; it is therefore used mainly for the manufacture of individual pieces and short runs. This does not apply to die casting and its use in the technological field of instrument and engineering design. It is eminently suitable for the mass production of small high-precision parts. But even the goldsmith makes little use of the possibilities of casting, although a cast gold ring can hardly be surpassed in the compactness and adaptability of its form.

The methods of casting are many, and vary greatly. They are determined by the shape of the mold, its nature, and its production. First, we must distinguish between solid and hollow casting. It is clear that molds are easier to make for solid castings than for hollow ones, in which a core inside the mold has to take up the hollow space of the casting. The fixing of the core inside the mold and its correct position, on which depends the uniform thickness of the walls of the casting, raise technical difficulties; these have been solved in a number of different ways as the method evolved.

The lost-wax method is the oldest and best for producing hollow castings for artistic purposes. It can be used only for casting in sand molds, which are destroyed after the casting has cooled, in other words they can only be used once. During the nineteenth century the lost-wax method was displaced by sand casting (see page 134). But most recently the best foundries have again reverted to the older method. A further development of the earliest casting in stone molds can be seen in chill casting (metal molds). Since the casting cools rapidly in metal molds, this method is particularly well suited for mass production *(Fig. 3-63)*. In centrifugal casting, where the mold is rotating at great speed, advantage is taken of the centrifugal force to obtain sharply defined results. The method, although its technical application varies a great deal, is used both for single-piece production by the craftsman and industrial mass production. Injection molding (of plastics) and die casting (of metals), on the other hand, in which the liquid casting material is also pressed against the walls of the mold to obtain density and definition of the casting, are wholly industrial processes *(Fig. 4-38)*.

Forging

The term "forging" (or working) is used for the shaping of metal both in the glowing (iron) and in the cold (gold, silver, etc.) state.

In the past, artistic forging in the hot state was the job of the smith and the locksmith. The role of forging, from its simplest application in the mobile portable forge to the industrial shaping of red-hot forgings with the matrices of huge presses and hammers can be ignored here.

Working in wrought iron (pages 118–127), contains technical explanations of the craft of hot forging.

Cold forging is often also called embossing because it is closely related to the process of embossing/chasing. For a metal object to be forged, a piece of sheet metal must first be hammered or rolled. In historical development, forging therefore followed the more ancient casting (see *Fig. 4-47*).

Sheet metal today is no longer hammered but rolled, and therefore has a smooth surface and uniform thickness. But not every shape can be forged. Simple basic shapes of round bodies offer the least difficulties. Practice should therefore begin with a hemisphere. Very sharp edges, marked reductions, small secondary shapes and ancillary features make the work more difficult. The strained metal sheet tears, and cannot be subjected to further rough treatment. This necessitates large designs with smooth, continuous surfaces.

The section on *Cold forging* (pages 138–144), contains a detailed description of the practice and conditions of this procedure.

Assembly

This term is newly introduced here. It is meant to cover all those methods of forming in which the object is not worked from a seamless piece, but assembled from several components and soldered. This comprises a number of processes which are today considered tasks for the brazier and sheet-metal worker in the narrow sense.

The coppersmiths and braziers of earlier centuries, already aiming at economical series production, found that to raise with a hammer the round body of a sheet-metal jug wholly from a single piece was too cumbersome. From a flat sheet of metal they cut the developed surface of a tube, and jointed and soldered it together. From this rough basic shape they embossed the shape of the body with the hammer by raising it in and snarling it (see *Fig. 4-64*). The copper jug *(Fig. 4-65)*, for instance, is made from such a section. It clearly shows a soldered seam, running from top to bottom on the side of the handle.

Assembly is the more obvious method to adopt when development results in a number of surfaces which do not have to be bent very much to produce the final form after assembly. Cubes, parallelepipeds, prisms, or, as functional shapes, rectangular boxes, are most simply shaped from the development of surfaces.

Edging and hemming are aids to sheet-metalworking. In conjunction with soldering and welding they are very advanced processes practiced by the sheet-metalworkers (plumbers, tinners) as part of their craft. In the sheet-metal industry (body builders for instance) work has become highly developed with the introduction of many types of special machinery. In the field of creative metalwork, the technical convenience of these methods, in particular, has recently resulted in a larger number of poor articles than good ones. Designs based from the beginning on the possibilities of the development of prismatic bodies have become more and more numerous. Thus the most complicated structures were made of sheet metal simply because this was easy. In the syllabus of practical training establishments and in constructional drawing, as taught in vocational training centers, development was gradually accorded excessive importance. Considerable time was devoted to its practice. This may have led to conceptual thinking, but the more important training, to create and foster a feeling for form, was neglected.

Turning and Spinning

Round forms can be formed on a turning spindle. If they are cut from a solid piece of material, the process is called turning. The machine used is a lathe. Sheet metal can also be formed into round, hollow bodies with a machine which is in principle identical.

The rotating metal sheet is pushed against wooden or iron chucks with a blunt hand tool. The craftsman or skilled worker using this method is called a metal spinner. Only a few years ago he was an important link in mass production, but now the drop forge press has taken over many of his tasks so that today he works mainly to produce models and test pieces rather than in production proper.

Since axial-symmetrical bodies such as jugs, cups, bowls, etc. are produced much faster and with higher precision on the spinning lathe than would be possible with the hammer or by casting, the design of the forms has no longer kept pace with their production. Old forms of craftsmanship were copied, and no advantage at all was taken of new possibilities. *Figs. 3-32* and *4-100* show examples of the clarity and beauty of form that can be obtained on the spinning lathe, provided that it is used properly.

Punching, Pressing, and Stamping

A kind of mechanized production developed from the minting or striking of coins, the punching of sheet-metal strips and rough-pressing of hollow bodies by means of cast matrices and patrices. At the end of the eighteenth century this led logically to the pressing of metalware by machine. The section on *Engraving* (page 177) describes the part the engravers played in this development. Presses of the most varied designs, such as screw presses, eccentric presses, hydraulic presses, etc., adapted in weight and size to the workpieces they had to process, are the machine tools used in this field; they are briefly described on pages 172–174. The essential feature of the operation, which in principle is always the same, is this: Two shaping parts, made of steel, move towards each other; they are forced and guided by the press so that a piece of sheet metal placed in between them is compelled by enormous pressure to yield to its shaping movements. Technical details, as far as they are necessary for the understanding of the process, follow in the paragraph below. It will also be seen why design and model must be based on technical feasibility.

Copper and its alloys (brass, red brass, mosaic gold) are particularly suitable for the deep-drawing process. But sheet steels, too, are subjected to this method, which is particularly well suited for mass production. Mechanical presses (for the toggle-lever type, see *Fig. 4-117*) and hydraulic presses are used in industry mainly for the forming of large metal sheets (automobile bodies, as in *Fig. 1-2*). Cylindrical hollow bodies like those shown in *Fig. 4-88* at various stages of deep-drawing can be produced by the press considerably faster and more cheaply than by the metal spinner. During the production of drawn brass pieces, for instance, drawing rates of up to 1m/sec. are possible. Drawing punch and die are the tools used in this process. The gap between them, the drawing gap, is very important. The dimensions of the drawing gap, the thickness of the sheet and that of the round must be precisely calculated to prevent the drawn pieces from cracking or folding. Depending on the strain they are subjected to by the shape and material of the workpiece, the drawing tools are made either of carbon steel or specially alloyed tool steel, even cast steel. Surface hardness and favorable behavior towards the raw material to be machined (avoidance of adhesion and hoop formation of the drawn pieces) determine the choice. Bronze tools are suitable for drawing stainless steel (kitchen utensils, *Figs. 2-12–2-13, 2-30–2-31, 3-59*). The metal spinner, too, machines such work with bronze tools (*cf.* page 166). Diluted soap solution helps the sheet-metal parts (copper alloys) to slide during drawing. Copper alloys for deep-drawing are supplied in various standard qualities as sheets, strips, rounds, wires, tubes, and rods, and designated according to their composition and suitability.

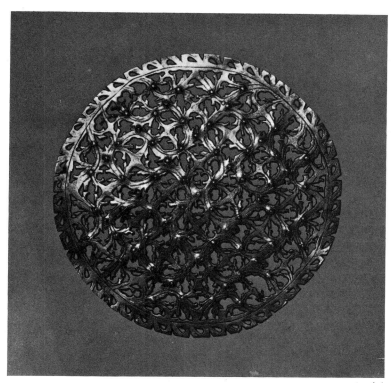

4-1

Fig. 4-1. Wrought-iron ornamental rosette, German, fifteenth century. Stamped and traced.

4-2

Fig. 4-2. Attempt at forging a rosette. A flat iron stood on edge was forged into a simple rosette by splitting it up. Top: First attempt. Bottom: Second attempt, with the number of leaves limited to six, which produces a clearer outline. Procedure: The narrow side of the flat iron is split, the slit is forced up through a round mandrel, the pattern notched, and finally the concave rosette leaves are embossed with a kind of ball punch (drift with hemispherical top).

Working in Wrought Iron

In this chapter the old term wrought iron has been retained, because the terms "structural steel" or "forged steel" have not yet become popularly accepted. It is difficult suddenly to call an eighteenth-century grille, hitherto known as a wrought-iron grille, a forged-steel grille.

The most important condition for wrought-iron work to become meaningful again is that it should be carried out and acknowledged as a pure technique of handicraft. The work as such is a preserve of the craftsman; the duty of acknowledgement, which is perhaps even more important for the cultivation of the craft, is incumbent on the client. Any association with mechanized or semimechanized techniques destroys the essential quality of forging. Although up to the end of the eighteenth century such techniques were freely employed, with, for instance, the frequent use of drop forging or of stamped plate, this is no longer possible today. During the Age of the Baroque, craftsmen still had no need to stint themselves in any way and, with their great ability and creative power, could afford to be guilty of occasional lapses in the use of unsuitable materials such as plaster, wood, and iron without coming to grief. We, however, must adopt a more cautious and modest approach, and look to earlier periods for our technical and artistic examples.

This is the occasion to mention Julius Schramm, a highly talented smith whose pioneering work should not be forgotten. Nobody has described the characteristic features of creative work in wrought iron better than Julius Schramm in his book *Über das Kunstschmiedehandwerk* (The Fine Art of Wrought-Iron Work) Berlin, 1938. The creations of his workshop make an even stronger impact. Although most of them appear perhaps dated now, his recognizable approach of the genuine craftsman is not. His most eminent pupil, Fritz Kühn, died in East Berlin in 1967. Inspired by modern sculpture, he found new means of expression in heavy forged deep-steel profiles. This excellent craftsman and individualist had great success not only in adapting his work to the functional architecture of the twentieth century, but also in decorating space with it and overcoming the prejudice against any ornamentation for its own sake. Kühn's success was due to his outlook, of which an appreciation appeared in a modern architectural journal: "The craftsman's mastery of his raw materials—brass, bronze, copper, aluminum have been added to iron and steel—remained the basis of his work. He thus claimed, in spite of his professorship, to be a craftsman and not an artist; in reality he represented the old master figure we know from the medieval associations of builders and whose work it is impossible to classify either as 'art' or as 'craft'". (*Bauwelt*, issue 34/35, 1967.)

Wrought iron can be hot or cold forged. But the characteristic of wrought-iron work is that it is formed in the hot and soft state with the hammer. This is the feature which distinguishes the smith's work from that of the locksmith, who fashions form and surface by cold processes: Filing, cold chiseling, sawing, drilling. Locksmiths' products can be bright, colored, or burnished and are evidence of skillful, patient toil with the cold work; but real smith's work always conveys something still of the fire and the direct, dynamic hammerblow. And the laws of wrought-iron working demand that this directness be preserved. Finishing with the file and any smoothing of the forged piece with cutting tools should therefore be considered with care. The same relation exists here as in casting between a form shaped in red heat from soft material, and the finishing of the hard material with cold working. Naturally, some of the old work seems to contradict these principles. Such exceptions can, however, be explained in terms of the superiority of an age based on an infinitely greater competence in the choice of its media.

The forge with its coal fire, kindled with the old bellows or a blower, is the place in the smithy to which master and work return as soon as the iron is no longer hot enough. For it must be forged only as long as it is hot, otherwise it develops cracks. The iron may be too cold for forging or it may burn in the fire—in between lies the correct forging temperature of the cherry-red iron. The smith must work swiftly and make quick decisions. It is the nature of the raw material which demands this. A hesitant or slow worker must heat the iron more often.

What is stressed again and again in these pages is of special importance in the work of the smith: The best and most original creative ideas occur during the actual forging, not on the drawing board. The design work of architects and other artists, little acquainted with the smith's work and its technical conditions and possibilities, presents the danger of using alien media and methods such as wood and casting, of failing to appreciate the means of expression proper to the working method—in other words, the natural one. Julius Schramm rightly points out that curves and scrolls in wrought iron are not a matter of period and style, but have grown organically from the technical process of forging and are part of the immutably valid expressions of form in this type of craft.

To exploit the creative possibilities of forging fully, the craftsman must first be familiar with them. The boring uniformity of new gates and lattices betrays not only economy, but also ignorance and intellectual poverty. Even the bar sections supplied by the rolling mill permit variation and contrast effects. It is by no means immaterial whether squares are set flat or overedge, flats flat or deep, or wide bars alternate with narrow ones. Such variations in the arrangement produce depth and strong shadow effects, which can be further enhanced by means of twisting or turning. More than in any other type of metalwork, the designer needs all the ideas flowing from the technical processes: The methods of riveting and faggoting of the bars and the proper use of the tools are described on the following pages.

The tools

The forge with the fire is the center of the workshop. It includes as fire tools the blast, the quenching tank, the fire shovel, the poker, and the brush. Smithy coal (small lumps of coal free from sulfur and phosphorus) should cake in the fire and form a solid layer (pancake). The smith distinguishes three degrees during the heating of the iron: (1) Red heat, (2) white heat, (3) welding heat.

The foot of the anvil is inserted in a steady block of (oak) wood; its cheeks are supported by it. It is made of cast steel or wrought iron, and has a cast-steel face welded onto it. The anvil face is the base for work like beating out and drawing. On the round horn the metal is bent round, and on the angular horn it is bent rectangularly. Forgings are upset by being tamped on a plate mounted between the jaws. The anvil base should be so rigid that the anvil does not spring back.

The vise must be able to resist heavy blows and should therefore not be a parallel one, but a heavy fire vise (bottle vise).

The hammers can be divided into three groups:

1. Hand hammers wielded by the smith in one hand, while the other hand holds the fire tongs and the work. The group comprises the small forge hammer weighing about 2 lb (1kg), and the large forge hammer

118

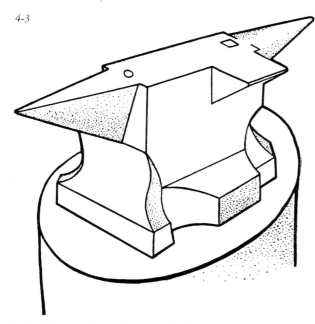

Fig. 4-3. Smith's anvil on the anvil block (wood), almost unchanged since the beginning of the Iron Age.

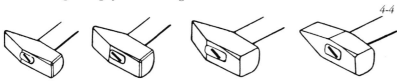

Fig. 4-4. Fron left to right: Small forging hammer, weight 2·2 lb (1kg); large forging hammer, weight 4·4 lb (2kg); forehammer, weight about 13·2 lb (6kg); cross-peen sledge, weight about 13·2 lb (6 kg).

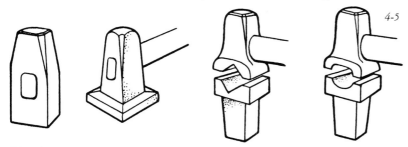

Fig. 4-5. From left to right: Set hammer; square flatter or planishing hammer, top and bottom swage for angular shapes, also useful as a support for opening; finally, top and bottom swage for oval shapes, for the attachment of pins, the drawing of rods, etc. The handles of the swaging hammers are not wedged.

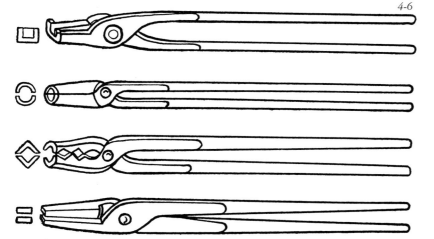

weighing 3·3–4 lb (1·5–2kg). The narrow face opposite the flat face of the hammer is called the peen. It is used mainly for beating out.

2. Hammers used by an assistant with both hands for striking. This includes the forehammer, about 13 lb (about 6kg), and the cross peen sledge of the same weight; its peen runs parallel to the direction of the shaft. It is used for the beating out and stretching of large workpieces.

3. Hammers only in name, which are not used for striking but are struck upon: These are the planishing hammer or square-face flatter, the plane bottom hammer, the ball hammer (for fluting) and the drop hammers. To prevent them from snapping, their shafts are not wedged.

The fire tongs must have long handles. They have differently shaped mouths for the secure holding of flats, rounds, and squares. There are small and large flat-jawed tongs, roundnosed tongs, pointed tongs, and the hollow-bit tongs—tongs whose mouth is of rhombic and serrated cross section.

Fig. 4-6. Forging tongs, jaws shaped to accept different cross sections of rod and bar. From bottom to top: Flat nose, open mouth, square, hollow bit (toothed, for various profiles), round, hollow bit (for rods and bars), forming bit (for small work). The pointed tongs and the riveting tongs are not shown. The tong arms are sprung.

4-7

4-8

Fig. 4-7. Mountings on a coffer in a church at Rydaholm, Sweden. Motifs taken from folklore; vigorous rhythm in the naïve but well-composed pattern.

Fig. 4-8. Components (identical sets of six individual shapes) of a cemetery gate at Scarl, Switzerland. Inserted in an old piece of rural architecture by students of the Swiss Locksmiths' Technical School at Basle.

Fig. 4-9. Stages in the execution of a part of the cemetery gate at Scarl. From left to right: Splitting off and stretching the scrolls, bending the centerpiece and scroll together, curling the scrolls.

4-9

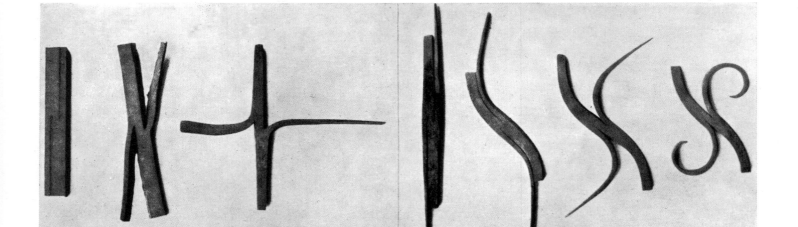

4-10

4-11

4-14

Figs. 4-10–4-13. Sections of old grilles (Fig. 4-11 is German, the others Swedish). Rhombic intersection of the bars, and decorative patterns filling the spaces.

Fig. 4-14. Rood screen, parcel gilt, Chartres Cathedral.

Fig. 4-15. Figure mountings on a chest, Voxtorp, Sweden. Crude nail heads contrasting with delicate chiseled line patterns on the figures.

4-12

4-13

4-15

121

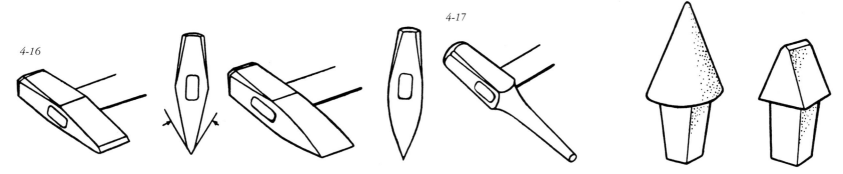

Fig. 4-16. *From left to right: Cold chisel, and hot chisel.*

Fig. 4-17. *From left to right: Drift, "cone stake", and hardie.*

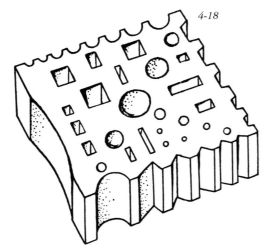

Fig. 4-18. *Swage block.*

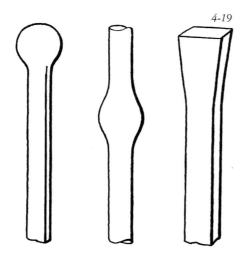

Fig. 4-19. *Forged pieces as examples of various possibilities of upsetting.*

Chisels and punches are made of hardened steel for cold working, and unhardened steel for hot working. We must distinguish between chisels with and without shaft. Cold chisels (angle of cutting edge about 60°) and hot chisels (angle of edge about 20°) have shafts. The anvil chisel is inserted in the square anvil hole. It serves for knocking off. Ordinary chisels without shaft: Cleaving chisels, straight and bent, of nonhardened cast steel. The burr has rounded edges, so that it produces no sharp edges during hole punching. The length of its edge depends on the thickness of the bars to be punched. As a rule it should be $1 \cdot 3$ times the thickness of the bar. The edge is curved so that the corners of the chisel do not get caught during punching. The slot is opened out to its final cross section with a mandrel which can be round or square, is made of unhardened steel and, depending on its size, should be $0 \cdot 02 - 0 \cdot 04$ in. ($0 \cdot 5 - 1$mm) larger than the final diameter of the hole, because this shrinks as the iron cools.

The swage block—a support for opening—and the twisting bar are further tools used by the smith. In addition to these specific tools, the smithy, especially that of the locksmith, will contain all the tools, implements, and machines necessary for cold working, including cold saws, cold chisels, files, and drilling machines.

Forging techniques

This survey does not follow the natural sequence of operations on an individual work, but compares the various possibilities.

Drawing and beating out

Forging means hammering the red-hot work on the anvil to lengthen or broaden it or its ends. The thickness decreases, and the piece tapers.

Upsetting

This is the opposite process: The red-hot piece is compressed along its longitudinal axis by blows or strikes. The length decreases, and the piece becomes thicker (drawing on the left).

4-20

4-21

4-22

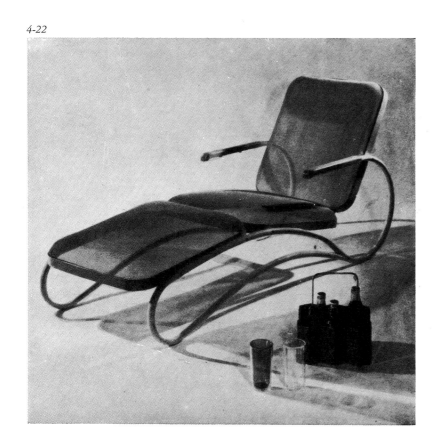

Fig. 4-20. *Chair and two stools for the garden, round steel. One stool with a cushion, the other with a glass plate, for use as a small table. Design: George Nelson. Manufacturers: Arbuck Inc., USA.*

Fig. 4-21. *Rocking chair of electrowelded steel rods and table of thin steel tubes, with wooden tips inserted. Design and manufacture: Ernest Race Ltd., London.*

Fig. 4-22. *Deckchair, tubular steel frame, seat and back rest fine wire mesh. Design: L. J. Zerbee and Don M. Hilliker. Manufacturers: Zerbee-Hilliker Company, USA.*

4-23

Figs. 4-25–4-30. Companion sets.
Design: George Nelson.
Executed by Howard Miller, Michigan, USA.

Fig. 4-23. Frying pan, with handle forged from a flat iron, and a wrought fish slice. Ends split, round forged, twisted and forge-welded. Siegfried Prütz.

4-25

Fig. 4-25. Companion set (shovel, poker, and broom). Design: George Nelson. Executed by Howard Miller, Michigan, USA.

Fig. 4-24. Flat iron bars, lower parts forged narrow and long, tops hot-drawn over the round-iron ring, form the basket for a log fire. Siegfried Prütz.

4-24

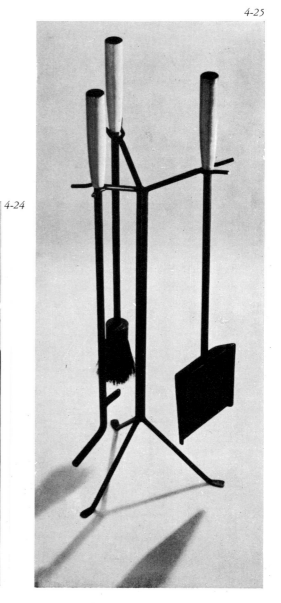

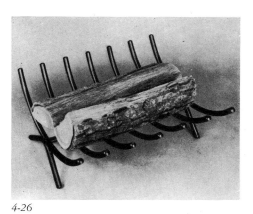

4-26

4-29

4-27

Figs. 4-26 and 4-29. This log basket of bent rods makes it easier to keep the fire going, because fresh logs slide automatically into it.

Fig. 4-27. Robust fire dogs, profile steel.

Fig. 4-28. Fire dogs made of steel rods.

Fig. 4-30. Fire dogs made of steel bars.

4-30

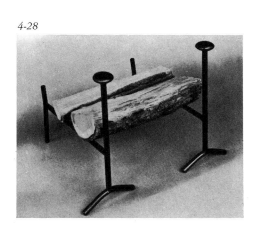

4-28

Splitting off

With the setter, a lateral piece is split off obliquely to the longitudinal axis of the bar without separating it from the bar altogether. The smith holds the work or the fire tongs with his left hand, the setter in his right hand; an assistant strikes a blow with the forehammer. The split-off piece can be further shaped into a scroll by rolling it *(Fig. 4-9)*, or into a leaf by beating it out. Splitting off or attachment by welding is a decision which must depend on the size and shape of the work.

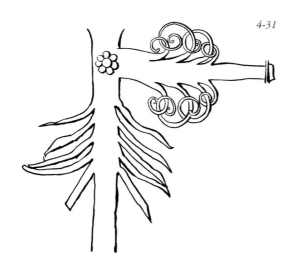

4-31

Fig. 4-31. Splitting off and curling of a flat iron (drawing based on a piece of work by J. Schramm).

Opening up

The same process as splitting off except that the work is split in the center instead of along the side, for instance to pierce it so that one bar can be threaded through the hole of another *(Fig. 3-56)*, or to upset and twist an ornament *(Fig. 4-2)*. Lastly, the end of a bar can be split in halves for the beating out of lugs for fastening with rivets *(Fig. 2-2)*. The setter for punching must be narrower that that for splitting off, and must have the appropriate ratio to the diameter of the hole. Before it is opened up, the iron must be upset where it is to be punched.

Cutting out and cutting in

Portions (incisions, recesses) can be chiseled out of the soft red-hot work, or depressions cut into it, with a setter and the aid of an assistant with a forehammer; this is necessary, for instance, with animal figures and similar forms.

Punching

The work is placed with the already heated, split-up portion on a circular hole. A round or square mandrel of suitable thickness is driven through the slit with hammerblows. It can be deflected into the hole of the swage block. When one rod is to be pushed through another, the site of the hole must first be upset and split up before the mandrel is driven in.

Bending and rolling

Right-angle bending of the red-hot iron round the edge of the anvil or in the vise. If the outer edge is to be sharp, the site to be bent must first be upset (edging). Round bending round the horns of the anvil. Rolling of split-off parts in scrolls. Scrolls formed from rounds are sometimes drawn over a spiral pattern.

Fluting and notching or ribbing

Furrowed modifications of the profile produced with the rounded hammer or the chisel. Depending on the cross section: Groove (fluting with rounded hammer), chiseling of notches (ribbing).

Turning or twisting

In the hot state, the rod clamped in the vise can be turned round its axis with the twisting bar. Clockwise or anticlockwise turns, even alternating on the same piece, create a spiral, very lively shadow effect. Turning can be combined with splitting up, even with flats.

Drop forging

A modern, strictly artisan movement in artistic wrought-iron work rejects the design produced with the aid of dies, because it rightly considers the forms created with blows of the hammer more appropriate to the process of forging, more solid, and more expressive. The die has for a long time been found convenient where a small ornament (leaf, rose, ball) was used repetitively. The richly ornamented wrought-iron work of the sixteenth and seventeenth centuries, in particular, would be unthinkable without labor-saving dies. Working methods were thus evolved, notably in France, which gradually led to the hot pressing of entire parts *(Fig. 4-4)*.

Techniques of joining the parts

Welding

Projecting or filling branches of bars which are too large to be split off are welded on. Welding is thus used for the attachment and joining of two forged parts.

The method is as old as forging itself. Two splayed pieces are joined by hammering them in white heat. Only the old manual forge welding is suitable for preserving the character of traditional wrought-iron work. Oxyacetylene welding, which softens the iron to its melting point, leaves shapeless bulges. Modern masters, influenced by contemporary sculpture, try to make use of these very effects. Thus the Italian Antonio Bennetton welded lattices in free-flowing curves. With this method, the bar shrinks irregularly as in welded gold jewelry *(Figs. 2-70, 2-73–2-74)*. The exact nature of the surface is deliberately destroyed in favor of an expression that appears organic and resembles casting.

Riveting

Riveting is not only a proper method of cold fastening and joining. It also imparts a rhythmically divisive and therefore decorative effect to the work. Rivets should therefore not be hidden, but remain visible. In old work and good new examples, the decorative character of rivets is emphasized through the beating of their heads into roses (*Figs. 3-56, 3-58*). Small pieces are cold riveted; for large ones it is necessary to heat the rivets in order to shape their heads with a hollow spherical tool.

Fitting collars

Where curved parts, rings, or scrolls touch, whether inside the panel or on the frame of a door, or in a grille, fastening by means of collars is indicated. As the drawing shows, the collar is prepared with beveled ends to overlap and to be wrapped or fitted hot, but not welded. The contraction of the iron during cooling is sufficient for a tight fit. Before it is fitted, the collar should be slightly shorter than the total circumference, since it expands a little when it is hammered in the hot state. In old French wrought-iron work strongly profiled collars, and collars with multiple profiles, were used; they have now become simple again, and most of them have only a single notch in the middle.

4-32

Fig. 4-32. *The use of collars in old work (rood screen, fourteenth century).*

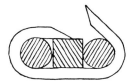 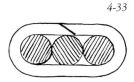

4-33

Fig. 4-33. *Hammering a collar. Left: Bar clamped with two rods. Right: Three rods.*

Casting

All the relevant metals can be formed by means of casting, if not in the pure, then in the alloyed state. In forming through casting, the properties of the raw materials play a less important part. The molten metal, whether iron or gold, readily assumes any form, which will be final after solidification. The formal character of iron and of silver castings therefore differs less than that of wrought pieces in the two metals. A sensitive designer will without doubt take advantage of the difference in color and luster of the surface effect for his work. Nevertheless it is easy to understand why contemporary gold- and silversmiths sometimes consider casting a method alien to craftsmanship, because of their preference for the realities of the wrought metal.

This attitude is still better appreciated when it is borne in mind that even those sculptors who were less experienced as craftsmen could at all times express themselves in metal casting. Thus large and small sculptures in bronze are the preserve of the artist, not of the craftsman. The paths of artist and craftsman have diverged more and more since the Renaissance. It was the highest ambition of Benvenuto Cellini (himself the most famous goldsmith of his day) to be compared with Michelangelo as a sculptor in bronze, and he wanted to be accepted as a sculptor more than a goldsmith. He therefore attached, whenever he could, cast figures to those of his works which he had not already cast himself.

This demonstrates that a casting is created in two completely separate stages: The production of the casting pattern is the purely artistic; the repetition of this pattern through casting, the reproduction, is the purely technical task.

Only a small area of the artistic task is dealt with in this chapter; we are mostly concerned here with the negative pattern, which still lends itself to execution by the craftsman. Artistic sculpture in the round, on the other hand, is beyond the scope of this book.

A similar limitation applies to the treatment of the second, the technical task. It does not extend to the description of metallurgical details, and the chemical reactions during melting are only touched upon. Casting in iron, bronze, brass, German silver, and tin, and lastly the various methods of casting in silver and gold, require a knowledge of theory and practice whose exposition is a matter for the purely technical handbook. Chapter 6, nevertheless, contains some observations on these questions. What follows is merely a survey of the most important processes.

Negative patterns for cast medals

Small relief representations on cast medals or seals are not modeled in high relief but cut as negatives (that is, hollowed out of solid material). The reason for this is that with positive modeling it is almost impossible to obtain clearcut, impressive forms in such small sizes; however, cutting the negative pattern in plaster, wood, stone, or slate offers the craftsman, in the technique of cutting and in the choice and handling of tools, the possibility of very dynamic expression. If modeling is impossible, it is replaced by cutting. For soft material such as plaster, wooden tools, for instance boasting tools, are adequate. For cutting in slate or steatite, semicircular steel scrapers of various sizes are suitable. They are best made by the user himself, for the shape of the tools determines the style of the work. (The expert would say he was making the tool to suit the character of the form at which he was aiming.) At any rate it is the direct, rough effect of the cutting tools that creates the appeal of the

work. The hollow shape must therefore not be smoothed; the pattern must remain as produced by the tool. This originality of the negative pattern explains why the tool is so important; it need not be expensive at all, any worn-out riffler, any scraper or cutter can be modified into a useful cutting tool without difficulty.

The working procedure corresponds to the last detail with any other negative sculpturing process, for instance with steel engraving. However, steel engravers, especially those attempting to cut negative patterns for a casting method in soft material, cannot be advised strongly enough never to attempt to trim the forms, as is normally the practice, because it is totally out of place here. The examples to be chosen should be the unspoiled and uncorrected cuts, as naïve as they are refined, of antique cameos and cast seals. To sum up, the relief intended for casting is directly cut in the negative without any preparation. Tool marks are preserved. Corrections during working are made with plasticine or wax, with which the offending feature is filled (Fig. 4-43–4-46).

Casting: First a positive is cast in plaster of the cut shell mold. This relief pattern serves the founder as a model for casting in molding sand. For bronze castings, such as plates and plaques, the conventional sand casting method is suitable. The founder dusts his sand mold with graphite powder to ensure a sharply defined cast. But not every founder is able to cast small items so cleanly that finishing is unnecessary. However, this is the very goal to be aimed for, because any finishing, let alone chasing, would completely change the appearance of the casting, and the character of the negative pattern would be destroyed. Thus only risers and fins must be removed and carefully cleaned up. To do any more would be deplorable—even the cleaner must have some feeling for the character of a cast surface and know that small pores of the casting need not be eliminated in every case.

Patinating (Fire gilding, page 137): There are many well-known recipes for the patination of bronze castings. Page 93 also contains information about the use of well-tried coloring agents, pickling and other solutions. But recipes alone are not much help. The main factor is the outcome of practical trials and above all the taste of the person conducting them. It is possible to color and patinate with abominable results. A technical hint: The patina should not be too thin, and the coat should be thick.

4-34

Fig. 4-34. *Bronze casting of an old door knocker with mask: The molder is about to cast the knocker (in the shape of a snake) and small accessories. In the foreground is an iron rammer.*

4-35

Fig. 4-35. *The two parts of the mold for the mask have already been dusted. Each is in a flask, whose frame with eyes and lugs permits the assembly of the closed shell mold. The incised vents are clearly visible. On the worktable are a rammer and slickers, used as forming tools. When the original on the right was molded, it left a hollow space corresponding to its thickness between the negative and the positive sand mold, to be filled later by the liquid metal.*

4-36

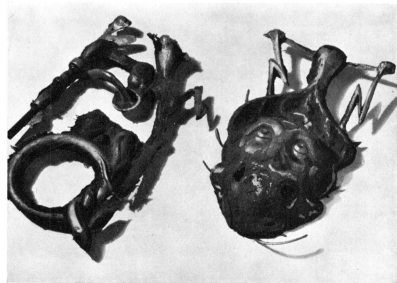

Fig. 4-36. *The cast pieces, photographed immediately after cooling. The sprue (gate) and the vents (also cast) are not yet sawn off. Only the molding sand has been rapped, or, where baked on, removed with a sandblast blower.*

Fig. 4-37. *Iron casting in functional form. A stove designed by Walter Gropius for Franksche Eisenwerke, Dillenburg, Hesse has given reliable service for more than 30 years.*

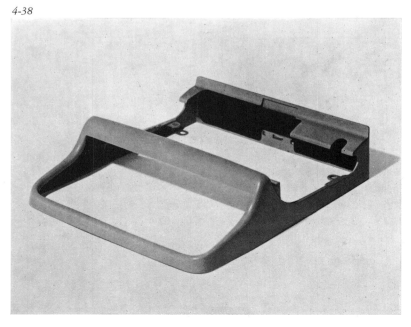

Fig. 4-38. *Aluminum as die cast metal. The frame of a famous typewriter, the Olivetti-Lettera 22.*

4-39

4-40

Fig. 4-39. *Romanesque candlestick, with Gothic socket added later. Bronze casting, not turned. Height up to the socket 4·6 ins. (11·2cm), height of socket 2·3 ins. (5·5cm).*

Fig. 4-40. *Fifteenth-century censer. Bronze casting, foot soldered on, height 8 ins. (19·3cm), diameter 4·4 ins. (10·5cm). Wall thickness varying between 0·15 and 0·2 ins. (3·5 and 5mm). Compare the description of the casting of a censer by Theophilus in his "Schedula diversarum artium".*

Fig. 4-41. *Figure of St. Ursula (picture motif: Medieval Virgin of Mercy). Left wing of a portal in Cologne Cathedral (see Fig. 2-8). Bronze casting, chased by the artist. Ewald Mataré, 1948.*

Fig. 4-42. *Door knocker (Jonah, vomited by the whale); a motif popular in the Middle Ages. Right wing of a portal in Cologne Cathedral (see Fig. 2-8). Bronze casting, chased by the artist. Ewald Mataré, 1948.*

4-41

The Casting Methods

The production of a casting again consists of several independent operations which are: Making the mold, melting the casting metal, and the casting process proper.

Development and improvement of the casting methods in the course of time were concerned above all with the quality of the mold, its functional construction, and the material of which it was made. This material must be pliable, in order to accept the most delicate details of the mold and transfer them to the molten metal. It must also have sufficient heat resistance and not affect the surface of the casting either chemically or mechanically. During the Bronze Age, such materials for molds were found in soft stones and burnt clay. A mold for an axe was hollowed out of the ground or modeled, and casts were made. In the description of the further development of molds it is necessary to distinguish between two different methods.

Solid casting and hollow casting

Examples: The axes of the Bronze Age *(Fig. 1-3)* and the figure of St. Ursula, a modern casting *(Fig. 4-41)*, are solid castings or massive cast parts. A two-part mold encloses the hollow space in which they are produced. Two-part molds of sand for solid castings are illustrated in *Fig. 4-35*. In one case *(Fig. 4-34)*, round works were formed in two symmetrical halves, in the other it was necessary, because of the plastic design of the mask, to make a smaller counter mold for the low relief (the distance between the two molds is the wall thickness of the casting). Medals really require only a single mold; the second part of the mold is a simple plane.

But the Romanesque censer *(Fig. 4-40)* is hollow. So are plastic figures. Their walls have a certain thickness. Such castings can be produced only with the aid of a third part of the mold, which is a core inside the shell mold; it must obviously be smaller than the mold. The distance between its surface and the walls of the hollow mold determines the thickness of the wall of the casting.

About 950 A.D. Theophilus in his *Schedula* (Nelson, London, 1961; a handbook of working in metal and glass in the Romanesque period) also described hollow casting with the example of a censer. According to his description, the lost-wax method was used during that era. It was most probably also used for bronze sculptures in Antiquity.

The lost-wax method

The craftsman modeled his work in wax on a clay core in full thickness complete with riser and vents (air channels). He covered the layer of wax with a complete layer of clay as an outer mold, which he burnt after allowing it to dry; during the burning the wax drained away, leaving the shell mold for casting. The necessary openings of the censer, also filled with clay within the layer of wax, constituted the required connection between core and mold shell. The mold was tamped into a pit and a cast made. To remove the casting, the mold had to be smashed. It was therefore not possible to cast a second piece in it; it had to be modeled anew (dead mold). This lost-wax method was also used in the casting of all the large and small bronze sculptures. From the sixteenth century onwards it was modified and improved, mainly to make further castings possible from the same mold. Cellini described the following improvement as his own invention.

A plaster cast is made of the sculptor's model in two or more parts. This hollow plaster cast is, as it were, the original mold which permits the repetition of any number of casts. It merely serves to make another mold, actually used for casting, as follows.

The shell mold is lined with a thinly rolled layer of clay already corresponding to the wall thickness of the casting; but this is no more than an aid to making the core. The core contains a frame of wires and iron rods and is modeled or cast, so that it fits into the rolled layer, in a mixture of clay, plaster, brick dust, and bone ash. After the core has been fired, the rolled layer can be removed from the shell mold. Wax is first poured into the spaces between the plaster part-mold and the core fixed inside it after the riser and casts of vents are cut. Only now has the original mold served its purpose. A second solid casting in wax is available, and can be finished and improved. Riser and vent casts, also of wax, are attached to it, and the whole is surrounded with a jacket of emulsified alumina, mixed with shearings and held together by iron bands. The wax can be melted, the mold obtained embedded in soil, and a casting made.

In his autobiography, Cellini describes the exciting venture of such a casting very dramatically. Similar methods were probably used in the casting of the great Renaissance and Baroque sculptures of Germany.

The modern casting process in sand molds described in the following paragraph was taken over from the iron foundry at the beginning of the nineteenth century.

Casting in sand molds

Since the nineteenth century, brass and bronze has been cast mainly in sand molds. Casting in cast-iron molds is suitable only for special series work (page 115). First, a model of metal, plaster, or other raw material must be available. *Fig. 4-34* shows how the mask of a lion was formed as part of an old door knocker that had also been cast. Here, then, the casting itself was in turn used as a pattern. The old mask can be seen on the right of the box with the low-relief mold. The thickness of its wall corresponds precisely to the space between the recessed and the raised sand mold. Placed in the mold, the mask completely fills this space.

Forming

The molder covers his pattern in a cast-iron molding flask placed on a level plate with a layer of fresh facing sand. This is a particularly fine sand, prepared with about 4–6% water. To fill the molding flask, less pure heap sand is quite adequate. It contains used and reconditioned sand from smashed molds. With a wooden or iron tamper the molder gradually tamps these layers so firmly that even the most delicate projections and depressions of the pattern are reproduced in the sand mold, which at the same time becomes more densely packed.

It is important for successful casting that the air displaced by the molten metal is effectively expelled from the mold, chiefly by means of special vents *(Fig. 4-35)*. But air must be allowed to escape from the back of the mold, too, through the layers of sand. To ensure this, fine holes are pricked into the sand up to about 0·4 ins. (1cm) from the pattern. After forming the front, the molder turns his flask round and forms the back of the pattern. He now removes this and cuts the sprue for pouring in the molten metal, and a sufficient number of vents, with the slickers (which resemble a spatula and are shown in *Fig. 4-34*). The arrangement and distribution of the vents depend on the kind of mold and its hollow spaces, and therefore require experience. There must at any rate be a sufficient number of them to allow the air to escape from the hollow spaces quickly and without obstruction during the rapid casting operation. *Fig. 4-35* illustrates how the sprue and the vents are cut into the negative mold.

The casting metal should not come into direct contact with the sand, which may affect it chemically and would also cake the metal surface. The sandy surface of the mold is therefore covered with graphite powder, called blacking, with a brush; often compressed air is used with the aid of a blastpipe. If the blacking is applied in liquid form (water + graphite), it is blown with a blowpipe from a vessel. Finally, a powder containing lycopodium (club moss) is dusted on the already blackened mold from a cloth bag, to prevent sweating of the surface. A small hand bellows on the molder's workbench merely serves to blow individual grains of sand off the mold. A vessel with water and brush is also at hand in case the sand is too dry, although it should be used as dry as possible. The finished mold is placed in a drying kiln, whose temperature rises up to 250°C. How long it stays in the kiln depends on its size and how moist it is.

A few tricks are used to influence the casting operation favorably and to obtain a smooth, unburnt cast: Petrol sprayed with the blacking produces a layer of gas in the mold during casting, which prevents contact between metal and sand. Another measure has a similar aim. Shortly before casting, the mold as well as the sides of the cast-iron flask are sprayed with paraffin; this, too, is designed to ensure a smooth surface of the casting by the ignition of pore-forming gases (zinc vapors). The paraffin burning on the outside of the flask in conjunction with ejected and burning gases is said to produce suction, which in turn accelerates the removal of air from inside the mold. This effect is further enhanced in art molds by the introduction of wood shavings on the sand, which, ignited by the metal poured from the crucible, burn up.

Sand molds for mass-produced articles (e.g. metal type) are now stamped in a press instead of by hand, which obviously speeds up the work considerably. Here, the patterns to be cast are made of metal to make them withstand the required high pressure.

Melting the casting metal

The metal is melted in cast-iron, graphite-lined crucibles. Smaller or larger crucibles of about 110 lb (50kg) capacity and more are inserted in melting furnaces, which are cylindrical crucible furnaces let into the ground, coke-fired and including a blast; they accept one crucible each. Since coke contains sulfur, which produces pores in the casting, the coke fire is allowed to burn down a little and purify itself before the crucibles are inserted.

With brass, casting temperatures range between 1080°C and 1030°C, with bronze between 1160°C and 1130°C. The melting temperatures reached in the furnace are about 50°C higher in each case. Before the casting, the temperature between furnace and mold is measured with special galvanic instruments, which have a probe that is immersed in the liquid metal. The lower the casting temperature used the better. This is easier with thick-walled castings than with thin-walled ones, which call for greater heat and a freer flow of the casting metal. Brass for casting is alloyed with lead (up to 3%), which influences the color of the patina.

Purification of the casting metal

Cuprous oxide forms in molten brass; this requires purification of the casting metal molten in the crucible by means of a special process: Copper phosfide is introduced into the molten mass in a bell jar. The quantity varies between 0·1–0·5% for bronze. Molten German silver receives an addition of about 0·3% cupromanganese and 0·1% magnesium for the same purpose.

Casting

As the metal melts in the crucible an oxide film (slag) forms on the surface of the liquid mass; it must be removed. To prevent further oxidation, small pieces of crushed glass are placed on the casting metal. The glass melts at once and forms a layer that isolates the metal from the air. Casting can now begin. The crucible, suspended from large tongs, is moved above the mold, tilted, and the jet of liquid metal poured into the sprue. Splashing, glowing drops indicate that the mold is full. The metal solidifies at once, and with small castings the pins of the flasks can be loosened after a few seconds; this enables air to penetrate the mold, causing further cooling.

Casting Methods of the Gold- and Silversmith

The various methods of gold and silver casting differ only in the choice of material for the mold. Naturally, all molds must have sprues and vents after the pattern has been formed, and the openings must be generous.

Sand casting

A modification of the sand casting method for smaller-scale working in gold is casting in the flask (obtainable through the tool trade), which is a small, two-part molding box. The pattern is shaped in the sand by the procedure already described. Finest coal dust can be used in place of graphite.

Plaster molds

The two halves of the plaster cast of the pattern serve as the mold, after being burned in a charcoal fire. Instead of the pattern being cast, a female form can be cut in plaster. This makes direct artistic composition possible (see *Negative patterns for cast medals*, page 128).

Sandstone molds

Unlike plaster casting, casting in sandstone demands the cutting of the recesses into the female form. It is therefore appropriate to work with the immediacy demanded by the negative cutting method (page 128).

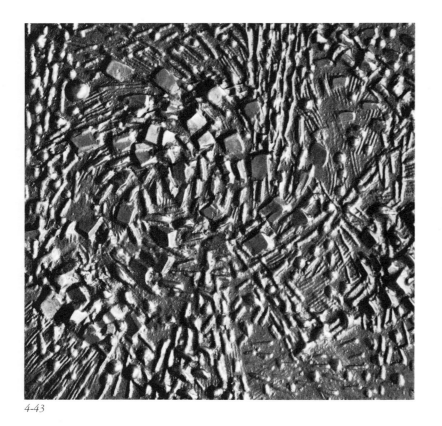

4-43

4-45

Figs. 4-43–4-46. *Bronze castings from cut plaster negatives. Four gilt relief plates, 3·4 × 3·4 ins. (9 × 9cm), chased by the artist. Alexander Gonda, 1967. Owners: Sammlung Bahlsen, Hanover, Manfred de la Motte, Berlin, Bund Deutscher Architekten, and Dr. Friedenberg, Berlin.*

4-44

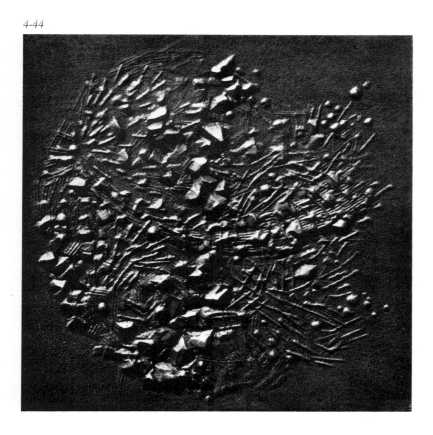

4-46

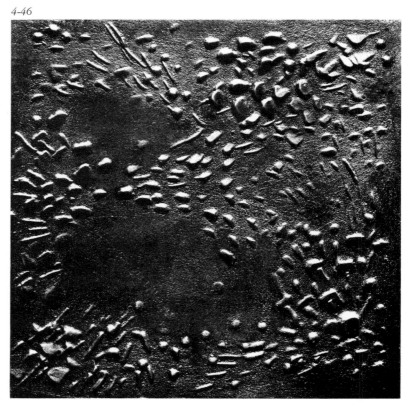

Os sepiae (cuttlefish shell)

Cuttlefish shell is the softest material for a small mold (ring). A metal pattern, even when the material is lead, can be cast in parts; it is simply pressed into the shell. The texture of the mold is, however, visible on the casting, which can, but need not be, finished. The method is unsuitable for delicate work not intended for finishing. The cuttlefish shells can be cut with a fretsaw. The pattern must be pressed in gently so that the shell does not break.

Centrifugal casting (Fig. 2-71)

Dental technicians, goldsmiths, and mechanical engineers take advantage of the effect of centrifugal force to obtain sharply defined castings. Using the lost-wax method, gold castings that need not be chased afterwards can be produced by hand centrifugally. Mixtures of plaster, whose composition is probably better established in the dental laboratory than in the modern goldsmith's workshop, are used as embedding substances for wax patterns. In addition to gypsum they contain asbestos, fireclay, quartz, china clay, etc. Their composition is based on modern methods of materials testing to allow for the shrinkage that occurs during the cooling of the casting. Although goldsmith's work does not always demand such precision, the experience of the dental technician versed in the practice of casting could provide many improvements.

Fire Gilding

by Andreas Moritz

Even today, we still admire the radiance and sparkle of old fire-gilt work from the Early Romanesque to the Late Renaissance period. It is without doubt the most beautiful, solid, and most truly craftsmanlike method of gilding. About the turn of the century it was displaced in the workshop almost completely by electrodeposition gilding; only in England, where silver is highly esteemed and tradition reigns supreme, is the professional water gilder still found today.

In most books on the gold- and silversmiths' craft, fire gilding is mentioned mainly to complete the picture and is described summarily. The practical hints given are usually very scanty indeed.

In fire gilding, mercury is used as an aid. It has the property of readily forming an alloy with gold, as with other metals. The gold alloy is called gold amalgam, and is a silvery-white paste which, because of its pliability, can easily be spread as a thin film on the metal to be gilt. The mercury can be separated from the gold as readily as it can be made to combine with it; it is removed by evaporation or by fuming it off; the gold then remains attached to the base.

Two substances must be prepared for the gilding process. First, the amalgamating fluid, which has to amalgamate the metal to be gilt and establish the chemical conditions for the adsorption of the gold amalgam; second, the gold amalgam itself.

The amalgamating fluid is prepared either from metallic mercury, of which $0 \cdot 1 - 0 \cdot 2$ oz (3–5g) are dissolved in a little nitric acid; to this, 1,000cc water are added; or from mercuric nitrate, of which $0 \cdot 4$ oz (10g) are dissolved in 1,000cc water. A turbid solution is cleared by the drop-by-drop addition of nitric acid. For potassium cyanide amalgamating fluid $0 \cdot 4$ oz (10g) potassium mercuricyanide and $0 \cdot 4 - 0 \cdot 9$ oz (10–25g) potassium cyanide are dissolved in 1,000cc water; it reacts a little more slowly, which may be an advantage with some types of work. The old masters used metallic mercury, a quick-acting and highly corrosive fluid.

The gold amalgam is prepared in a dull-red-hot fireclay crucible lined with fine, moistened alumina, or in a fireproof china crucible. Thinly rolled fine gold, loosely folded, is introduced into the crucible with the mercury, in a ratio of about 1:6; the crucible is now covered, taken up with the tongs, and shaken horizontally in a good draft until the alloy has formed; it is allowed to cool and its contents are poured into cold water. The paste obtained is kneaded thoroughly and kept under water in a glass bottle with a ground glass stopper. Amalgam which is too thin is pressed through a piece of sheepskin until the substance of the desired viscosity remains in the skin.

Gilding can now start. The work is pickled, scraped, and thoroughly degreased; above all it must be free from oxides. The surfaces to be gilt must be amalgamated with the amalgamating fluid already prepared, and thoroughly rinsed with water afterwards. A whitish film of mercury remains; if it is gray, it indicates lack of cleanliness. The approximate quantity of gold amalgam necessary to cover the area is now removed with a copper spatula and carefully distributed with a damp brass-wire brush; even density and thickness are important. The mercury is fumed off over a charcoal fire or a blowpipe flame (the angel, *Figs. 2-6–2-7,* was fumed off outdoors with two soldering guns). Heating must be done slowly. The coated surface will radiate in the heat like a silver mirror. Accumulating amalgam is distributed by continuous wiping with a plug of cotton wool. As the temperature increases, the mercury evaporates in the form of white fumes, the specular luster disappears, and the amalgam dries a mat white. After the mercury has been completely fumed off, a mat-gold, fine-grain film appears. The gold has formed a compound with the base. When it has cooled, the work is brushed to a mat luster with the brass-wire brush under soap and water. A lively sparkle is obtained by burnishing it with a piece of polished hematite. Minor unevennesses caused by distribution and wiping with cotton wool, and the fine surface granulation brought out by rubbing with hematite, are not removed. They are the hallmark of craftsmanlike fire gilding, whose attraction is unsurpassed by any other method of gilding.

That mercury and its compounds are poisonous is quite well known; precautions during handling are essential. The inhalation of mercury vapor is particularly dangerous and may cause the most serious damage to health. It is therefore best to carry out the fuming off outdoors in a downwind draft. If it is impossible to work outside the workshop, extensive safety measures must be taken. The first essential is a well-drawing flue. Sheets of tin foil (silver paper) can be suspended like flies in the flue above the forge. They attract the noxious fumes and by amalgamation prevent their condensation into liquid mercury.

Cold Forging

In the past, members of various crafts, among them the basin makers and the cutlers, were engaged in the forging of metals in the cold state. Even today, the copper- and silversmiths belong to this group, although within the trade they no longer do much forging proper; they usually assemble pressed parts, or, as specialists, carry out specific types of forging such as planishing and setting shallow silver bowls.

The term of forging as employed here covers all work with the hammer for embossing, chasing, or raising hollow bodies from sheet metal by hand. The sheet metal, of course, has not had to be beaten out by hand for centuries. Cast silver bars are beaten out under steam- or hydraulic hammers. The sheet metal is then rolled. Only those who hand forge silver cutlery—now really necessary only when a designer makes a pattern—have to beat out the thin material of the bowl with the hammer. It is not easy to distinguish between a wrought and a pressed work. The generally known mark of distinction, the so-called hammer finish, is not the most important sign. Furthermore, its typical surface effect, produced by the polished faces of the hammer, is unfortunately imitated in many a pressed work. Even more frequently, one finds pressed plates or bowls which were finished with the hammer and have thus been given the appearance of being hand-made. But this appearance is only superficial. The expert eye will always see that the object itself was created by a different method. There is no need to be over-strict in the judgment of such finishing work. In the past, too, hammer and press were sometimes combined without scruple. Here, too, the quality of the result decides the issue. It is the subsequent use of hammer finish for the purpose of deception which must be rejected.

The form appropriate to forging has an unmistakable, sculptured, yet soft outline. The ideal basic shape is the sphere, which, more or less modified, may be hidden in forged hollow bodies or their parts. The intrinsic laws of wrought forms can be explained even more simply and naturally in terms of the craftsman's handiwork, because almost all vessels are designed to be taken up and used by the hand. They are also fashioned by hand. It is therefore obvious that a form that fits snugly in the palm meets the demands of both its origin and its purpose. This character is revealed by many of the more recent wrought-metal objects illustrated in this book.

Rounded forms, however, also grew naturally from the tinsmith's work, shown in *Figs. 4-56, 4-58*; there was therefore no need to ill-use the material. A bowl can be shaped and chased without any technical difficulties.

Fig. 4-54 shows how a hollow sphere is gradually fashioned from the circular blank.

The tools

Hammer and anvil are also the tools of cold forging, but whereas in hot forging only a few types of hammer and anvil are required, here a large number of different striking tools are necessary. Both the anvils of every shape and the hammers must match the craftsman's objective. It may therefore be necessary to shape a special tool for an unusual hollow shape. Only the most important and widely-used hammers and anvils are mentiond here. The coppersmith and sheet-metalworker are as familiar with them as the silversmith; the goldsmith, too, knows most of them.

During work, the tools are inserted in a steady block of hard wood the height of a stool; they can also be clamped in a vise *(Fig. 4-58)*. The

4-47

Fig. 4-47. Copper engraving from an
eighteenth-century French technical book. Various
operations in a silversmith's are shown. On the left:
Melting and annealing forge with bellows. Next to
it the blowlamp under a vent pipe. (a) casting an
ingot. The two workers (e) are forging the red-hot
piece. The seated person (b) raises a hollow shape,
while the silversmith standing on the right (c)
embosses a flat plate. What the man sitting in the
corner (d) is doing is not quite clear. They all give
the impression of being left-handed, because the
copper engraver apparently engraved directly onto the
plate.

Fig. 4-48. Old shapes for hammers, from an
eighteenth-century French technical book.

4-48

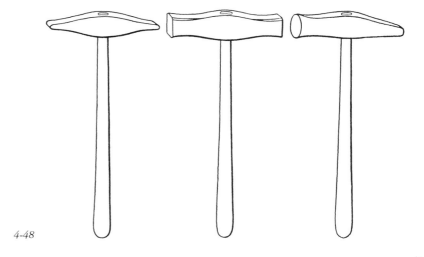

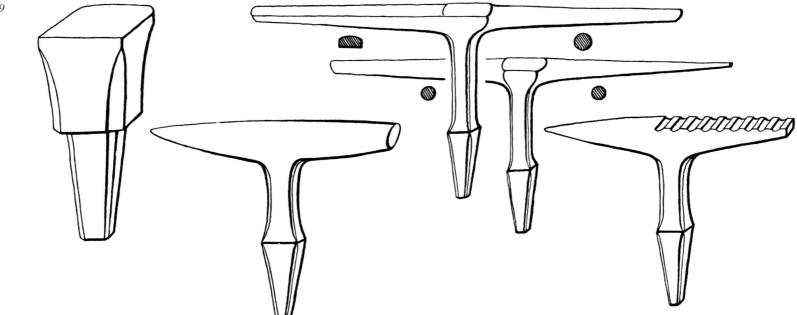

Fig. 4-49. From left to right: Square stake, double arm round stake, two beak horns of various cross sections, creasing stake.

tools are called horns, or beaks if they take up much space; their face is slightly convex, and their cross section circular or oval. The beak horn belongs in this category; the creasing stake and double-arm round stake are shorter and thicker. Sockets, flat, slightly or strongly convex, can be straight or cranked. The flat head, eminently suitable for the planishing of small pieces, is a kind of socket, but flat, with polished edges, and straight or arched sides. Roundheads and T-stakes are necessary both with a straight and with a curved face with acute and obtuse angles, for turning over rims and for folding (flanging). Snarling tools are used for rounding-out vessels (cf. Fig. 4-64). The tool most frequently used is perhaps the square stake, an anvil with a plane, square face. The working areas or faces of all these tools, like those of the hammers, are highly polished. They must be protected against rust and damage and therefore carefully looked after. The hammers can be divided according to the working stages into two groups. The first comprises the embossing, deepening, raising in, and raising hammers. The second group consists of square flatters, planishing, and setting hammers. There are several hammers common to both groups; they include hammers with one or two faces, and thick hammers.

Embossing hammers have a strong or weak convex ball peen and are therefore also called ball-peen hammers. The shape of the swaging hammers is illustrated in the drawing; those with a broad, flat, round face are used for raising in, and raising.

Square flatters, planishing, and setting hammers are the blackjacks proper. Their round faces can be flat, or a weak or strong convex

shape. Square faces are as a rule flat. When planishing hammers are used, fine differences in convexity are decisive if the hammer finish is to be evenly applied to different convexities of the work.

The working procedure

A wrought hollow body can be either embossed or raised. *Figs. 3-24* and *3-27* illustrate the difference between the two methods. In embossing, the circular sheet-metal blank is rounded with the ball-peen or deepening hammer from the center towards the circumference. In raising, the hammer work starts at the circumference, and the rim of the sheet is raised inwards against a wooden sectional chuck in stages.

Embossing requires robust material; the thickness of the rim remains unchanged. It is closer to forging from the solid and is thus the original form of sheet-metalworking; it originated in an age in which rolled metal sheets were still unknown. "This embossing produces the beautiful and strong rims so typical of old cups and never obtainable with soldered reinforcements." (Prof. Rickert.) The extent to which the material is stretched here can be clearly seen in the embossed bowl of any antique chalice; for "with embossing, the strong sheet-metal plate of which the vessel is made has a diameter which is not appreciably larger than the rim of the finished vessel. Hence the old pastime of beating coins into cups, on whose rim the marginal inscription of the coin is still legible." (Rickert.)

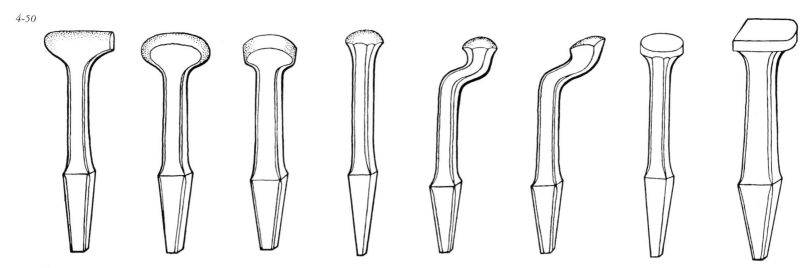

Fig. 4-50. *From left to right:* T-*Stake, two round heads, straight socket, two cranked sockets, two versions of flat head.*

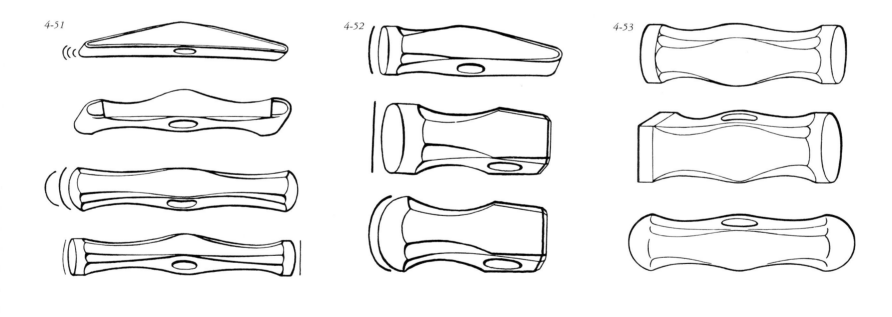

Fig. 4-51. *From top to bottom: Raising hammer with indication of various widths, collet hammer, embossing hammer with various convex faces, planishing hammer with a flat and a slightly convex face.*

Fig. 4-52. *Single-face hammers. From top to bottom: Spotting hammer, planishing hammer with one face, ball-peen hammer with one face.*

Fig. 4-53. *Two-face hammers. From top to bottom: Planishing hammer with one flat, round face, and one convex, round face; with one flat, square face, and one convex, round face; and two-face embossing hammer, various curvatures.*

4-54

Fig. 4-54. *Raising a ball from flat sheet in four successive stages.*

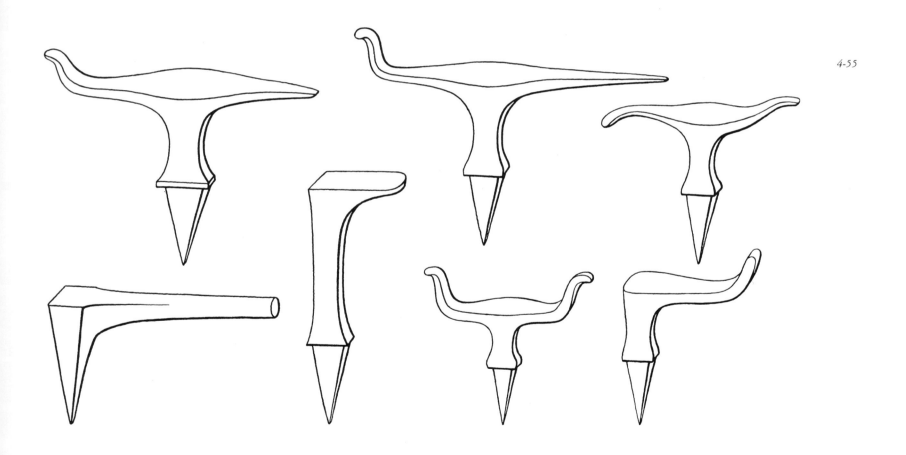

4-55

Fig. 4-55. *Old stakes for forging and embossing, copied from copper engravings in an eighteenth-century French technical book; their hand-wrought original shapes and profiles differ radically from the standardized types produced in modern tool factories.*

Raising can also be combined with stretching the sheet radially and upsetting it tangentially. Here, the sheet is stretched in the direction of the concentric circles beaten with the hammer and starting from the center of the circular blank. (They can be recognized in the top half of the object on the left, *Fig. 4-54*.) The angle at which the peen of the hammer strikes the metal depends on whether the thickness of the metal is to remain unchanged, to be reduced, or to be increased. If the hammer blows are vertical, the thickness of the material remains unchanged. If the hammer is inclined so that the blows come from the direction of the edge of the work (that is, the angle between hammer and sheet is narrower towards the edge of the work than between the hammer and the center of the blank), the material is upset, and its thickness increases towards the circumference. If the angle between hammer and sheet is larger towards the circumference of the plate (plate for the round blank) than towards the center, the thickness will decrease towards the circumference.

The creasing visible in several of the illustrations is not essential. There is a method of raising without pleating, but it is undeniable that the use of pleats speeds up raising. If a work is to be raised without pleating, the first stage must be embossing. With thin sheets, this is not without risk except in the case of shallow bowls. Raising, the more widely used method, is described below in detail, with illustrations.

The raising of a hollow sphere, shown in four stages (Fig. 4-54)

First stage: The work shows two different directions of the hammer blows and, as a result, two differently treated zones of the surface. The circumference of the still fairly shallow hollow form is wavy. In this part, the hammer blows are radial. They are part of the preceding stage, in which the sheet was pleated over a wooden saddle block, with the pleats radiating from the center towards the circumference of the blank. At the subsequent stage, after the work has been annealed and pickled, these pleats are flattened again with the same hammer (the swaging hammer) transversely to their direction. The diameter decreases during this operation, and the work gradually grows higher—it is being raised. The progress of the circular hammer treatment can be clearly seen: Up to the break with deep shadows separating the transversely hammered upper and larger zone from the still pleated lower section.

Second stage: The same operation is repeated at an advanced stage. Here, too, a transversely hammered upper section is separated from the lower one, where the hammer blows produced the existing pleats and were therefore longitudinal. The remaining pleats can still be seen along the circumference. This alternation of pleating and flattening is repeated until the approximate shape of a sphere is produced.

Third stage: This shows the work after the pleats have been completely flattened. To obtain the spherical shape, the bottom must be rounded out and the rim even more raised-in. In the illustration, the surface of the work appears mat because it has just been annealed and pickled.

Fourth stage: Corners, shallow depressions, and bulges have to be evened out, and the pure spherical shape produced, fashioned with a cut-out and filed template. During this stage the surface is also gradually evened with a planishing hammer. This last stage of forging, the planishing proper, is the most difficult part of the process.

Various wrought objects

The illustrations on the relevant pages show various shapes of vessels raised with a hammer (*Figs. 1-14, 2-27, 3-23–3-24*, etc.). All these hollow bodies are wrought in one piece; only the accessories (handles, knobs of lids, bottoms, and rim reinforcements) were added subsequently. Their profiles are determined by differences in the dimensions, not by deep recesses or bulges. The character of the design is the result of very carefully proportioned changes in the outline. Designs of this kind are based on the technical process of raising, to which any drastic change of volume and character of design runs strictly counter. Marked bulges and recesses cause difficulties and additional work, and also greatly tax the tensile strength of the material. If a sheet is excessively maltreated with the hammer, cracks suddenly appear on the margin or in the center of the bulge of an "ill-used" form.

The lessons to be learned for raising are that the processes of stretching and upsetting must be followed closely, and a feeling acquired for changes in the thickness of the sheet if unpleasant surprises are to be avoided. Naturally, the thickness of the sheet can and should be checked from time to time. But neither a micrometer nor a tenths' scale can enter deeply into a hollow body. Precisely where the risk of cracking is greatest, little can be done with measuring instruments. The amount by which the sheet is longitudinally stretched while it is being worked is a rough guide to the degree of reduction of its thickness. The radius of the round blank (the circle cut out of the sheet) is known. If the length of a wrought form is divided into small sections and arranged in a straight line, in other words, if the curves are developed, the difference can be determined. The radial dimension of the blank will always be found to have increased; this will show itself as the height of the form. Added to this longitudinal lengthening, there is also a diametrical lengthening if the sheet is slightly planished. The limits within which this lengthening can still be regarded as structurally sound depend very much on the shape of the work, the chosen metal, and the thickness of the sheet, as well as on the pliability and uniformity of the shaping and on careful tempering. Hard and fast rules therefore cannot be established. A lengthening between a quarter and a third of the maximum dimension can, however, be considered normal.

The pure hammered form chased from a seamless piece of material is only rarely the final functional form. Almost always other components (feet, handles, etc.) must be attached, riveted, or soldered on to make it ready for use. Exceptions are the drinking bowls (*Figs. 3-25, 3-27*), which, for the sake of the harmony of their design, are left without any attached parts. Their uncompromising, almost sacred, solemnity is based in part on their spherical or oval embossed form, which is not weakened by any interruption or ancillary feature. The difficulty of adding the suitable handle or knob of the lid to a vessel can be seen even in the best examples illustrated in this book.

Only the handle makes the vessel "handy", and must therefore be shaped to match the form of the hand and its function. But it must also combine with the existing functional shape to produce an integrated design. It can unobtrusively repeat the curves of the outline; on the other hand it may form a bold contrast. Base, lid, and reinforcement of the lid present further difficulties, because they are made by means of a process which differs from the chasing of the body; the difference shows. Bent from strips of sheet metal comparatively easily, and soldered, they lack thorough shaping with the hammer. Naturally, they too can be hammer-finished if their appearance is to be matched with that of the embossed hollow body. As we have already seen, however, the superficial effect of the hammer finish is not decisive. An edge produced by the joining of two separate parts is sharp and definite, and therefore looks totally different from the soft transition across a hammered bend or edge. Such scruples of the craftsman are out of place with work in copper. Tableware of beaten brass, too, readily combines with work of contrasting appearance. Often it is their very abruptness of difference that adds a dynamic element; a difference in color (copper handles, rivets, etc.) too, provides an attractive change. However, this does not apply to silver tableware. Here, careful design and adaptation of all parts to the character of the soft curves of hammer finish is essential. The teapot *(Fig. 2-27)* is an example where precise composition of the structure and practical, solid design of the details (the spout, the lid) are possible.

After all that has been said about the character of the chased work, it can easily be seen that a hexagonal or octagonal bowl, developed and bent, filed along the edges for beveling, soldered, and lastly hammered, differs from hammered work. It is the result of assembly. The metal sheet was subjected to less stress; moreover much time was saved. To work the bowl from a single piece, it would first have had to be chased round, the edges forced up and the panels beaten, which is a tedious process. It is easy to see that prismatic shapes do not go with hammer work. They are suitable for combinations of methods. We therefore must enlarge a little on hammerwork in combination with other, time-saving working methods. Here, as more modern pieces are compared with similar ones of the eighteenth century, it is worthwhile to point out that the apparently chased copper jug in *Fig. 4-65* really shows an overlapped soldered joint running from bottom to top beneath the handle. This is evidence that the piece had been bent from a developed sheet, soldered to form a body, and its form smoothed completely with the hammer. Here we have the working method of the coppersmith or the brassfounder.

Combined techniques

Occasionally, jugs are found which are not chased from a single piece (a flat sheet-metal disk), but shaped from a soldered sheet. This method saves time and labor. Here, too, the body was first raised-in at the top and bottom from a conical, soldered section, banged out at its greatest circumference, and finally planished on the convex anvil. The bottom of the jug can be soldered in place. This is possible with silver. In copper it would have to be hemmed (folded), since copper, once planished, must not be tempered if it is not to lose its spring hardness (acquired through hammering), and its consequent stability.

Banging out is the bulging out of a hollow body from inside with an embossing hammer. If this hollow shape is so narrow that it is impossible to work inside with the hammer, minor bulges can also be formed by means of snarling *(cf. Fig. 4-64)*. This calls for an iron bent at right angles and clamped in a vise. The top of the iron faces upwards and has a convex face. In snarling, the hammer blows are directed not at the work, but at a spot on the snarling iron close to the right-angle bend in the vise, so that its horizontal limb will vibrate. With sheets of moderate thickness, the desired bulge can thus be produced from inside.

The working of a shallow tray *(Fig. 3-31)* cannot be described in words. Practical guidance by an expert and much experience are necessary to know exactly where the hammer blows must be directed during planishing, so that the stresses in the sheet are balanced for the bottom to rest evenly on the support without springiness or wobbling. In addition, the character of the work is determined by the force of the hammer and the shallow or deep marks it produces on the metal surface. Whereas it was fashionable for a few years to emphasize the hand finish with the roughest possible hammer finish *(Fig. 3-24)*, this approach has been abandoned in more recent work. The delicate attraction of a regularly hammered surface increases if the hammer face is only slightly convex, but so does the difficulty of the technique. Each single blow with the highly polished hammer face produces a tiny, straight, polished spot on the work, standing out against the neighboring one at an imperceptible angle. A beautifully planished round shape thus feels like a smooth, naturally-grown fruit. This effect is at once destroyed if the finished work is pickled in acid—before it is silver-plated, for instance. This produces minute pores and blurred transitions between the individual, struck surfaces; this in turn will mean that the luster has gone. Machine grinding and polishing, too, should be used with care on hammer-finished work.

Fig. 4-56. The beginning of raising: The creases are beaten. The tools used are an embossing hammer, similar to the swaging hammer but rather blunt, and the wooden saddle block clamped in the vise, its groove just visible below the hammer. Instead of creasing the round and raising it directly, it can first be embossed on a round hollowed wooden block.

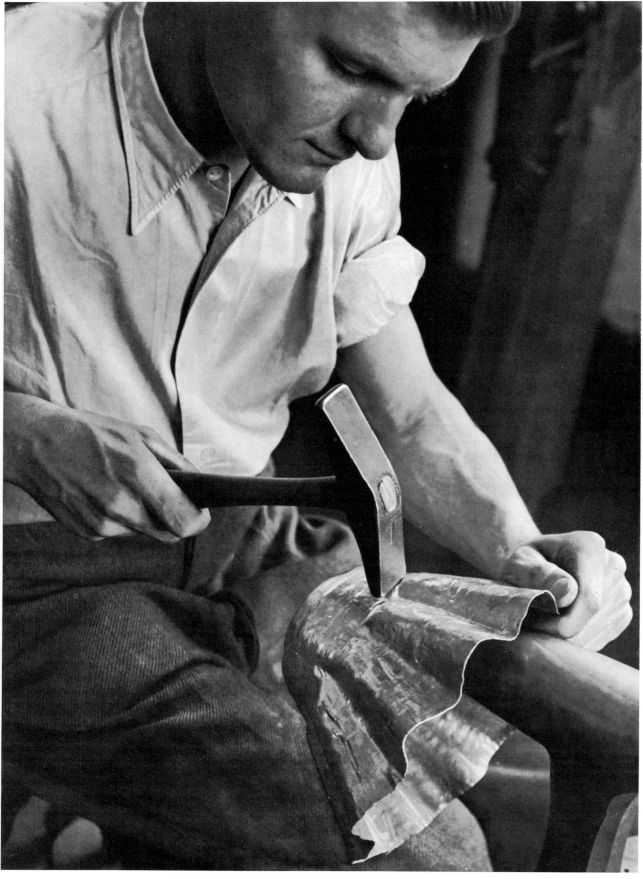

Fig. 4-57. *After each creasing operation, the shape must be beaten out again transversely to the direction of the crease. This produces marked swaging. This stage roughly corresponds to stage 2 of the operation in Fig. 4-54. The hammer is a raising hammer. Its corners are carefully rounded, because blow marks with them, caused by incorrect holding of the hammer, are almost impossible to remove during planishing. When a work is creased and beaten out repeatedly, care must be taken to beat a new crease where there was formerly a projection to ensure that the thickness of the sheet remains uniform.*

Fig. 4-58. The last task for the hammer. The hollow shape, now completely raised, is planished, that is, beaten out. The planishing hammer, with a round face on one side, and an oblong face on the other side (both faces are plane), corresponds in shape roughly to the center drawing in Fig. 4-48. The stake, again clamped in the vise, adapts itself to the round form of the work. It has a convex face, also planished. The work is turned with the left hand, on which depends the regularity of the hammer marks.

4-59

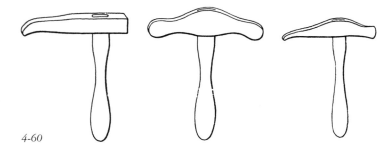

4-60

Fig. 4-59. *Casserole, silver, hand-forged, rosewood handles, diameter 5·8 ins. (14cm). Kay Bojessen, 1951. Neue Sammlung, Munich.*

Fig. 4-60. *Old shapes for hammers, taken from copper engravings in an eighteenth-century French technical book.*

4-61

Fig. 4-61. Silver fruit bowl. Beaten with chiseled border. Workshops of the City of Halle, Burg Giebichenstein.

Fig. 4-62. From bottom to top: Single face flattening, embossing, and planishing hammers. These are special coppersmith's hammers.

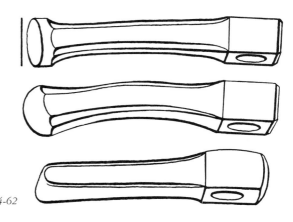

4-62

149

Fig. 4-63. *Jar, sheet brass, raised with the hammer. Workshops of the State School of Arts and Crafts, Schwäbisch Gmünd, 1948.*

Fig. 4-64. *Snarling. A tube, whose original width of 1·5 ins. (40mm) is indicated by the broken line, has been widened to the outlined form by means of snarling. The hammer strikes the spot marked by the arrow. Not only can a narrow hollow form be widened, but individual projections or continuous patterns can also be modeled. The worker modeling and directing the work presses it strongly with both hands onto the appropriately shaped face of the snarling iron, while his assistant produces the bouncing thrusts with his hammer blows.*

4-64

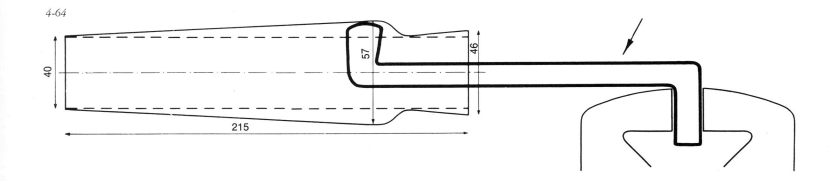

Fig. 4-65. Jug with open handle for clamping, copper. Dimensions: Height 8 ins. (19·2cm), diameter 4·5 ins. (11·8cm). Reputedly around 1700. Body from a single sheet, lapped soldered joint, reduced with the hammer. Thickness of sheet 26 gauge (0·4mm). Handle and reinforcement of rim made of a piece of about 0.12 ins. (3mm) thickness, fastened with brass rivets.

Assembly

The term "assembly" covers any kind of fitting together of individual components; the metal craftsman gradually took it over from the mechanical engineer, who mass-produces components (of an automobile, for instance), which he assembles only at the last stage of production.

Today, even the goldsmith speaks of assembled rings and assembled tableware, indicating that these objects, too, are assembled from individual, separately fashioned components (findings). Obviously, the kind of connection plays a part in this assembly. In industrial metalwork, screws, rivets, and welding are used to assemble the parts of a machine or of a steel bridge. The craftsman, too, knows and uses these techniques in his creative work; after all, he developed them himself long before the advent of mechanical engineering and industrial technology. The Gross Komburg Chandelier, for instance, was assembled from individual strips and joined with rivets (Figs. 5-18–5-19, 5-37). In most chalices the component parts, bowl, stem, and foot are screwed together, for the simple reason that it must be possible to dismantle them for the annual cleaning during Holy Week. For assembly of wrought parts by means of rivets, screws, and (hammer-) forge welding see page 126.

These methods of joining are supplemented by some others peculiar to sheet-metal working. There are two kinds of soldering: Soft and hard soldering. Soft soldering (with tin solders of low melting points) need not be described here since it is only rarely suitable for creative metalwork, with the exception of copperware. Any firm and durable joint calls for hard soldering. Although occasionally unavoidable (in repairs, for instance), soft soldering is rightly regarded in the goldsmith's workshop as botching. For hard soldering, gold, sterling silver, copper, and brass solders are used at working temperatures mostly above 800°C.

A mechanical cold joint is the folding and in-setting of rim edges, called hemming by the brass founder and the coppersmith. Riveting also belongs to this group.

Other work loosely associated with assembly proper consists of the preparatory steps of filing, drilling, sawing, and bending. For their assessment as working methods for the gold- and silversmith, an original view, confirmed by superb achievements, must be mentioned here; it has found acceptance among fellow craftsmen and may well induce the rising generation to look at their own work in a critical light.

One of the best and most successful contemporary gold- and silversmiths in Germany, who has tried out many techniques, has reached the following conclusions about the relations in his own work between raw material and technical and artistic form: Sheet metal, wire and granulation are the media of creative craftsmanship.

He regards the bending of wire and sheet as the first step of creative work with these media, in which the forms of the scroll, the wave, of knots, ribbons, and chains are evolved. Another element of form, in his view, is granulation (the grain). This is the level at which he sees the connection with the first beginnings of artistic metalcraft.

The cutting methods are associated with the second stage: Drilling, filing, turning, engraving, and grinding. They alter the original uniformity of wire and sheet, and their possibilities of expression are not as closely restricted as by the methods of the first group. The task, now made more difficult by differentiation, consists in imparting an artistic meaning to their technical character.

The third and final group comprises those techniques in which he sees a greater danger to the harmony of technical and artistic form,

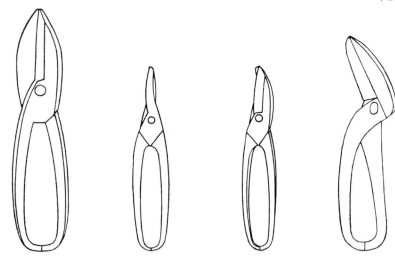

Fig. 4-66. Work begins with cutting the sheets. These are the tools (from right to left): 1. Hawk's bill shears, which do not bend or curl the sheet during cutting; 2. curved-blade tinners' hand shears for curved parts; 3. scroll pivoted circular shears; 4. Conventional straight-blade plate shears, length 6·6–10 ins. (16–25cm).

because they have departed from the original forms of metalcraft and favor the imitation of nature. These are forging, pressing, and embossing. For their use, he demands guidelines which must be the stricter the greater the freedom. And he seeks to establish these guidelines by adhering to the styles of the past.

Fig. 4-67. Milk can, sheet copper. Brass plate, iron handles and handle fixtures. Body bent from a developed sheet, with soldered joint. Neck raised from a disk, and hemmed over the upper rim of the truncated cone. Bottom also hemmed. The developed sheet was beaten and planished to round it evenly and to tighten it, and to make the copper spring hard. Franz Rickert, Munich.

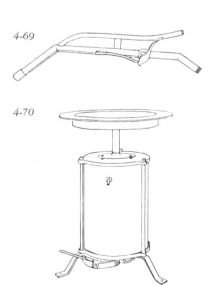

Fig. 4-68. *Hard soldering (brazing). A bottom section is being soldered. A fine-pointed flame from the soldering gun (from top right) heats the soldering joint. The soldering bar is held in the left hand. Binding wire prevents the section from slipping. The rotatable soldering bowl is filled with charcoal.*

Fig. 4-69. *Conventional soldering gun.*

Fig. 4-70. *Rotating soldering machine with built-in bellows and pedal for its operation.*

Riveting

In sheet-metalwork, riveting is used less often today than it was in the past, because the formerly laborious soldering methods have been simplified by technical developments. In addition, electric spot welding, which greatly favors mass production and the streamlining of manufacturing techniques, has been invented, and introduced everywhere in industry. But a certain prejudice against riveting, too, plays a role. A work whose parts are riveted together does not look as much one piece as a soldered one. There is a striking emphasis on the place where it has been joined; the rivet head sees to that. Such honesty is perhaps a little oldfashioned, but quite proper to the craftsman. The unselfconsciously decorative effect of a row of rivet heads is also a logical manifestation of craftsmanship. Even on the wings of a jet airliner (incidentally, an example of typical craft production) they suggest an ornamental pattern. The recent attitude towards riveting is based on an over-valuation of fined surfaces, which has, however, already been overcome in good examples of present-day craftsmanship. Certainly, riveting is unsuitable for joining parts subsequently to be plated with silver or any other metal. But where a handle, a knob on a lid, or something similar is to be attached to a brass or copper jug; or where a box-shaped container that need not be watertight is to be made of sheet metal, riveting is quite proper and can also be attractive (*Figs. 2-33, 4-7, 4-15*).

Soldering

(Hard soldering only is described here. For *Soft soldering* see page 262.)

Preparation

So that work and solder enter into a firm connection, to enable them to form an alloy along their contact faces, these faces must be metallurgically pure, in other words free from grease and oxides. Oxidation must also be prevented during heating. The first condition is met by fining—scraping or filing clean the joint, the second, by spreading or dusting it with soldering materials (borax, fluoron, pastes; see page 261), whose task is to prevent on the one hand any oxidation by its chemical action, and on the other to produce a liquid, vitreous coat to insulate the joint physically against air. These soldering materials are also called fluxes, because they favor the rapid, unobstructed penetration of the solder into the joint. The most important point in soldering, apart from thorough preparation, is to recognize, from observations based on past experience, the exact moment when the solder "shoots" into the joint like water after it has been just sufficiently heated. Competence requires much practice. The tying together of large parts of a work to be soldered (sections, handles, spouts, etc.) with iron binding wire also demands skill and thought. The direction in which the parts are to be tied together must ensure that they are held securely together, because they soften in red heat and tend to slide *(Fig. 4-68)*. On the other hand, however, the binding wire must not cut into the work or change its shape by excessive pressure. To prevent the dreaded shriveling (formation of wrinkles as melting begins) caused by overheating, the area adjoining the joint and the binding wires is brushed with clay paste.

Soldering equipment and how to solder

The ancient heat source for soldering was the charcoal flame, and for small pieces the single glowing charcoal, fanned into a flame with a blowpipe. Later, various types of blowlamps (methylated spirit, and more recently other fuels, too) were used, whose flame was also directed at the joint with a blowpipe. Today, the most popular source of heat is town gas. Workshops in remote areas rely on bottled gas and similar facilities. Depending on the size and raw material of the work, soldering is done with the soldering gun *(Fig. 4-69)* connected to a bellows or blower unit, in a charcoal trough (large workpieces), or on a wire grid, a single piece of charcoal, or in plaster (jewelry) with the goldsmith's blowpipe operated by mouth. The jet of air produced by the operator's breath (goldsmith) or bellows (silversmith) or blower unit (brass founder) has two purposes: First, to supply the flame with oxygen and thereby increase its heat, and second, to direct its effect and confine it to the joint. The blower unit converts it into a fine-pointed flame, whose outer cone is dim but very hot (oxidation flame), and inner, blue cone (reduction flame) considerably cooler. Those who are unaware of this use the blowpipe incorrectly and do not take advantage of the flame. At the beginning of soldering, the entire work is heated: A broad flame (little air) is evenly played on it; now the heat is increased at the joint by vigorous use of the blower unit and the pointed flame until the solder melts. The treadle-operated bellows, which can also be built into the cylindrical soldering hearth with rotating disk *(Fig. 4-70)*, permits more accurate adjustment of the air jet at the critical moment than a mechanical blower unit. The rotating trough lined with asbestos or charcoal is necessary for uniform heating of round bodies from all sides, and to make possible a steadily progressive sequence for soldering on the whole circumference of the work. During soldering, the stick of solder is held, with or without tongs, in the left hand, and the soldering gun in the right *(Fig. 4-68)*.

The solders
(*Soldering operation and table of solders see pages 242–243, 248, 261.*)

The solders used are alloys of the raw material of work with other metals, whose composition is precisely adjusted according to the desired melting point, and, with gold and silver, to meet legal requirements, according to the standard fineness of the work. Depending on the melting point, we distinguish between hard, medium, and easy solders. It must be mentioned that brass and copper work can be soldered with sterling silver solder without difficulty. Refineries supply the precious-metal solders in sheet form, but the user can also alloy them himself. Strips (soldering sticks) or small snippets (paillons) are cut from the sheet. Very hard solders are needed for enameling, so that soldered strips do not dissolve when they are fired in the muffle furnace, and liquid solder does not contaminate the enamel.

Fig. 4-71. *Oblong copper box, tin-plated inside, early nineteenth century. Typical coppersmith's work. One piece, with broadly lapped soldered joint in the back, bottom hemmed, lid with riveted copper hinge. All surfaces are hard-beaten.*

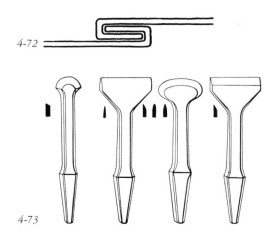

4-72

Fig. 4-72. *Sharp folded seam.*

Fig. 4-73. *Various hand groovers.*

4-73

Hemming, Crimping, Rounding-Off, and Folding

Fig. 4-73 shows some hand groovers. They have been used in these forms for centuries for folding plate edges, first with a wooden mallet, later with an iron hammer. The term "hemming" is a little ambiguous, and such a tool is therefore occasionally called a folding tool. A metal rim is hemmed to reinforce it, and to make it more rigid and less sharp. This flange can be open or folded (rounded or sharp). The round folding of a rim with thick or thin wire effect *(Fig. 3-40)* is blunt flanging, carried out on a tool with a convex face, and adapting itself to the dimensions and shapes of the work. The tools suitable for a given task are made by the user himself, who files or grinds them to the desired shape. Flat rims are folded across the edge of the square stake. Flanges to make folded seams, for instance for joining two sheets without riveting and soldering, are sharp *(Fig. 4-72)*. The tinsmith and the industrial sheet-metalworker use this kind of connection; so do coppersmiths and brass founders. It is therefore met with especially in copper vessels, because soldering is difficult here *(Fig. 4-71)*.

The metal spinner, too, hems on his spinning lathe: He folds edges with a notched spinning tool or a little rotating roller, also notched (see *Fig. 4-72*). Here, everybody has his own method. When a spinner force-fits a bottom, he pushes a flat round blank through the hemmed edge of, for example, a foot, which holds it in position.

In the sheet-metal industry, small and large flanging machines, hand- or power-operated, are used. They round, key, and fold; the work passes between two rollers, whose bulge and groove engage each other.

Hammered or rolled grooves of angular cross section are called creases. The swaging hammer is discussed at length in the section *Cold forging*, page 138. The appropriate anvil part, a horn with grooves, is called a creasing stake and is found among the tools illustrated in this chapter. The rollers of a flanging machine are interchangeable. Most of the hand-operated ones can therefore also be used as seam rolling machines.

Seam rolling and flanging machines, bending and beading presses for the reinforcement of sheet-metal parts, or for the preparation of riveting and welding positions, are necessary for shaping large mass-produced workpieces (automobile bodies, containers, etc.).

Sawing and Beading

Steel blocks can be sawn on machines like wood, except that sawing takes much longer. The locksmith, too, uses a steel saw. But it is gold- and silversmiths who use the most delicate saw blade, a kind of fretsaw known as a piercing saw, mainly to saw into sheets. Some masters of their craft are able to cut figures measuring only a few millimeters in linear fretwork design in the bezel of a gold ring. Others bend spiral scrolls, leafwork, and figures from strips with roundnosed and flat pliers (see *Figs. 4-74–4-75*).

Scrolls are not very popular today. Leaving the question of this well-founded objection or indeed questions of style aside, the unbiased judge must nevertheless accept sawing and bending as a perfectly proper technique of working in sheet metal. The end products of these techniques are a different matter. The exercises shown here— half-completed work by apprentices at a technical college—leave all the formal problems open. They are only meant to teach the pupil to saw and bend neatly; they have no creative pretensions.

Filing

Filing to smooth surfaces, to clean up soldering joints, and for similar purposes requires no detailed explanation. With gold- and silversmiths, brass founders, and related craftsmen it differs from the work of other metalcrafts (such as that of the locksmith, for instance) only in the choice of tools. The steel engraver uses the file perhaps most often; his files, of coarse or fine cut, that is, rough and smooth files, of square, flat, circular, or semicircular cross section, are the same as the mechanic's. In addition to these well-known and generally used large files, he also has a number of needle-files and rifflers *(Figs. 4-81–4-82)* among his tools. They are the types of file used also by other specialists engaged in delicate work. The cut of the files differs according to whether they are designed for silver or steel work. Whereas rifflers are required in the most varied shapes and cross sections resembling those of boasting tools (of which the drawings in *Fig. 4-81* show only a few), bent and cranked to be able to reach all the corners and bends of the work, needle-files are merely smaller and finer versions of the large files.

Creative effects based on filing are possible in gold and silver where a shape or a profile can be produced from the solid wire, or thick sheet *(Fig. 4-76)*. Such work, like all manual work, is of course expensive and worthwhile only in a unique, custom-made piece. Wrought iron should not be touched by the file. Cold working in blank iron as practiced in the past by the locksmith, on the other hand, is largely based on filing in addition to sawing, drilling, and chiseling. Many small objects (keys) thus acquired their final shape in the vise.

4-74

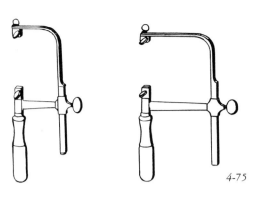

4-75

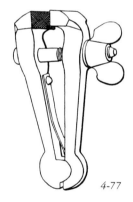

4-77

4-76

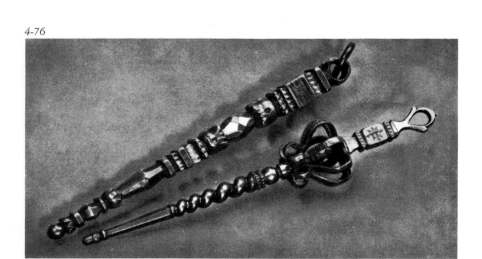

Fig. 4-74. Sawing and bending: Basic techniques of the goldsmith and of all sheet-metalwork. The illustration shows the progressive stages of bending with roundnosed pliers, upwards and downwards from the plane of the sawn-in sheet.

Fig. 4-75. Saw frames, on the left for small work, on the right for larger work.

Fig. 4-76. Individual forms produced by filing on stay pins. Eighteenth century.

Fig. 4-77. Filing vise for clamping and holding small work.

Fig. 4-78. Silver tea egg with strong lock and bent wire bracket for hooking over the rim of the teapot. Robert Fischer.

Fig. 4-79. Set of knife, fork, and spoon, silver, hand-wrought. The curled ends are filed and cut from the solid metal. On the right another hand-wrought silver set, in which the spoon handle was joined to the bowl with a long, pointed prong. Franz Rickert, Munich.

Fig. 4-80. Fish-knife and fork, silver, with cherrywood handles, filed and ground. Franz Rickert, Munich.

4-78

4-79

4-80

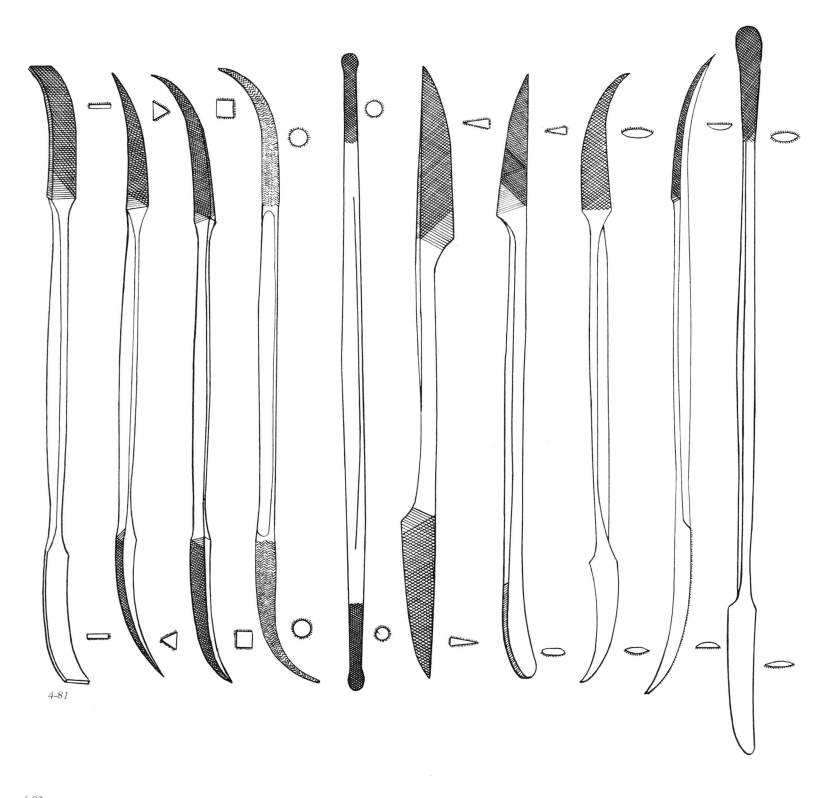

4-81

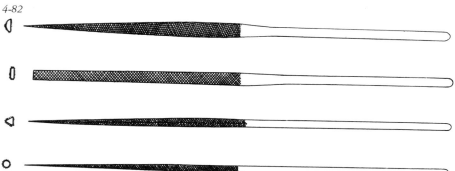

4-82

Fig. 4-81. Rifflers used by the steel engraver and (with a rougher cut) the silversmith. A small selection from a large number of forms.

Fig. 4-82. Needle-files of simple cross section. Sword-shaped and other cross sections are used for special tasks.

4-83

4-84

Fig. 4-83. Left: Pocket folding spoon, silver, fire-gilt, Germany, seventeenth to eighteenth century. The serrated end of the handle (called "Wildspur" or "pied de biche") was originally a result of the working process: The metal often frayed while it was beaten out. Right: Bronze spoon: Holland, seventeenth century.

Fig. 4-84. Hand-wrought knife, fork, and spoon, free adaptation of historical forms (spatular handle, knife blade, and knife handle). Franz Rickert, Munich.

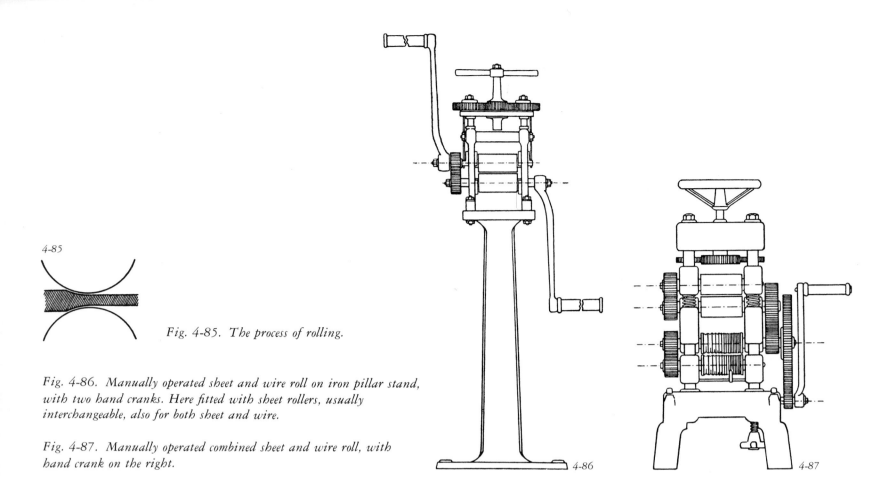

4-85

Fig. 4-85. *The process of rolling.*

Fig. 4-86. *Manually operated sheet and wire roll on iron pillar stand, with two hand cranks. Here fitted with sheet rollers, usually interchangeable, also for both sheet and wire.*

Fig. 4-87. *Manually operated combined sheet and wire roll, with hand crank on the right.*

4-86

4-87

Rolling and Drawing

During drawing, as well as rolling, the metal is stretched in the cold state. This can be done by hand: The goldsmith draws fine wires through the holes of a draw plate clamped in the vise, or he rolls a piece of sheet gold. In the huge rolling mills producing semifinished goods (tin plate, strips, tubes, wire, sections), these working methods have been enlarged to technological dimensions. The principles of the working methods are the same, the changes in the crystal structure of the raw material, too, are largely the same, whether the wire is drawn by hand or in modern, largely automatic machines.

Rolls serve above all for the production of sheet metal of the most varied thickness, of bars, and of sections. Here, the process is explained with the example of the production of sheet silver: When the bar is cast, measures are already taken to prevent the formation of pores and the occurrence of other flaws in the material. Rolling is preceded by dense forging under heavy spring hammers at temperatures of about 700°C. In this context, the description of material flaws and their origin is of interest (see page 246), because many a casting flaw will first appear during cold rolling. The drawing of wires and of solid rods differs from that of tubes and hollow drawn wire, where a drawing mandrel (draw spindle, *Fig. 4-89*) is built into the tube. In both cases, one end of the piece to be drawn is pointed, pushed first through the widest hole of the draw plate or drawing die, and drawn through by hand or machine. Here, the drawing cone performs the task of stretching proper. Lubricants are necessary to facilitate the operation. Progressively narrower holes are used until the final shape and dimension is obtained. Cold work hardening is eliminated by intermediate tempering.

To produce a basic form for the drawing of seamless tubes (silver), convex hollow bodies are first chased from stout round blanks under the press in several working steps (see *Figs. 4-88–4-89*). A draw spindle with mandrel (see *Fig. 4-89*) inside the tube is necessary to maintain the inside width. After each drawing operation, the spindle must be rolled off on a roll with an oval groove, which applies pressure only at two points and therefore loosens it, so that the drawn tube can be pulled off the spindle.

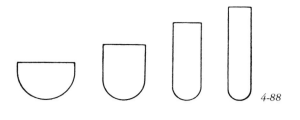

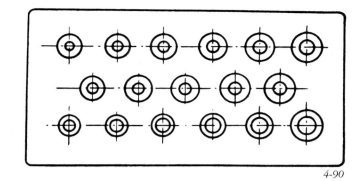

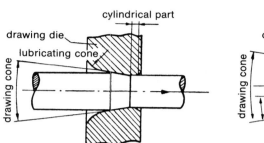

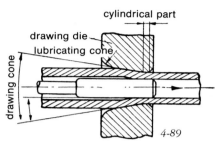

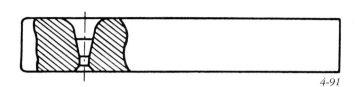

Fig. 4-88. *Preparatory work for drawing seamless silver tubes. Raising the sheet round under the press in several stages (four are shown).*

Fig. 4-89. *Left: Drawing wires and rods. Section through the drawing tool (drawing die). Right: Drawing hinges and seamless tubes; section through the drawing tool. The drawing mandrel in the tube.*

Fig. 4-90. *An oldfashioned draw plate.*

Fig. 4-91. *Section through an oldfashioned draw plate; outlined; Drawing cone and cylindrical part.*

Metal Spinning

This operation should really be called "sheet spinning", because it is not metal of any shape, but only sheets, and only sheets of certain thicknesses at that, which can be shaped by means of spinning. Hollow bodies such as cups, vessels, bowls, dishes, or parts of such bodies to be assembled, are produced with this method.

A hollow body can be spun only on a spinning lathe, which is a machine very closely resembling a lathe in principle. Over a clamped rotating piece of wood, whose shape he continuously changes by turning, and approximates to the final shape of the work step by step, the metal spinner hollows his sheet, which is also rotating, in several stages. He produces the shaping pressure with glass-hard steel tools having rounded and polished ends, during the revolutions of the wooden chuck and the sheet clamped on it. Like the craftsman hammersmith, he must temper his work after each stage of shaping, to remove the strains and stresses in the sheet and to reestablish the soft state. Whereas the hammersmith can produce any desired shapes (in other words, those whose cross section is other than round), the metal spinner—like the turner—is unable to spin any bodies except round or, with special devices, oval ones.

Spinning belongs to the category of noncutting forming. The sheet is shaped into a hollow body in the cold state without its thickness being altered through the removal of material with cutting tools. For this purpose, a circular disk must first be cut or stamped out of the metal sheet; its diameter must be calculated from the size of the work. Since the material stretches during working, the radius of the round blank is shorter than the length resulting from the development of a side of the work. The thickness of the sheet to be chosen depends on the purpose of the object to be made. Generally, the thicknesses of sheets for making spun brass, German silver, or copper vessels varies between 23 and 18 gauge (0·6–1·2mm). The most frequently used thickness is probably 20 gauge (0·8mm).

Compared with other possibilities of mechanical noncutting forming, spinning is still an act of craftsmanship insofar as the spinning tool, guided freehand and with considerable muscle power, forces the sheet

4-92

Fig. 4-92. This is how the metal spinner works: The wooden chuck, the wooden adapter between dead center and work, the support with pin (which can be inserted in a number of holes for use as a pivot and lever fulcrum), and the form of raising tool and the spun grooves on the work are clearly visible.

Fig. 4-93. *Spinning of the hemispherical hollow form visible in the initial stage in Fig. 4-92 is complete, and the work is being removed. A hollow chuck is required (see text) if the rim is to be reinforced, that is, folded.*

rotating on the lathe against the chuck rotating together with it. In addition, the metal spinner turns his patterns himself, according to drawings and templates, on the basis of his technological and craft experience. The drawing press is the much more highly mechanized rival of his working method, and more suitable for mass production. But, compared with it, the spinner has a wider range of possibilities. He can more easily produce difficult, composite, and repeatedly narrowing shapes; furthermore, his simpler tool is very versatile, whereas the drawing tools of the press entail separate and expensive outlay for each new shape. The metal spinner is therefore still indispensable for certain work, even in large plants in the sheet-metal industry. He produces single parts or short runs, difficult shapes too expensive for mechanized production, and finishes coarse-drawn workpieces.

His raw materials are sheet copper, brass, German silver, and aluminum. Sheet gold, silver, and platinum are less usual (unless for technical purposes), since these precious metals demand treatment appropriate to their value and beauty and by the craftsman only.

Sheet metal for deep-drawing is a type of material whose properties largely meet the requirements of drawing, whereas ordinary types of sheet iron are unsuitable. Unlike brass, German silver, and other metals, sheet metal for deep-drawing need not be annealed between the various stages of raising, since the frictional heat generated during the working process is sufficient to cause recrystallization, in other words to eliminate the brittleness and hardness produced. With sheet aluminum, too, annealing is pointless, as it does not make it more pliable. Copper alloys are beaten on iron with a wooden mallet to relieve internal stress before they are annealed, so that their spring temper is reduced and they do not crack during annealing. After annealing, the layer of scale must be removed by pickling (see *Acids*, page 260). Water is used for rinsing, sawdust for drying.

Spinning lathe and tools

The spinning lathe: Construction and operation are illustrated by the drawing below. On the one side are the headstock, spindle, and mandrel, whose thread accepts the chuck, which thus revolves at the same speed. A step pulley is necessary only when the spinning lathe is belt-driven through a transmission (older models).

If an electric motor is built in, it will have a step switch for various speeds of revolution. Opposite the headstock, on the bed way of the lathe, is the tailstock with the dead center and handwheel for the backward and forward movement of the latter. The support with pin, whose position can be altered by means of a number of bores, is also important in the operation. *Fig. 4-113* shows the way in which the metal spinner arranges the spinning tool, uses the pin as pivot and support, and thus produces a lever effect in his tool. Where the support with a simple pin is not sufficient to produce the necessary force, for instance with large workpieces and thick sheets, a simple lever transmission can be of help. Here the metal spinner uses, in place of the rigid spinning tool, a fork-mounted spinning roller to apply pressure to the sheet. This decreases friction, and makes work easier. Or he can, like the iron turner, clamp his tools in a carriage and move them to and fro by means of spindles and handwheels or crank handles, but this is no longer part of the spinning operation proper, in which body weight and body energy are used. The physical effort and the role played by a backrest (or a belt), which is part of the spinning lathe, are clearly illustrated in *Fig. 4-92*.

Turning and spinning tools: To turn his wooden chucks, the metal spinner uses the same turning tools as the wood turner. The most important of these tools are shown in the illustration: The tools for roughing and finishing the chuck, the straight lathe tool for the turning

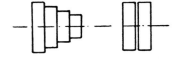

4-94

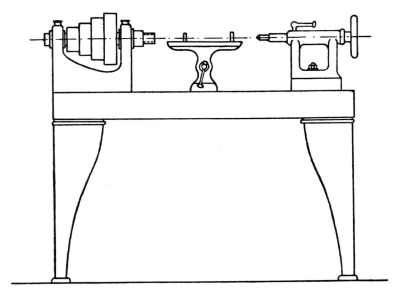

Fig. 4-94. Old-type spinning lathe with transmission drive (gear). On the left: Step pulley for changing the speed of rotation. On the cheeks of the lathe the sliding "support" with bores and lug. On the right: Headstock and dead center, spindle, and handwheel. Top: The transmission gear.

Fig. 4-95. Spinning lathe of more recent design with its own power; motor with step switch. The construction of the rest of the machine is unchanged. Model: L. Schuler A.G., Göppingen.

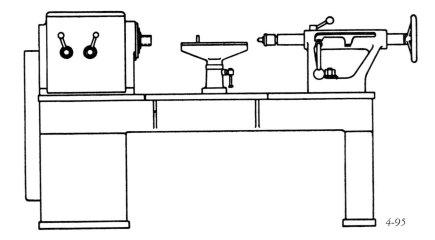

4-95

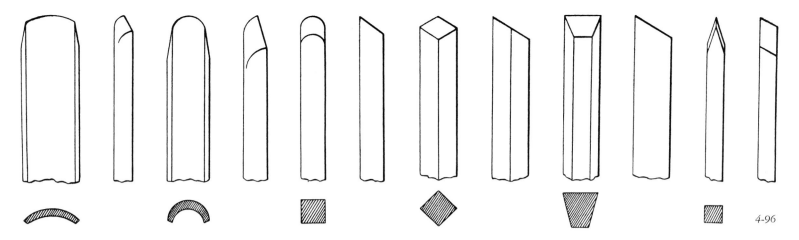

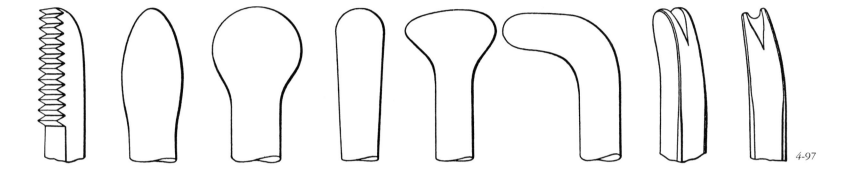

Fig. 4-96. *Turning tools used by the metal spinner. From left to right: Roughing and finishing tools, planing tools, flat blade and diamond-point tool.*

Fig. 4-97. *Tools used by the metal spinner: Threading tool. Raising tools as follows: Roundnose tool, ball tool, all-purpose tongue tool, planishing tool, raising-in tool. Beading fork, various aspects.*

of cylindrical shapes, the round turning tool, with which grooves and internal shapes can be turned, and the boring tool, whose cranked edge, shaped according to the nature of internal or hollow shapes, makes it possible to machine their inner walls. Threading tools, too, belong to this group, for the external and internal thread cutting of the chucks.

Whereas the turning tools must have sharp edges, the spinning tools, as already mentioned previously, are blunt, since they must not damage the sheet. Only a few of them are also used in a cutting capacity (usually on the already spun work), such as the cutter and the diamond-point tool, which are used to cut off edges and to cut away bottoms. With all the others—the true spinning tools—all possible aids are used to prevent them from reducing the thickness of the sheet. Their convex faces are therefore most highly polished. If the sheet to be worked is very hard, for instance a special stainless steel sheet, brass instead of steel tools (but of the same design) are used, so that the tool rather than the work is subject to wear. Brass and German silver sheets are greased with tallow during rotation, before the spinning tool is applied, so that the steel slides better on their surface. Before the work is annealed, this grease must be fumed off with a gentle flame.

The roundnose tool serves for raising the sheets during the first working stages; the all-purpose tongue tool, on the other hand, permits raising as well as finishing (smoothing). Grooves are made with the drawing hook. For opening out or lifting a shape, the raising-in tool is used.

The spinning chucks are generally made of wood. Only for the last, final raise, which is combined with smoothing, does the metal spinner prefer a steel chuck, especially when he has to spin a large number of identical pieces, or if severe raising-in subjects the chuck to considerable wear. Obviously the wood used for chucks must be hard, and must have neither cracks nor pores. Even marked growth rings would be a disturbing feature. Suitable types of wood are: Maple as medium-hard wood for chucks, whitebeam or hornbeam (suitable especially for patterns, see *Fig. 4-113*), and for internal chucks the softer alder. White hawthorn is hard, and therefore suitable for shapes and patterns. Pear and walnut would be suitable, but are expensive.

The chuck screwed onto the spindle, and therefore rotating at the same speed, forms the steady support against which the metal spinner presses his round metal blank. At the same time it represents the precise form of the work, but only at the last raise. For the sheet offers strong resistance to shaping and can therefore not be transformed from the flat blank into the finished hollow body in a single operation. Intermediate chucks are necessary *(Figs. 4-99, 4-101–4-110)*.

167

Fig. 4-100. *Work produced on the spinning lathe. Cocktail shaker, Workshops of the State School of Arts and Crafts, Schwäbisch Gmünd. Design: Karl Dittert.*

Figs. 4-99 and 4-101–4-104. *Chucks (wood) for part 1 of the constructional drawing.*

Fig. 4-99. *First raise.*

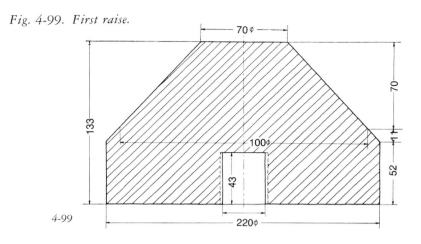

4-99

Fig. 4-98. *Constructional drawing for the cocktail shaker in Fig. 4-100. Note: ø in these drawings represents the spherical or cylindrical coordinate. Numbers in larger type refer to the various parts of the drawing. Measurements are all in millimeters.*

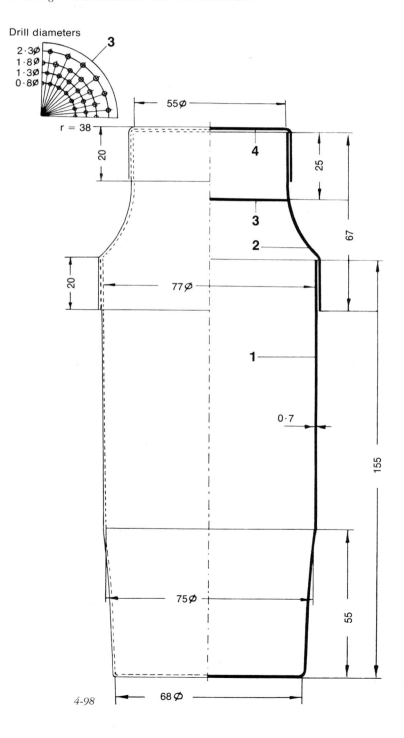

4-98

4-100

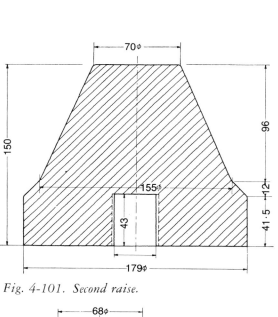

Fig. 4-101. Second raise.

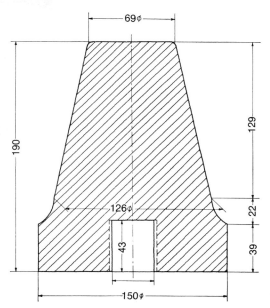

Fig. 4-102. Third raise.

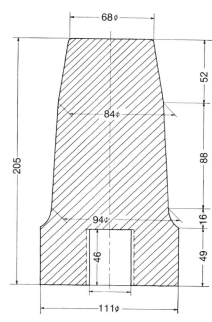

Fig. 4-103. Fourth raise.

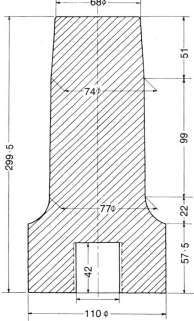

Fig. 4-104. Fifth and final raise.

Figs. 4-105–4-107. Chucks for part 2 of the constructional drawing.

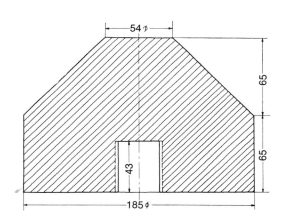

Fig. 4-105. First raise.

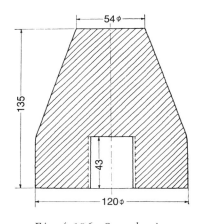

Fig. 4-106. Second raise.

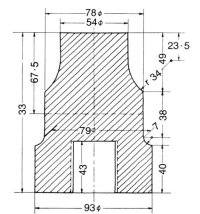

Fig. 4-107. Third and final raise.

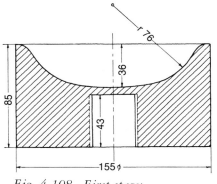

Fig. 4-108. First stage: Cupping (deep-drawing).

Figs. 4-108–4-110. Chucks for part 4 of the constructional drawing.

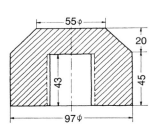

Fig. 4-109. Second stage: Raising.

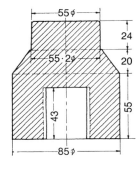

Fig. 4-110. Last raise.

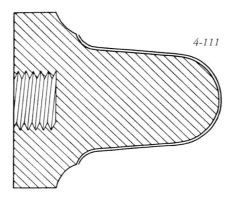

Fig. 4-111. *Section of a chuck which is not raised in, covered by the metal sheet: The work can be removed without difficulty.*

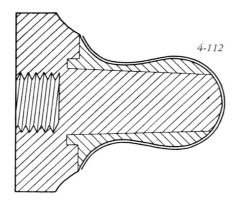

Fig. 4-112. *This chuck is raised-in in the shape of a tulip. It is therefore necessary to use a sectional chuck, which can be dismantled and removed from the raised-in work.*

Raising-in with the aid of sectional chucks

As long as hollow bodies of conical or hemispherical shape are spun, a solid chuck can be used. The finished workpiece can be removed from it without difficulty. The situation is completely different with a pear-shaped hollow body. It narrows, its diameter becomes smaller, and it must be raised-in (see *Fig. 4-113*). It would be impossible to remove a solid chuck through its narrow neck after the work is completed. Here, the chuck must therefore consist of several parts and be capable of being dismantled (*cf. Figs. 4-111–4-112*).

The metal spinner makes his sectional chuck by first longitudinally boring out (turning out) the solid wooden raised-in chuck. Into the bore he fits a slightly conical chuck in whose thicker rear part is cut the necessary thread for mounting it on the spindle. He now divides the (bored) chuck proper into several parts (see *Fig. 4-113*). One of these parts is wedge-shaped inversely to the others. It is called the key piece (arrow a). Because it can be inserted and removed from inside, it allows assembly and dismantling of the ring-shaped chuck. The cone inserted in the bore transforms the ring into a solid shape again. As the longitudinal section shows, the individual parts of the sectional outer chuck are inserted in an annular groove turned in the conical chuck. They cannot therefore fall apart. When the work is raised-in, that is, reduced and fully spun, first the conical chuck is pulled out, then the key piece; now the parts of the outer chuck ring can be removed individually.

Cupping

During the first stage of operation on the spinning lathe, the flat round sheet blank is often embossed first instead of directly raised from outside over a chuck. This applies particularly to silver work. A hollow chuck is required for cupping *(Fig. 4-108)*, for the sheet is worked on its inner surface and spun into the hollow. In this operation, the round sheet blank cannot be held in the headstock and adapter, because this is the very spot where the spinning tool is to do its work. It must be mounted on the hollow chuck with the outer edge doubled over. Basically, cupping on the spinning lathe resembles embossing with the hammer (described on page 143) in its relation to raising.

Hollow chucks are used also for the doubling of edges (hemming), and force-fitting of bottoms (joining by folding).

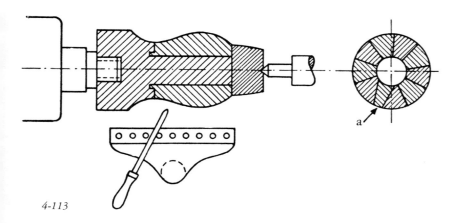

Fig. 4-113. *A sectional chuck for spinning raised-in work in longitudinal and cross section. The arrow points at the inverted conical key piece, with which the sectional chuck can be dismantled after extraction of the pin. The longitudinal section shows the more closely hatched "pattern" between the dead center and the sectional chuck, the spindle chuck with bush and screw thread, and the annular groove in which the various parts are held together.*

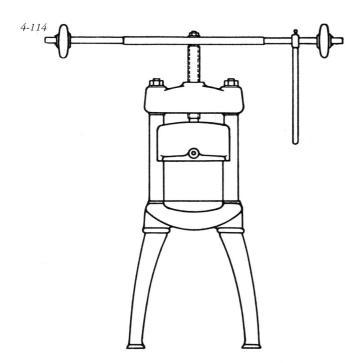

Fig. 4-114. The hand screw press, used since the seventeenth century. It has an advantage over the gravity-operated drop hammer in that its impact is more sustained. The metal has time to "flow". Press: L. Schuler A. G., Göppingen.

Spun workpieces

The cocktail shaker *(Fig. 4-100,* constructional drawing *Fig. 4-98)* spun in three stages is an instructive example of a design in which the potentialities of the spinning lathe have been correctly assessed. Functional austerity, severe surfaces, and carefully thought-out proportions result in a design appropriate to what the spinning lathe can do. The individual stages of spinning can be seen in the modification of the chucks.

Machines for Stamping and Pressing

The press plays a far greater part in the metalware industry than, for instance, in the glassware industry, where it developed in an ancient tradition of shaping (by means of primitive hand tools for pressing and stamping). Nevertheless, glassworkers succeeded in finding forms of pressed glass, which reflect the operation of pressing proper, not of any craft technique, whereas the press in the metalware factory is often expected to imitate the appearance of hammerwork, embossing, and chasing.

In the workshop of the silverware factory of P. Bruckmann Söhne, Heilbronn, Germany, dies dating from 1805 for pressing silver tableware were kept only a few years ago. This was roughly the period when machine pressing is said to have been used for the first time. Hand-made pressed articles were produced in stone molds or on metal patterns, and strip ornaments hand-stamped with metal stamps were made in the Middle Ages and indeed in Antiquity. From these primitive attempts at series reproduction, the methods of pressing and stamping have gradually developed. As already explained elsewhere (page 116), pressing is the shaping of sheet metal by means of bottom and upper die (swage and hubbing die), whereas stamping entails the impression of a relief, on one or on both sides of a thicker piece of metal, by means of recessed pressing dies (swages). (Full stamping.)

Dropwork: One of the earliest constructions for mechanical pressing and stamping is the dropwork, in which a suspended heavy steel block, the ram, strikes the work under its own weight after its anchorage has been released.

The handscrew press or pillar-type press is simple in construction and function. The pillar, a spindle with a flat thread, moves in the part of the upper frame which has a female thread. It is rigidly connected with the horizontal weighted rod on which a vertical handle is mounted. If the spindle is started by a vigorous pull on this handle, the head of the press attached to the bottom end of the pillar is raised or lowered according to the direction of rotation. Speed and impact of the head rapidly bearing down thus depend on the power of the drive, and are therefore adjustable. The pillar-type press has a further advantage over the dropwork with its sudden and harsh impact, in that its action on the die and the

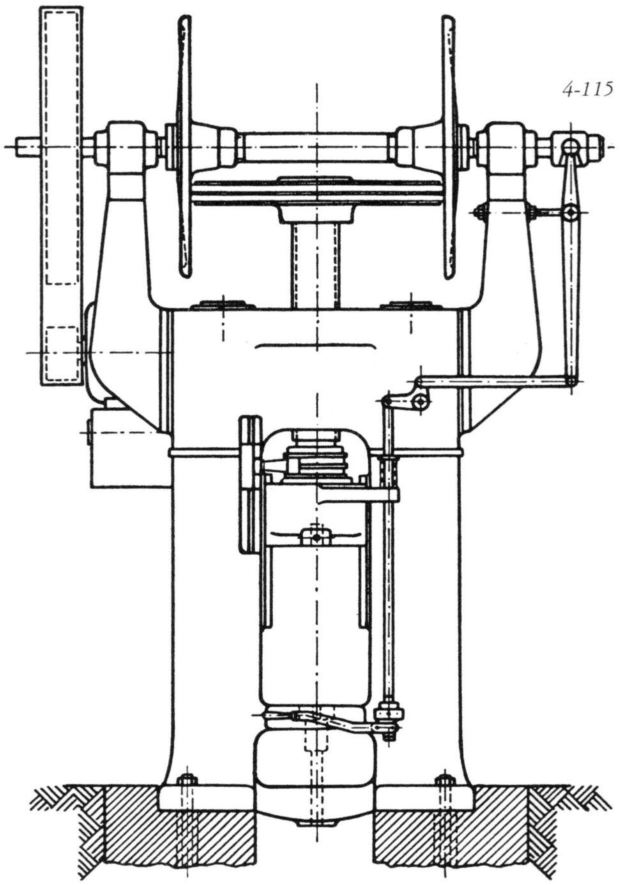

Fig. 4-115. The fine-pitch friction spindle presses are suitable for cold stamping hard metals. For hot stamping coarse-pitch presses are used.

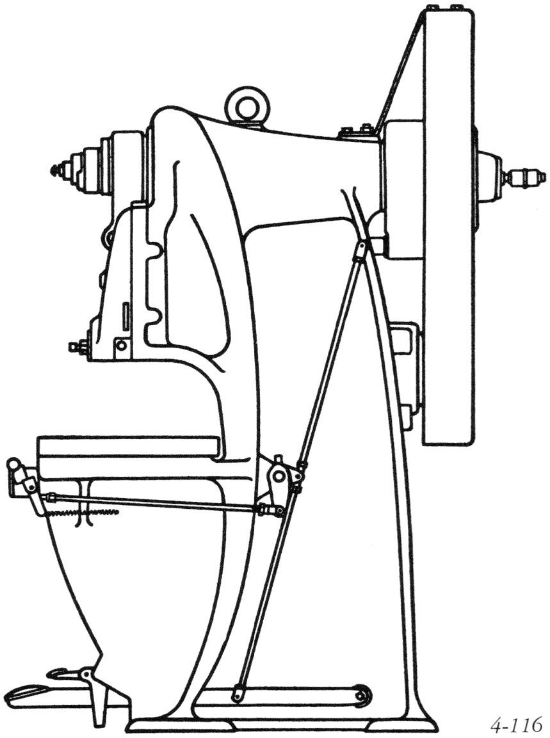

Fig. 4-116. Eccentric presses are more suitable for punching than for pressing and stamping. Small mass-produced articles, however, can also be stamped in an eccentric press.

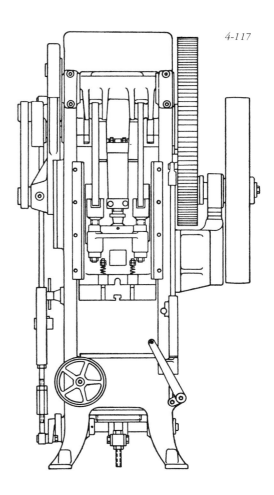

Fig. 4-117. In addition to its use in pressing holloware, the toggle-lever press is preferred for coining in closed dies (with guide rings).

work is sustained but more gentle, since the inertia of the mass is used instead of gravity. It is suitable for pressing small hollow shapes, especially jewelry. The matrix is clamped on the table, the key form on the movable head of the press, and the press is given its impetus by hand. The fact that such light presses are now no longer used except in small craft and industrial establishments needs no explanation.

The friction screw press functions on the same principle as the pillar-type press. Its head, too, is raised and lowered with a screw. But weight and performance have been increased, and manual operation has therefore been replaced by a power drive. As the name of the machine implies, the screw is driven by friction, generated by two disks (shown in cross section in the drawing) of which either acts with its speed of rotation on the leather cover of a horizontal flywheel rigidly connected with the screw. These friction plates can be horizontally adjusted by pressure on a lever via a rod linkage from below, so that they impart either clockwise or anticlockwise rotation to the screw, thus raising or lowering the head of the press. Within the distance between the horizontal drive shaft and the female thread of the frame, which determines the lift of the press, the flywheel sliding up and down on the friction disks can be

continuously driven or braked. This makes stamping action of the press possible, ranging from light to very heavy. Because of this possibility of controlling the stamp, friction presses are suitable both for pressing holloware and for the production of cutlery.

Unlike the friction screw press, the *eccentric press* executes jerky movements whose impact cannot be controlled. They are generated by the eccentric shaft, which converts the circular motion of a drivewheel into the vertical motion of the head of the press (ram), which slides between rails. Its property of executing identical blows in rapid succession makes the eccentric press particularly suitable for punching and stamping. Cutting tools and piercing tools, in which the flat and keen-edged over die engages in a precision-matched swage block for stamping strips and all kinds of small plates from sheet metal, are used mainly in eccentric presses. In machines of completely accident-proof design, in other words, those which do not permit interference by the operator, the press is actuated with a treadle. With work requiring or merely permitting interference with the tool by the operator, the machine is started by means of a two-hand starting device which forces the operator to remove both hands from the danger zone, thus preventing possible accidents.

Toggle-joint drop presses are double-action machines used for drawing where it is essential to clamp the sheet. The punch is guided in the blank holder ram, actuated by the crankshaft via powerful slides and toggle-joint transmission. The punch, too, is actuated by the crankshaft. The tools to be used consist of the tool base, blank holder, and punch. The inserted blank is held in position by the blank holder, which descends first; this prevents the formation of creases as the punch descends. The drive of the blank holder ram is powerful enough to permit cutting. The actuation of the punch by a strong crankshaft makes the exertion of high final pressures possible, so that bottom stamping, too, can be carried out on the drawn work.

This type of press is also largely accident-proof; safety controls are fitted which compel the press operator to keep his hands outside the danger zone when the tool descends.

Grinding and Polishing

Use, usefulness, and disadvantage

Before the invention of the machine with rotating grinding wheels and brushes, metalwork was ground and polished by hand. Old abrasives used in this way are pumice stone, coal, slate, etc. Even today, engravers and gold- and silversmiths hand-grind individual work when they have reason to fear that the less adaptable mechanical grinding procedure might be too risky. A delicate shape can be ruined within seconds.

Without doubt the great efficiency and saving of labor introduced by the machine has recently led to a considerable increase in (often unnecessary) grinding and polishing. Customers have thus been conditioned to look for the flawless, specular surface of the object they buy. Sparkle dazzles the eye and masks the shape. It would be salutary if polishing, too, were reduced a little, and matters of taste as well as usefulness could be accorded higher priority than the wishes of the already spoiled customers. Solid craftsmanship has long opted out of the race for such effective window display attractions; manufacturers, too, should set their aims higher.

These critical remarks are of course not meant to contest that grinding and polishing are quite proper to metallic materials; the latter, however, less so than is accepted today. It can perhaps be said generally that although almost all metalwork (except iron and castings) must be ground, polishing is, apart from a few cases of functional necessity, a matter of taste, and that the question of polishing depends on the character of the various metals. Bronze, for instance, does not lend itself to it; brass and copper objects, too, look better mat ground. The same applies to stainless steel objects. Pewter should never be polished, because its mat sheen is more beautiful than any polish. Silver, too, is unsuitable; although its polished surface is more resistant to tarnishing, it appears cold. Furthermore, the high gloss with its specular reflections breaks up the restful surfaces so desirable with silver. Unfortunately, however, silver tableware in particular has been polished increasingly for many years (first laboriously by hand, with hematite, and later by machine); customers have thus been conditioned to it, and must first be convinced of the error of their ways.

About the technique

The grinding machine or floor stand grinder has a horizontal spindle rotating at 2,800–3,000 rpm, powered by a built-in electric motor or a transmission. Interchangeable grinding disks and brushes are screwed to the ends of the spindle. A metal trough and protective casing surround the working area and largely prevent the pasty abrasives from splashing the area round about. Rags suspended from the machine serve the same purpose; nevertheless the operator will always be covered in dirt from head to foot.

Before pressed, annealed, or soldered brass is ground, hard oxide films covering the surface must be removed or softened in the pickling solution. Diluted acids are used for pickling the metals, but concentrated acids and mixtures of acids are used for dipping. (Dip: Nitric and sulfuric acid, to which hydrochloric acid or cooking salt and shining soot are added; composition, page 260.) After the work has been rinsed and dried with sawdust, coarse grinding begins with sea horse wheels and fiber brushes. Pumice powder and emery powder with oil are used as abrasives. If the work was rough-ground by hand, or filed, it is ground at an angle against the direction of the hand grinding or filing so that even the finest scratches stand out, because filing marks and scratches that are not completely removed during grinding will not be removed by polishing. They are found especially in inaccessible corners.

Rough-polishing follows grinding with the brush. For this, as for polishing, the so-called buff is used. This is a soft wheel composed of many layers of circular pieces of fabric, a mixture of various types of tissue for a hard or soft effect, and stitched to stiffen it. Buffs made of nettlecloth serve for rough-polishing; for polishing proper, flannel and molton buffs are used. The polishing agents are tripoli, French chalk, rouge, and special pastes supplied by the trade.

So far the abrasives and equipment suitable for the craftsman's workshop have been described. In industry, where manual work has long been too expensive (grinding, especially, is a weighty factor in pricing) these methods, too, have become mechanized and automated.

Today even cutlery and light-alloy builders' hardware are ground on automatic machines, sometimes with the aid of abrasive belts, sometimes in rotating drums (tumblers). The latter method, which has recently come into industrial use, is derived from an ancient goldsmith's technique. Utilizing centrifugal force, the material to be ground is tumbled in a paste of emery and oil, and the friction caused thereby produces a grinding action very suitable for round shapes.

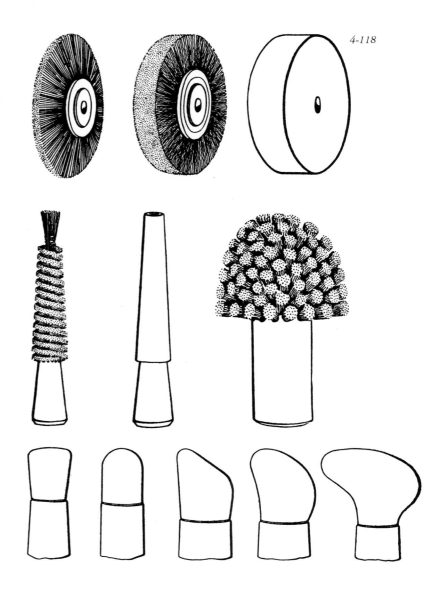

4-118

Fig. 4-118. Grinding- and polishing tools: Fiber grinding brush, crimped wire brassbrush, abrasive wheel, flue tapered bristle- and felt scratch brushes, goblet brush. Bottom row: Blood stones for polishing, in various shapes (mounted in wooden handles).

5-1

5-2

5. Decorating Techniques

Engraving

Engraving has the same meaning as "incising". The various activities covered by this term have one thing in common—all the changes in the shape of the work are brought about with cutting tools, such as chisels and gravers. The needle, which the layman thinks is the engraver's principal tool, is not used by him at all. Even today, the most widely-known examples of engraving are the monograms and letters on cutlery and tableware. They are the preserve of the metal engraver, who, like the copper engraver, engraves delicate and bold lines on the metal surface with the graver. Goldsmiths and many a painter in the fifteenth century used the graver with great competence, and even today every goldsmith is expected to have at least some skill in letter engraving. Masterly ornamental engravings on the mat surfaces of silver tableware, on plates and jugs of the type Lettré produced in his workshop, are only rarely achieved even by good goldsmiths.

Whereas the metal engraver practices his craft directly on the work, the steel engraver engraves only the dies and stamping tools in which coins, cutlery, pewterware, jewels, and thousands of other objects are stamped and pressed in large numbers. Since he works not only in one plane but shapes round forms, and is therefore also called a relief engraver, his activities often overlap those of the chaser; the only differences between them are that the former works in a different material, steel, and cuts instead of chases it. His engravings are always recessed, and only the hubbing dies necessary for stamping may be raised. The iron engraver during the sixteenth and seventeenth centuries engraved individual coining dies as well as raised figure and ornamental decorations. This makes him the predecessor of the steel engraver, whose craftsman's skill and achievement has now completely entered the service of the machine.

This summary of the modern engraver's craft will be followed by a detailed description of the work in the various branches, the craftsman's techniques, and the tools. It will give a comprehensive picture of this all too specialized and splintered, highly skilled group of workers, but this picture will be complete only when it is seen in the light of the comments in the section on the development of the metalcrafts, and in the section dealing with the role of the machine, on pressing and stamping.

Various types of engraving

To distinguish him from the relief or steel engraver, the ordinary engraver is sometimes called a metal engraver. His field of endeavor, too, has progressively contracted. Demands of an artistic kind are rarely made on him nowadays, or, conversely and more correctly, since he became independent, and detached himself from the craft of the artist-smith, he has lost his originally strong association with the workpiece and can therefore no longer offer any work he has created entirely by himself. As the man who completes the creative ideas of others, he has gradually become more dependent, merely an executive technician. This explains why even those of our contemporaries who appreciate the quality of solid craftsmanship are almost unaware of the potentialities of true engraving. As a result, there is hardly a metal craftsman, except the chaser, whose skill is in so little demand today.

Only those engravers who do not copy uncritically the letter, monogram, and decorative patterns in some (usually obsolete and tasteless) pattern book, but are themselves able to draw and design whatever is asked of them, and who conceive more original and better designs for their graver than the author of the pattern book, himself ignorant of the use of tools, are capable of convincing achievements. There are as many engravers today as there ever were in the past who have a confident and masterly control of their tools. What is lacking is equal taste, a rich imagination, draftsmanship, and a flair for style.

Nevertheless, the technical aspects must by no means be neglected. They receive prominent treatment in this chapter.

Tools and working methods

What the metal engraver needs first and foremost are good eyesight, a steady hand, and a carefully ground graver. Everything else is less important, and if need be can be dispensed with. The old type of graver

Fig. 5-1. Flat figure engraving, pure line pattern. Design and execution: Gerda von Herff, School of Arts and Crafts, Schwäbisch Gmünd.

Fig. 5-2. Egyptian signet ring, gold, cast and engraved. Bezel about $0 \cdot 8 \times 1 \cdot 3$ ins. (20 × 32mm) with round shank. Louvre Collection, Paris.

is called a burin (see *Fig. 5-3*). It was also used by copperplate engravers. Its cross section is a square or a rhombus, whereas the more modern single-point tool has a raised back and curved sides; its cross section is shaped like a shield. The single-point tool is the most important tool for linear engraving; but the engraver also uses flat and round scorpers. All gravers are relatively narrow compared with the steel engraver's tools, since they are used only for graving and cutting lines, not for scraping surfaces and round shapes. The multiple tool is a pointed tool with several faces. It produces parallel lines and is used for hatching (see *Figs. 5-5–5-6*).

The tool handle is made of wood, shorter than in the past, with a metal collar. The engraver splits its bottom half off so that it cannot interfere with his handling of the tool (see *Fig. 5-4*), because keeping to a uniform depth during engraving is difficult.

New factory-supplied tools are mostly too long and therefore springy. A feeling for the handiness of the tool, which is soon acquired, indicates the correct length. Sharpening of the tools is very important. The raised back, necessary to make the narrow tools rigid, must be ground down as shown in the drawing below. The cutting area (edge) will then only be about 0·04–0·1 ins. (1–3mm) high. Its inclination to the face is also of importance. For the engraving of hard metals (iron, nickel, and nickel alloys) it should be steeper than with soft metals as it will otherwise break. In such a case the engraver speaks of a bumpy edge. Coarse grinding can be carried out on the rotating, wetted grinding wheel, but this must be followed by the edge being honed on the oil stone. Heavy pressure must be applied to the cutting area to produce a perfectly plane instead of a curved face. An edge ground towards the point is considered sharper than that ground transversely to it. Lastly, in single-point tools, the face, too, can be raised (see *Fig. 5-7*) so that the handle and the hand guiding it move freely along the surface instead of digging down or sticking; it should slide evenly. The new face must be a straight-line continuation of the old, and its sides must be smoothly polished, first with fine emery paper, and then with French chalk or rouge on leather. Beautiful bright lines and cuts can only be obtained with polished faces. To master cutting, the fingers of the right hand must grasp the shaft and the handle correctly. *Fig. 5-14* shows how the thumb presses against the left side and at the same time forms the pivot of the control movements. It restrains excessive pushing. The base digits of the ring finger, and even more of the little finger, grasping the handle control the depth of the cut and lateral deviations from the straight line. The first exercises consist of cutting straight lines. The greatest problem is to prevent the tool from slipping, in other words to control the pressure on the advancing tool so that the cut does not overshoot the intended stop. Width and thickness of the curling cuttings are a sure guide of the depth of the cut. Once cutting straight lines is mastered, right- and left-hand curves should be attempted. Care must be taken to prevent the right hand controlling the graver from moving into the curve, and instead to push the work against it with the left hand in the intended direction of rotation—it is the work, not the tool, that is turned. The left hand is entirely responsible for the correct position and the required counterpressure of the work. If, together with the first cut of the line, or with a second cut with the single-point tool, a shiny broadening of one of the two cutting surfaces—a so-called bright cut—is desired, the tool must be tilted towards the intended side, so that it cuts into the metal not only with the point, but also with a side edge of the face.

Depending on the thickness of the single-point tool, and the cross section which accordingly is pointed or obtuse, the lines are fine or bold. Tools that are too pointed are difficult to handle, and thin lines are not conspicuous enough. This must also be borne in mind when the face is raised. For this reason, curves with a broad bright cut are preferably cut with the edge of a flat scorper, which is of course formed by sides at right angles. Lines of even width, on the other hand, are best cut with a round scorper. But here the character of the cut will be completely different. For engraving in inaccessible sites, on the inside of a ring, for instance, cranked tools are used.

With flat and round scorpers, but at different depths and with different effects, a characteristic technique of engraving, mostly used in a primitive manner, the so-called tremolo or wrigglework is possible. The hand guiding the tool rocks to and fro in an even rhythm as it slides forward, creating a zigzag line because the left- and right-hand edges bite alternately. This wriggling cut with the round scorper was used in the past as a test for the genuineness of the material, and can be found on the back of old silver spoons and utensils as an inspection mark next to the stamp. Wriggling was also employed for the decoration of cast pewterware, jugs, and cups. It does not require a great deal of practice, but equally does not offer any special possibilities of expression.

Clamping devices

While it is being engraved, the work must be secured both firmly and so that it can be rotated in any direction. Depending on its size and shape, it can be held and rotated on a sand-filled hide pad with the left hand. Otherwise, special clamping devices such as the engraver's ball and the engraver's hand vise take over this function. The engraver's ball, copied from the chaser's ball, but fitted with screw clamps, is mounted in a hide ring so that the work clamped in it can be tilted and rotated in all directions. It is illustrated in *Fig. 5-14*. The line drawing *Fig. 5-61* shows an engraver's hand vise. It is held with the left hand, and is particularly suitable for clamping stamps and small work. Sheets, spoon handles, and objects similarly difficult to clamp, or easily damaged, are cemented onto a piece of hardwood with some sealing wax, and can now be mounted in the ball.

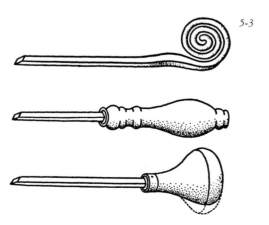

5-3

Fig. 5-3. Top to bottom: Antique, medieval, and modern graver for copper engraving.

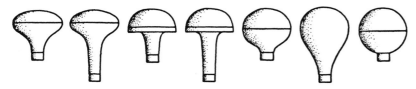

Fig. 5-4. *Various modern tool handles. The lower half is usually split off.*

Fig. 5-5. *Multiple tool without handle. Slightly curved, since here the face cannot be raised.*

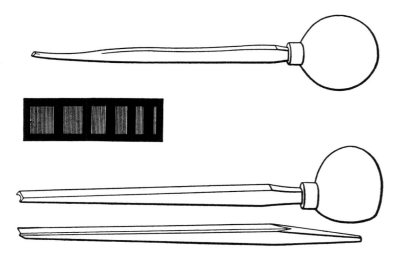

Fig. 5-6. *Multiple tools. The patterns they produce are shown in the black rectangle.*

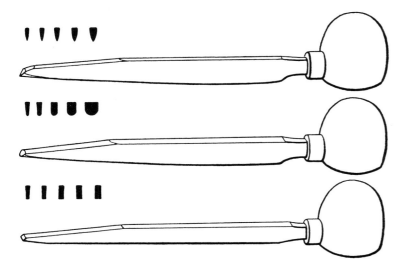

Fig. 5-7. *Single-point tool, round and flat scorpers used by the engraver and made by tool factories. Note the raised face.*

A polishing steel for the removal of slips and general tidying up has its place on the engraver's tool board together with a pencil and a gamboge bottle with brush, for it is not possible to draw on bare metal, and gamboge dissolved in methylated spirit (for less delicate work, powdered chalk or lithopone will be adequate) coats the specular metal surface with a mat, yellowish film which takes pencil lines. The subject of the engraving is drawn on or transferred to this film according to one of the common methods. With mass production (engraving of cutlery, for example), a reprint ensures the monotonous uniformity of execution desired today. The pattern of the first engraving is carefully rubbed with the polishing steel and printing ink or powdered graphite onto soft paper, in exactly the same way as a hand pull is obtained of a woodcut, and transferred to the other workpieces.

Up to now we have described the technique of pure metal engraving which engravers call damascening if it is used for the decoration of large areas with ornamental or figure motifs. Like so many others, this term, too, is somewhat ambiguous, because the sword blades artistically decorated in old Damascus (hence the term) were more often than not etched or inlaid rather than covered with engravings. Such restrictions and misnomers in the technical language, too, are evidence of the decline of craftsmanship.

As soon as the task of the engraver goes beyond this pure cutting of lines into surfaces, the relief work begins; at first, the graving tool still dominates, but other tools will come into their own with increasing height or depth of the relief. The techniques of relief engraving today form part of the steel engraver's domain. This does not mean that we no longer find individual engravers with a knowledge covering all these possibilities; but they have become rare. The intermediate field between metal engraving and specialized relief engraving, now concerned exclusively with steel stamps for pressing and stamping covers, for instance, brass stamps used for the gold embossing of book covers, or small dies for relief printing on paper, negative seals, and stamps.

Before we study the techniques of these modern specialists, a comparison between the past and present tasks of metal engraving is necessary to show up the weaknesses and potentialities of this technique. Here we must distinguish between the engraver, who at an early stage became a graphic reproduction technician, for centuries engraving almost exclusively from drawings by others, for instance, the copperplate engraver proper, and the engraver who contributes to the design of individual works of goldsmiths and silversmiths and other metal craftsmen. The process engraver in the graphic arts has almost disappeared; at most he engraves plates for banknotes or postage stamps from the design of a graphic artist. But the metal engraver of the second kind, too, has largely entered the field of reproduction. If he has remained an independent craftsman, he will be content to execute occasional orders, whose subjects are mostly modest imitations of old originals of seals, coats of arms, and inscriptions. Heraldry, however, is known only by a few experts (what little the engraver must know about it is contained in a condensed form in Chapter 10). Originals, engravings that owe their existence to the joy of the dynamic, sparkling interplay of the engraved lines and their inimitable elegance, have not been created in our century. We have nothing to show that compares with the superb draftsmanship, style, and force of expression found in engravings on chalices, altar crosses, reliquaries, even everyday pewterware. The claim that there is no demand from connoisseurs and patrons is unfounded so long as there is no supply. We therefore must repeat what was pointed out at the beginning of this chapter: The future of the engraver's craft depends less on technical training than on talent and truly artistic education of the young generation of craftsmen. By artistic education we do not mean an academic education aiming at the artist, probably an oil painter, but a live association with the tradition of craftsmanship and conscious cultivation of the creative gift, to be used for the benefit of the technique of craftsmanship. The more narrowly we circumscribe the profession, the more the study of figures and other drawings is concerned with the mode of expression of metal engraving, the better the prospect that one day we shall again see engravings evoking spontaneous acclaim and the wish to own them. This applies equally to functional work of practical usefulness, and to that which because of its self-sufficiency and abstraction begins to fall under the heading of works of art *(Figs. 5-1, 5-16)*.

Relief and steel engraving

The various sections of this chapter, like the practical work itself, overlap. One technique sometimes develops from another, becomes independent, and finally, unfortunately, specialized. We can fully understand it only when we know about its origin. For the complete appreciation of the steel engraver's work, a study of the sections on *punching*, *chasing*, and *metal engraving* is therefore indispensable.

It is possible to strike a coin with a negatively engraved upper and lower die. Whether this is done with a hammer or in a complicated press is merely a matter of technical development in mechanical engineering, and has little effect on the engraving itself. But the extent to which such engraved dies are used for the stamping and pressing of the most varied metal objects has been steadily growing as mechanical engineering and industrial production have progressed. Hand in hand with this has gone a multiplication of the tasks which the steel engraver had to master as the producer of such stamps.

A piece of metal placed between an upper and a lower die shows the picture in raised relief after it has been stamped. This explains the task of the steel engraver: With his tools he forces into the hard steel the low relief into which coins, cutlery, plates, buttons, medals, and a thousand and one other articles in daily use are pressed.

Example of a steel engraving

To make a spoon or a fork such as those shown in *Fig. 3-36*, two dies are necessary: An upper and a lower die (see *Fig. 5-8*). To produce this pair of dies is the steel engraver's task. First, a profile is planed from two rectangular steel blocks, which corresponds to the sweep of the cutlery parts. The die in which the bowl is raised is taken as the upper die. It is engraved first. Out of the rough-planed work the steel engraver, like the sculptor in stone, chisels the form of the bowl with a strong flat chisel. The chips fly under the powerful blows with a heavy, usually barrel-shaped sledge hammer. Here, the engraver must take great care to keep to the dimensions of this oval shape in steel within two hundred and fiftieths of an inch (tenths of a millimeter). He therefore checks his progress continually with templets of the longitudinal and the transverse curvature as well as of the outline. After the chisel he uses the file to smooth the raised oval shape; for the first rough work, small fine files of the usual kind will be adequate; for fine finishing, however, rifflers of suitable shape are used *(Fig. 4-81)*. Even the tiniest file marks can be removed with fine emery and polishing cloth or with soft wood adapted with a knife to the form to be ground, and with emery and polishing powder (French chalk, rouge) prepared in oil, until the oval bowl shape displays a specular luster. Now the spoon handle of the upper die is

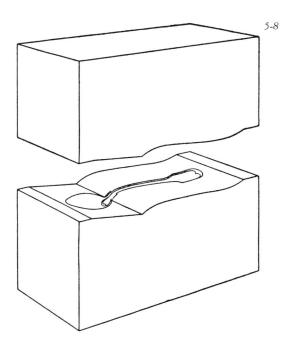

5-8

Fig. 5-8. Pair of dies for a spoon. Bowl raised (upper die), and recessed (lower die). The handle is engraved (recessed) in both parts.

engraved. The method and procedure of engraving depend entirely on the pattern, in other words on the design and model of the spoon to be created. The engraver now has to choose the tools he must use, the much finer pointed and round chisel, the curved and flat chisel; in this he is guided by his personal experience in his craft, individual sleight of hand acquired through many years' practice, and complete familiarity with the characteristics of his various tools. The engraving of cutlery designs with smooth handles is rightly regarded as very much easier than, for instance, a thread or bead pattern, let alone the richly ornamented features of copied styles. Since, like any true craftsman, the steel engraver values difficult tasks and stringent demands on his skill more highly than easy and unimaginative work, the designer is often faced with a situation he cannot understand, in which modern functional patterns without ornaments are unpopular and looked down upon. Owing to the hardness of the raw material, the most delicate effects of modeling, imperceptible transitions and highest precision, clarity, austerity of line and form, and thereby a regularity and coldness of execution have been developed in steel engraving more than in any other metalcraft. The manufacturing methods in the metalware industry, especially the process of pressing, in which the sheet is formed

5-11

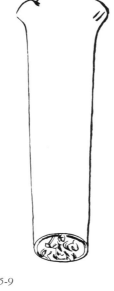
5-9

5-12

5-10

Fig. 5-9. Stamp for the one-sided coining of a bracteate.

Fig. 5-10. Silver bracteate depicting Otto I, Margrave of Brandenburg 1170–1184. Diameter 1·2 ins. (29mm).

Fig. 5-11. Silver bracteate, England, Middle Ages. Dynamic punch cut, unsharp coining on a soft support.

Fig. 5-12. Silver tetradrachmon, Syracuse, Sicily. Reverse shows the nymph Arethusa. About 438 B.C. Vertical diameter about 1 in. (25mm), weight 0·6 oz (17·33g).

within fractions of a second; and completely mechanized mass production, for which the steel engraver provides merely the tools but which has a strong feedback effect on his work, narrow the scope for the aesthetic appeal of any irregular work even further. The terms "strict" and "precise" are the ones that are heard most frequently at work. The engraving of stamping dies in steel has thus become precision work with the magnifier and the most accurate measuring instruments, whose technical conditions the designer, too, must know and take into account.

After the handle has been chiseled, it is engraved. It is again the hardness of his raw material that compels the steel engraver to use the gravers he scrapes with differently from the metal engraver. Only rarely can he apply the graver freehand for cutting and graving; usually he places a ring bent from a piece of wire or some other suitable object under the tool, thereby creating a lever action which reinforces his pressure. He can now scrape. Stamps, too, help to make the shapes more austere, to line up and smooth the beads and other patterns and bring them to the same depth. In a handle of a piece of cutlery, this depth is usually no more than a fraction of a millimeter. The steel engraver's stamps are shorter and stronger than the chaser's, otherwise they would vibrate. Stamps should, however, never be used excessively because the structure of the steel, eventually to be hardened, cannot stand chasing and upsetting; there is a risk that after the hardening process the parts will crumble under strain in the press. It is therefore considered bad workmanship to reduce portions from which too much "meat" has been removed by upsetting them with a flat punch. Corrections of any kind are, after all, almost impossible in steel engraving.

After cutting and graving, work begins with the rifflers, of which there are many forms with coarse and fine cuts. Whereas the steel engraver makes his own stamps and chisels as well as the large gravers and scrapers, this is less easy with rifflers; these are supplied by tool factories. Specialized and often completely novel requirements in the type and shape of engraving tools compel the steel engraver, too, to think continuously of new types of chisels, gravers, and stamps, to forge, file, and harden them, and to grind them into shape, indeed even to bend red-hot rifflers into shape and to harden them afterwards. He can therefore work only with his own tools and takes them with him when he changes his job. This custom is so generally accepted that every apprentice, on completing his apprenticeship, is as a rule given the tools he has acquired so far as a present or against payment of a nominal sum.

As he graves and grooves surfaces, the engraver changes the direction of his movement from time to time to avoid the formation of waves. He therefore graves or grooves transversely to the previous line, especially when an oblique glance at the engraving shows him a hint of waves. When the depth of the engraving is correct, its modeling perfectly resembles the pattern and is finally so smoothly grooved that even the most minute blemishes have disappeared, the steel engraver's work is done. What follows now—grinding and polishing with coarse, fine, and lastly ultrafine emery powder suspended in oil, with pieces of soft or hard wood cut to the individual shapes of the engraving—can be left to apprentices and semiskilled workers. It is an accepted rule that the surface of the grinding wood should be as large as possible; this eliminates the danger of grinding grooves and waves into the material.

The bottom die

Before the engraving of the bottom die is begun, the upper die must be hardened. Depending on the type of steel and its hardness specification, water-, oil-, or air-hardening must be used (hardening and tempering of tool steel, see page 255). For annealing in the tempering furnace, the work should be embedded in coal dust in an enclosed box to prevent scaling. Only after hardening will it be possible to match the profiles of the two dies; this entails laborious filing and control by rubbing against the soot-covered corresponding upper part, until the profiles of the two dies are such a perfect match and the visible pressure areas in the negative shape of the bowl in the bottom die so chiseled away that even contact is established at every point of the surface. This highly precise matching of the two dies in height, width, length, profile, outlines of the engraving, and lastly the careful maintenance of uniform thickness of the metal between the top and bottom of the bowl, are essential to the use of the dies, mounted in high-speed presses, as precision tools. The carelessness with which coins were struck in Antiquity, with complete disregard for matching between upper and lower die, would be catastrophic in industrial operation. The thickness of the sheet of the final spoon must be left between the two forms of the bowl, because, strictly, in this part of the two dies the ratio hubbing die : female form applies, that is, pressing occurs, whereas the handle of the spoon is shaped of stronger metal by two matrices, in other words it is really stamped in the manner of a coin. This, incidentally, is the difference between pressing and stamping: Sheet metal can be pressed between lower and upper die (hubbing die and female die), but a stronger piece of metal can only be

Fig. 5-13. Various sizes of chisel, wrought, filed, hardened, and ground by the steel engraver. From left to right: Pointed chisel, flat chisel, gouge and shallow-curved (stretched) chisel.

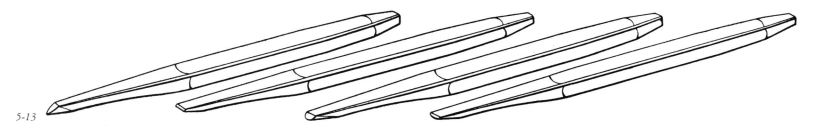

5-13

stamped, on one or both sides, with one or two dies, that is, recessed stamps.

What we have described so far may be sufficient to explain the regard the engraver must have in his work to the technical conditions of manufacture. The description is by no means complete. The graving of angle parts, so-called butts used in the pressing of holloware or bodies, is even more complicated and often demands endless trials of tools under the press. Engraving proper of the bottom die can begin when the examination for technical suitability is complete. It is carried out in exactly the same way as already described: Scooping out and modeling with the chisel, smoothing and fining of the shapes by scraping and cutting, stamping, and grooving. Finally the die is ground and polished. Intermediate trial pressings can be made in soft material (lead) to check whether the gap between the upper and the lower die of the bowl corresponds at all points to the desired thickness of the sheet. This applies when the bowl of the roughed, trial-pressed blank of the spoon is shiny throughout, without any mat patches and bulges. The trial pressing is also a means to check whether the contours of the handle match. During his work, the engraver continually watches the character of his negative engraving, the relief effect of the interior shape, with the simple aid of plasticine impressions, which he knocks off within seconds with a piece of wood and a hammer. Since with large engravings such replicas show only part of the work, he supervises the effect of the whole article from time to time with plaster or wax casts. The definition of wax casts is superior, but plaster casts are quite adequate for most work. To make the cast, the engraving is first rubbed blank with fine, dry emery powder and a rubber pad, and then lightly brushed with neat's foot oil.

Machines

Naturally, the steel engraver, too, avoids the hard work of chiseling whenever possible by using machines wherever the properties of his raw material permit it. Depending on the nature of the hollow shape to be chiseled, he drills, mills, or turns out the largest depressions. Hubbing dies can be reasonably well prepared on the planing machine. Often cutters, toolmakers, mechanics, and assistants relieve the engraver of the rough work. It has already been mentioned elsewhere that engraving and reducing machines also play a part in the preparation of the dies.

The engraving stage of a pair of blanking dies described so far is naturally only part of the production process, which is technically both more complicated and more economical in a modern, large factory. The purpose of the example is merely to give the layman an insight into the nature of a specialized occupation, which today is a peculiar mixture of creative skill on the one hand and adaptation to the conditions of working with machines on the other. Nor must it be forgotten that the steel engraver making blanking dies is only one among many specialists in his field, such as the steel engraver of holloware, of jewelry, etc., although he needs many years' experience to meet the demands of today. The fact that pressing is the most suitable means of mass production has up to now made the steel engraver indispensable in industrial processes, whereas his close relative, the chaser, still in great demand at the beginning of this century, is apparently about to die out. It was his adaptability alone that reduced his influence on design more than that of almost any other metal craftsman, and he now no longer engraves anything except reproduction tools. Thus the gap between the "artist" and the "craftsman" (here perhaps better "technician") has become most noticeable here.

Overleaf:

Fig. 5-14. Metal engraving. Engraver's ball with modern hide pad (cloth is inserted to increase friction). In the foreground: Three tools with handles split off at the bottom. Brass disk for practice: Cemented onto wood (chaser's pitch) and clamped. The ball with the work is rotated with the left hand for cutting curved lines. The tool is guided with the right hand. The use of the thumb as a brake on the working surface is clearly evident. The upper part of the letter, traced out in pencil, is engraved with the single-point tool. The shiny widening of the curves (bright cut) is cut with a narrow flat scorper, but can also be produced with the edge of the single-point tool tilted sideways.

Fig. 5-15. Steel engraving. Engraver's ball with hide ring and two clamping screws. Because the piece of steel for practice engraving is so small, it must be held between clamping jaws (additional clamping device). To keep the clamping jaws parallel, various pieces of steel are inserted underneath. The pointed chisel is guided with the left hand. A shaving can clearly be seen curling away in front of the chisel. The chisel is controlled with the wrist, and the ball of the thumb rests on the clamp. The right hand grips the thick, slightly curved end of the handle of the chasing hammer, whose plastic shape is determined by individual comfort and therefore made by the engraver himself. In the foreground: A home-made depth gauge with movable pointer. To the left of it: Two chisels, points towards the right. Directly next to it: The front portion of a single-point tool. Other tools with various handles are in the background.

5-14

5-15

5-16

5-17

Figs. 5-16 and 5-17. The Last Supper and other subjects of eucharistic symbolism. Engravings on a ciborium, about 1500. The draftsman's competence and the lively expression of the faces are evidence of the close association between goldsmiths' engraving and copper engraving at the time.

5-18

5-19

Chasing

The chaser does not cut, but chases the metal sheet. He forces it with the hammer and punches to yield on a soft support, so that lines or plastic shapes are produced. Both are described below. The finishing work on a casting roughly corresponds to the popular conception of chasing as a very careful filing and fining operation. The shape of solid castings in gold, silver, or bronze can no longer be appreciably changed at this stage; but surface blemishes caused during casting (cast seams, etc.) can be tidied.

Whereas the sheet metal chaser causes plastic changes in his work to the extreme limit of its ductility, the chaser of castings confines himself to finishing the solid or thickwalled casting true to pattern, or at best to decorating its surface with ornaments.

Fig. 5-18. Embossed figure of a knight, Gross Komburg Chandelier. Exemplary treatment of large, restful shapes (head) and delicate, lively structuring of the sleeve.

Fig. 5-19. Figure of a saint, Gross Komburg Chandelier. Embossed, thin sheet copper.

187

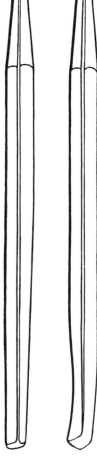

Fig. 5-20. *Chasing. Cast-iron chaser's (hollow) ball, universally rotatable, with practice sheet cemented onto it. The most important feature in this picture is the position of the fingers of the left hand. Thumb, index- and middle finger hold the punch. The middle finger applies pressure to the sliding and guiding ring finger, which curls in a* manner characteristic of experienced chasers. On the left: Tool box containing punches. Additional punches are on the workbench.

Fig. 5-21. *Two punches, natural size. Workface at the bottom, conically filed heads, beveled edges.*

The tools

Hammers and punches are the most important tools for both kinds of chasing. The chasing hammer (the steel engraver, incidentally, uses the same shape) has a circular, broad face and, on the opposite side, a ball peen designed, but only seldom used, for direct chasing (see *Fig. 5-20*). Its weight is important. The chaser therefore employs hammers of different weight for light, medium, and heavy chasing work. Like the more or less curved shape of the shaft, especially of its body, the weight of the hammer is a question of the individual feeling and hand; therefore even the apprentice shapes his own hammer shaft with the rasp or file, smooths it carefully with bits of glass, and finally soaks it in linseed oil.

Even more personal than the weight and shape of the hammer, which, like other special tools, is today supplied by tool factories as the finished article, is the shape of the punches. These are therefore almost exclusively made by the chaser himself. The apprentice begins with filing into shape, polishing, and hardening the punches he needs for his first practical work; he makes them from pieces of square tool steel of suitable thickness and about 4·4 ins. (11cm) in length (hardening and tempering of tools, see page 255). Even after many years in the trade, the chaser, having amassed a wide range of tools, has the occasional need to make an unusual, oddly-shaped punch for a special job. Thus the punch boxes become full as time goes on. For chasing widely projecting shapes softly and broadly, the chaser uses wooden punches, mostly of boxwood, which he shapes with a file as required. For such chasing the support must be softer than usual, and the pitch must be heated if it is already cold.

One example each of the shapes and types of punch needed most often is represented here. Each has numerous small and large, obtuse and pointed, long and short, convex and flat, versions of its own. Purpose and uses are briefly as follows.

The tracer is used for drawing or tracing delicate or bold, soft or hard lines. Its face can be pointed or blunt, long or short, straight or curved. It is also used for drawing definite and well-marked outlines, without soft transitions. *Figs. 5-20* and *5-25* illustrate the work with the tracer particularly clearly. It can be seen that the work was filled with chaser's pitch. The way the fingers of the left hand, which guides the punch, are held is also shown. The punch is held vertically with the thumb, index, and middle fingers. The ring finger, with its nail lightly pressed down by the middle finger, slides along the traced line. It maintains contact with it like a brake shoe and thus forms the connecting link with the work. Its steady advance, adjusted to the rhythm of the hammer blows, joins the individual incisions made by the punch into an uninterrupted even trace. The raised lines on a bronze belt buckle *(Fig. 5-29)*, the circles and wavy lines on the Eberswalde gold vessels *(Figs. 5-30–5-31)*, and the vertical, short line patterns on the foot of the bowl *(Fig. 5-28)* were all executed with the tracer.

Fig. 5-25 is an example of the use of flat punches and the typical manner in which this enlivens the surface. Flat punches can have a smooth, polished face, or they can—especially for the chasing of castings—be slightly roughened with a file, in other words slightly mat, when they will have a better grip on solid, cast surfaces.

The shape of modeling tools depends on their special purpose: They may be square or oblong with very rounded corners, oval, or round. Their depth, too, may differ: They may be flat or more spherical, from a slightly arched surface to the hemispherical shape of a bead. The latter shape constitutes another special type of punch, which plays an important part among the examples illustrated in the section *Punching*: The perloirs. Their shapes are identical, and only the diameters are different; they are more suitable for single blows than for modeling movements. In this respect they are intermediate between the versatile punches, to be used in many different ways, described so far, and the typical figure punches, which are really no more than stamps. The hollow perloir also belongs to this group. It is the negative version of the perloir: A shallow or hemispherical hollow with a raised, sharp edge. The figure punch proper may be a letter or numeral stamp, more often it shows an individual figure or ornamental representation: A palmette for instance, or some decorative pattern to be stamped in multiple repetition, as the basic feature of a series. The illustrations in the section *Punching* contain many examples of such uses.

Chasing on sheet metal

Two masterpieces of metal sculpture are excellent examples of the method of chasing and even more of the artistic potentialities of this very ancient technique. They were both made in the twelfth century. The chased high relief figure of a knight *(Fig. 5-18)* is a detail from the huge chandelier of Gross Komburg near Schwäbisch Hall, which is rich in such features. The figure of Christ in Glory, chased in gilt sheet copper, is the center of a number of figures of the apostles; the subject was designed to adorn the altar in the same monastery church as an antependium *(Fig. 5-24)*. Both works show clearly how the large body features of head and limbs were chased from the flat sheet from the back (repoussé) with punches. Where these shapes merge softly into one another, for instance in the face, on the hand, and on the sword-bearing arm of the knight, the first modeling was not sharpened and fined with any afterwork from the front of the figure. This is the character of pure repoussé chasing technique. The lines of the drapery, facial features, and the blessing hand of Christ, however, appear considerably sharper and better defined. Some drapes have quite sharp ridges, which show that afterwork (final chasing from the front) was carried out here. This demonstrates the two most important differences in the technique, which decisively influence the character of chasing.

If an inimitably soft effect, the appeal of uncorrected competent modeling, is desired, the only method is repoussé chasing. This is how the drapes in the knight's garment *(Fig. 5-18)* were produced, without any later correction from the front. The bold, coarsely drawn lines of the candle-holding Baroque angel *(Fig. 5-25)*, on the other hand, are evidence of work from the front. Many chasers of our day have been induced by competition with steel engravers' highly precise and sharp work in pressed relief to finish their work by too much detailed chasing from the front—much to the detriment of their work, because chasing cannot be compared with pressing and stamping. Its beauty rests on conditions completely different from those of cleanness and precision of line. As in the artistic hand drawing, the impulsive force of expression of the line is immediately destroyed by later improvements; as watercolor will not tolerate any corrective over-painting, so the object chased through the back by the master at the first attempt has an original appeal. It is true that the great masters of such small sculptures in sheet metal who created the figure ornaments on the Romanesque reliquaries enhanced the expression on the faces of their prophets and apostles by finishing them from the front. But they did this without any restraint, guided only by concepts of design and without sideways glances at dubious examples of relief engraving and pressing (apart from the fact that no such methods as yet existed in those days).

189

Fig. 5-22. Engraved representations (Martyrdom of St. Felix) on the
Abdinghofer portable altar, Paderborn, eleventh century, probably by
Rogerus von Helmarshausen. Gilt sheet copper, figures in opus interasile,
the edges therefore joined. Line drawings on the figures, frequently
(though not here) filled with niello at this time.

Fig. 5-23. Frontal (altar front) of Gross Komburg, gilt sheet copper,
twelfth century, figures individually chased and riveted in the enameled
ornamental frames. In addition to the superb rendering of the figures note
the delicacy of detail: Drapery, evangelists' symbols, and lettering.

Fig. 5-24. *Centerpiece of the frontal of Gross Komburg: Christ in His Glory. Cloisonné in the frames, champlevé lettering. The photograph clearly shows the technical details of the chased work, which are fully described on page 189.*

At present there are only few opportunities for large-scale chased figure work. The technical mastery of tasks of the magnitude illustrated in *Figs. 2-6–2-7* requires much experience and practice. It would be beyond the scope of this specialized book to describe the sequence of operations. The work is shown only to indicate the extremes to which this technique can be carried.

Unlike these individual achievements, far exceeding the limits of pure craftsmanship, it is the more primitive techniques of the simple tool and modest skill, so infinitely rewarding in their craftsman's possibility of application and expression, which are of prime interest here. The delicate ornament of the silver bowl *(Fig. 4-61)* shows with what little technical application even an apprentice can produce a superb piece of work if only he has taste and skill. Here, tracing was confined to the line drawing. The subject could serve as an exercise for a beginner. It is only the competence with which the punches were used which reveals that it is no first effort. Only those who are familiar with the chased work by the still unspoiled Mediterranean craftsmen and African artist smiths can appreciate how exaggerated the demands, even of the moderate among us, still are for insipid neatness (always judged with a furtive glance over the shoulder at machine finish). The work from Peru and Columbia should be compared with it *(Figs. 5-74, 5-76)*.

Sand bag, ball, and pitch

A round hide bag filled with sand serves as a support for large objects to be chased, but only rough shapes can be chased in this primitive way. More delicate work can only be executed on chaser's pitch, which is best prepared by the user himself. It is a mixture of pitch and powdered brick or molding sand, to which tallow is added according to the desired degree of suppleness. Wax and turpentine, too, affect the degree of hardness and elasticity of the pitch, whose most outstanding characteristic consists in the fact that heating makes it soft and yielding. It is very important for the success of the work to obtain the correct degree of heating or cooling of the pitch. This is the rule: Soft and warm for preliminary work with wooden punches, cold and hard for delicate chasing. The pitching of sheet metal requires experience; no air bubbles must come between metal and pitch. They would damage the work during chasing. It is therefore best to fold the edges of a plane sheet at right angles to form a shallow trough, to heat it to more than body heat and to fill it carefully with liquid pitch. As soon as this has cooled enough to have congealed, the full trough can be pressed without difficulty onto another soft pitch support of the ball or a piece of wood. The danger of air bubbles forming under the work is lessened by this procedure but it can recur if during subsequent heating of the work the heated pitch locally drains from under it. A certain amount of skill is therefore essential here.

The chaser's ball has the same purpose as that of the engraver: It permits the turning and tilting of the work in all directions during the process of chasing. It is a hollow, cast-iron hemisphere of 8–12 ins. (20–30cm) diameter, filled with liquid pitch. To make the latter go further, small pieces of brick or lead can be placed in it to weight it. It can easily be moved within a hide ring or a small triangular frame, as shown in *Fig. 5-20*. After the work is completed, or for repitching the workpiece (from the back to the front), parts of the hard pitch together with the workpiece are knocked off with a broad chisel. Damage to the workpiece must be avoided. Heat may first be applied with a soldering gun, using little air. Remnants of pitch that cannot be removed from the work with gentle knocks and blows must be burned off with the soldering gun or in the fire. They can also be wiped off with turpentine. If necessary, the work is annealed and pickled between the various operations.

A well-equipped chaser's workshop has a pitch hearth, in other words a small room in which the pan with liquid pitch is kept hot on a small flame. The room is also used for pitching and unpitching, to keep the dirt and smoke of the chaser's boiling pitch out of the workshop.

Chasing the casting

All the conceptions based on the everyday usage of the term "chasing" as fining, as improving and finishing the form by scraping, cutting, or filing it, and giving it the final appearance with punches, apply to the chasing of castings. Consequently today, when as a rule less care is lavished on molding and casting than in the past, and, on the other hand, patterns to be strictly adhered to leave no freedom at all to the creative intentions of the chaser, this kind of chasing has sunk almost to the level of mechanical fettling. The bronze relief of a portal of Cologne Cathedral *(Fig. 4-41)*, in contrast, shows brilliantly how freely a chaser of castings can trace his lines. The artist has not yet seen the purpose of chasing a casting in the production of uninspired smoothness and precision, which runs completely counter to the nature of chasing. It is, after all, the very appeal of a craftsmanship which is not precise in the technical sense that constitutes the value of chasing. Unfortunately this concept, which makes uninhibited use of all the possibilities of the tools, has given way to an unthinking routine based solely on tricks borrowed from styles of the past. One follows a certain way of giving acanthus leaves and other historical forms of ornament a "live" appearance through elegant lines made with mat punches: They are dressed up to look antique. Such nonsense is still taught in the teaching workshops of some technical colleges, even in modern training workshops, because it is, after all, easier to continue flogging a traditional course than to adapt a beautiful, old, but stale technique to the contemporary mode of expression. However, nothing is to be gained from the student's imitation of means of expression that cannot be separated from long-dead decorative forms such as the rococo cartouche. The minor and rare possibilities still open to finishing cast church plate, individual plaques, and medals by chasing must be attacked with fresh vigor and an original and creative impetus. To do this, it is above all essential to leave the craftsman chaser enough freedom, and to create in him enough renewed self-confidence that he can again begin to invent original and natural means of surface decoration from experimenting with his tools and raw material. If we fail to find this way, no person of taste will any longer be interested in a chased cast object, and the technique, already half-dead today, will completely die out. It is a pity that so far all trade journals and craft and technical instructions have taught techniques without conveying their meaning. They could at best point to old examples to be followed. However, only what serves the present and its needs has a right to exist. A craft that is dying can therefore be helped only if it is given a new task. But this must evolve organically. In the last resort, this is a demand that aims at the artistic education and training of the craftsman, which also includes the chaser, and must therefore be addressed first and foremost to the institutions concerned with craft education.

Fig. 5-25. Candelabrum angel, sheet silver, eighteenth century.
Dynamic, coarse chasing, use of broad flat punches for the garment, finest tracers on the wing.

Punching

The punch, the chaser's tool, described and illustrated in the preceding section, can also be used for the decoration of surfaces in a way that differs from that of pure chasing. Whereas the chaser who chases and models a figure looks at his punch for its suitability as a part form adapted to his model, here the punch is considered a decorative stamp in its own right. It is easy to see that this is the more primitive use of the tool.

This dual possibility of using the punch is most clearly apparent in the comparison of perloir and tracer. If the tracer is to produce a line, it must be moved. Each hammer blow is directed at a different spot, and the uninterrupted line is created by the flowing contiguity of the regular depressions. The situation is completely different with the perloir. This tool has not been created for movement. Its object is to chase the unique likeness of the recessed spherical bead projecting on the other side of the sheet metal. The tracer, too, can be used like this; however no line will be produced, but only a length of it of the size and shape of the punch. A tracer was used in this manner on the foot of the brass bowl *(Fig. 5-28)*: Recess follows clearly separated recess. Such a technique is called not chasing, but punching.

In addition to ordinary decorative punches such as tracers and perloirs, special design punches of an ornamental or figurative kind can be filed and cut, and rows of repetitive patterns punched into the work with them. For the linear arrangement, in other words the design, the continuous recurrence of the individual subject or of various subjects side by side is the essence of punching. Where a raised or recessed ornament is repeated several times, each identical in form, the design will mostly have been produced with punches of varying sizes.

The more artistic the subjects of the individual punches become, the more the originally primitive craft of punching will gradually approach the modern method of stamping and pressing, until the making of the punches itself becomes a special craft, practiced by the iron engraver, the punch cutter, and the modern steel engraver. From this point onwards, the further development is described in the section *Engraving*.

In the portion of a bronze belt buckle, dating from the eighth to sixth century B.C., found near Grossengstingen *(Fig. 5-29)*, the characteristics of pure punching can be seen very clearly. The prehistoric metal craftsman needed only six punches for his ornaments: A perloir, with which he punched raised dots, the beads, a tracer, with which he traced the lines, and lastly four punches for the ornamental designs alternately occupying the rectangular fields. We have only to compare these forms (human figure with outspread arms, animal representation, circular and rhombic symbols) with one another to recognize, especially from the continuously recurring minor irregularities, that they were made with punches. This shows us a very early example of that mechanization of the techniques which began with punching. It already reveals the germ of a development which ultimately and logically led to the steel punch, the die, and thus to pressing, stamping, and mass production. Certainly, the general appearance of this belt buckle, with its appealing irregularities, evokes the impression of pure craftsmanship. Yet that reproducing and labor-saving tool, the punch, had already been invented and was being used. In the same way, simple stamp dies were used and further developed to the end of the eighteenth century.

5-26

Fig. 5-26. *The two punches used in the work shown in Fig. 5-28. Left: Oval hollow perloir (repoussé). Right: Tracer.*

Fig. 5-27. *The prehistoric metalworker punched his sheet with the six punches sketched here (see Fig. 5-29).*

5-27

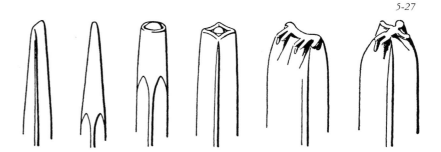

5-28

5-29

5-30

5-31

Fig. 5-28. *Fruit or confectionery bowl, brass, raised with the hammer, tin-plated inside. Extremely simple decorative pattern on the foot: A series of parallel lines was punched with a single tracer, and an oval hollow perloir used to fill the space. Work of an apprentice, Artisan's School, Geislingen, 1939.*

Fig. 5-29. *Bronze mounting for a belt (detail), eighth to sixth century B.C. Two-thirds natural size. Traced lines, punched beads, and pictorial symbols.*

Figs. 5-30 and 5-31. *Punched gold vessels, from the Eberswalde Treasure. Patterns with identical perloirs (repetitive arrangement of the same motif), divided and composed by a traced, i.e. "drawn", "chased", line.*

5-32

5-34

5-33

Fig. 5-32. *Silver inlaid in iron. Handle of a cavalry sword, seventeenth century. Example of inlay (rosettes and buttons) which is not flat, but cut in slight relief.*

Fig. 5-33. *Box, 835/1000 silver, hammer work, with twisted wires soldered onto it. Initials cut into iron disk, and inlaid with gold wire. The inlaid iron disk was blackened in fire with oil. Work of an apprentice, Artisan's School, Geislingen.*

Fig. 5-34. *Roman silver inlay in bronze. The many corners make execution easier.*

Inlaying

In metal techniques, too, the various colors of the raw materials can be used for decorative effects in a contrasting adjacent arrangement. What is known as intarsia when small pieces of wood are composed to form ornaments, and incrustation when stones of different colors are used in the same way, is called inlaying in metalwork. The colors of the metals can differ naturally, for example gold and silver, copper and tin, copper and iron, but the surfaces of the metals can be colored differently by means of chemical treatment. It is, however, not enough for the metals chosen to compose the pattern of inlay work to have different colors. They must also differ in their hardness, for the harder metal must form the base into which the softer metal can be beaten.

Fig. 5-33 shows a monogram inlaid in a round lid. The lines consist of gold wire, the lid is wrought iron, after inlaying burnt black to show the gold lines more prominently. In this instance, the design was engraved with chisel and graver in the iron plate as shown in the drawing below. The engraving had a dovetail-shaped cross section; the line broadened out in depth, the walls were inclined, and it thus became possible to wedge the softer gold in the harder iron. To make the physical connection between gold wire and iron base even closer, the latter was roughened with the chisel, and graver cuts and tiny barbs produced in which the gold wire was caught. A flat punch was used to force the wire bit by bit into its cut-out groove. Great care is necessary in this operation, since during its progress vibrations are set up which may make the whole wire suddenly come out again. This and many another experience can be gained only with hard practice. The guidance offered in this technical book can only go far enough to assure the student that he can master such technical difficulties quite competently at the very first attempt; in fact, the technical execution of inlaying does not make undue demands on craftsmanship and skill. If one can engrave a common-or-garden nameplate reasonably well, it will be possible to produce inlaid work that is technically solid and durable. Naturally, in this kind of surface decoration, based only on the contrast effect of various areas and colors, the design is of decisive importance, and the laborious work will be worthwhile only if it is at least balanced by the

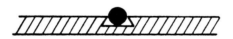

Fig. 5-35. The wire inserted in the undercut groove.

Fig. 5-36. After driving in. The softer metal of the wire has filled the groove.

intellectual and artistic standard of the design. Fertilization from graphic techniques and their mode of expression is quite likely. It must be borne in mind that the preparations required for proper inlaid work are far too time-consuming and therefore expensive, so that we cannot afford to execute any odd or banal patterns, chessboard fashion, for instance. We no longer have the infinite patience with which a sword cutler and armorer of the fifteenth century covered his armor with scroll work of inlaid ornaments. According to our taste, such precious work, original and rare in material and invention, should be isolated as a special ornament on a restful background.

To demonstrate as clearly as possible what we could achieve today with this beautiful ancient technique, we shall briefly outline its importance in the past.

Inlaid work in iron and steel, in conjunction with the techniques of iron engraving, sometimes also in etched low relief, was executed by devoted practitioners in Asia as well as in Europe. It was used on armor and weapons of all kinds by the armorers of Damascus and Toledo and the iron engravers of seventeenth-century Munich, such as, for instance, the Sadeler family of copperplate engravers. The famous sword guards by Japanese Masters reveal an individual expression in this technique of an exuberant richness in delicate plant motifs and the most exquisite elegance of execution *(Figs. 5-38–5-39)*.

Generally, the various technical possibilities of inlay can be classified as follows:

1. *Flat inlay:* The base is roughened crosswise with chisel, graver, or file. Thin wires and sheets, mostly gold and silver, are hammered down and adhere to the rough base. This method, although less solid, has been much used in Asia *(Fig. 5-38)*.

2. Inlay in a groove widening in depth like a dovetail fitting, practiced particularly by the Arabs. This technique makes fine lines and wider areas in the inlaid metal possible. After it has been hammered in, with or without the use of punches, the inlaid feature can be filed level with the base and polished. The metal color of the base, or, if desired, of the inlay also, offers further opportunities to enhance color contrasts *(Fig. 5-33)*.

3. *Relief inlay:* Method as before, i.e. chiseling and undercutting. The dimensions of the parts to be hammered in are kept so generous that they protrude. They are not filed level with the base, but plastically cut and, if required, chased *(Figs. 5-32, 5-39)*. For this, the metal driven in must of course be firmly lodged in the base. A second inlay, in another metal and another color, can be inserted in the area of the first inlaid metal.

Inlaying in steel is easier than in copper, bronze, silver, and gold. In the silver inlays in bronze of the Barbarian Invasion period, simple patterns of lines of various widths appear side by side, rhythmically breaking up the design. Often small fields, too, are inlaid. *Fig. 3-49* shows a modern gold and silver inlay in bronze.

Steel portions of an inlay are colored by means of heating, and burned off with oils, greases, and resins at temperatures between 200 and 400°C. The tempering colors are in this temperature range. In the past they were also used for coloring; steel, for instance, was "blued". Assyrian bronze plates, bronze utensils from Pompeii, Alemannic tomb finds, and Asian metalwork offer ample opportunities for studying the possibilities of inlay. Japanese inlay is famous. Its techniques are varied: Inserts, flat inlay, and relief inlay. Their stylistic judgment demands knowledge that is mostly inaccessible to Europeans.

5-37

Fig. 5-37. A tiny section of a great work of medieval craftsmanship. The hoop of the Romanesque chandelier of Gross Komburg near Schwäbisch Hall measures 17 ft 6 ins. (5m) across. Vertically it is made up of five bands; the illustration shows the middle three fully, the bottom one partly, and the top one not at all. Three of these bands—the middle, bottommost and topmost ones—are in opus interasile. The two bands with decorative texts directly above and below the middle one cover the iron framework supporting the sheet-copper hoop. The iron of the supporting frame and the sheet copper in which the creative work proper is executed are the raw materials, to which silver disks with nielloed figures were added; they have since been lost. With the exception of the letters, the entire hoop is fire-gilt. Twelve lanterns in riveted sheet copper, symbolizing the gates of Heavenly Jerusalem, support hand-sized, embossed and cutout figures of saints and knights (Figs. 5-18, 5-19).

Technique: The relief-like, opus interasile leaf and hunting motifs of the middle band (120 individual representations of different design, although the motif is occasionally repeated) are not punched (which would in fact have been possible then); every piece is chased. The two outer bands are flat and therefore more subdued, accompanied only in outline by chased (traced) lines. There is a technical explanation for why the two inscriptions were worked separately. They were burned with oil varnish (email brun) and the base between the letters scraped clean again; this accepted the gilding, whereas the brown varnish coating of the letters rejected it. The lettering thus stands out against the gold background as a dark, enamel-like tone, and in spite of having been buried in the ground for years has been perfectly preserved. The strength and compactness of this work (cf. Figs. 5-19, 5-24) are founded on the perfect harmony of technical competence and artistic intention.

5-38

5-39

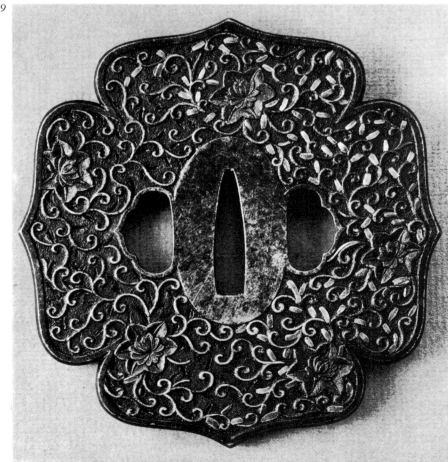

Fig. 5-38. Japanese guard: Silver inlay in steel. In this kind of inlay no groove was cut; the silver wires were hammered onto the surface, which was roughened to a file-like texture. The photograph shows that adhesion is poorer in this case. In some areas, the linear pattern is interrupted where the silver wire has become detached.

Fig. 5-39. Japanese guard. Here, the scrolls and flowers were cut out plastically, so that the differently colored metal forms a raised relief on the dark background.

Nielloing

The ornamental technique of nielloing in actual fact makes a virtue of necessity. The name is derived from the Medieval Latin *nigellum*. It uses in a decorative manner a chemical property of silver which is normally a nuisance. Silver is blackened by sulfur and its compounds, which also include the hydrogen sulfide present in the atmosphere. This is why a silver spoon becomes tarnished immediately it makes contact with (sulfur-containing) egg yolk, even when diluted in soup. The blackening of silver objects in the course of time, like the artificial blackening of silverware, wrongly called oxidization (still practiced to give it an antique appearance) is caused by sulfur-containing compounds. It is this coloration which is employed in the technique of nielloing, to produce not accidental, but quite definite and deliberate contrast effects, like drawings, between darkened inserts and the bright base of the original metal.

For this purpose, recesses are carved with a chisel or graver, and the mass of niello, colored with the admixture of sulfur, melted in. The most important difference from enameling is this: The niello filler substance is metallic, that is, a mixture of silver, copper, and lead. Metallic properties such as the ductility caused by the pliable copper and the soft lead are the most outstanding mark of distinction from enamel, which consists of glass and is therefore brittle and splinters easily.

Completely forgotten in the eighteenth century, when even the term niello was unknown, this decorative technique has again come to the notice of present-day gold- and silversmiths through the works of the Renaissance and the instructions which Benvenuto Cellini (see opposite) published about its use. But the technique is much older. Egyptian and Roman niello work is known; it also occurs in Indian and Persian metalwork. Industrial application of the technique in the nineteenth century in Tula in Southern Russia on boxes, spoons, and trinkets, and in Germany on watch lids and cigarette cases, devalued its artistic importance. The earlier, more primitive works are far better suited as examples for our own modern experiments than the sophisticated achievements of the High Renaissance, and since we normally trace the beginnings and origins in the fields of the arts and technology to build on them, a revival of the niello technique could be imagined most easily in the kind of austerely linear and figurative designs of Early Christian and medieval work. Granulation, too, luckily taken up again, was conceived by the earliest masters.

The author knows of no modern niello work involving figures and this is why only examples of oriental niello work are illustrated here. The choice was made after careful consideration, because the examples are intended by their style and technique to stimulate individual experiments, and therefore must be attuned to present-day taste. Hardly any of the simple objects which still display figure or ornamental decorations today are niello work. It is possible that craftsmen of good taste no longer derive any pleasure from this splendid old technique because of its indiscriminate, superficial use in the so-called Tula silver made by the jewelry trade.

The technical execution

The recesses into which the niello mass is melted can be produced in different ways. The craftsman making single pieces can use the graver for delicate line work, the chisel for bold, prominent designs, and lastly the tracer for work that does not cut, but merely displaces the metal (see *Tools: Chasing*). Both scooping out of material with the engraver's chisel, and recessing with chasing punches, permit not only line but also area nielloing. However, even the mechanical preparation of the niello recesses by means of etching, pressing, or guilloching does not necessarily lead to work in poor taste. Everything here depends on the design.

The tools used for producing the recesses were the graver, chisel, and punch, each of which decisively affects the character of the work. The historical development of the technique began with the contrasting areas of the earliest Egyptian nielloes: Deep pits in bronze or gold are liberally filled, and the colored inserts, together with inlay, resemble incrustation in their character (modern example of this style: *Fig. 3-49*). Gradually, in the course of time, engraving niello proper developed. Marc Rosenberg, in his book *Geschichte der Goldschmiedekunst auf technischer Grundlage* (Frankfurt, 1910), describes its historical progress in detail. He also gives interesting old recipes for the preparation of the niello filler and directions for melting. He includes a brief description based on the experiences published in 1921 by A. Wagner, who also established the following table of mixtures:

Mixture ratios

	I	II	III	IV	V
Silver	8	2	3	1	2
Copper	18	5	5	2	1
Lead	13	3	7	4	—
Sulfur	4	2	6	5	3
Borax	90	30	24	—	—
Ammonium chloride	—	—	2	—	4

Special properties of the various mixtures:
No. V is very hard (low copper content) and therefore takes on high polish, whereas No. I, because of its high lead sulfide content, is rather porous and lead-gray rather than black.

Production of the niello mass

Sulfur is melted and brought to boiling point in a graphite crucible inserted in an air furnace. Of the three metals silver, copper, and lead, the first two, because of their higher melting points, are used in the shape of wire or thin snippets, whereas the lead pieces can be pea-sized. As soon as the sulfur boils, the silver wire is introduced into the crucible. The silver and copper snippets are first brought to red heat on coals. The glowing metal burns in the sulfur fumes to silver sulfide, emitting strong light as it does so; the silver sulfide melts at once and sinks to the ground. After all the silver has been introduced, it is the turn of the copper, and lastly of the lead. The paste is stirred in the crucible with a clay rod to mix the metal sulfides intimately and to find out whether there are still any solid pieces left. When all the metal parts have melted, the niello mass is poured over a brushwood broom into a vessel filled with water. This divides the liquid metal into tiny droplets, which solidify immediately they enter the water. A niello mass is thus obtained that can easily be crushed. It is a thorough mixture of the various metal sulfides, and has a beautiful dark color.

The application of the niello mass

According to Cellini's advice, evenly crushed but not completely powdered niello is washed in pure water, and applied with a brass, copper, or wooden spatula to the cut, chiseled, or chased recesses in a uniform thickness. It should cover the engraving at about the thickness of a knife back, if the niello inlay is intended to be scraped down to the level of the bright surface, and polished. (In a few old pieces examples can be found of niello which does not completely fill the engraving.) Unless the borax has already been added to the mass, it must now be sprinkled on top.

Melting

The inlay is melted, and made to flow in the muffle furnace at temperatures ranging between 500°C and 700°C depending on the ratio of the mixture. A practical tip by Cellini suggests that, at the instant of melting, the niello mass should once more be pressed home and evenly distributed with the broadened end of a heated iron wire or spatula. After the entire engraving has been filled by the completely molten niello, the work is taken out of the furnace to cool.

Scraping, polishing, and after-treatment

Since niello is metal, it is cleaned, protruding bits are scraped off, and it is filed and polished like any other silver object. The treatment of any bubbles that might have formed is described in the following directions, published by Cellini in 1568. These, like any other recipe, can help the user with his own experiments, but cannot replace them.

Take an ounce of the finest silver, two ounces of well purified copper, and three ounces of the most solid and pure lead obtainable; and a small goldsmith's crucible large enough to melt the three metals in.* Now expose the ounce of silver and the two ounces of copper in the crucible to the flame of a blast furnace, and add the lead as soon as the silver and copper are truly melted and thoroughly mixed. Now rapidly withdraw the crucible, pick up a lump of coal with the tongs and stir with it. Because the lead always forms a certain amount of foam, remove as much of it as you can with the coal, until the three metals are intimately and purely mixed. Now keep a clay bottle at hand, about the size of your fist, and with a neck no wider than your finger; half fill it with finely crushed sulfur, and pour in the hot mass when it has become free-flowing. Quickly seal the bottle with a little damp soil. Pick it up in a thick linen rag or a piece of old sacking, and shake it to and fro while it cools. As soon as the mass is cold, take it out by smashing the bottle, and you will see that the sulfur has dyed it black. Be careful to choose the darkest sulfur you can find; the bottle may be one used for separating gold from silver. The shaking to and fro of the mass while it cools in the sulfur serves for mixing mass and sulfur as thoroughly as possible. Now

pour your niello, which will consist of many granules, back into the crucible and melt it with a grain of borax over a suitable flame. Repeat this twice or three times, breaking the mass after each melt to examine its structure. When this is fine and dense enough, the niello will be ready for use.

I must now teach you the way of using niello, but first I must say a few words about the engraved plate. This consists of gold or silver; nielloing is not done in any other metals. If you want the niello to be without holes, and of even and beautiful appearance, you must first boil the engraved plate in a lye prepared of water and very pure ash, preferably of oak wood. After you have boiled it in a vessel for a quarter of an hour, place it in a bowl of fresh, clear water, and brush it with a clean brush until you have removed all the dirt. Now attach the plate to a piece of iron long enough so that you can handle it in the fire; it must be about three palms long, or more or less, as experience will teach you with each work. But take care that the iron to which you attach it is neither too thick nor too thin, so that when you are about to niello your work in the fire it will be heated evenly. Because if either the iron or the work is heated alone first, you will not be successful. You must therefore take great care in this matter. Now crush the niello on the anvil or the porphyry stone, but hold it in a clamp or a copper tube so that it does not jump off; take care that it is not powdered, but only crushed, and very neatly, so that its grains are the size of millet or foxtail grains, and nothing is missing [sic].

Now place the crushed niello in a bowl or glazed cup and wash it thoroughly in fresh, pure water, until it is clean, free from dust and other dirt that may have been added during crushing. This done, spread it with a brass or copper spatula on the engraved plate, which should be evenly covered to the thickness of a knife back. Now sprinkle well-crushed borax on top, but not too much; place a few pieces of wood on coals so that you can set them alight with a bellows. Thereafter move the work slowly towards the wood fire and expose it skillfully to the heat until you see that the niello begins to melt. Take care not to heat it to red heat. If it becomes too hot it will lose its natural properties and become soft; the lead, making up the biggest portion of the niello, will begin to corrode your work, which is made of silver or gold. This may make all your labor in vain; to consider this with the greatest care is as important as to engrave the design well. Before we follow the process to completion, we want to have a closer look at melting. I must advise you, when you expose your work to the flames and see that the niello melts, to take up a piece of iron wire of medium thickness and move its flattened end into the fire. As soon as the niello begins to melt, quickly grasp the hot iron wire, slide it to and fro across the niello and endeavor to spread it everywhere like molten wax with the hot rod until it fills the engraved pattern completely. Allow the work to cool, and remove the surplus niello with a fine file. When you have filed the design of the plate almost down, place the work on hot ashes or glowing coals; as soon as it is too hot to touch, in fact even hotter, smooth the niello with the polishing tool of hardened steel and a little oil. Apply as much pressure with your hand as the work requires, according to its nature. The only purpose of this smoothing is to block up certain bubbles occasionally occurring during nielloing. With only a little patience and practice, these bubbles will be completely closed with smoothing. The engraved pattern is now fully revealed with a scraping knife. Now moisten tripoli earth and powdered coal with water, and, with a cone flattened down to the pith, rub your work until it appears flat and beautifully smooth. Do not be annoyed, patient reader, because of the long-windedness of my explanation; remember that I have not yet said half of what you must consider in this art. It indeed fully occupies a man

---

*Judging by Cellini's indications of the high lead content of his niello he must have used a mixture similar to the one listed under III in the table on page 200.

who undertakes to practice none other. As a youngster of fifteen to eighteen I worked much in the art of nielloing, always to my own designs, and was widely acclaimed for it.

Multicolored metal inserts of other kinds

Where lettering and craftsman's marks appear silvery on the dark background of, say, a brass plate, the engraved pattern has been filled with fine tin. This is a very simple method. The liquid tin is spread into the engraved lines with a soldering iron and scraped smooth after it has solidified. The brass base can be made dark-colored with various substances and in many different tones, without the tin losing its bright color.

The Technique of Granulation

by Elisabeth Treskow

The granulations of the Etruscans have always aroused the interest of experts and laymen alike, especially perhaps because the method of their production had been lost for centuries.

It is impossible to mention here all the goldsmiths who in the course of the last hundred years attempted to rediscover the technique of granulation. Some, however, cannot be ignored, for instance Augusto Castellani, who lived in Rome during the mid-nineteenth century and devoted many years of his life to the revival of the technique of granulation; he also believed to have found it. The results of his work will be described when the technical processes of granulation are explained. Castellani's experiments induced many goldsmiths all over the world at the turn of the century to practice the technique developed by him, and called at the time "Roman soldering".

When Marc Rosenberg wrote his book *Granulation* (Frankfurt, 1918) he, together with his co-author Franz Stanger, earned high praise because he raised anew the question of the technique of granulation.

Delicate granulated silhouettes, resembling those found at Vetulonia, were first made by Johann Michael Wilm of Munich about 1920 *(Fig. 5-40)*.

The author too, independently of others, spent years searching for the technique with which she succeeded in producing, about 1930, her first practicable and flawless work. As far as is known, many different methods today lead to the same result. These will be included in the description.

Nor must the author forget to mention in this context Mr. Littledale of London, whose lecture on his own granulations she was privileged to attend in London in 1936.

Apart from interest in the technical process of granulation, this possibility of surface decoration most emphatically deserves intensive study of its creative potentialities. Here, however, there is space only for the description of technical processes whose knowledge will allow conclusions about a method used in the past on equal terms with all the goldsmith's ornamental techniques. It had sunk into oblivion for several centuries. The problem of granulation, unsolved for so long, was this: How can a durable connection be established between fine and ultrafine grains and the supporting base? The antique granulations showed that this connection could not possibly have been brought about with solder, as we would normally do today. Chemical examination proved that grains and base of each work always consisted of the same alloy. It is true that the most varied types of alloy occurred in different works of different periods and different localities. In spite of the fineness of the granulated material used, a clear, amazingly plastic effect of the grains is preserved in antique granulations. The cause of this has been discovered: They are joined to one another and to the base only by a very minute amount of gold. When such a granulation is examined at eye level, daylight is visible even between the tiniest grains. To achieve this effect, it was necessary to distribute a solder so finely that the tenuous connection of the tiniest grains became possible.

The goldsmith Augusto Castellani, whose superb collection of antique jewelry and jewelry of his own production can be seen at the Villa Julia in Rome, probably used finely powdered solder in his work. In much of it, especially in a Mask of Pan (illustrated in Marc Rosenberg's *Granulation*, Frankfurt, 1918) it can clearly be seen that the grains are closely connected with one another without plastic outline, in an

Fig. 5-40. Box and ball, magnified about 3 times. Gold with granulation. J. M. Wilm, Munich.

Fig. 5-41. Antique granulation. One of the few examples of simple, linear arrangement; yet, because of the large number of parallel lines, the effect is not monotonous.

Fig. 5-42. Granulation by Ruth Koblassa.

indistinct, pasty consistency: Their pasty appearance is due to the fact that the intermediate spaces are filled with solder. The Etruscan granulations are striking precisely because of their clear plastic effect, produced by the shadows in the intermediate spaces.

No matter how finely powdered the solder, this method is therefore a failure. This made Marc Rosenberg and Stanger realize that it must have been a chemical reaction that joined the grains to the base. Rosenberg believed that, through being melted and subsequently annealed in charcoal dust, the grains became coated with a film of gold carbide whose melting point is about 160°C below that of the gold to be worked. The object would therefore be heated to the melting point of the gold carbide film during the soldering process; the film, running down as it were, connects the grains with one another and with the base.

For years the author has been eminently successful with this technique, using 22 carat gold, the rest of the alloy consisting of equal parts of silver and copper. Nor was it necessary to use any flux. The grains were coated on the base with a saliva-moistened brush: The mucins contained in the saliva acted as temporary adhesives. During the melting process, the adhesive contained in the saliva (an organic substance) burned to carbon, which reduced the melting point. Essential to the success of this technique, however, is the use of at least 22 carat gold, as has been discovered during experiments lasting several months.

In addition to this, another method can be described. During his experiments, Mr. Littledale also concluded that to join the tiniest grains to the base a mechanical division of metallic solder was impossible, and he therefore brought about a chemical division. The component which lowers the melting point of an alloy is copper. Copper alloyed with silver, like copper alloyed with gold, melts at 890°C, in other words it lowers the melting points of both the metals it is alloyed with. This is why we add copper to our solders. In the chemical solder used by Mr. Littledale, the soldering process was based on the fact that a copper salt that formed part of the solder was converted into metallic copper by being heated in a reducing flame; together with gold or silver it formed a chemical solder. But an admixture of an organic substance is necessary to produce the desired effect in the solder. This may, for instance, be Seccotine (a fish glue), which is converted into carbon during the melting process and causes the reduction of the copper salt to metallic copper. With stronger heating, this metallic copper forms a solder of pasty consistency together with the gold of the base and the grains. Diluted with water, this paste can be applied at thicknesses varying with the size of the grains.

Mr. Frey, a Capetown goldsmith, told of a third method. To the gold to be granulated, and to the grains, a higher proportion of copper than usual is added, actually at the alloying stage. Before the grains are applied to the base, both they and the base are strongly heated in an oxygen atmosphere, so that the copper is oxidized in the alloy, in other words grains and the metal of the base are annealed black. The grains are now applied to the base with a flux (borax or fluoron) and heated until the copper oxide melts, which again, as in the other experiments, lowers the melting point and enters into an alloy with the gold or the silver of the parts to be joined. The author checked and tried Mr. Frey's data and obtained the desired result with this method, too. Here one does not depend on the use of very high-carat gold, but can achieve the required results with cheaper alloys, too. There remains the production of the gold grains to be described, as well as the method of their temporary fixation before they are finally attached by means of soldering.

How the grains are produced

Finely rolled gold is cut into longitudinal and then transverse strips in the same way as solder, or drawn into very fine wires; these are bundled, and particles cut off the bundles; the sheet or wire cuttings thus obtained are distributed in a clay crucible filled with coal dust. The distribution must be in layers; the individual gold particles must be sufficiently isolated from one another by the coal dust. The clay crucible thus prepared is brought to red heat in the melting furnace. At the instant of melting, the gold particles contract into tiny grains, each of which is isolated from the others by the surrounding coal dust; they are left there until they are cool; then they are poured into water, washed, dried on blotting paper, and put through a set of sieves to obtain classes of grains, each of as uniform a size as possible.

A further problem is the temporary fixation of the grains to the base. Wax or honey, as Rosenberg assumed, does not work. Both substances would let the grains move during melting. The adhesive force of saliva is strong enough, if great care is taken, to produce sufficient adhesion even on spheres and strongly convex supports. Mr. Littledale, who added Seccotine to his copper salts, not only obtained considerably stronger adhesion to the base; as already mentioned, this fish glue also had the purpose of enriching the copper salts with carbon. Carbon causes the reduction of the copper salts to metallic copper. The type of copper salt used is immaterial. Copper sulfate, copper oxide, and copper chloride have been found successful. All these salts can be equally well used for granulating if mixed with Seccotine or some other organic glue. The author prefers the brown copper hydroxide, because, when mixed with Seccotine, it is possible to draw the pattern of the granulations on the base with it almost as well as with Indian ink. It is also important that the copper salt should cover only those areas that are eventually to be covered with grains. The empty areas must be carefully cleaned of all residue with a damp brush, because the copper salt would leave traces of melt behind on the base. During the arrangement of the grains in patterns, figures, or areas it should be borne in mind that they follow the law of smallest checkerwork—they automatically arrange themselves to fill the gaps. If this law is followed with the arrangement of the grains, there can be no failure in the distribution, nor is the stability impaired.

Conclusions about the likely methods the Etruscans employed can be drawn only from personal experiments. The author believes that they, too, used copper salts. As long as the author granulated only with grains there was no need to change the method described, but as soon as wires were attached together with granular material to the base, as is found on many Etruscan granulations, the method failed. Wire cannot be fixed to the base without copper salt, because it requires more solder for joining than the first method can produce. The elastic gold armlets from Etruria, which consist of narrow gold strips and bent wires, can only have been produced by the copper salt method, since any use of a metallic solder (whose copper content is lower) would necessarily have made it stiff. But the Etruscans often used round wires and flat wires together with granular material, not only on filigree bracelets, but also on brooches, earrings, and other jewelry, especially during the late period.

The Etruscans were the most eminent bronzesmiths not only of their own time, but perhaps of all time: Nothing is more natural than the assumption that they made use of a copper salt on which to melt their granular material. All they needed to do to achieve this was to keep the gold grains in copper vessels and expose them to the normal influence of the atmosphere. The film of copper oxide forming would cover the grains with a film of copper salts. Perhaps the Etruscans also made use of the copper salts they obtained during bronze forging to speed up the time-consuming process of natural oxidation.

The situation can be summarized as follows: After a number of experiments the technique of granulation was eventually rediscovered. One of the methods employed could be the Etruscan one, and it is thought that the use of copper salts would have been natural to these great bronzesmiths. Only during later periods, in which the gold used was less pure, was the role of the copper salt solders forgotten. Benvenuto Cellini even mentioned a similar copper salt formula in his book. From the Renaissance back through the Middle Ages and Antiquity to the Etruscans, who probably invented it, this rediscovered method was likely to have been in general use not only in granulation and wire soldering, but also in transparent filigree and cloisonné.

Filigree

The term is composed of the Italian *filo* (Lat. *filum*) and *grano* (Lat. *granum*) and denotes thread (wire) and grain. Filigree, then, is really wirework combined with granulation. It is, however, also possible that the term "grain" refers to the notching or granulation of smooth wires, because in filigree work the wire was often made more attractive by means of notching or knurling.

The old and original version of filigree probably consisted of wire soldering on a metal base *(Figs. 5-44, 5-66)*, although as early as about 800 B.C. the Etruscans made bracelets in woven and spun patterns solely of smooth, fine wire. Smooth, notched, and multiple knurled (twisted) wires have been used in metalwork for soldering onto a gold or silver base from Antiquity (since 2000 B.C.) through the Middle Ages to modern times. The goldsmiths of the Renaissance and the Baroque periods, too, practiced this technique, of which a fine Italian piece *(Fig. 5-45)* is evidence. The goldsmiths of the period of the Barbarian Invasions were particularly fond of filigree soldering. North African and Oriental metal craftsmen even today use knurled wire with immense skill. But the most delicate gold threads were probably spun and soldered into pieces of jewelry by the Indian and Chinese craftsmen.

From the seventeenth century onwards, a cheap, popular type of silver filigree appeared in Germany. The colorful fashions of the Baroque, still surviving here and there in some European folk costumes, were decorated with large ornamental pieces of silver filigree worn as headdresses, with stay pins, and with other trinkets. The wire had now become completely independent, was no longer fixed to any support, and airy, spiderweb-like patterns of fantastic shapes, fashioned from ingeniously bent wires, soldered where they crossed, were the outcome. Produced by an ill-paid cottage industry often relying on child labor right into the twentieth century, this kind of "popular art" still survives in a modest way in some Balkan countries.

More recent wirework

The goldsmith of today avoids the word filigree with its association with this somewhat down-at-heel cottage industry. He also avoids its dainty,

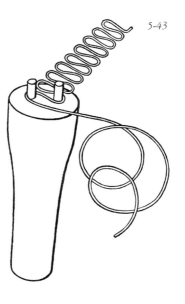

5-43

Fig. 5-43. A bending jig for making continuous wire loops.

5-44

5-45

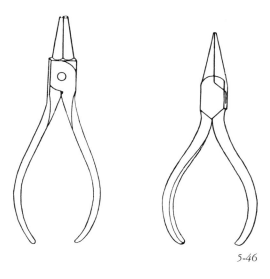

5-46

Fig. 5-44. Gold filigree. Bracelet of Queen Amanishakhete, treasure of Meroë, Egypt, first century A.D.

Fig. 5-45. Silver filigree on a Renaissance cup. Italian. Example of a balanced surface decoration, which at the time was also produced by means of damascening and metal engraving.

Fig. 5-46. Bending pliers for filigree work: Round and pointed pliers.

frivolous subjects, but he does appreciate wire as a creative element *(Fig. 3-13)*. He no longer tries to force it to represent leaves and butterflies, but finds in the simplicity of natural bent patterns, such as the wavy line, a more austere and at the same time more appropriate expression of wirework. He also takes advantage of the attractive interplay of light and shade on twisted wire *(Fig. 2-54)*, which, particularly on a restful background, looks so elegant and is evidence of true craftsmanship.

Here are some technical details: Flat and roundnosed pliers are used for bending smooth wire. A very simple little jig, a piece of wood with two metal pins, helps to bend wire into regular waves quickly. The wire is pulled taut round the pins; a uniform wave is thus produced, determined by the thickness of, and the distance between, the pins. With a larger number of pins and different distances between them, other and more difficult patterns can of course be bent.

Knurling or twisting

A simple flat wire can be twisted as a smith twists flat bars. Two or more wires can be twisted together like threads or a rope. The wires may be of the same thickness, or different. Already twisted wires can in turn be twisted together, in other words doubly twisted. But the appearance of the combination of identical wires, too, may differ depending on how strongly they have been twisted. The twisting machine, a clamping device with a hand crank, is used for this purpose (see *Fig. 5-47*). Its bottom is clamped in a vise. A jaw chuck holds the ends of the wires on one side, and a pair of heavy, flat pliers holds them on the other. When the hand crank is turned on the twisting machine, the jaw chuck is rotated through a gear, the pliers are held firmly in position, and the wires are twisted.

Other kinds of wire soldering

Another characteristic of modern goldsmith's work is the creation of austere line patterns of figures by means of wire soldering. It is the contour of cloisonné, which is used here without any association with colored enamel. The expression is therefore restricted to the square wire, bent according to the outlines of a line drawing. This technique requires as a design a drawing that is strictly confined to such bends as the wire will accept. It must be based on technical feasibility, above all on the wire itself, not on some natural shapes.

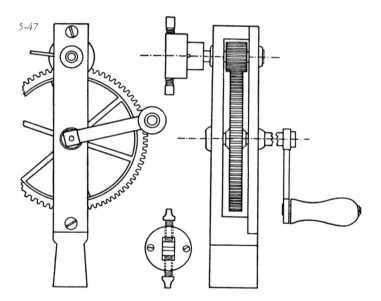

5-47

Fig. 5-47. Old-type twisting machine, to be clamped in the vise.

Etching

The treatment of copper plates during etching, described on page 68, has the purpose of deepening the drawn line so that it can receive printing ink. Conversely, etching can also be used for the production of raised drawings. Here, attention is focused on the unetched areas of the surface, which in their entirety constitute the pictorial representation. The etching procedure, therefore, is used to suppress the background of the drawing, or, indeed, to bring the drawing out by means of recessing and different inking of this background. This kind of etching can be called relief etching. Operationally, it differs in no way from the technical etching of the graphic artist. But the artistic means of expression of etching are very closely related to those of the graphic arts. The craftsman's involvement is not very deep: Ideas, draftsmanship and a flair for style are everything. This is perhaps also the reason why the modern craftsman makes no use of etching. The fear of dilettante effects and lapses into the exclusive preoccupation with drawing in, for instance, the Art Nouveau period, is not unjustified. Since each design for etching is a matter of personal perception, the—albeit fundamental—point must suffice that the two-dimensional character must always be preserved. Etchings of Arab art and also of the Renaissance period are exemplary because their arabesques and acanthus leaves do not simulate three-dimensional depth. This also applies to letter forms and consistently two-dimensional figure representations.

Protective coating and etching solution

The protective coating covers and protects those areas of the work that are not to be etched. It must resist the acid and be capable of being applied or rolled down as a thin film, and, if necessary, removed. Wax, paraffin, resin (mastix), and asphalt are suitable for this purpose. Wax in white sheets, the slow-drying bituminous varnish, to be diluted with turpentine, and lastly iron varnish, which dries more quickly when diluted with methylated spirit, are widely-used protective coatings. Generally known recipes of mixtures give various ratios of wax (10), mastix (5), asphalt (4), and colophony (2 parts). So that the protective coating adheres with uniform firmness to the surface of the work, the latter must be metallically pure before application. Depending on the nature of its surface, emery powder or finer grinding and polishing agents (French chalk, etc.), or methylated spirit and prepared chalk can be used to remove grease. Fingermarks should be avoided. For the rolling on of the protective coating the work is heated, preferably on an electric hot plate, until it hisses slightly when touched with a damp object.

The drawing

This can be produced on the plate in various ways, depending on its character: By tracing it and subsequently removing the etching ground with dry point and scraper, for strictly linear designs, or by applying the etching ground with a brush and leaving blank the areas to be etched, if the total effect is to be softer and more two-dimensional.

Etching

The metal is etched with dilute nitric acid, hydrochloric acid, ferric chloride, or various acid-free etching agents. Every acid etches more or less grainily, nitric acid more so than others. But degree of dilution and temperature of the etching fluid also play a part. Distilled water is used for diluting the acid; rainwater, or water softened by boiling are also suitable. The pieces to be etched are suspended or placed in china vessels so that they are covered by the etching fluid to a depth of at least two to three finger breadths. The intensity with which the acid attacks can be judged from the number and size of the rising bubbles, and above all from the rate at which new ones form. Violent bubble formation combined with effervescence of the etching fluid is a sign of dangerously strong action. The etching ground may be damaged along the rim and where it is thin. This, too, is indicated by rising bubbles. All bubbles must be carefully removed at short intervals with a goose- or chicken feather to avoid damage to the etching ground. If the acid etches too slowly (approximate guide: 1–3 hours depending on the depth) it may be poured off and concentrated; heating the etching liquid also speeds up the action.

Common and well-tried degrees of dilution

Metal	Etching reagent	Water
Gold	diluted aqua regia	—
Iron and steel	nitric acid: 1 part	6 parts
Silver, copper, brass	nitric acid: 1 part	3 parts
Tin (unsuitable)	nitric acid: 1 part	4 parts
Copper, brass, bronze	ferric chloride 400g (concentrated solution etches more slowly than diluted solution)	1,000cc
Glass (enamel)	hydrofluoric acid	—

Acid-free etching liquids (chlorine, bromine, and iodine salts, e.g. ferric chloride) have the advantage of forming no gases and therefore no bubbles. The danger of damage to the etching ground is reduced. Aluminum can be etched with ferric chloride (weak solutions). Etching reagent for iron and steel: 1 part bromine in 100 parts water, or 2 parts iodine, 4 parts potassium iodide in 40 parts water.

Enameling

by Walter Lochmüller

The desire to enrich the goldsmith's work with colors and to join ornamental and figure representations to the metalwork in contiguous colored areas led, even in Antiquity, to the use not only of individually mounted gems, but also of colored inlays of stones and glass, either inserted, mosaic-like, in cells, or filled into them in the form of pastes (Figs. 5-48, 5-51).

These powdered stone or glass incrustations, hardened with cement, are the direct predecessors of enamel work. Egyptian goldsmiths already knew cloisonné and champlevé inlays of this kind at an early date, but not melted glass until the middle of the first millenium B.C., although the faïence and glass techniques were already highly developed during the second millenium B.C. When and where the first glass powders were melted onto metal is not known.

5-48

Fig. 5-48. Gold bracelet, incrusted with colored glass pastes, height 4 ins. (10cm). Egypt, XIX Dynasty (1330–1195 B.C.).

5-49

Fig. 5-49. Early enameling. Purple glass in gold cells, lined with gold leaf, orange to cherry-red. Fibula of Prince Uffila, Alemannic tomb, Wittislingen, Swabia. Cast silver, gold leaf fastened with rivets. Made by the goldsmith Wigerig (650–700 A.D.), Longobard influence. Length 7·7 ins. (18·5cm).

Uffila wore this clasp in memory of his deceased wife; the beautiful Latin niello inscription on the back says: "Uffila, live happily in the Lord. I was innocent when I was carried off by Death, because as long as I was allowed to live, I was true to you with all my heart. Bear your fate with patience."

Fig. 5-50. *Cloisonné on a small box. China, around 1800.*

Fig. 5-51. *Falcon pectoral. Gold with lapis lazuli inlay (large wings), cornelian, and turquoise-colored inlay in the cells. Wing span about 6·2 ins. (15cm). Serapeum, Memphis, XIX Dynasty.*

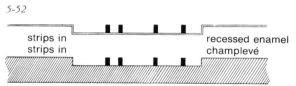

5-52

strips in
strips in

recessed enamel
champlevé

5-53

Fig. 5-52. *Bottom: The scooped-out trough with strips inserted. Top: The same principle, but here the troughs were stamped into the metal sheet (recessed enamel), hence the walls are thinner.*

Fig. 5-53. *Round enamel plate, roof of the Heribert reliquary. Champlevé with strips inserted (combination technique, see Fig. 5-52). Cologne, about 1170.*

Fig. 5-54. *Cloisonné bracelet in black and yellow. The loops and curves of the wire, bent with pliers, produce the pattern typical of Byzantine cloisonné. Walter Lochmüller, Schwäbisch Gmünd.*

5-54

211

A pendant with enamel has been found which belongs to the Cretan-Mycenean civilization. It is dated around 750 B.C., which does not rule out the existence of earlier work of this kind.

In about 50 B.C., Celtic metal craftsmen who loved the attraction of contrasts in material and colors used red, blue, and white enamel on bronze plates in shallow champlevé work (see *Fig. 9-14*).

Both in Oriental and in European art, use was made during the last pre-Christian centuries of the possibility of melting glass onto a metal base.

Whether special glasses were employed for this purpose, or the soft sodium glass of Antiquity met all the requirements, is an open question. Today enamel is a special colored glass, a lead-boron silicate whose melting point, coefficient of expansion, and adhesion make it suitable for melting onto metal, either covering only parts of it, or as a general coating.

It is used both on precious and on base metals, on the former as a decorative, on the latter, particularly on iron, as a protective coating. It is applied to the metal surface in powder or finely granulated form, usually mixed with distilled water, and melted on at about 800°C in the muffle furnace.

The enamels made in the various factories have the melting, adhesive, and expansion properties necessary for their application. Three groups of material must be distinguished:

1. transparent enamel
2. translucent enamel
3. opaque enamel

The basic material of all is a colorless frit, dyed with metal oxides and producing transparent colors. Opaque enamels are obtained by the addition of stannic oxide, fluorine, or bone ash, translucent ones by the admixture of fluorspar or cryolite.

Since some dyes enter into chemical compounds with the base metal and are therefore discolored during firing, the colorless enamel is often used as base enamel (flux). Silver requires a special silver flux, since the ordinary flux turns yellow and impairs the color and luminosity of the colored enamel.

The metals suitable for enameling and their preparation

Correct choice and treatment of the enamel base, the metal, is essential to the execution of enamelwork. Not all metals and alloys are suitable for this technique. Here are the suitable ones: Pure gold and its alloys, but if possible not below 16 carat; "electrum", used in Antiquity, a gold–silver alloy consisting of 400 parts fine gold and 600 parts fine silver; fine silver and silver alloys not below 900/1000, pure copper and enamel tombac (zinc content not exceeding 8%); and, for industrial purposes, iron.

When transparent enamels are used, the color of the base metal must be considered. Although gold is an ideal base for enamel, giving it high luminosity, all light-blue, gray, and green tones are changed towards yellow by the color of the support, whereas the color of yellow, brown, and red hues is intensified. The light, almost colorless silver is suitable for all hues, even pale and delicate ones, because of its own pale color. Since it affects many dyes chemically, these demand a silver flux base. Furthermore, silver has the highest expansion coefficient of all metals suitable for enameling, and, as it expands during annealing, it contracts again as it cools, which causes the enamel to split off easily. This can be countered by the use of thin sheet silver with uniform counter-enameling. Nor must the comparatively low melting point of silver be

forgotten. With copper and enamel tombac, as with gold, the metal color can be expected to show through.

The various metals require various pretreatments. Pure gold and pure silver are annealed and brushed with a glass brush in water or in a caustic potash lye. Engraved or guilloched plates are not annealed, only brushed in caustic potash lye.

Silver alloys are boiled in diluted sulfuric acid after they have been annealed. It is recommended to repeat this process once or twice with alloys below 950/1000. Gold alloys are treated like silver alloys; in place of sulfuric acid, dilute nitric acid is used for boiling. Copper and enamel tombac are annealed once and boiled.

The copper objects are now scratched with a brass brush, dried in sawdust, and pickle-polished. The polishing pickle used for this consists of equal parts of pure nitric and sulfuric acid and a small addition of cooking salt and shining soot, but the mixture ratio varies. The pickle is prepared in earthenware vessels: First the nitric acid is introduced, and then cooking salt and shining soot added. This is followed by the sulfuric acid, poured in a thin jet and continuously stirred. Because the chlorine fumes are noxious, pickling must be carried out under the flue, or, in its absence, outdoors. The pickling fluid must also be kept in a tightly closed vessel. The object is briefly immersed in the pickle, and immediately thoroughly rinsed and dried. After each treatment in acid, the metals must be carefully cleaned in boiling water (better still distilled water) and brushed for a short time, since acid residues make the enamel gray and porous. Nor must the metals prepared for enameling be touched by hand, since the slightest trace of grease repels the enamel during application and spoils it during pickling.

Careful preparation and scrupulous cleanliness are essential to the success of this work.

Dark patches appearing on soldered objects near the joints after pickling are surplus solder discolored in the pickle, and must be completely removed. Afterflowing solder produces stains and incrustations. The joints must be clean fits, and solder should be used as sparingly as possible.

Preparing the enamel (Fig. 5-55)

The factories usually supply the enamel in pieces that can be crushed in a steel mortar of 1·6–2 ins (4–5cm) diameter. Larger pieces, wrapped in cloth, are first broken up with a wooden mallet. The enamel crushed in the mortar is sieved into the porcelain mortar and finely ground with the addition of water. In the mortar, or better still in larger glass vessels, it is well washed; fresh water is added, and the enamel mass stirred with a glass rod or an applicator. After the enamel has settled, the water is poured off, and the process repeated until the water is quite clear. Distilled water should be used for at least the last two or three washes.

Transparent colors should be even more carefully washed than opaque ones.

Old colors, namely those that have been kept in the ground state for a long time and have already been mixed with water, must be reground and washed before use. It is recommended to add two or three drops of concentrated nitric acid to the first washing water. Washing must be repeated once again with much water so that no acid remains. The test for freedom from acid can be carried out with a piece of litmus paper. Washing with nitric acid makes the enamel a little harder to melt: Colors that flow too softly can be hardened by repeated addition of nitric acid to the washing water. This increases the luminosity of trans-

Fig. 5-55. *After being crushed in the steel mortar, the enamel must be ground and washed in an agate or porcelain dish.*

parent hues. The washing water to which no acid has been added is poured into large vessels. The enamel settling at the bottom can then be used for counter-enameling (enameling on the back of the metal sheet).

Application (Fig. 5-56)

Very finely ground enamel must be used for the first application to ensure a thin, even coat. Coarse grains do not make close contact, so that the blank areas of the metal oxidize during firing, producing dark spots that are difficult and tedious to repair.

Thin plates for cloisonné and painter's enamel must be enameled on both sides to prevent their buckling and the splitting off of the enamel. Wholly enameled objects (bowls, boxes, vases) must likewise be enameled on both sides, unless the metal sheet is thicker than 19 gauge (1mm) and thinly enameled. A general rule should be observed: Thin metal (28–20 gauge, i.e. $0 \cdot 3 - 0 \cdot 8$mm) and thick enameling on both sides, or thick metal and thin enameling. With champlevé and basse taille enameling, which is carried out on thick metal, no counter-enameling is necessary.

Before the enamel is applied to the back, which is always done first, and to steep walls (boxes, etc.) the metal is coated with a quince seed or tragacanth solution, which binds and retains the enamel coat so that it does not drop off during firing. It is not recommended to mix the adhesives with the enamel mass, except in special cases. Even application of the tragacanth solution by brush is followed by application of the enamel, of even thickness and not too dry, also with a brush or an applicator. The surplus water is dabbed off with filter paper or clean pieces of old linen; it collects along the rim and the enamel settles densely and evenly when the object is tapped or rapped with the applicator. After the water has again been dabbed, the plate can be turned and placed on a support of filter paper. The enamel is now applied to the front in the same way, but without the use of tragacanth.

With large areas or objects, very fine, dried enamel can be riddled through a sieve onto an object that has been well and evenly moistened with tragacanth. The inner surfaces of narrow vases, which are unsuitable for application or sieving, are washed with very finely ground, several-days-old enamel. Here, tragacanth solution must be added to the enamel.

Whereas the finest-ground enamel is used for the first application, coarser-ground enamel is satisfactory for further work. It is also

possible to rinse finely ground enamel of a different color into granular enamel; during firing this produces delicate veins, whose decorative effect may be desirable.

The mixing of colors, e.g. yellow and blue to produce green, is not possible. Intermediate hues are not the result of direct mixture, but of glazing, the coating of a different transparent color on top of a fired color. This process can be repeated in several layers and firings. However, care must be taken that the hardness and expansion of the various layers of enamel do not differ greatly, because this leads to the cracking or scaling of individual parts. Color tests must precede such complicated work. It is often impossible to top a color up to the level of the wires or champlevé depressions, because the thicker a transparent layer of color, the darker it will appear. To obtain the desired tint in such cases, a glass-clear, medium-hard flux is added until an even surface ready for grinding is obtained. Thin layers of color, which may easily be ground away, are also covered with such a flux; this must not be as finely ground as that used for a foundation; if ground too finely it becomes dull, especially on dark colors. Tests must always precede the use of flux for topping up. The flux must be thinly applied. Deep troughs which cannot be filled with a thin application must be filled again.

Firing (Fig. 5-57)

The enamel-covered object is fired on thin fireclay plates, wire or iron grids. Various supports and props, to hold up at the rim the objects to be fired, or at a few points only to prevent the enamel on the back or outside from baking to the base, must be made individually to suit the size and shape of each object. Smaller plates, whose back is invisible after they have been mounted, can be fired on intermediate sheets of mica (isinglass) which can be detached from the counter-enamel almost without leaving a trace.

All the water must be slowly evaporated before the object is inserted in the muffle, which must be heated to at least 950°C. With the exception of the counter-enamel, which is lightly cemented with tragacanth or quince seed solution, the enamel now covers the plate as a loose layer of powder. The plate is placed in the muffle gently, without jolt or shock. Firing is observed through an inspection window in the door of the furnace. When the object appears bright-red and the surface of the enamel smooth and mirror-like, it is quickly removed from the furnace.

Large work must usually be turned, since the heat in the muffle varies. This must be done quickly and the work returned at once to the furnace. Sometimes an object must also be tilted; here again, it must be protected against knocks and not be subjected to pressure, as it will bend easily in the red-hot state. Damaged areas on the back of a bowl can be repaired with dry enamel, which is riddled onto the red-hot work through a sieve. It immediately bakes onto the work and is made to flow briefly in the furnace. When the firing is complete, the object is allowed to cool slowly on its support near the furnace.

When firing on a silver base, the melting point of silver must obviously be taken into account. But especially on silver the enamel should be fired briefly and sharply rather than slowly and gently, since the colors will become more fiery with the first method. Firing, to the enameler, is not a necessary evil, no matter how often it may end in failure, but the main attraction of the process. Only in the fire does the enamel acquire its sparkle and bloom. Cloisonné and champlevé are ancient techniques. A recent development in enameling, particularly, has created a special characteristic appeal through the process of melting. The firing of one color through another (oxidation firing), for example of white on a copper base, leading to delicate green tints, or the melting together of various coarse and fine grains of different colors, which after firing solidify into strange colored structures, are fascinating in their effects. In the firing and the utilization of the melting process the expert enameler will be distinguished from the mere dabbler.

In principle, short, sharp firing is better than slow firing. There is only one notable exception: During the stage of covering with flux described in the section *Application*, gentle firing in not too hot a furnace is recommended, so that the flux sinters only on top of the colors without burning into the basic hue.

Sharp firing leads to the formation of patches, because the coarse covering flux breaks up the basic color. However, this effect can also be aimed at in special cases, for the purpose of brightening and adding sparkle to a color.

The furnace (Fig. 5-57)

Charcoal and coke furnaces are now little used since their replacement by gas-fired or electric furnaces, both of which reach muffle temperatures of 1000°C. The electric muffle furnace is generally preferred now. The choice of muffle size depends on the work to be carried out. Even where large pieces form part of the work, the purchase of a small furnace for samples and small objects is always advisable. The muffle is externally wound with the heated filament embedded in grooves, and is encased in a well-insulated sheet-metal housing. All the better-quality furnaces have a drop- or draw-door which is quick and easy to open. The muffle is formed of fireclay and hard burned. The door, too, has a fireclay insert on the inside. Since occasional dropping-off of the counter-enamel must be expected, an interchangeable sheet-nickel bottom is recommended for the protection of the muffle. The bottom of the muffle is additionally protected by a spread of grog. Cracked muffles, more frequent in gas-fired than in electric furnaces, are troweled off with grog, which is stirred into a thick paste with the addition of waterglass. For the secure insertion of the work in the furnace, and its quick withdrawal with tongs after firing, fireclay plates are placed on the floor of the muffle, unless this has longitudinal grooves for this purpose. They support the grid carrying the objects to be fired. Electric furnaces without automatic temperature control must be switched off from time to time to prevent the filament from burning through.

Fig. 5-56. The spaces (cells) enclosed by wire are filled with enamel. The fine-grained enamel particles are clearly seen; the second dish from the right contains adhesive made of quince seed softened in water.

Fig. 5-57. Firing. The work with the enamel applied is carefully introduced into the muffle furnace (electrically heated here). It can easily be moved on the small wire grid.

5-58

5-59

Grinding and polishing

The enameled object is usually ground to obtain a smooth surface. With cloisonné and champlevé, care must be taken to fill the troughs or cells level with the wire or the metal before grinding is begun. For grinding, square carborundum stones of various grain sizes are used, beginning with the coarsest.

The work, resting on a soft support, is ground under moderate pressure with the stones moistened in water; both grinding stones and work must always be kept sufficiently moist. After it has been rough-ground with coarse stones, the work must be thoroughly rinsed before grinding is continued with finer carborundum; the aim is an evenly mat surface. Grinding, too, is an operation that must be carried out with care and attention, especially when several layers of enamel have been coated one on top of another.

After the grinding stage, the enamel work must be thoroughly rinsed with water and washed out with a glass brush to remove the grinds from the fine pores. This is particularly important if, after grinding, firing is to be repeated to obtain a shiny surface. Here, it is best to brush the enamel with hydrofluoric acid after the first wash, and allow the acid to act briefly on the enamel, which is then washed carefully again with a glass brush and distilled water. Because of the damaging effect of the hydrofluoric acid on skin and respiratory organs, the operation must be carried out with the greatest care; hydrofluoric acid must never come into contact with the skin. The hands must always be washed immediately after work.

In enamels which are not to be glaze-fired but are to remain mat or semiglazed, small glazed areas too deep to be roughened without damage to the general surface can be matted with hydrofluoric acid.

Ground enamel becomes dull. Waxing gives it an attractive velvety surface. The object is slightly heated, thinly coated with wax, and after cooling rubbed down with tissue paper.

Unless glaze-firing is preferred, the object can be polished to bright luster with tripoli earth and water on basswood wheels, to be followed by colorless polishing paste on felt and leather wheels. Such work must first be rough-ground with the finest stones. Polishing is much more tedious and time-consuming than glaze-firing, but produces an even smoother surface because some enamels settle during glaze-firing. Naturally, every firing operation involves a certain risk.

The techniques

The two classical techniques of enameling are *cloisonné* and *champlevé*.

Cloisonné originates in the Byzantine gold cloisonné, practiced as relief enameling or as full enameling at the Imperial Court at Byzantium, from where it spread to the monasteries of the west. In Italy and in the Rhine and Meuse region it was taken over almost unchanged; it also entered the realm of the Greek Orthodox Church, the Balkan countries, and Russia.

Fig. 5-58. Boxes with heraldic motifs in cloisonné. Franz Rickert, Munich.

Fig. 5-59. Champlevé on turned and etched tea caddies. Workshops of the City of Halle, Burg Giebichenstein.

In relief enameling, the area to be enameled is recessed with a stamp. Within this recessed, simply outlined area the internal pattern (face, hands, and drapery) is formed by thin gold wires on edge, of the same height as the depth of the recessed area. The enamel is applied to the full height of the wire and is flush with it and the metal rim.

In full enameling, the same type of wire is used for patterns and color boundaries; the colors are filled up to the rim in the cells, except that here the entire metal base is covered with enamel—in relief enameling it is enclosed by a metal surface.

Figs. 5-54 and *5-58* illustrate more recent work in cloisonné technique. Variations of cloisonné are wire enameling and ridge enameling *(Fig. 5-53)*, in which the wires are inserted flat and on edge as in ordinary cloisonné, but the wires are usually stronger. In both wire and ridge enameling the enamel coat is thin, so that the wires stand proud of the enamel surface. During firing, the enamel creeps slightly up on the wires, so that the cells form little reflecting troughs.

In contrast to the old method, in which the wires were soldered onto the metal base as described by the monk Theophilus in his essay *De Electro*, they are now melted onto a base enamel. The wires are fixed with tragacanth solution onto the plate covered with base, carefully dried, and fired. They are bent so that they form a closed shape which stays in position. When the enamel melts, the wires sink into it, and when the work leaves the furnace they are pressed into the flux while it is still soft. Because the wires may be intended for future gold electroplating, it is important that they should be pressed in far enough to make contact with the base metal.

In steep-walled vessels it is advisable to attach the main wires of the pattern with a small amount of solder, since if held only by tragacanth solution, they easily drop off. Finer connecting wires can also be fixed on enamel and melted in, as they will be held in position by the soldered wires. The wire pattern must be adapted to the technical conditions. It is not the aim of enameling to produce naturalistic little pictures. The wire must be used so that it is correctly braced and bent and retains its character. The beauty of old cloisonné rests not least on the lines evolved by the play and the character of the wire.

On partly enameled sheets and objects, a strong wire soldered in position can serve as a frame forming a large cell which encloses other wires to produce the pattern.

Champlevé. It has already been mentioned that Celtic metal craftsmen used enamel in shallow troughs on bronze plates. Opaque red, blue, and white predominated. The effect was two-dimensional and full of contrast. Romanesque champlevé on a copper base, too, has a two-dimensional tendency. As opposed to cloisonné, whose pattern is determined by the uniformly thin line of the wire, champlevé permits a variation in the width of the line, which can broaden out into areas also in the pattern within the cell. The contrast between metal area and colored area is the dominating feature *(Fig. 5-60)*.

In the Romanesque champlevé of the twelfth and thirteenth centuries, both enameled figures on a gilt background and gilt figures with rendered internal pattern on an enamel base are found. The antependium of the Eilbertus portable altar shows metal figures on an enamel base on the side panels, whereas the figures and the arches surrounding them on the plate in the center panel are enameled. The most famous work by the group of craftsmen using gilt figures on an enamel base is the Klosterneuburg Altar by Nicholas of Verdun. Here the complementary harmony of blue and gold predominates. The gilt figures with blue internal pattern are on a blue background, and in the flesh parts the pattern changes into a deep brown-red. In both variations the recess engraved in or chiseled out of the plate determines the pattern. In spite of the abundant possibilities of creating naturalistic designs with engraving, Romanesque champlevé has an austere simplicity derived from an original flair for the technique of engraving. Today the preparation of the champlevé plate is a matter for the engraver, but in old pieces it was the goldsmith himself, master of all these techniques, who did this. This ensured unity of expression and meaningful use of the medium.

In Romanesque champlevé, only copper plates served as support. In contrast with cloisonné, which is based on thin sheet gold, the troughs to be filled with enamel in champlevé are scooped from strong sheets of 15–13 gauge (1·5–2mm) thickness with the graver. After enameling, the metal parts are fire-gilt.

The colors of the limited scale available are without exception opaque. Usually several colors are used within a trough; often they become brighter towards the metal base. The colored areas are not sharply outlined, but worked so that they gradually blend into each other. *Fig. 5-53* is an example of this. The tiles of the roof are formed by bent wires. This mixed technique of champlevé and cloisonné is found occasionally.

Champlevé was practiced mainly in the Lower Rhine and Meuse region and at Limoges. Today champlevé is the most widespread enameling technique, because all enameled badges and plaques are champlevé, although the troughs are pressed instead of engraved. Their depth is about 1/80 ins. (c. 0·4mm). The enamel is applied at least twice, so that it stands slightly proud of the metal surface, and ground. Fine, narrow line patterns within a metal area are filled to overflowing to prevent the enamel from incrusting or burning in the fine lines. However, care must be taken to ensure that the enamel not only covers the troughs but also fills them without any air bubbles; only then will it be free from pores and clear after it is ground. *Fig. 5-59* shows etched champlevé. The slightly frayed contour peculiar to etching was not subsequently engraved, but advantage was taken of its artistic appeal as well as of the uneven etching of the base, which when transparent colors are used increases their luminosity. The troughs of the tea caddy in the center were turned out.

Transparent enamel colors were already being occasionally used for champlevé during the Late Romanesque period.

Basse taille enameling. Basse taille enameling on silver developed during the Gothic period in the middle of the fourteenth century. The greater luminosity of enamel on silver, above all on an engraved base, led initially to work in which the base was enlivened with hatched or rhombic patterns in deep-cut engraving. In basse taille enameling, also called deep relief or silver enameling, the representation is cut into the silver sheet as a negative relief and covered with translucent enamels. In the deep portions the color becomes thick and darkens, whereas it covers the high portions of the relief in thin layers, thus shining brightly. This produces effects of magic luminosity through the refraction of the light and the differences between light and dark within a color tone, especially when the modeling is not soft, but consists of sharp cut edges and has great depth. In this technique, too, the enamel is ground and has a mirror-smooth surface. Basse taille enameling was practiced in Northern Italy, on the Upper Rhine, and in Paris during the fourteenth century. "Esmalta parisiana" is a descriptive term which is misleading because of its undue emphasis on Paris as the place where this type of enameling was practiced. Not much more need be added about its technical execution. The relief portions are filled repeatedly, fully up to the level of the surface. The luminosity of a color increases when it is applied thinly and repeatedly. Thick application carries with it the risk of the enamel becoming turbid; in this technique, especially, absolute transparency is essential. Dark hues are unsuitable for silver enameling because they offer too few light-dark variations. Light-to-medium blue, green, gray, and violet hues are particularly beautiful.

When enameling is used for modern industrial products on guilloched bases, advantage is also taken of the attraction of the light-dark effect of transparent colors on deeply engraved bases, and of the luster of cut metal, which lends reflections and fire to translucent enamel work. Punched and chased areas, too, can be enameled with this method. Such a base does not have the luminosity of bright-cut metal, but tonal modulation is produced by the different peaks and troughs.

Foils. It has already been pointed out that translucent enamels on metals of different colors yield different hues. This effect has been used in enameling techniques since the Renaissance: Gold- and silver foil is introduced between the base and the enamel. The use of small gold and silver shapes, called paillons, is also due to the desire to take advantage of the contrast in color and luster between different base metals.

The use of foils and paillons is described less for the sake of its artistic value than in the interest of complete coverage of the various enameling techniques.

The foil is cut between sheets of paper and glued with aqueous tragacanth solution to the surface to be enameled. It must adhere closely and not crease. To allow air and water vapor to escape from under the foil, little holes are punched in it with a fine needle. The foil is melted down at moderate heat in the furnace, and lightly dabbed with a brush while hot. For large surfaces, it is recommended to repeat the firing after the hot foil has been rubbed on with an engraver's burnisher. The fired-on foil is now covered with the desired color, and this in turn is fired.

Paillons are attached in the same way, except that these small pieces are not perforated like the foils.

Enamel en ronde bosse, used on small figures even in Antiquity, was revived in the fifteenth century. This covering of figures in the round, which was very popular during the Renaissance, presents no new technical features. The application of the enamel is a matter of great skill, and this kind of work is classed as artistry rather than art.

Some studios and masters of our own century deserve praise for having infused new life into all these ancient techniques. Other technological facilities available today have been used, and new means of expression found. As in many fields of craftsmanship, appreciation of the original character of ancient work has led to its revival, and evolved new forms from historical study and traditional application.

In addition to the modification, expansion, and merging of the old techniques, new possibilities were discovered, in which, as already mentioned, the utilization of firing plays a part unknown and technically impossible in the past.

Those familiar with the material and endowed with creative ability are not tied to any technique and are not dependent on recipes; they will find new solutions for new tasks and new experiments. The aim of the author is merely to encourage such an approach; to describe this or that new technical experiment does not lead any further along the path.

Fig. 5-60. *Champlevé plates (Four Apostles, Annunciation, Visitation, Birth of Christ, and Presentation in the Temple) from the portable altar (top of the mensa) by the Cologne master Eilbertus, about 1150–1160. The forceful pattern is typical of the cutting technique. The Eilbertus portable altar is part of the Guelph Treasure.*

Enamel painting

An exception, however, is the technique of enamel painting, which differs from enameling proper and deserves to be dealt with briefly.

It is mostly executed on a white-opaque enameled base. In contrast with the enameling techniques discussed, in which enamel paints are used, metal oxides stirred with turpentine and essential oil of petroleum on a porcelain palette serve as paints, which are applied in the manner of china painting. All that enamel painting has in common with enameling proper is the metal base on which a layer of enamel is fused, and firing of oxide paints on this; and if necessary covering with flux. Many limitations imposed on representation in enamel are avoided in this painting technique, which is used mainly for copying paintings in miniature, from the works of well-known masters down to the cheap colored picture postcard.

In this technique too, however, good work can be produced especially when restraint is practiced.

A special variation of enamel painting is Limoges painting, so called after its place of origin in France where it was developed and practiced during the fifteenth and sixteenth century.

Limoges painters use the grisaille manner on a dark base—black, blue, or brown. A thin coat of white underpaint is applied to the dark enameled base; firing turns it into a gray tone determined by the base; it is brightened through medium tones to white highlights by means of the required number of further applications. Finally, the work is covered with a soft flux, which should be chosen and applied to the dark ground with the greatest care.

In addition to much practice this technique demands excellent draftsmanship and a flair for painting. Its strength and refined effect lie in the restraint with which it is executed.

Setting

Goldsmiths in the Middle Ages had a relation to gems different from that of their present-day successors. They loved the colored stone, ground to a cabochon shape, which they set in a simple bezel, or in a wire coronet, fashioned after the bezel. They also set them in claws shaped like leaves, and in galleries, that is, in small architectural forms made of sheet metal and wire. Set in this way, the stone was a feature independent of the metal support. *Fig. 5-65* shows the effect of large stones in old settings. But even earlier, during the period of the Barbarian Invasions, colored gems were already treated as inserts and incrustations. Almandites were most commonly used, inlaid in rows of troughs or cells *(Fig. 5-49)*.

The settings of the earlier kind are the ones really appropriate to the goldsmith's technique in an older sense of the term. The stones are mounted above the base in little casings specially set for them in their variegated design, attractive decorations in their own right. Another way of setting stones developed from the incrustation technique of cellular inlay; it truly came into its own with the jewelry that became fashionable during the eighteenth century. The working technique of the jeweler, after all, established itself in sharp opposition to the intentions of the old goldsmiths and after violent economic struggles, in which the old goldsmith's craft largely succumbed. The jewelers set the stones, faceted to increase their light refraction, so that the light also had access from the back on an openwork base *(à jour)*. The French names still used for the various setting techniques clearly indicate their place of origin.

Small stones, ground round or angular, let into the metal support must fit very precisely in the hole drilled for them. A special tool with an oval face is used to cut or to adjust the bore to the shape and size of the stone. The fixing of the stones in the solid metal base, described below, demands as much skill, practice, and experience in the handling of the borers, tools, bezel pushers, and other setting tools as fitting itself, and because of the need for very delicate and highly accurate work, here, too, many specialized branches of setting have developed.

The tools

The work is either clamped in the setting vise or cemented onto a handy piece of wood. The jeweler's drill (see *Fig. 5-61*) serves for drilling with the most frequently used pointed drills and center bits, which the worker makes himself. Millers and drills can also be bought in tool shops. After they are drilled, the settings are cut with the same tools as engravings, with single-point tools, hollow and flat scorpers in various widths, and with a multiple tool for some work in silver. A very narrow single-point tool with straight sides is used for the finest cutting. The tool used most often, however, is the oval tool specially prepared for the work in hand. In addition to cutting implements, a number of blunt tools are required with which to force, rub, or push the stone into the setting or to fix it with beads. These include the grinder, filed to a point and hardened and resembling a nail, as well as pointed and blunt pushers and the creaser (see *Fig. 5-64*), which are filed, hardened, and fixed in a handle by the user himself. The use of the various beaders will be described below. These tools, too, are mounted with handles and are made of old needle-files or other round steels. They resemble a hollow perloir in that they have a hemispherical pit. To drive this pit into the flattened point of the beader, a matrix is necessary, which contains various grain sizes from very small to very large. The millegriffe tool is similar to the beader.

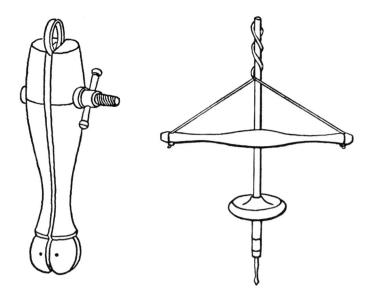

Fig. 5-61. Left: Hand vise, a tool for clamping rings and small trinkets, similar to the filing vise. Right: Jeweler's drill for boring and milling.

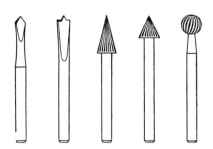

Fig. 5.62. Drills and milling cutters. From left to right: Common bit, center bit, acute-angled countersink, obtuse-angled countersink, spherical cutter (cherry).

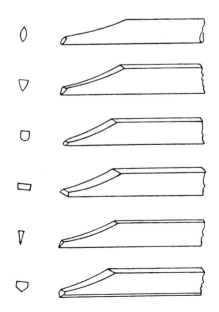

Fig. 5-63. From top to bottom: Oval tool, point tool, round tool, flat tool, knife tool, beveling tool.

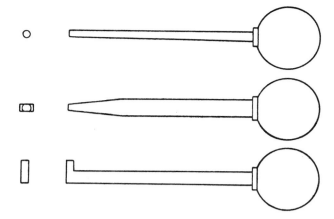

Fig. 5-64. From top to bottom: Beader, millegriffe iron, creaser.

Tools which are less important but make work easier are used for the handling of small stones. These tools include the set pin, a copper needle with recesses to press small stones home, and the dop, containing wax for moving the stones during work. Moistening with nitrobenzene considerably improves the efficiency of the drill.

To describe the numerous kinds of modern setting would encroach too much upon the field of industrial jewelry manufacture and the mass production of fashionable trinkets. Only the most important ones are briefly mentioned.

The old goldsmith's settings still in use are:
(a) the bezel setting,
(b) the scalloped setting, a simplified claw-, prong-, crab-, or leaf setting.

The bezel setting

The term is derived from the way the stone is set in a soldered strip, the bezel, in which the stone is precision-fitted. Making the bezel is the goldsmith's task. The setter adjusts the stone in position and presses the bezel over its girdle. This overlapping rim can be pressed on, lightly pushed with a punch, and finally trimmed with cutters.

The scalloped setting

This term is not used in this context to denote the mass-produced scalloped bezels, marketed by wholesalers for insertion into costume jewelry, although the terms scalloped bezel and mass production have almost become synonymous. The basic shape for a scalloped mount is the bezel, which is sawn out and filed in a kind of scalloped line; this produces a number of prongs (claws), which can be pushed over the stone, holding it in a circle. Making this is again the goldsmith's task. A scalloped setting of ornamental design is called a gallery. Ready-made galleries, too, can be obtained from metal merchants. The setter cuts the base on which the girdle of the stone rests on the inside of the claw ring, unless it had already been filed before the setting was assembled. When the stone is set, all the claws are pushed firmly over it with the creaser, one claw always being followed by its diametrical opposite in the ring, and trimmed with a flat tool.

Fig. 5-65. *Old goldsmith's settings of gems cut en cabochon. Part of a cross from the Fritzlar Cathedral treasure. The highly magnified photograph shows bezel settings of various kinds, combined with filigree work.*

Fig. 5-66. *A simple, basic rhythm breaks up the face of this fibula with set stones and soldered wire. Gold, fourth to fifth century A.D. Alemannic-Frankish, Heilbronn.*

Fig. 5-67. *Ring, gold, set with suspended white sapphire. Andreas Moritz, Würzburg.*

5-66

5-67

Incrustation settings

This is the name covering all those types of setting in which the stone is let into a bore in the metal base and fixed with the aid of tiny prongs—beads—raised with the cutter from the base. The true jewel settings belong to this class. There are many kinds of incrustation, largely determined by variation in arrangement of the stones for two-dimensional effect. What they have in common, technically, is that they require the highest precision, which demands a very practiced, sure, and steady hand, especially for the difficult recessing and raising of the beads. These little columns, raised from the base material next to the bore with an oval tool and cut to shape, are pressed over the girdle to hold the stone in position. The previously mentioned beader with its hemispherical hollow is used for pressing the raised bead into a round shape.

Channel mounting, too, is an incrustation setting; the stones in their settings form a row. *Pavé* settings are probably still familiar from the old garnet jewels. Their "paving" covers entire areas in parallel intersecting rows giving the impression of a fine sieve.

Since jewelry is very subject to the whims of fashion, setting, too, is affected by its changes. Unlike jewelers, whose work is usually aimed at making a superficial impact, contemporary goldsmiths seek even through their settings to regain contact with expressive designs of their ancient craft. An example of this is the new work shown in *Fig. 3-17*. These experiments, stimulated by artistic intentions and a new stylistic approach, are supported by the technical expertise of the setters, highly developed by specialization. Today it is an executive, purely technical activity, which is adapted and subject to the alien idea of form; its operations are sophisticated in the extreme, yet dependent on the finest manual flair and skill.

5-68

Fig. 5-68. *Large nose plug, Columbia. About 13·3 ins. (32cm) long,
6·2 ins. (15cm) high. Opus interasile with welded twisted wires. The
jewel is probably made of tumbaga, a gold-copper alloy popular because of
its low melting point, and its hardness which is superior to that of pure
gold.*

Fun in the Technological Age
and Pre-Columbian Technology

The confrontation of the oldest works of the goldsmith's art known to us with the latest works by a contemporary artist permits interesting observations. Comparisons force themselves upon us. To begin with, apparent similarities of form and technique, and later, much that is different, strike the eye.

Both the new and the museum pieces were made on the American continent: The new ones in the USA, and the old ones in Peru, Columbia, and Mexico. The former are the anonymous witnesses of an integrated civilization grown through centuries, the latter are the intellectual fun and games of modern artistic individuality. And it must be assumed that Calder was no less fascinated by the small ancient metal sculptures (which, because they are often sacrificial gifts, cannot be wholly regarded as jewels) than Picasso was by the wood carvings of the South Sea Islanders.

Alexander Calder became world famous through his mobiles (Sartre called them: ". . . strange structures of stalks, palm branches, disks, feathers, and petals.") and stabiles; in his life's work, jewelry (if indeed we can call his small pieces of metalwork this: For because of their strange proportions they are hardly suitable for wearing) plays only a minor role. But it is just as much fun as everything else this *homo ludens* touches. A consistent further development of Calder's wire sculptures is that, unlike the American Indian goldsmiths, he refuses to join any parts by melting processes and thus is satisfied with the simplest mechanical possibilities, wire bending and cold forging, conceding at most a rivet here and there. His large sculptures, too, are cold forged and riveted, never welded.

All this is deliberate reduction of a technique that has become all too clever, a preference for the primitive, the undifferentiated.

Where, then, does the undeniable strength of this metalwork reside? Not only its technique, but also its imagery is elementary. There is the symbolic bird, which Braque would have translated into metal. Boldly outlined forms of leaves are created from wire as if by accident, beaten out and cold forged. What looks like a Baroque glory, suggesting to the uncritical eye cast volutes *(Fig. 5-81)*, is, like the wavy band of a comb *(Fig. 5-80)*, and the scroll pattern of *Fig. 5-82* resembling a strange insect, the result of shrewd license: Wire will curl into scrolls when it is "tortured" like this.

Their technical development places the ancient American goldsmiths' works of the pre-Columbian era on a different level. In all the main areas of various techniques and styles (Columbian Andes, Peru and Bolivia, Mexico and Guatemala), all the possibilities of working gold (various casting methods, sheet-metalwork based on forging and embossing, also with matrices, soldering and welding, chasing, punching, and engraving) were already developed to fine arts. The solder the American Indian goldsmiths used was a mixture of copper salts and glue (see the notes by E. Treskow, page 204). Forge welding and alloying techniques were also mastered. In Columbia and Southern Central America tumbaga (a Malayan term) was particularly popular as a gold-copper alloy (low melting point, good hardness). The tools, however, were extremely simple, often made only of stone or bone, at best (in Peru and Bolivia) of bronze.

Special thanks for information and permission to reproduce illustrations in this chapter are due to Mr. Perls, Perls Galleries, New York, and Dr. Eisleb, Museum für Völkerkunde, Berlin-Dahlem.

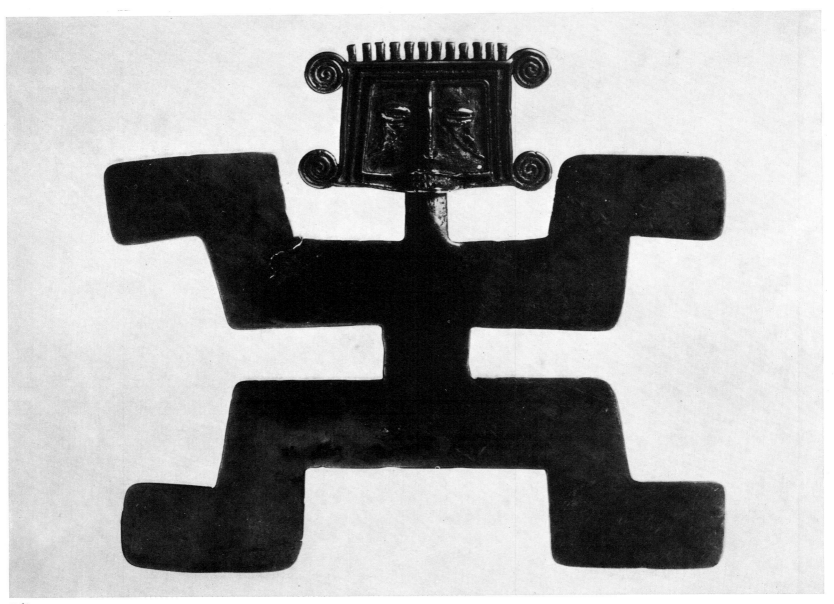

5-69

Fig. 5-69. *Gold pectoral, Columbia, presumably tumbaga amulet. The technique poses a riddle: Whereas the head is obviously cast, the broad extremities, judging by their surface and thickness, seem to have been beaten out afterwards.*

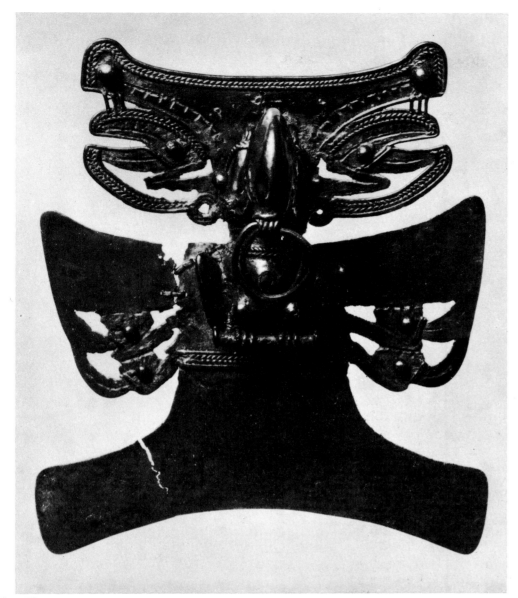

5-70

5-71

Figs. 5-70 and 5-71. Soldering, welding, and casting were techniques with which American Indian goldsmiths were quite familiar. Since they combined the most varied techniques in one and the same piece they produced strange effects, which were difficult to interpret. A porous, unfined surface is just as likely to be the result of the casting as of subsequent welding. On the left: Pectoral. On the right: Ritual figure offering, designed to be dropped into lakes or ponds. Gold alloy, Columbia, age indeterminate, probably immediate pre-conquest period.

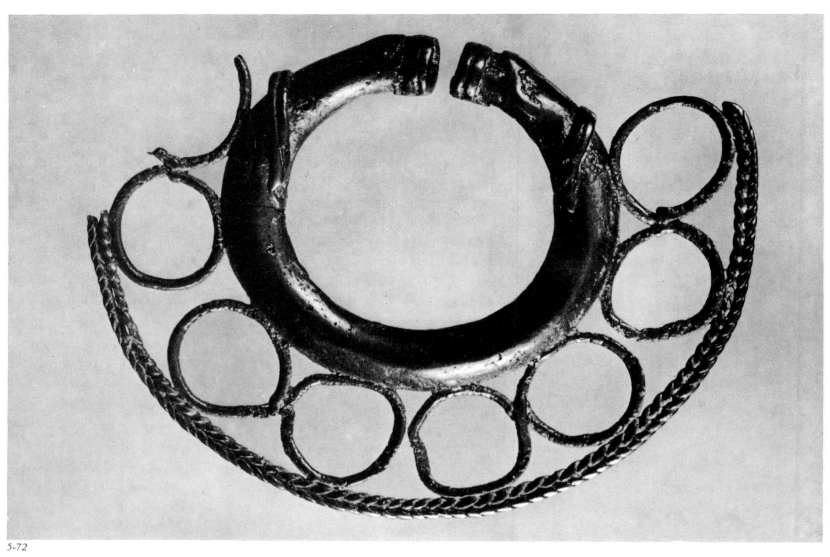

5-72

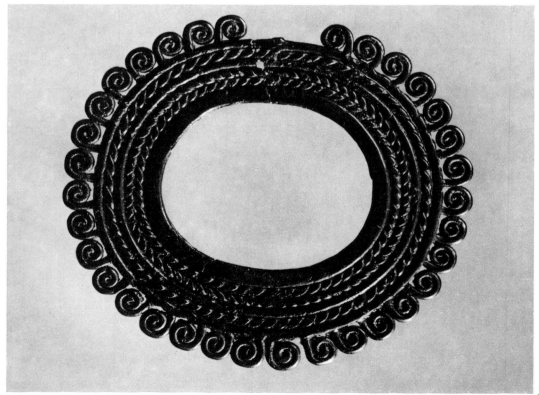

5-73

5-74

Figs. 5-72 and 5-73. Columbian nose ornament in two different designs: Whereas the solid ring (Fig. 5-72) is without doubt cast, the double loops and the outer ring with its plaited pattern are more likely to have been soldered. The working methods of the object shown in Fig. 5-73 can be determined with greater certainty. The outer volutes show that the casting was finished with a chisel.

Fig. 5-74. Four different ornamental elements, all embossed thin sheet gold; the variety of arrangement results in a contrasty, very three-dimensional effect: Large, smooth-beaten bossy squares contrast with richly embossed masks and small gold beads. Peru, about 1000 A.D.

5-75

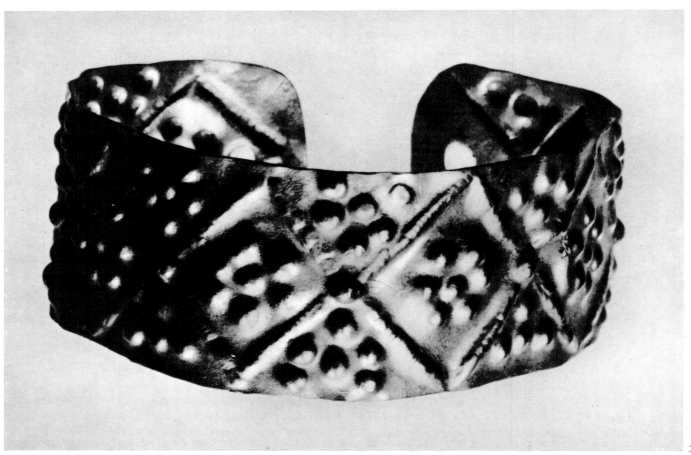

5-76

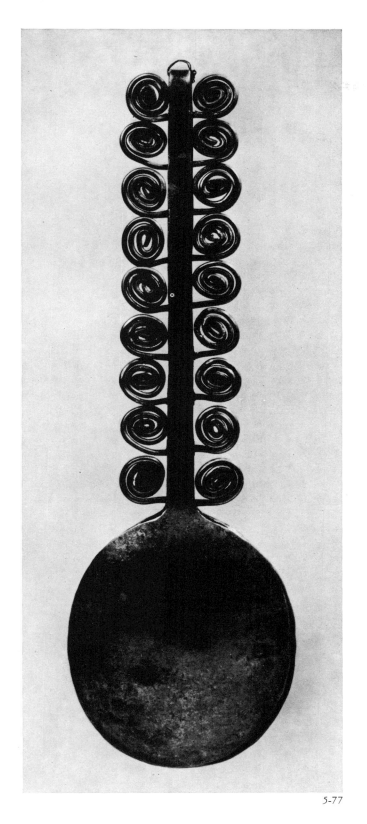

5-77

5-78

Fig. 5-75. Eagle. Dress ornament (to be sewn on), Peru, about 700–1000 A.D. Inner pattern punched with large ball punches, the linear parts chased with tracers.

Fig. 5-76. Gold bracelet, Peru, chased with the same technique. The globular rosettes and their lozenge-shaped framers are embossed from the back (repoussé). Magnification about one-third. As it is open, it yields to pressure to fit the wearer's arm.

Fig. 5-77. Beard plucker, probably not for practical use. Beaten sheet gold, with bent wire spirals. Peru, immediate pre-conquest period.

Fig. 5-78. Ear pendant (?), Mexico. Gold or tumbaga. Vulture's head and centerpiece cast, pattern of the mask chiseled. The ring-shaped links prove that soldering and welding were well mastered. Almost natural size.

231

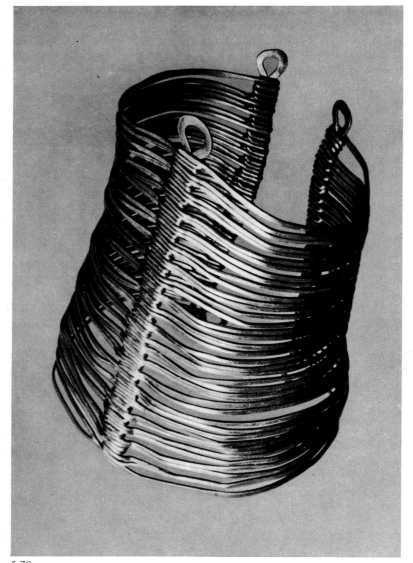

5-79

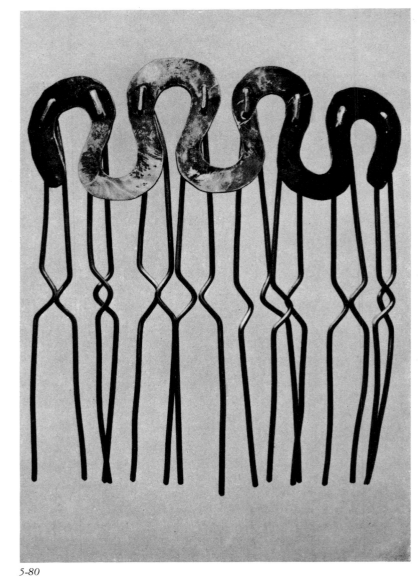

5-80

Figs. 5-79–5-87 show jewelry by Alexander Calder.

Fig. 5-79. "Fighting" bracelet (cuff), brass wires beaten flat. Joined by bending and beating; no solder is used anywhere.

Fig. 5-80. Decorative comb, round and beaten-out silver wire. Here too, the round wires are threaded and beaten, without any soldered joints.

Fig. 5-81. The broad collar is based on the principle of uniform structure: Wire is beaten flat and bent into spirals and thus connected, without any soldering. About three-quarters natural size.

5-81

233

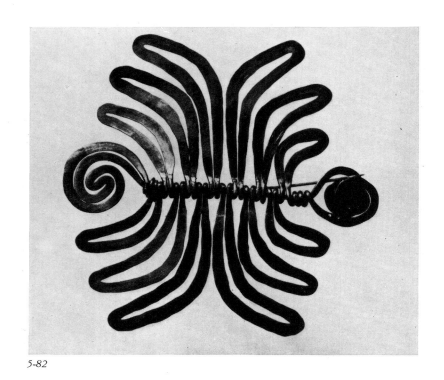

Fig. 5-82. Brooch, silver wire, bent into spirals and beaten into flat volutes and wings. About half natural size.

Fig. 5-83. Brooch, flat beaten silver wire, bent into spirals. Much reduced.

Figs. 5-84 and 5-85. The brooch in Fig. 5-84, like Calder's mobile and stabile designs, also derives its appeal from the strong and unusual silhouette effect. About natural size. Technically the artist confines himself to the possibilities of connecting the basic material (here, silver wire). Beyond this he might just accept the rivet (Fig. 5-85).

5-82

5-83

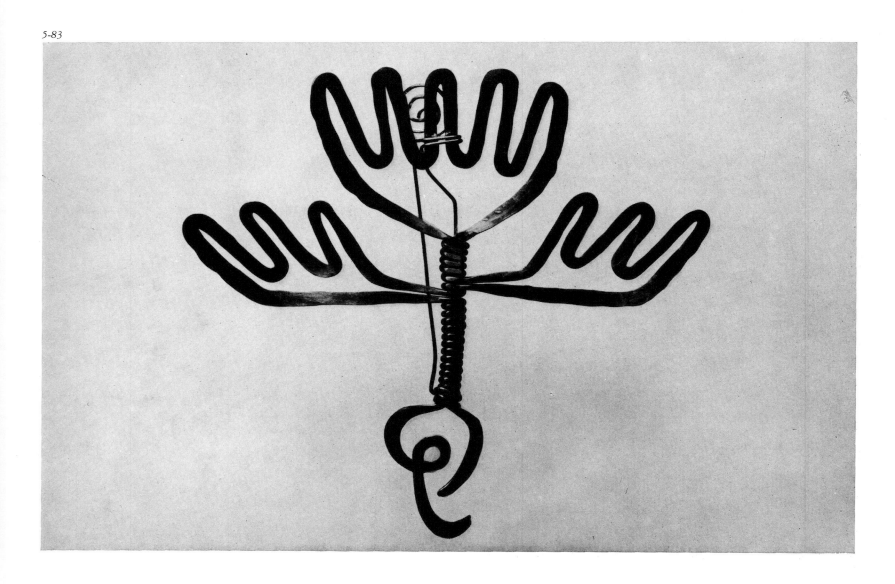

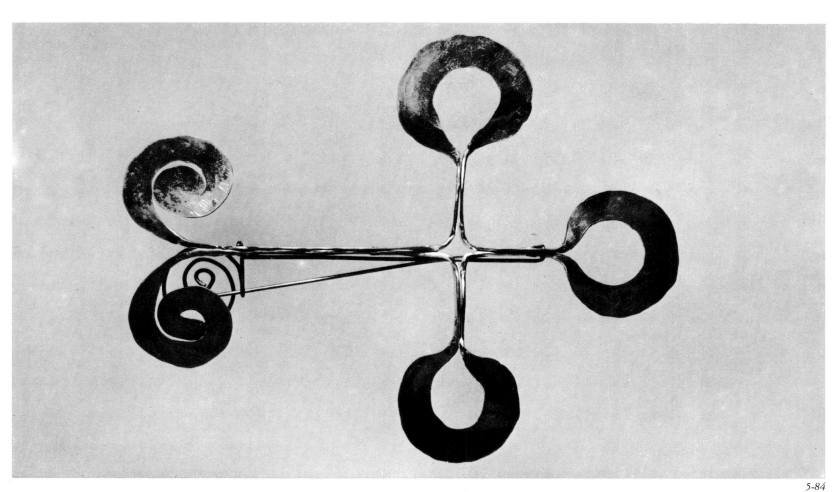

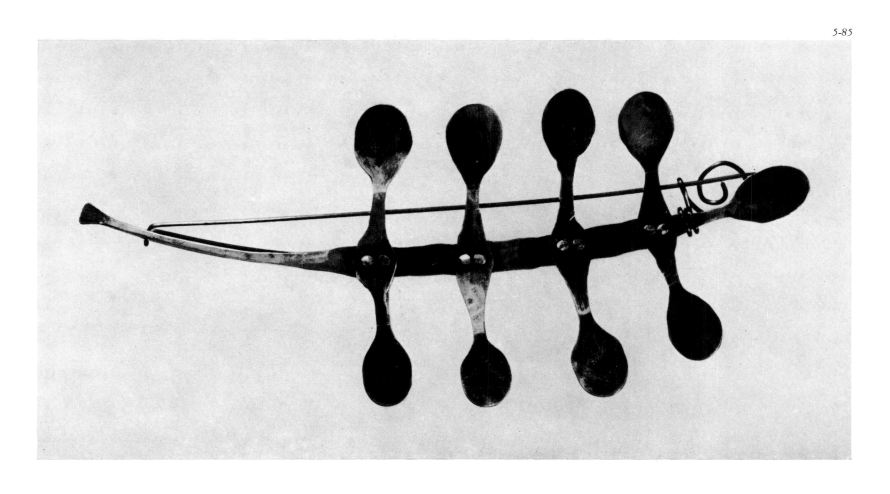

5-86

5-87

Fig. 5-86. *Broad collar, silver. As in all his jewelry, the artist has confined himself to essentials both in formal design and in technique: Lanceolate leaves, beaten out of thick wire without any further working, form a wreath of unusual dimensions. About one-third natural size.*

Fig. 5-87. *Here, too, unusual dimensions. A bracelet, again technically confined to bent wires and beaten leaf shapes. About half natural size.*

6. Metallic Raw Materials and Expendable Materials

by Dr. Werner Plate

General Properties of Metals

Metals are chemical elements. Of the one hundred elements (approximately) or basic substances known to us, they form the vast majority. The most outstanding characteristic in which they differ from the nonmetals (such as sulfur, oxygen, phosphorus, etc.) is that they are efficient conductors of electricity and heat. It is true that electroplating baths, too, conduct electric current; but whereas here the passage of current involves material transfer, which leads to the deposition of metallic films, conduction in metals is not connected with any transport of material. Metals are therefore called first-class conductors, electroplating baths second-class conductors.

Only a few of the large number of metals are suitable as raw materials for metalwork. Knowledge of their properties is absolutely essential if any forming is intended. The forming process, however, is applied mainly to alloys, not so much to the pure metals. Alloys are mixtures obtained when two or more metals are melted together; the melt is allowed to solidify.

The branch of applied science concerned with the internal structure of such alloys is called metallography. Its methods of investigation have shown that the smallest particles (atoms) in a piece of metal or alloy are not scattered at random, but arranged in so-called crystal lattices according to definite structural plans. The simplest of such crystal lattices is a cube whose corners are occupied by the individual atoms. Innumerable such cubes joined together result in a visible piece of metal. When an alloy is produced, it is possible that an atom of one metal in the crystal lattice is replaced by one of another metal, or that the lattice of one metal additionally accepts atoms of the other metal. In both cases, so-called mixed crystals (solid solutions) are formed. Sometimes, however, the two constituents of an alloy do not affect each other, when all that happens during solidification is the formation of fine-grained mixtures of the two metals. But a third case is much more frequent: One metal is capable of dissolving only a certain quantity of the other, or vice versa. This is called incomplete or partial solubility of the two components in the solid state. Examples of the first case are alloys of silver and gold, and of the third case those of silver and copper.

The concept of the chemical compound originated in inorganic chemistry: Two elements, such as sodium and chlorine, form a new substance, cooking salt ($NaCl$), combining at definite ratios of weight. This substance is something entirely new, in no way resembling the corrosive alkaline metal sodium and the poison gas chlorine.

Metals, too, form compounds; they are called intermetallic compounds. They are typical in that the atoms of the components combine to form a different crystal lattice at certain weight ratios and tempera-

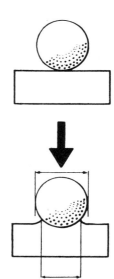

Fig. 6-1. Brinell test: The hardness of the test piece is determined from test load, sphere diameter, and sphere impression (dimensional arrows).

tures. This new arrangement usually leads to strains and stresses, hardening and embrittlement, which have a very adverse effect on the working of the metal compounds.

We distinguish between chemical and physical properties of metals and their alloys. The chemical properties, such as behavior with acids, oxidation, corrosion, etc. will be discussed later, along with the various individual metals, but a few general remarks about the physical properties are appropriate at this stage. In particular the mechanical and thermal characteristics must be mentioned.

The formability of metallic raw materials is expressed in various terms for their mechanical properties, such as hardness, strength, ductility, brittleness, toughness, elasticity, etc.

Hardness is the resistance a body offers to the penetration of another body. In hardness testing, materials are used for indentation which are much harder than the work under test. The Brinell Hardness is calculated from the impression a hardened steel sphere produces in the surface of the test piece at a certain pressure (load). In Vickers Hardness tests, the indenting bodies consist of regular, square diamond pyramids, which leave a square impression after the test.

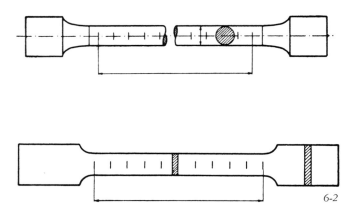

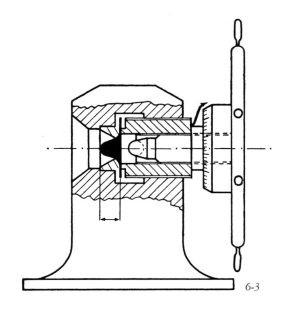

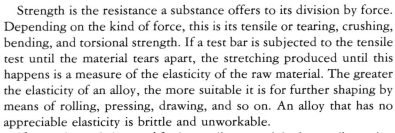

6-2

6-3

Fig. 6-2. Test rods for tensile strength tests.

Fig. 6-3. Erichsen depth gauge. The test piece is colored black.

Strength is the resistance a substance offers to its division by force. Depending on the kind of force, this is its tensile or tearing, crushing, bending, and torsional strength. If a test bar is subjected to the tensile test until the material tears apart, the stretching produced until this happens is a measure of the elasticity of the raw material. The greater the elasticity of an alloy, the more suitable it is for further shaping by means of rolling, pressing, drawing, and so on. An alloy that has no appreciable elasticity is brittle and unworkable.

If a metal sample is tested for its tensile strength in the tensile-testing machine, it will usually be found that the test bar stretches according to the load it is subjected to, but that it contracts again as soon as the load is removed. This kind of springiness of a raw material is called its elasticity. If, however, the load is further increased, there comes a point during stretching when the limit of elasticity is exceeded. The test bar begins to stretch out of all proportion or, as the technical term has it, to yield. The stretch beyond the limit of elasticity is permanent. Any further increase in the tensile load produces fracture.

Since the formability of a sheet, for example, can be determined only vaguely because of the difficulty of applying an even load, the so-called cupping test is more widely used in practice. The sheet is cut according to certain dimensions and mounted in the Erichsen cupping tester between an annular holder and a matrix. It is then cupped with a hemispherically-rounded stamp until fracture occurs. The depth of the depression is a measure of the formability of the raw material. Naturally, knowledge of the elasticity of a material is particularly important to the worker, especially if he has to make complicated hollow shapes.

The mechanical properties of metals and alloys are altered by cold working and heat treatment. As the degree of cold working increases, the material becomes harder and more brittle. This is brought about by various operations, such as rolling, drawing, plastic deformation during bending, and so on. To understand these changes in properties, one must know that in metals the transition from the molten to the solid state always involves the formation of crystals. Since during solidification all these crystals mutually interfere with their growth, we do not obtain those beautiful geometrical forms we know from the world of gems, but a conglomeration of irregularly shaped crystal "cripples" called crystallites or grains. These are sometimes recogniz-

able with the naked eye, but usually their boundaries can be seen only under the metallographic microscope after the surface of the specimen has been etched.

Because of its inhomogeneity, the cast structure is unsuitable for working. It is therefore broken up by noncutting shaping: Rolling, hammer forging, embossing, etc. During rolling, the fragments of the crystallites stretch in the direction of rolling; they interlock with one another. The structure becomes hard, and is also unsuitable for working because of its internal stresses and strains. The metal to be worked is now annealed. This gives the atoms the necessary kinetic energy to enable them to arrange themselves in new crystal lattices and therefore new grains. The result is the working structure proper, the recrystallization structure. It is homogeneous, strain-free, and very fine-grained. If annealing is prolonged or the annealing temperature too high, however, the grains coalesce into coarse structures measuring up to ⅖in. (10mm) across; the structure becomes coarsely crystalline and unsuitable for working because of its tendency to crack along the grain boundaries.

The refinement of the raw material by mechanical and thermal deformation is particularly important. Operating conditions often vary considerably with the various alloys and uses. It is therefore not possible to give generally valid data concerning working methods, or the number of intermediate annealings required.

The high degree of workability (plasticity) of the metals and their alloys is an outstanding characteristic that distinguishes them from the other elements. Of the other physical properties of metals, heat conductivity, electrical conductivity, heat expansion, etc. are of less interest here. However, a few physical data must nevertheless be mentioned, because they are particularly important in the characterization of the various metallic raw materials: These are specific gravity, and melting and boiling points.

The specific gravity of a substance is the ratio of its weight to that of an equal volume of water (at 4°C). Since 1cc water weighs 1g, we can also say that the specific gravity is the weight of 1cc of a substance. We therefore have the following simple relationship: Specific gravity × Volume in cubic centimeters = Total weight. In pure metals, the values vary slightly depending on the working. The position of the melting points (solidification points) of the pure metals is sharply defined. They are the points where the vibration of the atoms of the solid metals is sufficiently increased by the heat supplied to break the crystal lattices. The metal melts. The atoms now move more freely. If heating is further increased, the individual atoms in the melt acquire so much kinetic energy that they eventually overcome the surface tension of the liquid metal and shoot into space. The metal evaporates.

In alloys, melting and solidification points usually do not coincide. When a molten alloy is allowed to cool, a point is reached where the metal begins to solidify. First, crystals of a certain composition form in the melt; in contrast with pure metals, the entire substance does not solidify at once. This point of incipient solidification, clearly evident in a leveling-out of the cooling curve, is called the liquidus of the alloy. During further cooling the crystal deposits increase, until a second point is reached, at which the alloy has become completely solid. This temperature point is called the solidus. In some alloys, the temperature difference between liquidus and solidus, the melting range, is very considerable and can be several hundred degrees Centigrade.

Finally in this context, the extremely important fact must be mentioned that an alloy can have a melting point that is lower than that of any of its constituents. Thus an alloy of 75% gold and 25% copper (i.e. 18 carat red gold) begins to melt as low as 883°C, whereas the melting point of gold is 1063°C and that of copper 1083°C. The extent of the melting range, the position of the solidus and of the liquidus depend on the percentage proportions of the components of an alloy.

The Precious Metals

There are altogether eight precious metals: Gold, silver, and the six platinum metals platinum, iridium, osmium, palladium, ruthenium, and rhodium. Their special distinction from the other metals is due to their high chemical constancy. The eight elements exhibit a characteristic inertia to reactions, so that they enter into chemical compounds only with difficulty.

Man has known gold and silver for thousands of years. Gold ornaments have been found that were made 7000 years ago, and the oldest coins found were struck during the second millenium B.C. The technological use of precious metals, on the other hand, is very recent. The possibility of obtaining these metals at great purity, and their resistance to any kind of corrosion, makes them particularly suitable for physical measurements. It is well known that the standard measure and the standard weight, kept in Paris, consist of a platinum-iridium alloy. The precious metals play a special role particularly in electrical engineering and in the chemical industry. In the form of alloys, electro- or mechanical plating (rolled gold), they increasingly replace or protect the base metal as raw material. In medicine and dentistry, the precious metals have become largely indispensable. It must also be pointed out that the high value accorded to the precious metals has not only led to their use for coins; right up to the present time they are the basis of most currency systems.

Gold

Faith in the value of gold has survived all the quarrels and frictions in the history of mankind, the continual fluctuations of values, and all the vicissitudes of time. Its general esteem is based on the very assumption that everybody else considers it valuable.

Gold is man's oldest decorative metal. Since because of its precious character it occurs mainly in the pure state—although never completely pure, but contaminated with copper, silver, platinum metals, etc.—it attracts attention on account of its yellow color. Furthermore, its extraction requires only a little skill. We distinguish between the free gold in a primary field, and placer or river gold in secondary deposits, for instance in river sands, deposits of pebbles, or in the detritus of auriferous rocks.

South Africa produces 71–72% of the world's production of gold (in 1961, 1079 tons excluding the USSR). In the quartz deposits of the Transvaal (Witwatersrand near Johannesburg) the gold is extracted from rock seams of 6–30 ft (2–10m) thickness, known as reefs. The USSR, Canada, USA, Australia, Ghana, and Rhodesia are next in the quantity of gold produced. The world's greatest hoard of gold is heavily guarded in Fort Knox, a fortress in the forests of Kentucky, USA.

Many river sands contain gold: The Rhine was famous for its richness in gold (The Hoard of the Nibelungs). The rivers washed the gold into the oceans. Although each cubic meter of sea water contains only about 0.01 mg of gold, the total content of the oceans is many millions of tons.

The oldest method of gold extraction is washing, a purely mechanical separation of gold from sand. Today, manual work has been replaced by machines. The auriferous ores are subjected to the process of amalgamation, in which they are kneaded with mercury, which dissolves most of the gold from them. The residual ores are then treated with sodium cyanide (cyaniding); the gold is dissolved, forming a complex salt, and precipitated from the solution with zinc shavings. The crude gold is now further refined by means of electrolysis.

Gold is the most ductile of all metals. Some gold leaf is only 0.1μm thick (1μm = 0.00004 ins. or 0.001mm). 0.035 in. (1g) gold can be drawn into a wire 1.2 miles (2km) long. Its specific gravity is 19.3, its melting point 1063°C, its boiling point 2710°C. It is not attacked even by hot lyes and acids, and is soluble only in aqua regia (3 parts hydrochloric acid + 1 part nitric acid). Since gold is very soft, it is usually alloyed with copper or silver. Pure gold is called 24 carat. The name carat is derived from the Latin for the carob tree, *Ceratonia siliqua*. The seed of this tree weighs about 0.007 oz (0.2g) and was used as a unit of weight by Arab gold merchants.

Because of its corrosion resistance, gold is used not only for jewelry, but also for surface finishing. Base metals are protected by means of electroplating, fire gilding, only rarely used today, and mechanical plating (rolled gold).

Gold alloys

For the manufacture of jewelry, gold alloys of the most varied compositions are used. It is this composition which determines the properties of the raw material, its mechanical qualities, and its color. Although the goldsmith, with the benefit of many centuries' experience to fall back on, knows how to handle these alloys, processes were investigated and explained by modern metallographers within the last few decades for which there had previously been no explanation.

Faults of gold alloys

When industrial gold alloys are made into sheets or wires, faults often occur which make further working impossible. To avoid disappointment, therefore, it is important to the goldsmith to become familiar with the causes of such faults. The following are the main reasons why a casting becomes unsuitable for further forming treatment.

Even wrong pouring into the mold can produce pores (cavities) in the casting. If, for instance, a melt is poured from the crucible high above the mold, particularly if the mold is standing upright, the long jet of melt has ample opportunity to capture air mechanically. This air enters the mold. As the pouring progresses, it is driven into the marginal zones of the casting, where it becomes trapped because the rapid solidification in this zone prevents its complete escape. This often produces large bubbles in the entire cross section, but particularly in the marginal zones. They frequently become evident only during shearing off. Bubble formation is prevented if the pouring ladle is held directly over the mold, which should be tilted, heated, and greased at the sprue.

Another kind of cavity, the pipe, is caused by the fact that all alloys are subject to a loss of volume as they pass from the liquid into the solid state. If the outer zones of the casting are already solidified, contraction of the solidifying core necessarily produces such cavities.

Even small additions of other metals can make the gold alloys so brittle that they crack and become useless even during rolling. This applies especially to the addition of bismuth, lead, and tellurium. If gold alloys are made of scrap and of old material, there is a danger that lead will enter the material from soft-soldered pieces. An admixture of as little as 0.05% lead, however, makes further working of the alloy impossible.

Industrial gold alloys usually contain, in addition to silver, base metals, mainly copper and often zinc, cadmium, and nickel as well. The alloy thereby loses the resistance to oxygen characteristic of pure gold. At high temperatures, the base metals in the alloy form oxides with the atmospheric oxygen. These are largely soluble in the melt, but when the alloy solidifies they separate out as solid, brittle parts in the material. Especially when the oxide particles are not regularly distributed in the raw material, but form lines, objectionable weaknesses occur in the alloy, along which it cracks during rolling, or which produces scaly fractures in the sheet. The oxides are particularly hard. If the particles are directly on the surface, the work cannot be polished, because they remain proud of the polished surface; during further treatment they break out, leaving comma-shaped holes. Naturally, special difficulties arise in engraving and guilloching.

Similar difficulties can be caused by other foreign inclusions. Fine emery grains or material from poor-quality crucibles, too, can freeze into a solidifying casting as separate particles. Only during surface treatment will they become evident—and a nuisance.

Finally, there are faults directly connected with the special composition of the alloy, and not caused by any foreign inclusions. They can easily be avoided if the material is correctly treated. Thus the shanks of rings made of alloys of low gold content suddenly fracture. A typical feature is that the fracture faces become mutually displaced. The reason for this must be sought in the fact that the individual components had previously undergone different degrees of deformation. This sets up internal stresses, to which are added the corrosive effect of perspiration and of the atmosphere while the ring is worn, and leads to the eventual fracture. It is almost always enough to heat such objects to 250°C for some time (½–1 hour) to relieve the internal stress.

Another problem occurs in particular with alloys of a high gold content. Work of 18 carat gold often exhibits cracks when it is processed after the annealing stage; during rolling they widen to zigzag fractures. With further mechanical stress, deep cracks form through the whole sheet. As a rule this phenomenon is observed in red gold, in other words, in alloys free from or poor in silver, when the material is only lightly rolled before it is annealed. But if the work is rolled down to at least 50% before it is annealed, no cracks will form. In practice, therefore, the rule is observed that 18 carat red gold alloys should be annealed only after they have been rolled sufficiently for small cracks to appear along the edges because of overstress. The metallographic investigation of the alloy shows that, when a piece that has been only lightly worked is annealed, very large grains will form. This pronounced grain growth leads after further processing to cracking along the grain boundaries. The same brittleness can also be seen in sheet metal only lightly worked before it is annealed. But if the metal is heavily worked and then annealed, crystal grains will form which are so fine as to be almost invisible. Such material is obviously perfect to work.

Color gold alloys

There are two ways of determining the color of gold alloys. Either an alloy is melted which as a whole already has the desired hue, or the hue is produced on an existing gold alloy by suitable surface treatment.

Of all the metals only two, gold and copper, are really colored. Small quantities of other metals quickly deprive gold of its saturated yellow color. The addition of silver lightens the yellow, the addition of copper reddens it. About 10% palladium or nickel is enough to color the gold almost white. Most hues within the realm of possibility are obtained with the gold–silver–copper system. Goldsmiths have been familiar with these alloys from time immemorial, and their production raises few difficulties.

Color gold alloys whose properties are firmly established are tabulated below with their physical data. Obviously it is always difficult to determine the colors, since the more delicate differences in hue depend, after all, very much on the personal ability to differentiate, and language cannot express such fine nuances.

The transitions between alloy colors of both tables are continuous. The alloys are melted in a graphite crucible, which is heated to about 1100°C; first the copper is introduced in the form of a little block or wire, then the silver is added in granulated form, and lastly the gold in sheet form. The whole is covered with charcoal.

It is important to chill thick pieces of 18 and 14 carat gold alloys in methylated spirit as the red heat disappears. As they cool slowly, the mixed crystals of gold and copper decompose below 370°C to form the two compounds $AuCu_3$ and $AuCu$, which are both very brittle and render the raw material hard and unworkable.

For the production of green gold alloys, we depend on the addition of cadmium. The hues of cadmium-free compositions usually have a noticeable tendency towards yellow.

Since the boiling point of cadmium is as low as 770°C, losses owing to evaporation must be avoided as the alloy is prepared.

Many of the low-carat gold alloys are produced with the addition of brass, which means that these alloys contain not only copper and silver, but also zinc. Small amounts of zinc result in a definite lightening of the color. Addition of zinc to yellow gold alloys produces pale gold.

Attempts have also been made to obtain blue gold alloys. After hopes had at first been vainly based on iron-containing gold alloys, a blue, brightly shining substance was produced in the gold–indium alloy ($AuIn_2$) which, however, was very brittle and therefore unworkable. The so-called amethyst gold, which appeared on the market in 1948, had to be withdrawn only a year later because of its unworkability and rock-like character. It was the beautifully violet compound Al_2Au, corresponding to a pure gold content of about 785/1000. In spite of this considerable proportion of gold, the $21 \cdot 5\%$ aluminum predominates quantitatively, which makes the alloy much baser than one would expect from the number of carats.

For cheaper jewelry, manufacture in special colored gold would be too expensive. Here the second method, that of surface coloring, is preferred. This can be done with electroplating. Today, we know a large number of colored gold baths with which the most varied hues between red and green can be produced. Very attractive effects can often be achieved by a succession of parcel gildings in various colors.

A very simple method of yellow coloring is hot pickling. This consists in the dissolution of the ugly brown cuprous oxide and the black cupric oxide formed on the surface during the various annealing procedures and the sulfides of copper and silver (both black) by means of a pickle composed of a mixture either of equal parts of concentrated, chlorine-free nitric acid, and distilled water, or of equal parts of nitric acid, sulfuric acid, and water. Silver and copper, too, are dissolved by these pickles, the copper first. Treatment is continued in the hot pickle until the hue of pure gold is obtained. Alloys consisting of gold and copper only are hot pickled in a 1:1 dilution of sulfuric acid.

There are only three metals whose addition can suppress the yellow body color of gold and produce white, platinum-like working metals: Palladium, nickel, and manganese: The last-named has the least coloring power and is therefore only rarely used as an admixture.

White gold with nickel (Ni) and palladium (Pd) was first developed in the laboratory at the turn of the century, to save expensive platinum.

Palladium white gold today is available in all purities from 333/1000; its workability is perfect. As little as 160/1000 Pd produces a radiantly white alloy. 140/1000 Ni is completely adequate for a perfect white gold; whiteness reaches it maximum at 160–170/1000 Ni.

A comparison between palladium white gold and nickel white gold reveals that the former, although more expensive and requiring higher melting temperatures, is considerably softer, more ductile, pliable, and corrosion-resistant than the baser white gold with nickel. The main advantage is that palladium white gold does not scale during annealing, nor does it acquire tempering colors, so that its radiant white color is fully preserved.

The tables of alloys I–IV were first published in the *Mitteilungen des Forschungs-Instituts Gmünd (Information Bulletin of the Research Institute, Gmünd)* 6th year, No. 1, 1932.

I. Yellow gold alloys

Gold	Silver	Copper	Liquidus (°C)	Color
750	145	105		yellow
750	125	125	905	bright-yellow
750	83	167	893	reddish-yellow
585	249	166	857	bright-yellow
585	207	208	845	yellow
585	166	249	853	dark-yellow
585	138	277	867	orange-yellow
585	125	290		dark-yellow
585	104	311	885	reddish-yellow
333	667		1030	pale-brass-yellow
333	445	222	790	pale-yellow
333	333	334	823	bright-yellow
333	267	400	856	straw-yellow
333	167	500	904	yellow
333	95	572	926	orange-yellow

II. Red gold alloys

Gold	Silver	Copper	Liquidus (°C)	Color
750	104	146		red
750	36	214	902	orange-red
750		250	885	intense red
585	82	333		red
585	59	356	907	orange-red
585	42	373		very red
585		415	922	intense red
333		667		intense red

III. Green gold alloys

Gold	Silver	Copper	Cadmium	Liquidus (°C)	Color
750	250			1038	pale-yellow-green
750	214	36		991	bright-yellow-green
750	167	83		968	greenish-yellow
750	165		85		green
750	125		125		green
750	115	95	40		green
585	356	59		903	bright-green
333	534	133		866	pale-green

IV. Pale gold

Gold	Silver	Copper	Zinc
585	224	141	50
333	425	202	40
333	303	304	60

Fig. 6-4. Goldsmith's blowpipe.

Gold solders

Metals can be joined in two different ways: By welding, and by soldering. Welding is the direct connection of workpieces in the molten, liquid, or high-temperature plastic state under pressure or impact, that is, without metallic bonds, whereas soldering is the joining or build-up of heated, but solid, metals or alloys by the melting of metallic adhesives called solders. Perfect soldering is possible only if the constituents of the solder diffuse into the metal or the alloy, in other words, if they dissolve in it. Soldering, therefore, means the establishment of a more or less distinct layer of an alloy. The connection therefore is not based on pure adhesive force. A solder is neither a cement nor a glue.

The ability to dissolve the metals or alloys to be soldered and to form a layer of alloy with them is therefore the first requirement all the solders have to meet. Secondly, of course, the solder must have mechanical properties that make its technical use possible; it must penetrate well, flow easily into the joint, and be noncorrosive. Thirdly, it is obvious that the melting point of the solder must be lower than that of the alloy to be soldered. Solders whose upper melting point (liquidus) is about 50°C below the lower melting point (solidus) of the alloy are called hard. In medium solders this temperature difference is greater, and work with them therefore easier. Solders of very low melting point are called easy. Although these are very safe as regards the scorching of the work metal, they present the danger of flowing during future treatment of the work and are therefore used only for repairs. Medium solders serve mainly for resoldering. It is therefore generally necessary for the liquidus of the solder to be at least 50°C lower than the solidus of the alloy to be soldered. When the solder is completely liquid, there is still a latitude of 50°C before the work itself begins to melt. Soft solders become liquid below 400°C. They are usually based on lead and tin, with a solidus at 183°C, so that they can be applied with a soldering iron. The hard solders (spelter solders) are mostly silver solders, whose melting points range between 650 and 930°C, and certain brass solders.

Whereas the conditions listed here apply to all solders, gold solders must meet two additional requirements. They must be of the same fineness as the work, and their color must approximate that of the work as closely as possible. Gold solders are usually gold–silver–copper alloys with additives, particularly to low-carat compositions, that lower the melting point; the usual choice is zinc and cadmium. With 14 carat gold alloys, the maximum limit of these metallic additives is 6%, and with 20 carat alloys 20%.

It is not possible in practice to deduce from the data for the solidus and liquidus the all-important correct soldering temperature at which the solder rapidly penetrates the joint. In the American literature, the term "free flowing temperature" has therefore been adopted. This is the temperature the work must reach so that the solder flows freely on it. The position of the free flowing temperatures varies considerably within the melting range of the many solders: Naturally it is always above the solidus of the solder, but usually not very much; sometimes it is near the liquidus, rarely above it. The free flowing temperature for the various solders is experimentally determined in the laboratories; it cannot be calculated.

In the pure gold–silver–copper alloys for 750/1000 gold, it is found that the location of the solidus (the beginning of melting) moves with the silver:copper ratio. No appreciable change, however, is found initially with increasing silver and decreasing copper content. But from 150/1000 silver and 100/1000 copper upwards, the solidus rises considerably if the silver:copper ratio continues to move in favor of silver. This means that alloys whose solidus has thus been raised can be soldered with gold solders of the same number of carats, whose silver–copper content is varied in favor of copper. Solders that contain no other metals than the work to be soldered, yet have the same gold content, are matching solders. These are available also for 585/1000 and 333/1000 gold. The only important point is that the silver:copper ratio does not determine a solidus of the alloy to be soldered that lies near the absolute minimum. Here, of course, the beginning of melting could no longer be anticipated by a matching solder. This applies, for instance, to 750/1000 gold, if the work contains 250–125/1000 copper. With the lower-carat gold alloys, too, melting ranges are found for which matching solders cannot be produced.

Matching solders are particularly useful. Although their color differs from that of the alloy of the work, their composition specially favors alloy formation and close integration of solder and the metal of the work. This in turn renders the joint particularly resistant to mechanical stress. Intimate diffusion is also helped by the closer proximity of the melting points of work and solder. Nonmatching solders, on the other hand, may cause corrosion.

Such alloy formation, incidentally, requires not only a certain temperature, but also a certain time. It is wrong to turn off the supply of heat as soon as the solder just begins to flow. Letting it flow (flash) for a few more seconds assists the diffusion of the two alloys.

If, for reasons of the melting point position or of different colors, matching solders cannot be used, zinc and cadmium are added to the alloy. This not only lowers the melting point of the solder at will, but also changes its color characteristically. Whereas yellow and green gold alloys merely become paler in color, the red gold alloys show an appreciable shift towards yellow.

Soldering is a very ancient working method. The practice of hard soldering of gold with gold was established as early as the third millenium B.C. in Sumeria and in Central and Southern Babylon. The Egyptians soldered with alum and flux around 2000 B.C. The ancient Greeks and Romans used a highly developed soldering technique. During the first century A.D., perfect soldering was practiced in Central and Northern Europe.

Gold alloys are soldered with material of the same number of carats (check solders) so that the fineness regulations are not contravened (see *Hallmarking*).

It should be noted in this context that it is easy to calculate how much the fineness of the whole piece changes when the gold content of the solder differs from it appreciably. The greatest care must be taken when solder formulae are copied from the literature that their fineness is the same as that of the material to be soldered.

A few gold solders are listed below. The tables were published in the *Mitteilungen des Forschungs-Instituts Gmünd (Information Bulletin of the Research Institute, Gmünd)*, 9th year, No. 10, 1936.

Gold solders

Gold	Silver	Copper	Cadmium	Zinc	Liquidus	Solidus
750	75	175			895	880
750	120	80	50		887	826
750	90	60	100		743	776
750	90	60		100	883	730
750		150	82	18	822	793
750	28	112	90	20	760	738
750	28	112	20	90	788	747
585	200	215			845	827
585	103	242	70		831	792
585	88	227	100		780	751
585	242	103	70		822	789
585	227	88	100		813	752
585	250	125	40		840	788
585	235	120	60		829	771
585	118	257		40	854	816
585	103	242		70	836	804
585	257	118		40	818	786
585	242	103		70	808	765
585	49	256	90	20	760	738
585	49	256	20	90	837	790
585		295	98	22	793	748
585	80	220	94	21	776	744
333	400	267			780	780
333	350	217	100		741	710
333	300	167	200		709	635
333	350	217		100	759	725
333	300	167		200	704	695
333	18	494	102	23 +30 tin	776	689
333	405	170	26	66	749	722

This table contains three solders consisting of gold, silver, and copper only. These are the lowest-melting solders of these three metals for the three different carat values.

Concerning the technique of soldering, it must be stressed that absolutely clean and oxide-free joints are essential. The joint must be close-fitting and free from impurities of all kinds. Joints of excessive width should not be filled with solder. It is best first to introduce small pieces of the same alloy and to solder these together. Special fluxes (borax, soldering pastes) serve to ensure freedom from oxide during the soldering, and further exclusion of oxygen.

Gold coating

By covering base metals with a layer of gold, one can take advantage of the high corrosion resistance of the precious metal at considerably reduced cost.

Fire gilding is an old method of covering base metals with gold, and is still used today for individual hand-made articles. Gold amalgams (alloys of gold and mercury) are applied to the work; the mercury is evaporated through heating. The result is a thick, firmly adhering layer of gold. The method is injurious to health because mercury vapor is poisonous; the fumes must be removed through a direct flue (see page 137).

Gold plating (rolled gold)

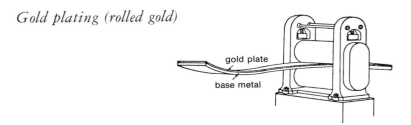

gold plate

base metal

A much more important role, especially in the jewelry trade, is played by the compounds called rolled gold, obtained by means of the plating process. These are materials, base metal or silver, onto which a thin sheet of a gold alloy has been welded. The base is usually a copper alloy. Light-alloy (e.g. aluminum alloy or zinc) articles require intermediate layers of copper, silver, or nickel. The sheets of base metal and gold plate are fitted with extreme precision and kept air-tight in a steel casket. The edges are covered with a boric acid paste to protect them from oxidation. The block is heated to welding temperature—about 850°C—in an annealing furnace, and pressed in a hydraulic press at about 200at. This is followed by rolling and intermediate annealing. During this process, the covering layer is rolled down extremely finely. During the welding operation under pressure, alloy formation clearly occurs along the contact face of cover and base metal; further promoted by the rolling process, this ensures an intimate connection between the two metals.

One of the advantages of rolled gold, plated on one or both sides, is that the gold plate can be applied in any desired thickness and color. Especially in view of any future mechanical stress, a certain hardness of the plating is desirable. The gold content of rolled gold can be accurately indicated, and is expressed in degrees of fineness. Rolled gold of 30/1000, for instance, means that 1000g of the compound contain 30g pure gold, irrespective of the number of carats of the alloy containing these 30g.

The quality of the rolled gold is specified not only by the proportion of gold it contains. Fineness and thickness of the coating are also important. In practice, the fineness of the coating ranges between 417/1000 and 750/1000, that is, between 10 and 18 carat. The thickness is stated in micrometers (μm). A 10μm plating of 585/1000 gold lasts about 5 years with average wear.

With watch and cigarette cases, cufflinks, etc. it is usually the thickness of the plating, or the gold content which is stated.

Special care is necessary in rolled gold manufacture to prevent damage to the thin film of gold. Absence of damage to and evenness of the rolled layer are more important than its thickness. Supplementary electroplating is often necessary, since the cut edges and soldered joints of the sheet do not contain any gold.

The production of gold films by the pressing or gluing of very thin sheet metal onto the base is of little importance today. Gilding can be done both with genuine and with false gold leaf.

In the rubbing-on method, small damaged areas that have become evident in plated gold are dabbed with gold powder produced by burning a linen rag soaked in a gold nitrate solution. The powder is rubbed in with a piece of moist leather. This method of gilding is of course not very durable, and it cannot be used for large blemishes.

Gold electroplating

Electrolytic gold plating or galvanizing is as important a method as the mechanical method of plating.

If a chemical compound, an acid, a base, or a salt is dissolved in water, the constituents separate. Each particle (molecule) still has the properties of the compound. The individual copper sulfate molecule, for instance, has the formula $CuSO_4$. But owing to the effect of the water the molecules, too, divide further, not into the atoms that make up the compound, but into positively and negatively charged particles called ions. In the example here, the molecule of the copper sulfate splits up into positively charged Cu ions and negatively charged SO_4 ions. This process of decomposition of a chemical compound in aqueous solution is known as electrolytic dissociation. The positively charged ions are called cations because during the passage of a current they move to the negative electrode, the cathode. All metals and hydrogen form cations. The nonmetals and acid radicals (such as the SO_4 group) form the anions, which move to the positive electrode, the anode, during the passage of an electric current. If, then, electrodes are immersed in a copper sulfate bath and connected to a current source, the Cu ions move to the cathode. There they cease to exist in the form of ions, in other words they become neutralized and pass into the atomic state. The SO_4 ions move to the anode where, if the anode consists of copper, they form fresh copper sulfate.

This is the principle on which all galvanic metal deposition is based. Certain metal salts are dissolved; the metal ions thereby produced are induced by the electric current to coat the article wired as a cathode. The kind of plating and its quality naturally depend on a number of factors, such as the composition of the bath, the temperature, the current density, the voltage, the preparation of the surface of the work, the distance between the electrodes, etc.

A distinction is drawn between gold baths which give the work effective protection against corrosion, and those designed to plate it with gold of a certain color. The former are called gold plating baths, the latter color gold baths. It is generally impossible to obtain both corrosion protection and a certain decorative effect in the same bath simultaneously. Gold plating baths do not produce any desired color, nor is the color of their deposits constant in the long term. But they do yield pore-free coatings of 20μm thickness. Color gold baths produce only thin films ($0 \cdot 1$–$0 \cdot 2\mu$m), which are not free from pores and therefore have no protective action. But the deposits are lustrous and their color is constant.

By means of certain additives, both types of gold bath can be converted into hard gold baths. Smooth and fine-grained platings are obtained from deadly poisonous gold cyanide baths. The salts are obtained ready for use from the dealer, and the gold plating is carried out strictly according to the enclosed instructions.

Hot gold plating and electrogalvanic gilding

To complete the section on gold plating, the methods of hot gold plating and of electrogalvanic gilding must be discussed. In hot gold plating, the articles are immersed in boiling gold salt solution without the use of electric current. Since the base metal of the work goes into solution and a corresponding quantity of the precious gold is precipitated, thin films of gold are obtained, which may be translucent to even a strongly colored base metal such as tombac. Electrogalvanic gilding differs from this method in that the work in the bath is touched with zinc, which in certain conditions enhances its base character compared with gold. What is known as a local cell is formed: Zinc goes into solution and gold is precipitated, not only on the work, but also on the zinc. The gold deposit must be scraped from the zinc from time to time.

It is clear that, unlike the production of rolled gold and electroplating, the other methods play only a very minor part.

In the past, rolled gold was distinguished from electroplated gold by the appearance of its underside: The mechanically welded surface of the former had a brownish color owing to the formation of an alloy, whereas that of the electroplated gold was lustrous and golden. Nowadays electroplated gold, too, is usually heated afterwards to make it diffuse into the base metal; this also produces the color of the resulting alloy. The end of this distinction has also led to the search for other differentiations.

First, one can demonstrate the characteristic rolled texture of the gold by means of X-rays if it has not been fully annealed. Secondly, the microscope can be used to distinguish between rolled and electroplated gold on finished articles. Here, the fact that rolled gold is already plated on the semifinished article, whereas with the electroplating method the gold is deposited only on the finished one, is of significance. Cut edges of rolled-gold items which were stamped, for instance, are free from gold or, if gold electroplating was carried out at a later stage, covered only with a thinner layer of it. With electroplating, on the other hand, the cut edges are throughout as thickly gold-plated as the rest of the work. Likewise, electroplated soldered joints are covered with the same thickness of gold, but with rolled gold the joints are either not covered at all, or only very thinly plated subsequently. Chains, for instance, which consist of many separate pieces, tend to be badly electroplated, if at all, where they make contact with the next link; with rolled gold they have an even plating. Where pressed articles are electroplated, the strongly protruding parts receive a thicker coating than the recessed and shaded ones. Articles which, on the other hand, have been mechanically gold-plated have an almost uniformly thick layer of gold both on the raised and on the recessed portions of the pressings and ornaments. It is almost always possible to find some of these distinctions with the microscope, so that a clear difference between electroplated and rolled gold can be demonstrated.

The following distinctive feature is particularly striking: Whereas a coating of rolled gold may have any degree of fineness, with electroplating it is difficult to deposit alloys of less than 750/1000 gold content. If the fineness of a sample is lower than 18 carats, it is most probably rolled gold.

Silver

Silver has been known as a decorative metal since the earliest civilizations.

As a precious metal, silver, like gold, is often found in nature in the pure state. But it usually occurs in compounds in the form of silver ores or argentiferous ores. The following are the more important silver ores; often, however, they contain no more than a few per cent of silver: Argentite Ag_2S, proustite Ag_3AsS_3, pyrargyrite Ag_2SbS_3, antimonial gray copper, tennantite, and cerargyrite $AgCl$.

Among the argentiferous ores, galena (PbS) plays the most prominent role; it contains from $0 \cdot 01-1\%$ silver, usually as Ag_2S. Copper pyrites, too, very often contains silver.

The largest quantity of silver is produced in the refinement of lead, gold, copper, and zinc. Mexico accounts for about 30% of world production (in 1950 about 1,528 tons of 5,400 tons world production). In 1961 world production was 7,357 tons; Mexico's share was 1,255 tons, USA 1,081 tons, Peru 1,045 tons, Canada 969 tons, USSR 900 tons, Australia 447 tons, Japan 220 tons, and East Germany 150 tons. The most important mines in the USA are in Nevada, and in Canada those near Quebec and in Ontario.

Today, only very rich silver ores are subjected to the amalgamation process (see *Gold*). Silver is usually obtained by means of the cyanide process, already described under gold; the material, ground to a fine sludge, is washed in a $0 \cdot 1-0 \cdot 2\%$ solution of sodium cyanide ($NaCN$) with good aeration; silver, silver chloride, and silver sulfide go into solution as a complex—sodium silver cyanide; from these solutions the silver is precipitated with stirred-in zinc or aluminum powder. The press cake contains 95% silver. Pure silver is obtained from this by electrolytic refinement.

Refining cupellation

Fig. 6-6. Cupels in various sizes.

The so-called refining cupellation is the oldest method of obtaining silver. The metal is melted together with lead, which must be added to the ore unless it is already present in it in sufficient quantity. Silver and lead are separated on the refining hearth by the transformation of lead into litharge (lead oxide), brought about when hot air is conducted across the melt. In the molten litharge, however, the silver is insoluble. Two separate molten layers form as a result: The litharge floats on top of the silver, absorbing all the metallic impurities; it is decanted or allowed to drain away in the porous bottom of the hearth. The silver remains. The same process is used for the analytical determination of silver in alloys. The weighed quantity of the alloy is melted in the muffle furnace in lead foil bags inserted in cupels, which are small bowls made of pressed bone ash. The oxides of the base metals dissolve in the lead oxide being formed, and drain away with it in the porous cupel. The remaining silver grain is weighed.

The well-known method of Parkerizing is used to enrich the silver during the dressing of ores of low silver content; it is based on the fact that an addition of zinc can remove almost all the silver from the lead.

Properties

Silver has a specific gravity of $10 \cdot 53$, a melting point of $960 \cdot 5°C$, and a boiling point of $1980°C$. It is a metal of white luster, soft, ductile, and eminently suitable for polishing. Like gold, silver can be worked very well at ordinary temperatures, and rolled into thin leaf of $1\,\mu m$ thickness. Of all metals, silver is the best conductor of electricity and heat, and, in the freshly polished state, has the highest reflecting power in visible light. It is therefore particularly well suited for mirrors and reflectors.

Molten, pure silver dissolves about twenty times its own volume of oxygen. During cooling, the gas is ejected again with sputtering. Silver alloyed with base metals does not behave in this way, because the oxygen in solution reacts with the base additive, forming compounds with it. Air and water do not appreciably affect silver even at elevated temperatures. The oxide film, covering silver exactly like base metals when exposed to air, cannot be seen with the naked eye. But its presence plays a part in the well-known bactericidal (oligodynamic) effect of silver, of which we take advantage in medicine for disinfection, or the sterilization of drinking water, etc., because silver oxide is soluble in water at a certain ratio, forming silver ions as it does so.

Silver is dissolved by nitric acid, and hot, concentrated sulfuric acid. In aqua regia, silver chloride is produced, which protects the metal from further attack of the acid (passivation). Its solubility in potassium and sodium cyanide plays an important part in the extraction of the metal from its ores, when the double salts $KAg(CN)_2$ or $NaAg(CN)_2$ are formed. Solutions of these double salts in turn produce the electroplating baths from which silver is precipitated for plating a large variety of articles. Pure silver anodes replenish the silver content of the baths. Not only base metals, but also silver-copper alloys are silver-plated electrolytically. This improves the color and resistance to chemical attack (for example, silver plating of cutlery made of 800/1000 silver-copper alloy).

The tarnishing of silver

Sulfur and sulfur-containing compounds react readily with silver even at normal temperatures, producing firmly adherent sulfide films. Other sulfur compounds, too, can be formed; they are the cause of peculiar sensations of smell and taste which occasionally occur with silverware or cutlery.

The formation of sulfide films, however, results in tarnishing and is therefore of the greatest practical significance. Depending on their thickness, the films are yellow, brown, purple, violet, bluish, or black. They may evenly cover the surface of the article if they are produced by gases; or they may form patches with concentric rings if they owe their origin to solid dust particles.

The speed of tarnishing depends on many factors, knowledge of which is obviously of great importance for the care of silverware. The following points must be borne in mind.

Mirror-finished silverware is much more resistant to reactions with sulfur than mat silver. Atmospheric humidity favors tarnishing. Atmospheric ammonia and sulfur dioxide are also noxious. Bright light greatly accelerates tarnishing, as can be readily seen on the parts of silver articles exposed to it. Temperature, too, has an effect. The higher the temperature, the more quickly are sulfide films formed. Turbulent and dusty air also promotes tarnishing. Silverware should therefore be stored in a dark, cool, dry, dust-free, and draft-free place.

In addition, one is faced with the question of how silver itself can be rendered immune to tarnishing. There are two basic possibilities: Either alloys resistant to tarnishing are compounded, or the articles must be surface-coated with a suitable, resistant film.

All efforts to produce nontarnishing silver alloys have failed because it is impossible to meet all eight of the following conditions:
1. The alloy must not react with sulfur; this also applies to the other alloying constituent.
2. The warm color of the silver must, if possible, be preserved.
3. The other alloying constituent must be able to alloy with silver, i.e. it must mix in a liquid state with liquid silver. Many metals are unable to do this.
4. It must be possible to produce the alloy industrially. Too large a number of alloying constituents is undesirable.
5. The alloy must not be too expensive (e.g. through the addition of gold or platinum).
6. The alloy must be easy to work.
7. For reasons of hallmarking, the other constituent(s) must not amount to more than 200/1000.
8. The alloy must not be sensitive to overheating, which can occur during annealing and soldering.

The old and well-tried silver–copper alloys therefore continue to be used. They are protected against tarnishing by:
1. Suitable wrapping paper.
2. Special protective paper for silver.
3. Storage in transparent bags.
4. Invisible surface films according to the Thomas Price process or the dipping process devised by Dr. Finkh.
5. Clear silver varnishes, i.e. nitrocellulose (nitro-) varnishes, synthetic varnishes, and combination varnishes; a distinction is made between air drying and furnace-drying varnishes (annealing lacquers).
6. Rhodination, i.e. electroplating with the platinum metal rhodium. Here the warm color of the silver is sacrificed, but rhodium, too, appears warm although its reflecting power is 20% lower than that of silver. Rhodium affords complete protection from tarnishing. The high price of the metal also makes rhodinized ware more expensive.

Finally, it must be mentioned that in practice much use is made of the possibility of giving an article a pure silver coating by pickling (blanching) or electroplating it. Apart from the fact that even pure silver is prone to tarnishing, it must be remembered that such silver plating shows little resistance to mechanical wear and tear because of its softness.

The industrial silver–copper alloys

Silver alloys are used for jewelry, coins, and utensils. Pure silver plays a subordinate role. The fineness of the alloys is stamped on the metal in parts per 1000. The most important silver–copper is 925/1000 silver (sterling silver). No alloy containing less silver than this can be stamped, either in Great Britain or the USA. The second alloying constituent is usually copper.

Silver and copper form mixed crystals only to a limited extent. In the alloys most important in the industrial field, the silver and copper particles are therefore mixed at random. These alloys, then, are heterogenous, meaning that their structure is nonuniform. Only in the alloys richest in silver (e.g. sterling silver) will a uniform structure of mixed crystals be obtained with quenching from high temperatures; it is called homogeneous.

The alloys for silverware are melted mostly in coke ovens. Graphite crucibles are generally used. The raw material is normally obtained from scrap metal melted together with virgin melts. The scrap is often strongly oxidized owing to the repeated annealings it has undergone. Even if grains of pure metal are the starting material, granular silver must be expected to contain mechanically trapped air that was included during the process of granulation. Granulated copper often contains oxygen compounds (cuprous oxide). During the melting process itself, and the subsequent annealings of the alloy, further effects of the atmospheric oxygen must be expected. But the influence of oxygen is of decisive importance for the workability of the alloy.

The silver–copper melts combine with the oxygen to form cuprous oxide (Cu_2O), which is red (cupric oxide, CuO, is black). This is the basis of the ability of copper to prevent the silver splitting. Cuprous oxide, because of its great hardness, especially when it occurs in nests and bands, weakens the alloy locally, and fractures easily occur in areas of such weakness when the sheet is worked. Hard nests of cuprous oxide resist the forming of the raw material while it is worked. Bands of cuprous oxide may cause cracks and brittleness in cast ingots, which are first hot forged so that they may break up into several pieces under the hammer. If the working of sheets is continued by cold rolling and intermediate annealing, surface cracks will sometimes appear which cannot be explained in terms of excessive stress of the raw material during rolling. Although they, too, start at the edges, they enter far into the material. The cause of this is also concentrations or bands of cuprous oxide, a substance that is produced mainly in alloys containing 800/1000 to 835/1000 pure silver. During annealing, it forms an even surface layer of scale which is not very permeable to oxygen, so that the metal it covers is protected to some extent, but not completely, from further oxidation. Alloys of finenesses of 900/1000 and higher form mainly the blue-black cupric, instead of cuprous, oxide. Its hardness makes it as objectionable as the cuprous variety. The protective scaly layer characteristic of cuprous oxide formation does not occur with alloys richer in silver. As a result, the copper in the finer alloys is more highly oxidized during annealings than in the 800/1000 alloys. Silver as rich in oxides as this cannot be polished. The oxide portions produce gray or blue patches on the surface, which are impossible to remove. The alloy is said to have blue spots.

It is well known that the scaly layers of cuprous oxide split off when the work cools, or splinter during subsequent rolling. This does not happen, however, with excessively long or hot annealing. Here, the splinters are rolled in. During subsequent annealing they form lines: These in turn cause scaling and shelling of the surface, and the notorious fish-scale fracture of silver alloys. During polishing, the tiny rolled-in splinters may produce the well-known and unattractive comma silver. Because they are very hard, polishing does not remove the splinters, and they remain proud of the rest of the surface; eventually they break out, leaving comma-shaped pits behind. Other hard inclusions, however, such as particles of iron, quartz, or alumina, are possibly a more frequent cause of comma silver.

Obviously, great efforts are therefore made to remove all oxygen during the production of silver–copper alloys. If virgin metal is used for this, no special deoxidants, that is, agents that remove the oxygen from the melt, are needed. The conventional protective measures such as melting under a layer of charcoal, correct and quick pouring, etc., are normally adequate. A deoxidant needs to be used only when the necessary care is not taken during working, and particularly when scrap material is melted. The deoxidants must combine more readily with oxygen than with copper. The oxides they form must be volatile or separate as slag on the melt.

Experiments have shown that, of all the possible elements, phosphorus and lithium are most suitable. Both deoxidize at a high rate, both oxides rapidly separate from the metal melt, and any excess of both elements remaining in the alloy has no adverse effect on its industrial properties. In industry, phosphorus is preferred because of its cheapness, and used exclusively as a copper alloy (copper phosphide) with 10–15% phosphorus. Generally $0\cdot07$–$0\cdot2$ oz (2–5g) 15% copper phosphide is added per $2\cdot2$ lb (1kg) crucible charge. The molten metal is well stirred after the addition of the deoxidant; the crucible is covered and further heated after three minutes; only then is the metal poured off, to allow sufficient time for the deoxidation process.

The following reactions take place in the melt: (1) The phosphorus reacts with the cuprous oxide, forming phosphorus pentoxide gas and metallic copper; (2) the pentoxide (P_2O_5) formed in turn reacts with the cuprous oxide, producing copper metaphosphate ($CuPO_3$), which is practically insoluble in the melt and slags completely.

The properties of the silver–copper alloy undergo little change if phosphorus or lithium remain in it: Ductility and cuppability are slightly increased, tensile strength falls off a little with higher content. Excess phosphorus makes bubble free casting easier. The temperature of intermediate annealing can be lowered and the duration of the process shortened. When the work is annealed above 646°C, distinct hot-shortness develops, but disappears again completely when it cools. For if the constituents are present in certain proportions of weight, the silver–copper/copper phosphide system forms a mixture which melts at the above-mentioned temperature and thus loosens the cohesion of the structure. The phosphorus-containing alloys therefore tend to form coarse crystal grains and segregations. After electrolytic degreasing, phosphorus-containing silver–copper alloys can no longer be perfectly silver-plated, so that a different method of degreasing must be chosen. Fatty acids, such as acetic acid, attack phosphorus-containing alloys far less than phosphorus-free material.

A special problem is the freedom from oxygen during intermediate annealing in the course of the production process. In large factories, silver alloys are not only cast, but also subjected to intermediate annealing, in high vacuum. Heat is supplied in the form of electric resistance heating, with low-voltage currents passing through the metal at a very high amperage. The process is ideal; it saves time and, in the long run, money.

This method, however, is too expensive for small factories. Annealing can be carried out in protective gas; town gas is suitable for this purpose if the alloy is completely oxide-free (in other words, if it has gone through a deoxidation process). If oxides are present, town gas is unsuitable because the hydrogen it contains diffuses into the alloy, forms water vapor with the oxygen of the oxides, and disperses the metal, because the large water molecules are unable to escape from the material. This is known as hydrogen embrittlement.

For silverware, charcoal is still best as protection against oxidation. If the material to be annealed is covered with pieces of charcoal, the atmospheric oxygen combines with the latter to form carbon monoxide gas (CO); because this is poisonous, good ventilation is essential.

Silver solders

Because of their excellent properties, silver solders play a very important part in all branches of the metal industry. The manufacture of jewelry, especially, would be unthinkable today without the use of silver alloy hard solders.

Silver solders consist of alloys with at least 8% silver. The other constituents are usually copper and zinc. The working temperatures range between 600–870°C. For special purposes, small quantities of tin, cadmium, nickel, or manganese are sometimes added.

Compared with the properties of the important brass solders, the rheological properties of the alloy and the mechanical properties of the soldering are improved by the presence of silver in solders; furthermore, it greatly increases corrosion resistance. For soldering stainless steel, the addition of nickel is recommended, because this hardens the solder and raises its melting point. The color of the solder becomes more like that of the steel. Tin considerably lowers the melting temperature, but workability suffers.

Industrial silver solders usually contain less than 50% silver. But in the jewelry and silverware industry, solders with 60–80% silver are used. In contrast with gold, no proper check solder is available for silver. For reasons of melting technology, the silver content of the solders is lower than that of the alloys qualifying for hallmarking. Thus the hard silver solders contain only 64–86%, the easy ones only 48–50% silver. In the silver-rich solders the copper:zinc ratio is 3:2. Silver-poor solders with only up to 25% silver contain more than 50% zinc; they are brittle. If some of the zinc in silver-rich solders is replaced with cadmium, the working temperature rises. It sinks with solders containing little silver.

The abundance of solder formulae is confusing. A few of these solders are described below.

Silver solder with 7–8% silver, and less than 55% copper. The rest is zinc. Working temperature 860°C. For coarse work with iron, steel, and brass.

Silver solder with 26–28% silver, and less than 40% copper. Less than 6% nickel and less than 10% manganese are added. The rest is zinc. Working temperature 840°C. For stainless steel and hard metals. It is chosen if high corrosion resistance is essential.

Silver solder with 48–50% silver, less than 18% copper, less than 8% manganese, less than 5% nickel. The rest is zinc. The working temperature at 690°C is considerably lower. The solder is suitable for use with stainless steel.

Silver solder with 66–68% silver, less than 26% copper. The rest is zinc. Working temperature 730°C. This and the following three solders are suitable for silver alloys.

Silver solder with 66–68% silver, less than 13% copper, and less than 11% cadmium. The rest is zinc. Working temperature 710°C.

If maintenance of the proportion of silver is not critical 60% silver solders are used:

Silver solder with 59–61% silver, less than 28% copper. The rest is zinc. Working temperature 710°C.

Silver solder with 59–61% silver, less than 25% copper, less than 3% cadmium, less than 3% tin. The rest is zinc. Working temperature 680°C.

Most silver alloys have their solidus at 779°C. It is therefore important that the working temperature of the solders should not exceed 730°C; this affords a latitude of 50°C before the work shrivels.

Silver solders are three to ten times as expensive as brass solders; but since the cost of soldering depends on the operating time, silver solders are the most economical. Their advantages are:

1. Low working temperature, therefore fast-working. Good workability, therefore available as sheets and thin wire and economical in use.
2. Easy, smooth flow. Effective penetration of the finest joints. Little need to clean up the joint.
3. Great firmness of the joint.
4. Good corrosion resistance.
5. Good conductivity of heat and electricity.

The melting ranges of the industrially important silver–copper alloys are given below, for comparison.

Silver content	Liquidus	Solidus
935/1000	904	840
925/1000	896	779
900/1000	875	779
835/1000	838	779
800/1000	817	779
720/1000	779	779

Platinum Metals (Platinoids)

The following elements are platinum metals: Ruthenium, rhodium, palladium, osmium, iridium, and platinum. The three first-named metals, of the palladium group, are the light platinoids, and the three others, of the platinum group, the heavy ones.

All six platinoids are usually found together in the pure state. Raw platinum contains only 2–5% of the other platinoids. The Canadian nickel ores from Sudbury have a comparatively high palladium content. Since the metals usually occur in association, and have also closely similar chemical properties, the extraction of the individual elements in the pure state presents considerable difficulties. Tedious separating methods must be used, which are based on the process of chemical analysis. The platinoids are melted with a blowpipe or in a high-frequency furnace. For platinum and palladium, a town gas–oxygen blower is sufficient. Oxyacetylene must be used for the accompanying metals of higher melting points. If no osmium is present, the temperature of an oxyhydrogen blowpipe is sufficient. Whereas small quantities of metal can be melted on a thick piece of quartz with a hand blowpipe, heat-resistant calcium oxide crucibles are used for larger quantities. Melting in the high-frequency furnace allows easy control of the entire melting process. The melts are usually cast in slightly warmed graphite molds.

Platinum

Occurrence

The name of the precious metal is derived from the Spanish *platina*, a diminutive of *plata* = silver.

The deposits of platinum and its accompanying metals are either primary or secondary. The platinum content of the primary deposits (iron, nickel, chromium, and copper ores) is very low. The most important such deposits are the nickel–copper–magnetic pyrites of the Sudbury region, Ontario (1 ton of ore contains 2·4 oz. (68g) of platinum metals). Other primary deposits are found in the Transvaal and the Ural mountains.

The most important secondary deposits (weathering and placer deposits) occur also in the Ural mountains, near Sudbury, and in the Transvaal, as well as in the Choco region of Columbia.

In 1957 the world output of platinum (free platinum and placer platinum) was 25·9 tons (26,395kg), of which 14·2 tons (14,472kg) came from South Africa, 6 tons (6,099kg) from Canada, about 4·5 tons (4,600kg) from the USSR, 0·8 tons (808kg) from Columbia, 0·4 tons (387kg) from the USA.

Properties

The metal has a beautiful luster; its color is gray-white. The melting point is at 1774°C, the boiling point at about 4350°C, the specific gravity 21·45. The mechanical properties of platinum are very favorable. The pure metal is relatively soft but highly ductile. Both platinum and palladium are easily worked both hot and cold. In practice, the two metals are first hot forged or rolled at 800°C, and then cold rolled to produce sheets, or cold drawn to produce wire. Foils down to a thickness of 0.0001 ins. (0·0025mm) and wires down to 0.006 ins. (0·015mm) are thus made. Minor impurities of other metals reduce ductility and increase hardness. Platinum starts to get soft at about 700°C. It can easily be welded in white heat if it is forged with the hammer at the same time. The solders used consist of alloys of platinum and copper, of palladium and gold and silver, or simply of pure gold.

The precious character of the platinum metals is demonstrated by their behavior to oxygen and resistance to acids. Like silver, platinum, when exposed to the atmosphere, acquires an extremely thin oxide film, which heat decomposes again. These oxide surface films protect the metals against external chemical effects. Of all the platinoids, platinum itself has the least tendency to enter into compounds with atmospheric oxygen. Apart from the covering film already mentioned, invisible to the naked eye and easily removed, solid platinum remains practically unchanged in air. Like silver, liquid platinum has a high affinity for oxygen, which, as the melt cools, is expelled again, spitting during the process.

Platinum is unaffected by acids. Only aqua regia dissolves the solid metal, although more slowly than gold. But the behavior of platinum towards acids changes considerably when it is present in very finely distributed form or in alloys with silver, copper, etc. Treatment with hot nitric acid, for instance, leaves clear traces of chemical attack.

At red heat and in the presence of oxygen or oxidants, a considerable quantity of platinum dissolves in the melts of caustic soda and of caustic potash. Melts of sodium carbonate and niter, which give off oxygen themselves, must be specially mentioned here. This reaction of platinum with oxidizing salt melts is particularly important in connection with the refining melting process used in industry.

At high temperatures, platinum readily alloys with carbon. Platinum utensils should therefore never be allowed to come into contact with sooting flames. Sulfur, too, attacks platinum at red heat.

Because of its great stability, easy workability, and attractive appearance platinum is very popular in industry and in the jewelry trade. During World War II, as much as 40% of the total consumption went into jewelry. Not until 1951, when the price of platinum rose to 2·5 times that of gold, did the consumption of the jewelry trade fall to 12%. Main consumers today are industry and dentistry.

The comparatively low hardness of soft annealed platinum (about 47 Brinell units) can be very easily increased by alloying additions, so that the resistance and firmness necessary for practical use are achieved without detriment to its working properties. Hardness measurements carried out in the Forschungsinstitut für Metallchemie (Research Institute for Metal Chemistry), Schwäb. Gmünd produced the following results:

Metal added	5%	10%	15%
Iridium	80	105	140
Rhodium	80	83	88
Ruthenium	105	158	unworkable
Palladium	65	70	73
Copper	110	135	145

The figures indicate the Brinell Hardnesses of the soft annealed alloys. It is seen that platinum is hardened from 47–110 Brinell degrees by the addition of 5% copper.

As a rule, no copper is added to platinum for jewelry.

The various commercial types of platinum are as follows.

Fineness degree 4: Minimum content 99·99%, available as sheets and wire.

Fineness degree 3: Minimum content 99·9%, available as sheets and wire.

Fineness degree 2: (Platinum for instruments), minimum content 99·7%, iridium content up to 0·3%, other metals no more than 0·1%, available as sheets.

Fineness degree also 2: (Technically pure platinum), minimum content 99·0% but at least 99·5% platinum metals, supplied in the form of sponge, sheets, wire, and ingots.

Fineness degree 1: (Jewelry platinum), minimum content 95·0% platinum (for reasons of stamping 96·0% platinum is the commercial quality). Supplied as sheets, wire, and tubes. Example of use: Jewelry.

The Accompanying Metals

The five metals accompanying platinum are used mainly as alloying additives to platinum. The table below shows their physical constants compared with those of platinum:

Metal	Melting point °C	Specific gravity
Ruthenium	2370	12·4
Rhodium	1966	12·35
Palladium	1554	11·97
Osmium	2700	22·5
Iridium	2454	22·4
Platinum	1774	21·45

The Canadian nickel ores contain all these metals (mainly palladium) except osmium. Like platinum, its various accompanying metals are obtained not by metallurgical methods but by wet chemical processes.

Ruthenium

The name is derived from Ruthenia, in the Balkans. It is a gray metal of little luster. Shaping of ruthenium by means of rolling or forging has so far failed, because the metal is very hard and brittle. It is attacked very little by aqua regia, and not at all by other acids. It is sometimes used in place of the expensive iridium for hardening platinum.

Rhodium

Because of the rose-pink color of one of its salts, the metal was named after the Greek word for a rose. It is even more corrosion-resistant than platinum and is not attacked by any acid, not even by aqua regia. Its color is aluminum white. Of all the platinoids, it has the highest reflectance in visible light, and is therefore particularly suitable for use in reflectors and as a nondiscoloring plating for silverware. Rhodium does not, however, equal silver in luster and color; after all, its reflectance is 20% less. In the hot state, rhodium is easy to shape. At red heat it can be forged if it is very pure; it can be drawn into wire and rolled into sheets. Cold working properties are poor. The importance of rhodium as

protection against the discoloration of silverware of all kinds is constantly increasing in the jewelry trade.

Palladium

In the jewelry trade, palladium plays the most important role of all the platinum metals. It owes its name to the small planet Pallas, which was discovered two years before the metal. Its color is very similar to that of silver. The luster of molten palladium is particularly bright. When heated to red heat, it shows tempering colors owing to slight oxidation; at still higher temperatures, they disappear again. Nitric and sulfuric acid attack palladium comparatively easily, especially when it is in a finely distributed form. Its mechanical properties are favorable and similar to those of platinum. The color-improving effect of palladium admixtures is especially well known. For instance, it brightens the gray color of platinum considerably. Furthermore, the addition of palladium greatly increases the tensile strength of platinum.

An alloy of striking whiteness consists of 900/1000 platinum and 100/1000 palladium. This alloy cannot be stamped. Another white alloy contains 960/1000 platinum and 40/1000 palladium. A jewelry palladium with 850/1000 palladium, 100/1000 rhodium, and 50/1000 platinum is recommended. The rich palladium finds in America led to the so-called white fashion, as a result of which the jewelry trade there greatly favored the white precious metals, making not only settings, but also wedding rings, watch chains, armlets and buttons of palladium alloys or of white gold.

Osmium

Osmium is bluish-white, and the element of the highest specific gravity. Osmium powder oxidizes slowly in air. The oxide has an unpleasantly pungent smell, to which the metal owes its name, derived from the Greek word for stench. Osmium does not react with acids. As an additive to platinum, it is outstanding in its hardening action; but the working properties of the alloys are less favorable, although their elasticity increases. Alloys with about 2% osmium are used in the jewelry trade. Like ruthenium, the pure metal is brittle and no method has been found so far of noncutting forming.

Iridium

Because of the many colors of its salts, the metal was named after Iris, Goddess of the Rainbow. It is white and very lustrous, and highly resistant to chemical attack. It is alloyed with jewelry platinum to increase its hardness. The metal is difficult to work. It is brittle, very hard, and wire drawing is impossible. The treatment of iridium is easiest at white heat. About 50% of the metal produced is used by the jewelry trade.

Palladium and platinum are frequently alloyed with gold, and more rarely with silver and copper. The alloys have good working properties and often serve as platinum-substitute metals. The gold–platinum and platinum–palladium alloys, especially, are extraordinarily resistant to chemical attack. Their gold content ranges from 8 to 20 carat.

Alloys of platinum with the other platinoids can, as already mentioned, be considerably harder than pure platinum.

The Base Metals

Copper

Occurrence and extraction

The prehistoric era of the Neolithic Age (4000–1750 B.C.) ended with the introduction of copper utensils. The so-called Copper (Chalcolithic) Age should therefore be fixed from 2000 to 1750 B.C. The subsequent civilization of the Bronze Age in Central and Northern Europe is assigned to the period from 1800 to 900 or 800 B.C. In Southern Europe, it began a few centuries earlier. Thus more than a thousand years of the history of civilization bear the name of copper or of one of its alloys. Copper was the first metal ever used for the manufacture of weapons and implements. It was preceded by stone, and succeeded by iron.

Copper, named after the island of Cyprus, which in Antiquity had important deposits, occurs in North America, Chile, and Australia as pure metal in the form of lumps, plates, and sheets; volcanic deposits, especially, contain copper in its pure form.

In compounds, copper is found mainly as sulfide (sulfur compound) or as oxide (oxygen compound). The most important sulfidic copper ores are copper pyrites ($CuFeS_2$), erubescite (Cu_3FeS_3), and chalcocite (Cu_2S). A very important oxidic ore is red copper ore (Cu_2O). The effects of water and atmospheric oxygen readily convert the copper sulfides into the water-soluble copper sulfate ($CuSO_4$). In the presence of carbonic acid, the copper is precipitated from the aqueous solution as basic carbonate, i.e. as malachite [$CuCO_3.Cu(OH)_2$] and as azurite [$2CuCO_3.Cu(OH)_2$].

The richest copper ores are found in Arizona and Montana, where copper occurs mainly as erubescite and chalcocite. The Chilean deposits are mostly of volcanic origin; they occur on the western slopes of the Andes. The third place among copper-producing countries is occupied by Zaire and Zambia, which are followed by Canada, Mexico, and Japan. World production per annum exceeds 3 million tons.

In the depths of isolated sea areas, copper sulfate dissolved by dead animal matter can be reduced to sulfide, which produces deposits of copper schist at the bottom of the sea. This is how the well-known Mansfeld copper schist was formed. (Mansfeld, near Halle, lies on the eastern slopes of the Harz Mountains in East Germany.)

Properties

Copper has a specific gravity of $8 \cdot 93$, melts at 1083°C and begins to boil at 2350°C. Apart from gold, it is the only colored metal. Pure copper is red, but it glows blue-green when heated. After silver, it is the best conductor of electricity and heat. It is hard, but at the same time ductile and tough. Fine wire and thin foil can therefore be produced without difficulty. The best solvent of copper is nitric acid; a blue solution results. The gases emitted during this reaction (oxides of nitrogen) are poisonous.

In the course of decades the metal, when exposed to the atmosphere, acquires a patina of beautiful green basic copper sulfates, basic copper carbonates, or basic copper chlorides. With acetic acid, copper forms the well-known verdigris. Another well-known salt is the blue copper sulfate (blue vitriol), the copper salt of sulphuric acid. The alloys of copper are of outstanding importance.

Copper Alloys

Copper alloys in almost any proportion with most metals, except with chromium, iron, and lead, with which its miscibility is limited. The copper–zinc alloys are remarkable because of their good casting and forming properties. Tombac contains up to 20% zinc, yellow brass 20–50% zinc. Copper–zinc alloys with more than 50% zinc are called white metal; this is very brittle and therefore cannot be machined; but it is readily cast. All copper–zinc alloys bear the generic name of brass. But in practice only yellow brass is as a rule known by this name. Brass containing tin is also known as *cuivre poli*. Copper alloys with about 25% nickel are used as coinage metals. Copper is the main constituent of German silver, which consists of 60% copper, 20% zinc, and 20% nickel. Since this alloy, which has acquired considerable importance as an industrial metal, is white owing to its nickel content, it is usually classed as a nickel alloy. Alpaca is either German silver or silver-plated German silver. Alloys of copper and tin, called bronzes, are very important. Unlike copper castings, bronze castings are free from bubbles; bronze is therefore used for bell casting. Aluminum–copper alloys are called aluminum bronzes. The 5–10% aluminum they contain has a hardening effect. Although they have considerable corrosion resistance, they discolor in the atmosphere and do not look as beautiful as tin bronzes. There are silicon bronzes with a maximum silicon content of $0 \cdot 05\%$, which are outstanding through their high solidity. Manganin, nickelin, and constantan are special copper alloys for industrial uses.

The importance of copper as an alloying constituent with precious metals has already been mentioned. The copper content has the special purpose of increasing hardness and the mechanical resistance of the precious metals. Gold coins usually contain 90% gold and 10% copper, silver coins 90% silver and 10% copper.

Brass

As already mentioned, all copper–zinc alloys can be called brass. The zinc content rarely exceeds 45%. Zinc improves the casting properties and increases the hardness of the metal, although not as much as tin. But brass can be rolled better than bronze.

There are two distinct types of brass:

Brass with more than 63% copper consists of only one kind of mixed crystals (known as alpha phase).

Brass with less than 63% copper contains, in addition to the alpha mixed crystals, a second type of mixed crystals (known as beta phase).

These two kinds of brass differ, to begin with, in their corrosion resistance. It has been found that two types of alloys are particularly corrosion resistant, i.e. (1) compounds, and (2) alloys consisting of only one type of mixed crystals, homogeneous alloys. It has already been pointed out at the beginning that compounds are only rarely suitable for industrial purposes, since they are very brittle. Alpha brass, with only one type of mixed crystals, can be worked very well and is more resistant to corrosion than the second type of brass. For all objects which are exposed to the corrosive effects of the atmosphere and water, alloys containing more than 60%, and mostly 70%, copper are therefore used. In commercial artwork involving deep etching by chemical means, it has been shown that in alpha brass the etching is cleaner than in alloys that also contain beta mixed crystals. The reason for this is that the beta crystals are more rapidly attacked by the chemicals than the alpha crystals, so that in the type of brass containing more zinc the base is unevenly etched.

At ordinary temperatures, brass with more than 63% copper can be more easily shaped than the type richer in zinc with the two kinds of mixed crystals. On the other hand, the latter type can be worked better at red heat than the type richer in copper. We therefore distinguish between the cold forging and the hot forging alloy.

The cold forging brass, with more than 63% copper, is used in commercial art because of its golden hue. It can be easily rolled, pressed, spun, or stamped at room temperature, provided it is not too contaminated by foreign metals. Rigidity and hardness are greatly increased by these shaping processes. The internal stresses thereby set up can be eliminated if the alloy is annealed at 200−300°C. The hot forging brass, richer in zinc, is used as casting material, as well as for the manufacture of rivets and screws, watch wheels and springs, sheets, parts of locks, etc. A hot forging brass with about 60% copper is called Muntz metal.

For the gold- and silversmith, only the brasses with a higher copper content, mainly the tombac alloys, are suitable. Their colors range from coppery-red to brassy-yellow. The various brasses comprise enamel tombac (95% copper), red tombac, gilding metal, and light-red tombac, or low brass. These alloys are supplied in the form of strips, sheets, or wires to the jewelry trade and commercial artists, and for decorative purposes.

Brass objects have been known since the third century B.C. Cicero was outraged at the dishonesty of some of his contemporaries, who sold brass as gold. Pliny the Elder used the name of "aurichalcum", which later became official, for brass. Since the Late Roman period, and especially in the Middle Ages, the Rhine and Meuse districts were famous for their brass work: Church plate, baptismal and holy water fonts, lecterns, monumental brasses, aquamanilia, candlesticks, mortars, and bowls were made of brass. St. Sebaldus's Tomb, by Peter Vischer's workshop (begun in 1508), is a particularly famous example of Nuremberg brass art. The so-called Dinanderies, brassware made at Dinant in the Belgian province of Namur since the middle of the thirteenth century, are also very well known.

Bronzes

All copper−tin alloys with more than 78% copper are called bronzes. They are chemically very stable. Whereas in dry air the metal does not change at all, in the presence of humidity it produces a beautiful, green, pore-free surface film—patina—which protects the layers it covers from corrosion. In addition, the tin content makes the alloy very hard. Whereas a bronze with 6% tin can still be rolled, higher proportions of tin create considerable difficulties when the material is to be worked. Bronzes with 10–20% tin are therefore used almost exclusively in molding shops. Phosphor bronzes usually contain small quantities of phosphorus added to the melt in some form or other to expel any residual oxygen compounds. For rolling alloys, the phosphorus quantity to be added is generally calculated so that only a slight surplus remains in the deoxidized bronze.

Alloys containing other material, such as aluminum instead of zinc, are sometimes also called bronze. In this case it should be called expressly aluminum bronze. Special brasses, too, whose properties often resemble those of the bronzes, are sold as zinc bronzes by some firms; but this description is unacceptable because the term "bronze" expressly implies a minimum copper content of 78%. Bronzes for art casting consist of 75–90% copper and 25–10% tin; mostly small quantities of zinc are present. The so-called coinage- and medal bronzes are composed of 90–96% copper and 10–4% tin.

Alloys of copper, tin, and zinc (often with small quantities of lead) are called gun metal or leaded semired brass.

For bell casting, bronzes have been used with more than 20% tin since time immemorial. The alloys are hard and rather brittle; when struck they emit a clear note. Even higher tin content (up to 40%) produces radiantly white alloys; like the bell metals they are brittle and hard, but accept a beautiful polish. They were therefore used for bronze mirrors even in Antiquity, and are today called speculum (mirror) alloys. For a time, cutlery was electroplated with this material as a substitute for silver plating, which tarnishes; but it did not fulfill expectations, because the brittleness of the plating makes it unsuitable for this purpose.

Zinc

The most important zinc ores are zinc blende (ZnS) and zinc spar ($ZnCO_3$); red zinc ore (ZnO) and siliceous calamine ($Zn_2SiO_4 H_2O$) are of secondary importance. The world's richest deposits are found on the Missouri-Kansas border in the USA, and at Broken Hill in Australia. Zinc ores also occur in Upper Silesia, near Aachen, and in the Harz Mountains in Germany. The USA is the world's leading zinc producer (world production more than $3 \cdot 3$ million tons per year), followed by the USSR, Canada, Australia, Mexico, Peru, Japan, Poland, Italy, Zaire and West Germany. Zinc is usually extracted by means of roasting the zinc blende to oxides, and reduction (oxygen removal) with coal. Recently, electrolytic production of the metal has been gaining more and more ground, because metallurgically the roasting and reduction process is rather imperfect.

The metal has a specific gravity of $7 \cdot 12$, and its melting point is 419°C; it begins to boil at 907°C. Zinc is lustrous, white, and brittle. It is more base than iron, and easily dissolved by most acids. Yet galvanization constitutes an effective surface protection for iron, since zinc protects itself against corrosion by forming a layer of hydroxide or carbonate. The brittleness of commercial zinc is due to foreign metal impurities. The purer the zinc, the more easily it can be rolled down. This is done between 90−150°C.

Zinc is used not only as a rolling metal, but also as a casting and molding metal. The zinc alloys, too, can be rolled and molded; as a rule, the other alloying constituents are copper, aluminum, or tin.

Zinc and zinc alloys can be soldered with the soft solders used for brass, unless the aluminum content is higher than 1%. But the best method of joining zinc and zinc alloys is welding, which can be carried out either with oxyacetylene or electrically. Because the solders mostly contain tin or lead, soldering has the disadvantage of making future scrap utilization and recycling into useful material more difficult, since, as already mentioned, zinc and its alloys are very sensitive to contamination with foreign metals.

The great importance of zinc as a plating material for iron must be particularly emphasized. The protective action of the zinc coating is based on the fact that it completely prevents contact between the iron and the atmosphere because it is free from pores, and therefore eliminates all corrosive action.

Of all the methods of zinc plating—hot galvanizing, electrodeposition, sherardizing, spray galvanizing, etc.—hot galvanizing is by far the most important. Almost half of all crude zinc today is consumed by the hot galvanizing industry; this protective measure annually preserves about 7 million tons of iron from rusting.

Hot galvanizing consists of the following steps: First the surfaces of the iron parts are pickled, which means that the adherent layers of scale (films of rust, etc.) are removed with hydrochloric or sulfuric acid. The metal is then dipped in the galvanizing bath containing molten zinc at a temperature of about 450°C. The surface of the molten zinc is divided in two by the immersion of a metal sheet. One half is covered with a layer of flux (ammonium chloride–zinc chloride salts), through which the iron parts pass when they are immersed in the bath. Thus the surface is once more cleaned before the iron comes into contact with the molten zinc. After a few minutes, the galvanized material is lifted out of the side of the bath not covered by the flux. Of all the zinc used for galvanizing, almost 98% is taken up by the hot galvanizing method.

Zinc electroplating today has come very much to the fore in the technology of galvanizing. It is possible to choose the thickness of the plating at will. Alkaline or acid baths are used. Electrolytic zinc sheets are the anodes. Bright zinc baths produce deposits of a beautiful, bright color.

Small, finished articles are sherardized. They are pickled and then rotated in drums with a mixture of sand and zinc dust heated to about 400°C.

With spray galvanizing, the pickled articles are roughened with sand jets to ensure better adhesion between the zinc particles and the iron base. For the plating process, spray guns are used with compressed air.

As a rolling material, the so-called commercial quality designates rolling zinc with a zinc content of 98·5–99%; it is used for plumbing, spinning, and stamping. The material can be stamped and pressed. The fine zinc quality contains 99·5–99·99% zinc and is used for spraying, spinning, and stamping. Special qualities, lastly, are mixtures of rolling- and fine zinc. The zinc content therefore lies between 99–99·5%. The material is sold in a soft, medium hard, and hard state, and is used for drawing and spinning where higher demands are made of shaping properties.

Cadmium

Cadmium is an accompanying metal of zinc and also extracted together with it. The world production of cadmium (1960: 9,857 tons) is higher than the demand.

The specific gravity of the metal is 8·64, and its melting point rather low at 321°C; it boils at 767°C. The vapors oxidize to form brown flakes of cadmium oxide, and if inhaled are injurious to health. For alloying, chemically pure cadmium of a minimum content of 99·8% is used. The metal serves as an additive to lower the melting point of alloys. Some precious metal solders contain cadmium. Alloys of cadmium and lead, tin, and bismuth have particularly low melting points. Thus Wood's Metal (12·5% cadmium, 25% lead, 12·5% tin, 50% bismuth) melts at 71°C, Newton's Metal (10% cadmium, 28% lead, 17% tin, 45% bismuth) at 70°C, and Lipowitz's Metal (10% cadmium, 27% lead, 13% tin, 50% bismuth) at 60°C—in other words, these metals actually melt in hot water. Soft solder, consisting of 25% lead, 25% cadmium, and 50% tin, melts at 149°C.

Cadmium plating is produced either mechanically or electrolytically. Even a thin film (0·9 oz. cadmium per 1·2 square yards, or 25g per square meter, is enough), as long as it is dense, provides an iron substrate with complete protection against rust. At a given plating thickness, cadmium plating is more resistant than zinc plating, although it is slightly softer. The rapid loss of luster is a disadvantage. The method is used increasingly for tools, automobile parts, etc.

Tin

Occurrence

Tin comes mainly from the ore deposits of the Malaysian islands Banka and Billiton. Cassiterite (SnO_2) is mined, from which tin is extracted by reduction with coal. Considerable quantities of tin are also found in Bolivia. The deposits in Cornwall, from which Caesar obtained his tin, are economically insignificant today. The world production is about 184,000 tons per year; a third of it comes from the Federation of Malaysia. Next in importance are China, Bolivia, the USSR, Indonesia, Thailand, Nigeria, and Zaire.

Properties

The lustrous, silver-white metal (melting point 232°C, boiling point 2270°C) is rather soft and not very strong. Its ductility, on the other hand, is considerable; tin can be beaten and rolled into thin foil (tin foil, silver paper) to a thickness of 0.001 ins. (0·0025mm). From the melt, tin crystallizes as "white tin" in a certain tetragonal type of crystal (See *Systems of crystallization*). In this form it has a specific gravity of 7·28. When tin rods are bent, as the crystal faces rub against one another they emit a crunching sound called tin cry. At lower temperatures, a second form of the metal occurs, the so-called gray tin, a gray powder which has hardly any metallic properties; its crystals are cubic. The decomposition into this second type of crystal proceeds like a contagious disease and increases with further cooling. This tin pest is a dreaded museum disease to which much pewterware has fallen victim. The specific gravity of this gray tin is about 5·75. Air and water do not attack tin at ordinary temperatures. The metal is therefore used as a protective coating, especially for iron. Tin plating is produced either electrolytically, or by the simple method of hot tin plating: The cleaned sheet iron is dipped into molten tin (tin plate, cans). The corrosion resistance of tin to organic acids as well (acetic acid, for instance) and its nontoxicity explain the use of the metal for beautiful utensils, tableware, pitchers, etc. from the Middle Ages to the present.

Alloys

Tin readily forms alloys with most metals. Of special importance are the tin-containing soft solders and soldering materials, the bronzes mentioned already, bearing metals, and Britannia metal (90% tin, 8% antimony, 2% copper). Antimony makes the metal brittle and hard.

Additions of zinc, too, make it brittle. Zinc and lead spoil the color, lead and copper have a hardening effect, and iron makes the metal friable.

In the past, Britannia metal was a pure antimony–tin alloy (91–94% tin). Today, copper is almost always added (up to 3%), and often also a little lead, bismuth, or zinc. Some Britannia alloys bear fancy names. Emperor tin is an alloy containing 93% tin, 5·4% antimony, and 1·6% copper. Cast Britannia metals are a little poorer in tin (e.g. 82%).

Bearing metals are alloys from which bearings are made for machine shafts. The main constituent of these alloys is tin, copper, or lead. Printing types (type metal) consist of a tin–lead–antimony alloy.

The soft solders consist mainly of tin and lead; almost all tin solders melt below 300°C; they are therefore unsuitable when the soldered objects are at any time exposed to higher temperatures. Lead is a poison, and tin cans must therefore not be soldered with tin–lead solders. The common soft solders begin to melt at 183°C. The solder with 62% tin and 38% lead has only one melting point at 183°C (eutectic).

Nickel

Among the white gold metals, nickel is used as an alloying constituent. The addition of nickel not only shifts the color of gold strongly towards white, but also has a stronger hardening effect than that of platinum or palladium. The main consumer of nickel is the steel industry. Nickel steel is particularly hard and tough, and used, for instance, in the manufacture of guns and of armor plate for warships.

Occurrence

Canada, with its huge deposits of nickel-containing pyrrhotite (FeS, NiS) near Sudbury, where platinoids, too, are mined, is the world's leading producer of nickel with a share of 60% of a world production totalling 355,000 tons. It is followed by the USSR and New Caledonia. Other important nickel ores are niccolite, white nickel ore, gersdorffite, nickel blende, and garnierite, a nickel silicate which is found among other ores in Silesian mines. From these ores nickel, like copper, is obtained through roasting after the iron is sintered, and through reduction with coal.

Properties

The color of nickel is silver-white with a slight yellow tinge. Its specific gravity is 8·9, and its melting point 1455°C; it begins to boil at 2730°C. Nickel can be forged, welded, polished, stretched very well, and rolled down cold or hot into sheets of 0.001 ins. (0·025mm) thickness.

The resistance of nickel to atmospheric influences is outstanding. Oxidation, which makes the metal friable, does not occur below 500°C. Its resistance to strong lyes, not too concentrated organic acids, water, vapor, and many gases, is also considerable. Because of this corrosion resistance, the use of nickel in industry is widespread. The metal is a very popular raw material not only in the food-processing and chemical industries, but also in the production of coins, in commercial art, in the manufacture of tableware, ashtrays, candlesticks, wall cladding, etc. Baser metals, especially iron, are nickel-plated to protect them against corrosion. This can be done by means of electroplating. To prevent tarnishing and dulling, nickel plating in turn is mostly covered with a thin layer of chromium. Nickel can also be joined to the base metal by means of hot rolling, a method which produces a particularly intimate connection between nickel and steel (because the welding temperatures of both metals are very close together).

Alloys

The most important nickel alloys contain iron, copper, and chromium. Alloys including certain other admixtures, in addition to 67% nickel and 28% copper, are called Monel metals. They have outstanding mechanical properties and are therefore very widely used. Alloys of nickel, copper, and zinc are called German silver.

German Silver

The ratios of the three alloying constituents move roughly within the following limits: Nickel between 8–20%, copper between 45–70%, zinc between 12–50%. Perfect workability, high corrosion resistance, and its silver-white color are the outstanding characteristics of German silver. Hardness and resistance to tarnishing increase with the nickel content, while copper makes German silver ductile and easy to roll. Zinc, too, increases the hardness of the alloy; it also facilitates casting. German silver can be welded and soldered.

The alloy, whose hardness and strength is superior to that of brass, is usually cast in plates and rolled down into sheets.

This material, known also as alpaca, alfenide, white copper, pack fong, argentan, nickel silver, etc., is used mainly for the manufacture of cutlery. Knives, forks, and spoons are stamped from the sheet metal. The material can be readily silver-plated. Last, but not least, its poor heat conductivity favors its use for cutlery. For this purpose, the alloy normally contains about 18% nickel and 20–30% zinc.

German silver is also used in watchmaking (clockwork, chains, cases), and in the electrical engineering and building industries (bannisters, wall cladding, fittings for restaurants, dining cars, ships, etc.). Here are a few examples of commercial German silver alloys (*Nickel Handbook*, Frankfurt 1939):

Type of alloy	Ni	Cu	Zn	Additives	Field of application
Rolling	25	60	15		Bar fittings
alloys	22	60	18		Cutlery and
(homogeneous	18	62	20		tableware,
alpha structure):	15	63	22		Oriental work
sheets, bands,	12	65	23		
rods,	8	70	22		
wire	26–28	54	Rest	Fe	Electrical
	20–22	58	Rest		resistances

Type of alloy	Ni	Cu	Zn	Additives	Field of application
Hot pressing alloy (heterogeneous alpha + beta structure): Profiles	11–13 8 13	45 45 45	Rest Rest Rest	Fe, Mn Al Pb, Fe, Mn, Al	Metalware, building fittings, shop-fittings, measuring instruments, watches
Cast alloys Molding	19–22 13–15	65 50–55	Rest Rest	Mn, Si, Al Pb, Sn, Fe	Armatures, sanitary installations

Iron

Iron is one of the most common elements. Its ores are as varied as its deposits. The most important ones are magnetic pyrites ($FeS+S$), magnetite or magnetic iron ore (Fe_3O_4) from Northern Sweden (Gellivare and Kiruna), siderite ($FeCO_3$) from Great Britain and the Sieg district of Germany, limonite or brown iron ore [$Fe(OH)_3$] from Luxembourg and Lorraine (Minette), red iron ore from Lake Superior (USA), hematite or specular iron ore (Fe_2O_3) from Elba, the knobby oolitic limonite from the Swabian Alps, the bog iron ore [$Fe(OH)_3$] from the North German plains, etc.

Pure iron is used only in exceptional cases. But alloys of iron and carbon are of the very greatest importance. Here, three main kinds were distinguished in the past: (1) The gray or white pig iron with $2 \cdot 7 - 5 \cdot 5\%$ carbon (cast iron if it is destined directly for casting without any further refinement), (2) wrought or rolled iron with $0 \cdot 4 - 0 \cdot 95\%$ (cooled), and (3) steel with $0 \cdot 4 - 1 \cdot 7\%$ carbon (chilled).

Today the only type of iron differing from steel is the nonworkable pig iron of more than $1 \cdot 8\%$ carbon content.

Extraction

Iron is extracted from its ores by reduction of the oxides with coke in tall blast furnaces. The products of blast furnaces are: Pig iron, slag, and waste gas. The pig iron contains $2 \cdot 5 - 4\%$ carbon, and varying proportions of silicon, manganese, phosphorus, and sulfur. When pig iron is cooled slowly, the carbon separates in the form of graphite: The result is "gray pig iron". During rapid chilling (in molds, for instance), the carbon remains in solution as cementite Fe_3C: White pig iron is obtained. Here, a higher content of manganese than of silicon is necessary, since the manganese prevents the separation of graphite. This manganese-containing pig iron is processed into steel.

The production of steel

Pig iron is brittle because of its high carbon content. It can be neither wrought nor welded. To transform it into wrought iron, it must be decarbonized to less than $1 \cdot 7\%$ carbon. Decarbonization into steel can be achieved either by the removal of all carbon, and a certain amount of recarbonization, or by carrying the process to just the desired percentage content of carbon. The first method is used in the "air purifying process", the second in the "charcoal hearth process". Air refining is carried out in Thomas converters or Bessemer converters, hearth refining in Siemens-Martin furnaces.

Heat treatment

Steel of carbon content between $0 \cdot 5 - 1 \cdot 7\%$ can be hardened by means of heating it to 800°C, followed by chilling. The hardening is due to the conversion of the finely distributed mixture of iron and cementite present in ordinary steel into a solid solution of cementite in iron (austenite). During slow cooling, the austenite decomposes again, and separation occurs. But if the steel is quenched, the original phase is partly preserved (martensite). It is the martensite, of needle-shaped structure and extremely hard, which hardens the steel.

Since the martensitic structure is not only very hard, but also very brittle, the quenched steel is heated, in other words drawn to remove internal strains and stresses. This produces intermediate structures called troostite and sorbite. Hardening followed by drawing is called tempering.

For the tempering of simple tools in the workshop, the tempering colors appearing on the steel approximately indicate the temperature.

blank	20°C	dark-blue	290°C
pale-yellow	200°C	cyaneous	300°C
straw-yellow	220°C	light-blue	320°C
brown	240°C	blue-gray	350°C
purple	260°C	gray	400°C
violet	280°C		

Steel alloys

The steel obtained by means of refining is further improved by after-treatment and alloying additives. Aftertreatment consists of remelting in graphite crucibles (crucible melting process) or in electric furnaces with arc or induction heating (electric steelmaking process). Alloying additives are silicon, titanium, phosphorus, vanadium, chromium, molybdenum, tungsten, manganese, nickel, etc. Nickel makes the steel tough. 25% nickel permits an expansion of 100%. 36% nickel produces invar steel, which hardly expands at all when heated.

Chromium makes the steel hard. Chromium and nickel together, therefore, result in hardness and toughness. The well-known V2A steel contains 71% iron, 20% chromium, 8% nickel, and $0 \cdot 2\%$ each of carbon, silicon, and manganese. It is extensively used, because of its high resistance to chemical attack, for utensils of all kinds (stainless steel). WT4 steel is an invar steel containing some chromium; it is used for sealing filaments into electric light bulbs, as it has the same expansion coefficient as glass.

Tungsten prevents softening at the beginning of red heat. It is therefore added to material used for high-speed steels (tools for lathes). Molybdenum and vanadium have a similar effect. The addition of silicon improves the acid resistance of the steels.

According to the types of treatment, we distinguish between oil-hardening steel, water-hardening steel, and air-hardening steel, depending on the necessary rate of chilling (oil chills five times more slowly than water). Steels are classified according to their purposes as structural steels, tool steels, special steels, high-speed steels, etc.

Chromium

Occurrence and extraction

The main producers of chromium are South Africa, Rhodesia, Turkey, the Philippines, the USSR, Cuba, New Caledonia, and Albania. The deposits in the USA are exhausted. World production is about 1·6 million tons. The metal is obtained from its ore, chrome iron ore $[Cr_2(FeO_4)]$, by the thermite method: The oxide is mixed with aluminum powder and the mixture made to react in a refractory crucible by means of a primer composition. The oxide is now reduced to the metal, because the aluminum powder avidly combines with the oxygen, and burns to form aluminum oxide.

Properties

Chromium has a silvery luster, can be easily wrought in the pure state, and is very hard. Its specific gravity is 7·1, its melting point is about 1765°C and its boiling point 2300°C. The compact metal is rarely used. But it is important as an alloying constituent, especially with iron. Chromium- and nickel-chromium steels are extremely tough and hard (high-speed steels). Chromium is especially important as surface protection of other metals. Electroplating with chromium is rapidly gaining ground today. The somewhat bluish color of the deposit, rejected in the past because of its very close resemblance to steel, has quickly become accepted in view of the excellent properties of the plating. Since chromium becomes passivated as it acquires an invisible skin of oxide, chromium plating does not tarnish. Chromium-plated surfaces are therefore weather-resistant, and more resistant to acids and gases than nickel-plated ones. Chromium deposits are extremely hard and can be produced in any required thickness. At sufficient thickness, they are a good protection against rust. They do not oxidize at all readily; up to 500°C the surface shows no change.

Reflectivity is higher (65%) than that of nickel (55%) and does not (as with silver and nickel) decrease with time. All metals (except electrum, an aluminum–manganese alloy) can be chromium-plated, either directly or indirectly. The plating adheres very strongly to its support, and because of its low surface adhesion its mechanical wear and tear is low. It cannot, however, be soldered, and does not accept paint or varnish. It is difficult to electroplate other metals on chromium surfaces. But in view of the advantages listed here, these disadvantages are insignificant. Since the color of the metal remotely resembles that of platinum, chromium plating has been taken up by the jewelry trade within the last 20 years. Silver and silverware are chromium-plated for use in the tropics to prevent tarnishing; this applies to an even greater degree to cheap products made of brass, German silver, and similar alloys.

Lead

Occurrence and extraction

Lead ores are usually associated with zinc ores. The most important of them is galena (PbS), which sometimes contains silver compounds. Anglesite $(PbSO_4)$, cerussite $(PbCO_3)$ and red lead ore $(PbCrO_4)$ are also ores from which lead is extracted. Australia and the USSR together supply about a quarter of the world production of 2·35 million tons per annum, followed by the USA, Mexico, Canada, Peru, and Morocco. Lead is often mined and smelted together with zinc. The metal is obtained by reduction with coal after the ores have been roasted.

Properties

Lead is a bluish-white metal: Its specific gravity is 11·34. It melts at 327°C, begins to boil at 1740°C, and is so soft that it can be scratched with the fingernail. In air, lead is very resistant; it is soon covered with a thin protective film. The resistance of lead to sulfuric acid, in which it is coated with a film of lead sulfate, is particularly important. Apparatus and containers for the storage or reaction of sulfuric acid are therefore made of lead.

The corrosion resistance of lead in air makes it suitable for use as a protective coating. The method is actually called lead coating: The pickled and rinsed articles are immersed in the melting bath at about 350°C. Today, homogeneous leading is important: First, the carefully cleaned surface is tin-plated, and the lead melted on. The layer of tin must not become completely liquid, as this would impair the adhesion of the lead. Lead coverings of thicknesses of 0·04 ins. (1mm) and more are thus produced.

Pure lead can also be separated electrolytically; the covering is perfectly compact, but very soft. Lead plating by means of rolling the lead onto the base metal is used only for objects made of zinc. For some purposes, spray leading is chosen: As with spray galvanizing, a stream of molten metal atomized by a compressed-air jet is forced against a sand-blasted surface, where it adheres with the base metal without forming an alloy, simply by mechanical interlocking. The covering produced in this way is not free from pores.

Lead effectively protects an iron surface against corrosion only when the coating is completely compact. If moisture penetrates through any pores, the base metal will be attacked more strongly than if it had not been leaded.

Lead is smelted in coke ovens or in electric furnaces. In air, the molten metal forms a thin covering film of oxide. It is cast either in blocks (for pressing and rolling), or in sand molds, or in ingot molds. Lead parts, sheets, pipes, etc. are joined by means of welding. If no special demands are made regarding corrosion resistance, tin solder can be used for soldering.

Tin solders are soft solders consisting of tin and lead. The table below lists the constituents of a number of them, in percentages.

Tin	Antimony	Iron	Copper + Arsenic + Nickel	Working temperatures °C	Specific gravity
8	0·50			305	10·8
25	1·70	0·05	0·10	257	9·8
30	2·00	0·06	0·12	249	9·6
33	2·20	0·07	0·14	242	9·5
35	2·30	0·07	0·15	237	9·5
40	2·70	0·08	0·16	223	9·3
50	3·30	0·09	0·18	200	8·8
60	3·20	0·10	0·20	185	8·5
90	1·30	0·10	0·20	219	7·5

The remainder is always lead.

Aluminum

As an alloying constituent, aluminum has recently become more and more important. After oxygen and silicon it is the most widespread element in the earth's crust. Aluminum minerals, feldspar, horn blendes, mica, etc. form the largest part of the earth's solid surface. Carborundums, rubies, and sapphires, as well as common emery, consist of aluminum oxide. The pure metal is obtained mainly from its important ores, cryolite (Na_3AlF_6) and bauxite [$AlO(OH)$].

Properties

Aluminum is silvery-white, very ductile, and very malleable. Its low specific gravity ($2 \cdot 7$), good resistance to atmospheric influences, also explained by passivation, and excellent conductivity of heat and electricity account for its widespread use in all branches of industry. In addition, its workability is excellent; it is easily cast, spun, rolled, forged, polished, and welded.

Most aluminum alloys can also be rolled and pressed. These shaping processes increase their strength considerably. Copper, magnesium, zinc, silicon, iron, tin, nickel, and manganese are suitable alloying additives. For molding, alloys with copper, magnesium, or zinc are mostly used. In casting, iron and nickel reduce the tendency of the cast aluminum alloys to form cavities. Additions of tin facilitate the further working of the alloys, of which the best known are duralumin and silumin. The latter contains, in addition to aluminum, 5–25% silicon (mostly $12 \cdot 5\%$); the alloy is very strong and tough. Duralumin consists of aluminum and $0 \cdot 5\%$ Mg, $3 \cdot 5$–5% Cu and $0 \cdot 5$–$0 \cdot 8\%$ Mn, and is chemically very resistant; it is interesting that the strength of duralumin increases during prolonged storage.

Shaping

Aluminum is usually melted in glazed graphite crucibles. During solidification, the metal contracts by about 7%. A coarse formation of cavities is therefore found, which is evident in contraction in the pouring gate or in the formation of undesirable blowholes. The melting point is at 658°C. The metal is cast either in sand molds, or in permanent iron molds.

The properties of aluminum and its alloys, like those of all other metals, depend on whether the raw matierial was cast, was hot or cold worked, or had received thermal aftertreatment. Tensile strength and hardness increase with cold working, which, like hot working, consists of stretching, bending, upsetting, rolling drawing, forging, or pressing. With increasing temperature, the strength steadily decreases, whereas plasticity considerably increases. Material in the cast state is very difficult to work cold, because it is very brittle; it should therefore always be hot worked first; the upper temperature limit for this should be the solidus of the aluminum alloy in question.

Hardening

The alloys of aluminum are hardenable. They contain constituents which at high temperatures are more readily soluble in the aluminum crystal than at lower ones. By means of solution heat treatment at about 500°C, as much as possible of the hardening additive is dissolved; rapid quenching in cold water (rarely, in oil) prevents the separation of the solute component. This results in considerable hardening. The increase in strength, whether it was achieved with hardening or with cold working, can be reversed with heat treatment at about 300–500°C. To save annealing costs, semifinished products are usually obtained in a soft annealed state if major shaping is intended.

Soldering

Alloys are used for hard solders which contain 70–90% aluminum, and the additives to lower the melting point are silicon, zinc, or tin. Silumin, for instance, melts at 570°C. The corrosion resistance of the hard solders is almost as high as that of the welding joint, and greatly superior to that of soft solders. Soft solders containing heavy metals are especially prone to corrosion. Without a protective coat of varnish they can be used only when the parts remain absolutely dry, in other words they must always be kept indoors. The strength of soft solders is also low.

Anodizing

The special importance of aluminum rests on the fact that it can be easily coated with protective films by the electrolytic oxidation method. Anodized aluminum is found everywhere today (largely as a substitute for the heavy and expensive German silver), in anodized jewelry, interior decorations, window display fittings, etc. This excellent material is widely used in the food processing, textile, metal, and automobile industries, architecture, mechanical engineering, instrument making, and the optical industry.

The material for anodizing is aluminum with a degree of purity of $99 \cdot 99\%$. This high-purity metal is particularly resistant to chemical influences of all kinds. However, its strength and hardness are much inferior to that of ordinary pure aluminum. Whereas even small additions of iron, copper, or silicon reduce the corrosion resistance of super-purity aluminum, magnesium increases the strength considerably. More than $2 \cdot 5\%$ has no such effect. Addition of as little as $0 \cdot 2\%$ magnesium, however, is never made, because it prevents the formation of the desired luster during chemical or electrolytic glazing.

The possibility of glazing and anodizing high-purity aluminum and the aluminum–magnesium alloy, and of coloring the hard layer of oxide obtained, is one of the main reasons for the increasing popularity of aluminum. Completely compact films of very high corrosion resistance can be produced. In Europe, more than 150 tons of aluminum are used every year for watch cases, reflectors, and fittings.

Articles made of high-purity aluminum and aluminum–magnesium alloy are polished before anodization; all surface irregularities (scratches, drawing grooves, abraded areas) would otherwise remain visible in the oxide film. The luster of the finished goods thus depends on the degree of polishing. Only now are the articles anodized.

Eloxation is the *el*ectrolytic *oxidation* of aluminum. The aim of the process is to strengthen the natural oxide film, which is only 0.00002–0.00001 ins. ($0 \cdot 0004$–$0 \cdot 0002$mm) thick. If we consider that rubies and sapphires consist of aluminum oxide (Al_2O_3) and have the hardness 9, the hardness of the film thus produced and its corrosion resistance are not surprising.

The finished work is dipped in an acid bath through which a current passes. The anodically suspended articles are covered with an oxide skin 10–15μm thick. As this is porous, it takes up organic and inorganic dye solutions like blotting paper. After the coloring stage the pores are closed (sealed) in some processes. The surface is now as compact as glass and as hard as ruby.

Anodized jewelry appears on the market in deceptively golden colors. It needs no maintenance, does not tarnish, blackens neither the skin nor the clothing of the wearer, and is very cheap. Naturally anodized jewelry, as cheap costume jewelry, has a market of its own.

Finally, aluminum plays a role in the composition of precious stones. Rubies and sapphires have already been mentioned. But the beryls (emerald and aquamarine) and the chrysoberyls (alexandrite), too, contain aluminum [as alumina (Al_2O_3)], as do the spinels, tourmalines, topazes, and many garnets.

Magnesium

Of the minerals containing magnesium, carnallite ($MgCl_2KCl6H_2O$), magnesite ($MgCO_3$), and dolomite ($MgCO_3\ CaCO_3$) are important sources of the pure metal. Olivine, serpentine, and meerschaum, which play a certain part in the lapidary trade, are magnesium silicates. The metal is obtained by the transformation of magnesite into magnesium chloride, followed by smelting flux electrolysis.

The metal is sold in the form of wire, strips, or powder (flash powder). Magnesium generally has a degree of purity of 99·7%. At 1·74, its specific gravity is extraordinarily low. Its melting point is 650°C, and its boiling point 1102°C. In dry air, magnesium is stable; it tarnishes, like zinc, only superficially. Heated beyond its melting point, it burns with a dazzling bright light to oxide. As an industrial raw material, the metal is used only in the alloyed state. The most widely employed alloying additives are manganese, aluminum, zinc, and silicon. The electrum alloys, especially, play an important role in technology.

Whereas electrum in the exact sense is an alloy of 90% magnesium and 10% aluminum, in industry all important magnesium alloys, as far as they are products of the dyestuff industry, are known as electrum metals. With few exceptions, however, aluminum is the most important alloying partner of magnesium. Aluminum, zinc, manganese, and silicon are alloyed to the specially purified magnesium in varying quantities. Between 350 and 400°C the alloys are pressed into shape and rolled into sheets.

The table below lists the constituents, in percentages, of the most important alloys.

Similarly to aluminum, electrum, when exposed to air, acquires a surface film which protects the metal substrate against corrosion. Additions of manganese considerably increase this corrosion resistance. With the chrome mordanting process, a yellow chrome compound is deposited on the surface, which not only protects the metal effectively, but also makes all varnish coats adhere firmly. The alloy can be painted with a great variety of colors by means of certain mordants.

Electrum alloys are melted in steel crucibles. A certain salt mixture protects the metal against oxidation during the melting stage. Casting takes place in sand or in iron molds at a temperature between 720–770°C. Injection molding is more economical for mass-produced articles. The easy workability and light weight of the casting electrum alloys account for their extensive use in all branches of technology.

Forging and pressing considerably improve the mechanical proper-

ties of the alloys. Rolling is usually carried out at temperatures above 300°C, forging at about 350°C. The material is not suitable for cold working. Electrum metals can be welded.

Magnesium as a raw material first became important in 1909 when a German chemical manufacturer marketed the first alloys of a specific gravity of only 1·8. Another German manufacturer supplied the needs of almost the whole world up to about 1930.

Al %	Zn %	Mu %	Si %
7·5	—	0·3	0·1
7·9	0·4	0·3	0·2
8·5	0·4	0·3	0·2
9·5	0·4	0·3	0·2
3·0	1·0	0·3	0·2
3·9	2·9	0·3	0·2
5·9	2·9	0·3	0·2
—	—	1·8	0·2
—	—	—	1·1
10·0	—	0·3	—

The rest is always magnesium.

Protective Metal Coatings

Plating

The purpose of protective metal coatings, apart from the aesthetic one of obtaining a beautiful finish, is to protect the base metal they cover, which is less resistant to the corrosive influences of the atmosphere. There are several methods of producing such metallic coatings. In the section on gold, plating was described, that is, the mechanical production of compounds by means of pressure-welding thin sheets of precious metals onto thicker sheets of base metals. The main difficulty here is how to prevent the formation of oxide films. Compounds of precious metals and copper alloys, of nickel and iron, of nickel–chromium steel and iron, of aluminum and aluminum alloys, and of nickel and copper alloys play an important role in technology. The coatings are even, dense, adhere firmly, and can be of any desired thickness.

Dipping

The simplest method of producing metal coatings is dipping. The metal to be protected is simply dipped into the melt of the coating metal. If the two metals form an alloy (e.g. copper and zinc), this is a straightforward matter; the coatings adhere with particular firmness, provided that no brittle intermediate layers form, resulting in scaling (zinc on iron). If the two metals do not enter into an alloy, dipping must be preceded by certain surface treatments (roughening, pickling, etc.) to ensure adhesion of the coating (leading of iron).

Spraying

A further method consists in the spraying of liquid metals onto the metallic surfaces to be protected. The coating metal emerges from the spray gun in the form of a wire or powder, is immediately melted with a blower as it emerges, and is atomized into miniscule droplets by means of compressed air. To make the droplets adhere better, the surface of the articles to be sprayed is first roughened by pickling or sandblasting. In some conditions, it may be necessary to preheat the article. Since the droplets oxidize in air, the coatings are always interspersed with oxygen compounds unless the work proceeds in an inert-gas atmosphere. The coatings do not adhere very well if they are very thick. The spray method is generally used with zinc, aluminum, lead, cadmium, and tin.

The diffusion method

Metal coatings can also be produced by the diffusion method, which is based on the fact that penetration of one metal by another results in the formation of a protective alloy film on the surface. The coating metals are mostly used in powder form. At a suitably high temperature, the atoms in the crystal lattice become so mobile that they are able to enter the other metal onto which they have been pressed. The metals most suitable for the diffusion method are those with a low melting point, provided that they form an alloy with the base metal.

Enameling

Enamel layers, too, are used as protective coatings of metals. Enamel is an easily liquefiable vitreous flux containing boric acid. Usually, certain metallic oxides (of aluminum, zinc, magnesium, or zirconium) are added to improve acid resistance. (Art enamel is not relevant in this context.) With the exception of aluminum, almost all important metals for practical use can be enameled. It is of course important that the coating has the same expansion coefficient as the base metal, so that it does not splinter off when heated. The ground enamel is coated at about 800°C, the top enamel at temperatures above 1000°C. This is followed by glazing. Freedom from pores is an important consideration in all enameling work.

Electroplating

Electroplating is the most important method of producing metallic coatings.

Compounds whose atoms are held together merely by electric attraction are separated into the components of their molecules by water. Such atoms are called ions, that is, atoms with a free positive or negative electric charge. The electrical nature of the ions is demonstrated particularly well when the two poles (electrodes) of an electric current are immersed in the solution. The positive ions migrate to the negative pole, the cathode (hence cations), where they become neutralized by taking up the appropriate quantity of negative charge. The negative ions migrate to the positive pole, the anode (hence anions), giving up to it their negative charge. Thus negative electricity disappears at the cathode and is given up at the anode. It follows that an electric current flows in the solution (bath) from the negative to the positive pole. These baths are therefore called second-class conductors or electrolytes (metals are first-class conductors). It has already been mentioned that all metals and hydrogen form cations, and all nonmetals and acid radicals anions.

In the electroplating bath, the metal intended for plating forms the anode, the article to be plated the cathode. Usually, however, another (insoluble) material serves as anode. Here, the metal to be precipitated exists only as a part of a salt dissolved in the bath. The electrodes are connected to the poles of a current source (storage battery). A certain potential, measured in volts, is necessary to operate the bath; this voltage depends not only on the reactions at the electrodes, but also on the conductivity of the electrolyte (which is influenced by its temperature, concentration, etc.), as well as on the surface area of the article and the path length between the electrodes. Additional liberation of hydrogen greatly depends on the voltage; it plays an important part in most metal depositions.

The state of the surface of the article to be plated is important for the production of good plating. The coatings adhere only to an absolutely clean and perfectly pure metal surface, free from all traces of grease and oxides. Polishing dust, sweaty hands, and residual degreasing agents endanger the precipitates and cause them to flake off. Furthermore, a certain current density must be maintained during plating; this is the current intensity, measured in amperes per unit area, and in electroplating this is usually 1cm^2. A specific quantity of each metal is deposited on the cathode per ampere per hour. A part of the electrical energy, however, is always lost in the baths without benefiting the deposition of metal. The ratio of the true weight of metal deposited to the theoretical value calculated on the basis of current intensity is called the electrolytic efficiency.

Current density, composition, temperature, concentration, and agitation of the bath are not only responsible for the quantity, but in particular for the quality of the deposit also. The metal coating can turn out mat or rough, spongy or knotty, brittle or tough, hard or soft, shiny, porous, or solid. Working instructions will therefore differ from one case to the next.

The deposition of the metal on the article passes through two stages of development. At the beginning the first solid particles, called nuclei, are deposited; these grow in all directions into crystals until they are inhibited by a neighboring crystal. If, therefore, the rate of nucleation is slow, but the growth rate fast, large crystals will form. But if a large number of slowly growing nuclei are produced, the deposit will be very fine-grained. In very dilute baths and at moderate current density the deposit forms slowly and becomes coarse-grained, because only comparatively few ions come to be discharged on the cathode, where they form nuclei. Conversely, high current density, high bath concentration, and high temperatures produce fine-grain deposits.

The behavior of the plating metals during electrodeposition varies greatly. It depends largely on the salts used. The hydrogen almost always present in the baths is not only liberated at the cathode like a metal, but also forms alloys like a metal with many other metals. This makes the situation very difficult to assess. A simultaneous deposition of two metals has been known, resulting in the plating of an alloy, as in the industrially important electrolytic brass plating. Alloy plating is successful if conditions favorable to the deposition of both metals can be created with the choice of the correct current density and suitable composition of the bath. There is no external difference between electrolytically deposited alloys and those that have been melted. But the internal structures are different.

The most important industrial baths are chromium, zinc, copper, and nickel baths. But there are a number of other metals suitable for plating: Platinum, gold, rhodium, silver, tin, lead, cadmium, cobalt, tungsten, and others.

With all the methods of metal plating described here, it must be borne in mind that the plated metal is truly protected only if it is covered completely. This applies especially when the plating metal is more precious than the plated one. If the plating contains pores, corrosion spreads further and further, starting in the minute areas of imperfection, and forming local cells. The damage becomes greater than if there had been no plating at all.

Coatings of other kinds

Finally, it should be mentioned that metal coatings are not the only means of protection against corrosion. A large number of well-known oxide coatings (for example with the eloxation method) as well as organic coatings, varnishes, greases, tars, rubber, oil paints, and similar substances are available.

Nonmetallic Aids

Acids

Acids are chemical compounds which contain hydrogen. In aqueous solutions, the hydrogen is split off as cations (positively charged ions). The remainder is called the acid radical, which forms anions with corresponding negative charges. The hydrogen atoms in the acid formula, which become ions in aqueous solution, determine the acid character. It is the H-ions (hydrogen ions) which are the cause of the acid taste of the acids and the red staining of litmus paper. Acids which in aqueous solution split off almost all hydrogen atoms as H-ions are called strong acids, and those which split off few or hardly any of these atoms medium-strong or weak acids. Acids whose formulae do not include oxygen are called hydracids, and those which in addition to hydrogen also contain oxygen are called oxacids.

The acids important in this context are hydrochloric acid (HCl), nitric acid (HNO_3), sulfuric acid (H_2SO_4), hydrofluoric acid (HF), boric acid (H_3BO_3), and hydrocyanic acid (HCN).

Sometimes the salts of the acids are of greater importance to us than the acids themselves. The salts are obtained if all or part of the hydrogen atoms in the formula are replaced by atoms of metals. Thus HCl becomes NaCl (common salt).

Hydrochloric acid

Hydrochloric acid is a solution of hydrochloric gas in water. The concentrated acid is about 37%; it fumes in air as it emits hydrogen chloride, and is therefore called fuming hydrochloric acid. The commercial acid is about 25%. The gas formed has a pungent smell. The acid is colorless and very strong. The strength of a solution is best determined by means of its specific gravity. The two values have a quite accidental relation: $S = 1 + p/200$ (S is the specific gravity, p is the percentage content). A mixture of 3 parts hydrochloric and 1 part nitric acid is called aqua regia, which is used to dissolve gold and platinum. The salts of hydrochloric acid are called chlorides.

Nitric acid

Nitric acid, too, is a very strong acid. The liquid has been used from ancient times for the separation of gold and silver, since it dissolves silver readily, but does not affect gold and platinum. The acid is colorless. Pure, concentrated HNO_3 is 68% and is also sold in this concentration. It rapidly destroys organic substances. Its salts are called nitrates. When metals are dissolved in the acid, brown fumes are emitted, which are highly injurious to health. The pickle used for brassware consists of equal parts of nitric and sulfuric acid. Usually, a little hydrochloric acid and cooking salt are added to it.

Sulfuric acid

Sulfuric acid is an oily liquid, in the pure state as clear as water and colorless. It is easy to determine its concentration by finding its specific gravity. Industrial sulfuric acid is usually colored yellow or brown by impurities. It must be treated with the greatest care at all times, as it too is very strong. Water must never be added to concentrated sulfuric acid, because so much heat is generated during dilution that the small volume of water is quickly brought to the boil, and as it evaporates it carries the acid with it, splashing it over a wide area. When concentrated acid is to be mixed with water, the acid must be added to the water slowly, in a thin jet, and continuously stirred.

Sulfuric acid is one of the most important pickling acids. The purpose of pickling a metal is to remove scaly layers, rust, and oxide skins formed during the manufacture of the workpiece. Metal objects are carefully degreased and pickled, especially before they are electroplated. Mixtures of concentrated acids, one of which is nitric acid, are used, especially for the pickling of copper and its alloys. Sulfuric and hydrochloric acid are the most important pickles for iron and steel. For aluminum, strong alkalis such as caustic soda and caustic potash, too, are suitable (first pickle). Besides the chemical pretreatment of the material, a mechanical method—scraping with strong steel wire brushes—is known.

Hydrofluoric acid

Hydrofluoric acid is an aqueous solution of the colorless, pungently-smelling hydrogen fluoride gas. The concentration of the industrial acid is normally 40%. Since hydrofluoric acid attacks almost all metals except platinum, as well as porcelain and glass, it is kept in gutta percha or plastic bottles. Searing of the skin causes painful, very malignant injuries, which heal very reluctantly. The property of the acid of dissolving silicates is used in enameling and staining techniques. The effective constituent of de-enameling baths is hydrofluoric acid.

Boric acid

Boric acid is of interest in this context only because of one of its salts, borax (see *Soldering agents*). The industrial acid consists of fine scales of a mother-of-pearl-like luster. It is one of the weakest acids.

Hydrocyanic acid

The importance of hydrocyanic acid, too, is based on its salts, potassium cyanide (KCN), and sodium cyanide (NaCN). Both salts are used for leaching gold and silver ores, since they dissolve these metals. The acid and its salts are lethal poisons. Fractions of a grain cause death if they enter the stomach.

Bases

Bases or lyes are chemical compounds which split off OH groups in aqueous solutions. These OH groups are the cause of the alkaline or soapy character of the compounds; they also stain red litmus paper blue. The most important alkalis (lyes) in metalwork are caustic soda, caustic potash, and liquid ammonia.

Caustic soda (NaOH) and caustic potash (KOH) play an important part as degreasing agents during the chemical treatment of the metals prior to electroplating. These lyes have the effect of transforming traces of grease or oil adhering to the objects into water-soluble soaps or of

mechanically detaching them by emulsification. The alkalis are usually sold in the form of little white pellets, which, dissolved in water, produce the lye. Bases must be treated with the same care as acids. The eyes are protected by goggles. It is a general rule that acid splashes should be neutralized by rinsing with very dilute ammonia, and alkali splashes by washing out with very dilute acetic acid. Eye injuries must be washed with running water, and medical advice sought immediately after this treatment.

Liquid ammonia (NH_4OH) is a solution of ammonia gas in water. The lye is very much weaker than caustic soda or potash. Since there is a constant escape of ammonia gas from the solution, the base is most easily identified by its characteristic smell.

Soldering Agents

It is well known that the cleanness of metal surfaces to be joined is extremely important. The most frequent impurities are oxide skins or other nonmetallic films formed in the course of shaping. Although scraping or filing produces metallically blank surfaces, it does not prevent the development of fresh oxide films during the soldering process. The soldering agents should therefore have not only the property of dissolving existing layers of oxide and impurities, but also the ability to prevent the formation of oxides on the joints during soldering. The solder, too, must be protected from oxidation, for those metals, especially, which lower the melting point would otherwise burn and cause undesirable changes in the flow characteristics of the solder, or in the position of the melting point. Lastly, the soldering agent should assist in immobilizing the solder where it is required, and in preventing it from flowing to neighboring parts of the work, which may lead to moving parts being soldered together.

The soldering agents can be divided according to their effects into those which dissolve oxides, and by covering the metal surface prevent the formation of fresh oxide, and those that confine the flow of the solder to the soldering joint. The first are called fluxes, the second solder-inhibiting agents.

Fluxes

To offer effective protection against oxidation, it is necessary for the melting point and the working temperature of the soldering agents to be below the melting point of the solder. The melting temperatures of the fluxes vary according to type and composition. If they are too high, the solder balls up, but is prevented from flowing by the undissolved oxides. At higher temperatures, however, the flux, too, would melt, which, of course, would nullify the advantage of the low melting point of the solder.

Flux can be bought in solid or in liquid form. In the liquid agents, the solvent medium evaporates; the solute remains behind, and becomes liquid exactly like a solid flux when it is heated further. All fluxes are expected to be easily removed after the soldering process (solubility in water or in dilute acids).

Common fluxes for soft solders: Soldering fluid, ammonium chloride, hydrochloric acid, colophony, soldering salt, and mixtures of tallow and sal-ammoniac.

Soft soldering

Soldering fluid consists of 27 parts zinc chloride, 11 parts ammonium chloride, and 62 parts water. The zinc chloride acts as a solvent of the oxides. In heat, ammonium chloride decomposes into ammonia and hydrochloric acid, which in turn also dissolves oxides. At the same time the salts form a covering layer, thus offering protection against further oxidation. With zinc and tin, pure hydrochloric acid alone is sufficient as flux, since it converts the oxides present into chlorides.

Ammonium chloride (NH_4Cl) on its own can be used as flux for soldering brass and copper. As already mentioned, when heated this produces a mixture of ammonia (NH_3) and hydrochloric acid (HCl) which dissolves the oxides covering the exposed metal surfaces, forming ammoniacal compounds and volatile chlorides. The salt dissolves readily in water.

Colophony (rosin), used for violin bows, is a residue of the distillation of turpentine. It does not dissolve, but merely covers oxides, and serves particularly for the soldering of lead; it is difficult to remove afterwards.

Soldering salt is a mixture of equal parts of zinc chloride and ammonium chloride. The hydrochloric acid liberated from the ammonium chloride not only reinforces the oxide-solvent action of the zinc chloride, but also etches the metal surfaces, favoring alloy formation between the solder and the metal base.

Mixtures of tallow, colophony, and a little ammonium chloride are sold in the form of pastes. They are easily removed after soldering.

To simplify soft soldering, the solders are often combined with the soldering agents.

Hard soldering or brazing

The best-known flux is borax.

Borax is a salt of tetraboric acid ($H_2B_4O_7$), which forms from boric acid (HBO_3) when heated; water is set free in the process. In the crystalline state, borax contains water of crystallization, which it gives off at about 400°C, strongly expanding. At 741°C, the salt melts and is transformed into a vitreous, solid mass. Borax thus acts as a solvent of metallic oxides and as a protective cover through the formation of hard coatings of light specific gravity. After soldering, these can be removed by boiling them off. Borax is used for hard soldering most metals and also for soldering gold and silver. For soldering, borax paste, which is prepared by stirring borax cones into water on a clay plate, is popular. For extensive work (e.g. silversmith's), borax powder (dehydrated borax), is used; potash is added to make it cheaper and to lower its melting point. Boric acid, too, is occasionally mixed with borax powder to lower its melting point. Thus boric acid (waterglass), which consists of 3 parts borax and 1 part boric acid, melts at 610°C.

Today, borax is being progressively displaced by branded liquid fluxing agents.

Occasionally cryolite, a mineral consisting of sodium, aluminum, and fluorine, alone or associated with ammonium phosphate, is also used as a hard-soldering agent.

Solder-inhibiting pastes

To prevent the solder from flowing to where it is not wanted, substances are used which, on the one hand, are not displaced by the liquid solder, and on the other are easy to apply, do not become liquid at the usual soldering temperatures, and withstand heat without becoming inflated. In practice, the materials used mostly are tripoli, clay, chalk, and iron oxide.

Chalk ($CaCO_3$) in its finest form is stirred with water or methylated spirit and carefully applied as near as possible to the joint. Entry of the solder into the joint, however, must remain unobstructed.

Tripoli consists of about 90% silicon oxide (SiO_2); in addition, alumina (Al_2O_2) and iron oxide (Fe_2O_3) can almost always be found. The mineral originated in the shells of unicellular plants (diatoms) and is therefore also called diatomaceous earth. Its name is derived from the Lebanese city of Tripoli, where large quantities of it were marketed in the past. Today, most of the material comes from deposits in Bavaria, the Tyrol, Czechoslovakia, and Saxony. Tripoli is used mainly for polishing metals, gems, and glass, and for the manufacture of molds. In addition, a large variety of other types of siliceous deposits are also suitable, such as the so-called rotten stone from Derbyshire, England. The yellowish, yellowish-gray, or reddish mass (the color depends on the iron content) is stirred into water as a fine powder; the resulting paste is applied as a solder-inhibiting substance.

Iron oxide is obtained when iron is burned in a stream of oxygen. Its chemical formula is Fe_3O_2. Very strongly annealed, it is sold as caput mortuum (painter's body color: "Colcothar"). In this form it is almost insoluble in hot, concentrated acids. Because of its hardness, the oxide is very widely used for polishing glass and metals. Finely powdered, it is made into polishing pastes. The color of the oxide depends on the manufacturing temperature and small quantities of additives. According to the various hues, the material, generally known as polishing red, is also called rouge, Pompeian red, or Venetian red. As a mineral the oxide is known as hematite, blood stone, kidney ore, or oligiste iron ore. The island of Elba is red with it. Polished pieces of hematite (blood stones) are used for obtaining a high polish on silver. Crocus is artificial oxide produced from iron filings. The iron oxide powder rubbed to a paste with methylated spirit is a useful solder-inhibiting substance on sites which are difficult to reach.

Clay, like tripoli, is also used as a solder-inhibiting paste. The substance consists mainly of alumina, silica, and water. The color varies between yellow and brown according to the content of iron.

Abrasives and Polishing Agents

Grinding and polishing are processes of flattening. The luster of metal surfaces, on which their attractive appearance is based, cannot be produced if the surfaces are uneven, wavy, or rough. To obtain a smooth, plane metal area and thus a specular sheen, the raised portions can either be planed off or rolled down under pressure. In grinding, certain abrasives, which consist of particles with hard crystal faces and sharp edges, are used to remove all raised portions on the surface by a kind of cutting action. Material is also removed by smoothing and polishing with polishing agents, whose particles are often round. The second method, that of pressing or rolling in raised portions, consists in using the polishing stone (blood stone) or the engraver's burnisher, and in drum polishing with mass-produced articles.

Generally, metal is polished on rotating wheels of wood, leather, felt, or, for burnishing, of muslin, wool, chamois leather, or natural silk. Depending on the nature of the base metal, certain abrasives or polishing agents are glued onto the wheels.

For the first grinding (coarse grinding), natural emery, silicon carbide, or corundum are glued on the periphery of the grinding wheel. Natural emery contains 55–80% alumina (Al_2O_3), 15–35% iron oxide (Fe_3O_2), as well as calcium oxide (CaO), silicon dioxide (SiO_2), and water. Iron oxide makes the abrasive tough, but reduces its hardness. Corundum consists of 90–95% alumina (Al_2O_3); it is considerably harder than emery, but is in turn surpassed by silicon carbide (SiC), whose hardness approximates that of the diamond. The artificial abrasives are generally harder than the natural ones, because they are purer. Artificial corundum, obtained from bauxite through an electric melting process, is sold under such names as alundum, abrasite, or aloxite. Silicon carbide is known as carborundum.

For finishing, during which the grinding cracks of coarse grinding must be removed, the abrasive is also emery, but of very fine grain. Finishing is followed by brushing, for which a very viscous emery paste is required; it consists of fine emery powder stirred into machine oil. The work is first rough-polished, and then burnished. In the final stage, the film of grease left behind from the preceding stages is removed from the shiny surface.

Pumice stone is a popular abrasive, especially for silver and even wood. When pressure drops in the interior of the earth, the masses of molten rock, which under pressure had many gases forced into them, begin to foam like bubbling champagne. Pumice is the solidified result of such bubbling magma. The mineral is sold in coarse pieces or in powder form.

As already mentioned, the abrasive power of the various materials depends on the hardness and sharpness of the edges of the individual particles. A certain toughness of the granules is also desirable; brittle particles splinter too easily. Oils, resins, ceramic substances such as clay or china clay (kaolin), a waterglass-sodium carbonate cement, and even rubber serve as vehicles for abrasives. The less vehicle used, the greater the abrasive power, but the less the firmness of the grinding wheel. Oil as a vehicle makes the material sharp in attacking the object to be ground, but softer. A rubber vehicle renders the wheels less sensitive to uneven pressure. Ceramic vehicles, on account of their own hardness, also take part in the grinding process.

The polishing agents usually come onto the market as rough-polishing pastes and as burnishing pastes. The agents mixed with oil or grease are more economical than liquid ones. The effective components of these polishing pastes, known by a great variety of trade names, are tripoli (especially finest American tripoli), alumina, polishing red, polishing green (chromium oxide), French chalk, polishing chalk, precipitated chalk (natural chalk from the island of Rügen), calcite ($CaCO_3$) from Lower Bavaria, magnesia (MgO), os sepiae—white cuttlefish bone—tin oxide (SnO_2), etc. Materials of noncrystalline, comparatively soft rock, or synthetic materials are preferred. Polishing is usually done with French chalk, which is produced as a rod-shaped paste. The vehicles are stearin oils or tallow. For the precious metals gold and silver, as well as for iron and steel, pastes which contain finest-grained polishing red or polishing green are popular. Silver is sometimes burnished with soot suspended in alcohol.

In the precious-metal trade, the question of material lost in the grinding and polishing process is of interest. Naturally, reliable values are hard to come by here since the loss of material depends on the quality of the substance, the polishing agent, the duration of the treatment, and the pressure on the wheel. The coarse-grained chromium oxide removes more material than the more gently acting polishing red. Experiments have shown that sheet silver, after having been ground on both sides with oil and pumice powder and burnished

on one side with polishing green and a cloth buff, weighed only about 21 oz (600g) per piece instead of 21·4 oz (612g) before the procedure. This meant a loss of 0·1 oz (0·6g) of material per 0·2 sq in. (1cm²) of ground and polished area of pure silver. In practice, the loss is probably much greater.

As already described, the second method of making metal surfaces smooth consists in the pressing and rolling of any raised portions into the metal by the use of the engraver's burnisher, blood stone, or steel balls in drums (tumblers) for polishing. The drums are usually made of wood. Burnished balls of hardened chromium steel, whose surface must be absolutely flawless, are introduced into these drums. If the balls are too large, they touch only parts of the surface of the work to be polished; if they are too small they may jam. The work is polished by pressure. The size of the drum depends on the pressure the work can stand. In addition to absolute cleanness of the drum and its contents, the choice of correct polishing substance is important. Firms specializing in this field supply a wide range of polishing salts, powders, and soaps. These are dissolved in water, and the solution poured into the drum. The duration of the process depends on the work to be polished and the polishing agent. Gold- and silverware is treated for about two hours. The work and the polishing agent should take up about three quarters of the volume of the drum. The work should represent about one third of the contents, the steel balls about two thirds. Drum polishing can also be carried out without steel balls, in other words, when the shape of the workpieces is such that they polish one another in the polishing liquid in the rotating drum.

Polishing with blood stone and engravers' burnishers also produces a very high gloss on the surface of the work. The polishing stones are available in all possible shapes, so that strongly profiled objects, too, can be polished without difficulty.

7.   Calculation of Alloys

Normally, the many tasks occurring in practice can be reduced to one of the following basic types:

Conversion of Carat and Half-Ounce into Millesimals

Fineness today is expressed in millesimals (parts per thousand). The value therefore indicates how many grains of pure gold or pure silver are contained in 1,000g of alloy. The expressions carat and half-ounce, also measures of fineness, are gradually becoming obsolete, and in the interest of international commerce should eventually disappear altogether. The number of carats indicates how many parts of gold are contained in the particular alloy. The alloy is divided for this purpose into 24 parts. Pure gold is therefore 24 carat. The number of half-ounces indicates the proportion of pure silver in 16 parts alloy. Hence pure silver equals 16 half-ounces. Conversion of carat and half-ounce is therefore based on the simple Rule of Three:

Example: How many millesimals are 9 carat?

$$24 \text{ carat } = 1,000 \text{ millesimals}$$

$$1 \text{ carat } = \frac{1,000}{24} \text{ millesimals}$$

$$9 \text{ carat } = \frac{1,000 \times 9}{24} = 375 \text{ millesimals} = 375/1000 \text{ gold}$$

Example: How many millesimals are 12 half-ounces?

$$16 \text{ half-ounces } = 1,000 \text{ millesimals}$$

$$1 \text{ half-ounce } = \frac{1,000}{16} \text{ millesimals}$$

$$12 \text{ half-ounces } = \frac{1,000 \times 12}{16} = 750 \text{ millesimals}$$

$$= 750/1000 \text{ silver}$$

Millesimals are converted into carat or half-ounces accordingly:

Example: How many carat are 250 millesimals?

$$1,000 \text{ millesimals} = 24 \text{ carat}$$

$$1 \text{ millesimal } = \frac{24}{1,000} \text{ carat}$$

$$250 \text{ millesimals} = \frac{24 \times 250}{1,000} = 6 \text{ carat}$$

Example: How many half-ounces are 600 millesimals?

$$1,000 \text{ millesimals} = 16 \text{ half-ounces}$$

$$1 \text{ millesimal } = \frac{16}{1,000} \text{ half-ounce}$$

$$600 \text{ millesimals} = \frac{16 \times 600}{1,000} = 9 \cdot 6 \text{ half-ounces}$$

Calculation of the Constituents of an Alloy

In these problems we have an alloy of a certain fineness in a certain quantity. The so-called standard (in gold alloys the quantity of pure gold present, and in silver alloys the corresponding quantity of pure silver), and the additional weight, that is the weight of the other metals constituting the alloy, are to be determined. If certain information about the additional metals is available, these can be separately calculated.

Example: According to the assay report, 750g alloy contain 485/1000 gold and 143/1000 silver. The rest is copper. How many grams of each metal are present?

1,000g alloy contain 485g gold, 143g silver, and 372g copper.
   1g alloy contains $0 \cdot 485$g gold, $0 \cdot 143$g silver, and $0 \cdot 372$g copper.
750g alloy contain $0 \cdot 485 \times 750$g = $363 \cdot 75$g gold
   $0 \cdot 143 \times 750$g = $107 \cdot 25$g silver
   $0 \cdot 372 \times 750$g = $279 \cdot 00$g copper.
The alloy contains $363 \cdot 75$g gold, $107 \cdot 25$g silver, and 279g copper.

Example: Calculate the constituents of 200g 333/1000 gold.
The alloy also contains 30% silver; the rest is copper.

Gold	$0 \cdot 333 \times 200 =$	$66 \cdot 6$
Silver	$0 \cdot 300 \times 200 =$	$60 \cdot 0$
Copper	$0 \cdot 367 \times 200 =$	$73 \cdot 4$
		$200 \cdot 0$g

Calculation of the Fineness of an Alloy

The fineness is denoted by the number indicating how many times the full weight is contained in the standard. The fineness can therefore be obtained whenever it is possible to calculate the standard and the full weight of an alloy:

Example: The following metals are melted together:

60g 585/1000 gold	standard $0 \cdot 585 \times 60 = 35 \cdot 10$g
40g 333/1000 gold	standard $0 \cdot 333 \times 40 = 13 \cdot 32$g
25g pure gold	standard $25 \cdot 00$g
75g silver	—
80g copper	—
280g = full weight	standard $= 73 \cdot 42$g

What is the fineness of the gold alloy obtained?

Fineness = standard divided by full weight = $73 \cdot 42 \div 280 = 0 \cdot 262 = $ 262/1000 gold

Production of Alloys from Their Constituent Metals

A certain alloy of gold, silver, and additional metals is to be produced. Either the weight of the alloy to be produced or a certain quantity of one of the constituent metals to be used is given.

Example: 200g of a silver solder of 646/1000 silver, 162/1000 copper, 100/1000 brass, and 92/1000 zinc is required.
How many grams of each constituent metal are required?

200g silver solder contain
$0 \cdot 646 \times 200 = 129 \cdot 2$g silver
$0 \cdot 162 \times 200 = 32 \cdot 4$g copper
$0 \cdot 100 \times 200 = 20 \cdot 0$g brass
$0 \cdot 092 \times 200 = 18 \cdot 4$g zinc

together $200 \cdot 0$g silver solder

$129 \cdot 2$g silver, $32 \cdot 4$g copper, $20 \cdot 0$g brass, and $18 \cdot 4$g zinc are required.

Example: 585/1000 gold with 300 parts silver, the rest copper, is to be produced from 450g pure gold. How much silver and copper is necessary and how much alloy is obtained?

1,000g alloy can be obtained from 585g pure gold

$\frac{1,000}{585}$g alloy can be obtained from 1g pure gold

$\frac{1,000 \times 450}{585} = 769 \cdot 2$g alloy can be obtained from 450g pure gold.

These $769 \cdot 2$g alloy contain

$0 \cdot 585 \times 769 \cdot 2 = 450 \cdot 0$g pure gold
$0 \cdot 300 \times 769 \cdot 2 = 230 \cdot 8$g silver
$0 \cdot 115 \times 769 \cdot 2 = 88 \cdot 4$g copper
total $769 \cdot 2$g alloy

$230 \cdot 8$g silver and $88 \cdot 4$g copper are required; melted with the 450g pure gold they make up $769 \cdot 2$g of the desired alloy.

Remelting Without a Preselected Gold Color

Two alloys are to be melted together to produce a third alloy, whose fineness obviously must be between those of the two original alloys. Either the weight of one of the two original substances or that of the alloy to be produced is given. If, in the case of gold alloys, one of the two original substances is pure gold, the calculation is based on 1000/1000 gold; if one of the original substances is copper, 0/1000 gold is entered in the equation.

The calculation is schematically carried out according to the diagonal rule, which is based on the consideration that, to obtain alloy C from alloys A and B, the largest quantity of that original metal is required to which the proportion of C is closest. There thus exists an inverse ratio between the quantities required and their distances from C.

A and B are the two original alloys, and C is the desired one, whose fineness must be between those of A and B. D is the difference between B and C; E is the difference between A and C. The sum of D and E is F, hence $F = E + D$. The rule means that Dg of A and Eg of B must be alloyed to make Fg of C.

Example: 3,000g 800/1000 silver are to be remelted to 835/1000 silver by the addition of 900/1000 silver. How many grams 900/1000 silver must be added? How much alloy is obtained?
According to the diagonal rule it immediately follows

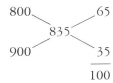

that 65g 800/1000 alloyed with 35g 900/1000 produce 100g 835/1000. But if 35g 900/1000 must be alloyed to 65g 800/1000, 3,000g 800/1000 require

$$\frac{35 \times 3,000}{65} = 1615g \qquad 900/1000.$$

4,615g of the desired alloy are obtained. To prove this, the fineness of the alloy can be determined that is obtained when 3,000g 800/1000 and 1,615g 900/1000 alloys are melted together.

In the above example, the weight of one of the original materials was given. In the example following, a certain weight of the new alloy is required, i.e. F is given:

Example: 200g 750/1000 gold are required from 430/1000 gold and pure gold. How much of the two original materials must go into the crucible?

The diagonal rule says

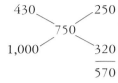

$$430 \diagdown \diagup 250$$
$$750$$
$$1,000 \diagup \diagdown \underline{320}$$
$$570$$

that 570g of the new alloy is obtained, if 250g 430/1000 and 320g fine gold are alloyed. Thus the following Rule of Three is obtained:

$$570\text{g } 750/1000 = 250\text{ g } 430/1000 + 320\text{ g pure gold}$$
$$1\text{g } 750/1000 = \frac{250}{570}\text{g } 430/1000 + \frac{320}{570}\text{g pure gold}$$
$$200\text{g } 750/1000 = \frac{250 \times 200}{570}\text{g} + \frac{320 \times 200}{570}\text{g pure gold,}$$

i.e. $\qquad\qquad 87 \cdot 7\text{g} + 112 \cdot 3\text{g}$

87·7g 430/1000 gold and 112·3g pure gold are placed in the crucible. 200g 750/1000 gold are obtained.

Proof:

87·7g 430/1000 gold	fineness	$0 \cdot 430 \times 87 \cdot 7 = 37 \cdot 7$
112·3g pure gold	fineness	$\underline{112 \cdot 3}$
	fineness	$150 \cdot 0$

Fineness: full weight $150 \cdot 0 : 200 = 0 \cdot 75$ or 750/1000.

Example: 500g 900/1000 silver are to be made into an 800/1000 silver alloy by the addition of copper. How much copper must be added?

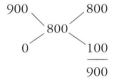

$$900 \diagdown \diagup 800$$
$$800$$
$$0 \diagup \diagdown \underline{100}$$
$$900$$

Thus 100g copper are required for 800g 900/1000

$\dfrac{100}{8}$g copper $\qquad\qquad$ for 100g 900/1000

$\dfrac{100 \times 5}{8}$ copper $\qquad\qquad$ for 500g 900/1000

i.e. 62·5g copper.

It is useful to know that, when the scheme is set up, it is immaterial which of the two starting materials is placed top left and which bottom left. When A and B are interchanged, D and E on the right must also be interchanged.

Remelting for a Preselected Gold Color

The diagonal rule cannot be used if a certain color of gold is required, because here the ratios of the addition metals to one another are fixed. The quantity of each additive must therefore be calculated separately. The correct procedure is to compare the constituents of the original alloy with that of the required one.

Example: 500g alloy of 605/1000 gold, 300/1000 silver, 95/1000 copper are to be remelted to 585/1000 gold, 115/1000 silver, and 300/1000 copper. What must be added in the crucible to the original alloy?

First of all, the constituents of the 500g original alloy are calculated:

Gold	$0 \cdot 605 \times 500 =$	$302 \cdot 5\text{g}$
Silver	$0 \cdot 300 \times 500 =$	$150 \cdot 0\text{g}$
Copper	$0 \cdot 095 \times 500 =$	$\dfrac{47 \cdot 5\text{g}}{500 \cdot 0\text{g}}$

We now deal with the metal whose content is most reduced in the new alloy. Here the gold content is slightly reduced (from 605/1000 to 585/1000), the copper content increased (from 95/1000 to 300/1000), and the silver content considerably reduced (from 300/1000 to 115/1000). The question now is how much of the new alloy can be produced with 150g silver:

With 115g silver, 1,000g of the new alloy can be produced

with 1g silver, $\dfrac{1,000}{115}$g of the new alloy can be produced

with 150g silver, $\dfrac{1,000}{115} \times 150\text{g} = 1,304 \cdot 4\text{g}$ of the new alloy

can be produced.

Now the constituents of 1,304·4g of the new alloy are calculated:

Gold	$0 \cdot 585 \times 1,304 \cdot 4 =$	$763 \cdot 07\text{g}$
Silver	$0 \cdot 115 \times 1,304 \cdot 4 =$	$150 \cdot 01\text{g}$
Copper	$0 \cdot 300 \times 1,304 \cdot 4 =$	$\dfrac{391 \cdot 32\text{g}}{1,304 \cdot 40\text{g}}$

A comparison with the original alloy shows:

	Gold	Silver	Copper
1,304·4g new alloy	763·07	150·0	391·3
500·0g old alloy	302·50	150·0	47·5
	460·57	—	343·8

500g old alloy, 460·57g gold and 343·8g copper enter the crucible.

If, instead of one original alloy, two alloys whose weights are indicated are given, calculations are the same as in the previous example, treating the two original alloys as melted into a single alloy.

Finally, here is an example of the use of pre-alloys, which are particularly popular for the low boiling point metals zinc and cadmium:

150g yellow gold is required with 333/1000 gold, 390/1000 silver, and 200/1000 zinc. For remelting, tombac with 15% zinc and 85% copper is to be used. How much tombac, gold, silver, copper, and zinc must be mixed in the crucible?

The constituents of the required alloy are:

Gold	$0 \cdot 333 \times 150 =$	$49 \cdot 95\text{g}$
Silver	$0 \cdot 390 \times 150 =$	$58 \cdot 50\text{g}$
Copper	$0 \cdot 077 \times 150 =$	$11 \cdot 55\text{g}$
Zinc	$0 \cdot 200 \times 150 =$	$\dfrac{30 \cdot 00\text{g}}{150 \cdot 00\text{g}}$

Copper and zinc are contained in how many grams pre-alloy?

Copper: $\dfrac{100 \times 11 \cdot 55}{85} = 13 \cdot 6\text{g}$; zinc: $\dfrac{100 \times 30}{15} = 200\text{g tombac.}$

The constituents of $13 \cdot 6$g tombac:

Copper	$0 \cdot 85\text{g} \times 13 \cdot 6 =$	$11 \cdot 56\text{g}$
Zinc	$0 \cdot 15\text{g} \times 13 \cdot 6 =$	$2 \cdot 04\text{g}$
		$13 \cdot 60\text{g}$

The following quantities enter the crucible:

Pure gold	$49 \cdot 95\text{g}$
Silver	$58 \cdot 50\text{g}$
Tombac	$13 \cdot 60\text{g}$
Zinc	$27 \cdot 96\text{g}$
	$150 \cdot 01\text{g}$

150g new alloy requires:

	Gold	Silver	Copper	Zinc
	$49 \cdot 95\text{g}$	$58 \cdot 50\text{g}$	$11 \cdot 55\text{g}$	$30 \cdot 00\text{g}$
			$11 \cdot 56\text{g}$	$2 \cdot 04\text{g}$
	$49 \cdot 95\text{g}$	$58 \cdot 50\text{g}$	—	$27 \cdot 96\text{g}$

Proof:

Fineness = standard: full weight

$49 \cdot 95 : 150 = 0 \cdot 333 = 333/1000$ gold.

Hallmarking

The hallmarking laws differ widely in the various countries. The hallmarks differ, the permitted tolerances differ, and often even the alloys that may be hallmarked differ. In many countries hallmarking is obligatory, in others optional. Whenever jewelry is to be exported, the hallmarking laws in force in the country of destination must be observed. The precious-metal-trade associations and the chambers of commerce and industry supply the necessary information.

The hallmarking law in the United States requires that any article of merchandise that is made of gold or silver or any alloy of either metal, and offered for sale, must carry the maker's trademark. That trademark must be registered with the government. All articles must also bear a quality mark (in the case of gold, the number of carats in the alloy, e.g. 14K). No more than half a carat variance from the declared content is permitted.

In Great Britain the law requires that any gold- or silverware made there, or imported, and subsequently sold, shall be submitted to a Hall (assay office) for hallmarking. The maker must register his own personal mark with one of the various Halls. If the assay of a silver piece is successful, it will be stamped with the maker's mark, the assay mark, the assay office's own mark, and a date letter. If the piece is of too low a standard, it will be broken up. Gold articles are stamped with their carat rating and its decimal equivalent.

8. Precious Stones

by Dr. Werner Plate

Chemical Composition

Precious minerals which play a role as decorative stones are selected according to aesthetic precepts. From a mineralogist's point of view they do not, therefore, form a scientific category. Their composition varies widely. The old belief in the existence of a particularly valuable precious-stone soil has been destroyed by chemical analysis. It was found that it is the most common and widespread elements of the Earth's crust whose compounds produce the beauty of gems.

According to chemical criteria, they can be roughly divided into the following groups:

The only gem that consists of a single element is the diamond. It is cubically crystallized carbon. Graphite, too, is crystalline carbon, although it is hexagonal instead of cubic.

The property of some minerals of occurring in various crystal forms and characteristics, in spite of identical chemical composition, is called polymorphism.

Sulfides

Sulfides are compounds of elements with sulfur, such as the polymorphous iron sulfides (FeS_2); they occur cubically as pyrites, and rhombically as marcasite.

Oxides

Oxides are compounds of elements with oxygen; this category includes quartz (SiO_2), corundum (Al_2O_3), spinel ($MgO.Al_2O_3$), chrysoberyl ($BeOAl_3O_2$), opal ($SiO_2.NH_2O$), and hematite (Fe_2O_3) (blood stone).

Fluorides

Fluorides are compounds of elements with fluorine. Here, the calcium fluorides, called fluorspar (CaF_2) must be mentioned.

Phosphates

These are more complex compounds, in which, among others, the PO_4 radical of phosphoric acid occurs. Examples are brazilianite, lazulite, turquoise, and apatite.

Carbonates

Carbonates are salts of carbonic acid (H_3CO_2). The CO_3 radical therefore occurs in all its compound formulae.

Examples are calcite, azurite, malachite, rhodochrosite and zinc ore. Calcite occurs in the trigonal form as calcite or in its rhombic form as aragonite. Pearls may consist of either variation.

Silicates

The silicates, salts of the silicic acids, constitute the most important and numerous class of minerals, which also includes the majority of precious stones: Andalusite, benitoite, beryl (emerald, aquamarine, etc.), cordierite, dioptas, disthene, precious scapolite, precious topaz, epidot, euclase, feldspar (orthoclase, adularia, moonstone, sunstone, microcline, labradorite, etc.), garnets (pyrope, demantoid, almandite, spessartine, grossularite, hessonite, melanite, etc.), nephrite, olivine, prehnite, jade, rhodonite, hiddenite, kunzite, tourmaline, vesuvianite, zircon, and many others.

Most precious stones contain, in addition to the elements indicated by their formulae, minute admixtures of metallic oxides, which are often the cause of color in gems. Thus chromium colors the ruby red and the emerald green; titanium oxide produces the blue of the sapphire. Besides chromium and titanium, iron, manganese, nickel, and copper are the main chromogenic metals.

Mechanical Properties

To identify an unknown precious stone, it is useful to determine its specific gravity and its hardness accurately.

The specific gravity is the weight of 1cc of a substance. 1cc ruby, specific gravity $4 \cdot 08$, weighs $4 \cdot 08$g. Since 1cc water weighs 1g, it can also be said that ruby is $4 \cdot 08$ times as heavy as the same volume of water. This fact is used in the determination of specific gravity. The stone is weighed first in air, then in water. In water, the stone has become lighter by the weight of the volume of water it displaces. The loss of weight of the stone is calculated by subtraction of the two values determined. The weight in air is now divided by this loss of weight; the result is the specific gravity.

Example: A stone weighs $2 \cdot 15$g in air, $1 \cdot 65$g in water; the loss of weight therefore is $2 \cdot 15 - 1 \cdot 65 = 0 \cdot 50$g. Now $2 \cdot 15$ is divided by $0 \cdot 50$, to give $4 \cdot 3$. The specific gravity of the stone is $4 \cdot 3$. [The stone is in fact a zircon (cf. table).]

In actual practice, a simple goldsmith's balance is used, one scale of which is suspended so high as to leave space for a second one below, attached to it with a thin thread (or hair) and immersed in a vessel filled with water. The stone can thus be weighed first in the top scale in air, and then in the bottom scale in water.

Specific gravities of the most important precious and semi-precious stones

hematite	$5 \cdot 30 - 4 \cdot 90$	vesuvianite	$3 \cdot 45 - 3 \cdot 27$
pyrites	$5 \cdot 10 - 4 \cdot 84$	diopside	$3 \cdot 38 - 3 \cdot 23$
zircon	$4 \cdot 70 - 4 \cdot 65$	dioptas	$3 \cdot 36 - 3 \cdot 28$
zinc spar	$4 \cdot 55 - 4 \cdot 30$	jade	$3 \cdot 35 - 3 \cdot 30$
green zircon	$4 \cdot 33 - 3 \cdot 96$	fluorspar	$3 \cdot 25 - 3 \cdot 10$
rutile	$4 \cdot 30 - 4 \cdot 20$	spodumene	$3 \cdot 20 - 3 \cdot 10$
spessartine	$4 \cdot 25 - 3 \cdot 98$	andalusite	$3 \cdot 20 - 3 \cdot 10$
almandite	$4 \cdot 20 - 3 \cdot 83$	tourmaline	$3 \cdot 16 - 3 \cdot 00$
corundum	$4 \cdot 10 - 3 \cdot 94$	euclase	$3 \cdot 10 - 3 \cdot 05$
malachite	$4 \cdot 00 - 3 \cdot 70$	nephrite	$3 \cdot 06 - 2 \cdot 94$
demantoid	$3 \cdot 85 - 3 \cdot 80$	prehnite	$2 \cdot 95 - 2 \cdot 85$
pyrope	$3 \cdot 80 - 3 \cdot 65$	rosaberyl	$2 \cdot 88 - 2 \cdot 78$
chrysoberyl	$3 \cdot 75 - 3 \cdot 65$	turquoise	$2 \cdot 84 - 2 \cdot 60$
grossularite	$3 \cdot 70 - 3 \cdot 60$	beryl	$2 \cdot 76 - 2 \cdot 66$
hessonite	$3 \cdot 70 - 3 \cdot 60$	labradorite	$2 \cdot 72 - 2 \cdot 69$
rhodonite	$3 \cdot 70 - 3 \cdot 40$	calcite	$2 \cdot 72 - 2 \cdot 70$
rhodochrosite	$3 \cdot 70 - 3 \cdot 30$	quartz	$2 \cdot 66 - 2 \cdot 64$
benitoite	$3 \cdot 68 - 3 \cdot 65$	cordierite	$2 \cdot 66 - 2 \cdot 57$
spinel	$3 \cdot 65 - 3 \cdot 53$	chalcedony	$2 \cdot 65 - 2 \cdot 60$
precious topaz	$3 \cdot 58 - 3 \cdot 50$	orthoclase	$2 \cdot 58 - 2 \cdot 54$
epidot	$3 \cdot 53 - 3 \cdot 28$	moonstone	$2 \cdot 58 - 2 \cdot 55$
diamond	$3 \cdot 53 - 3 \cdot 51$	opal	$2 \cdot 22 - 2 \cdot 05$
olivine	$3 \cdot 45 - 3 \cdot 35$	amber	$1 \cdot 10 - 1 \cdot 05$

In practice, the use of what are known as heavy solutions, of known specific gravity, is popular for the determination of the specific gravity of small stones. A search for a solution in which the stone just floats, and for one in which it just sinks, produces the approximate specific gravity of the stone; it must be between those of the two solutions. This method is sufficiently accurate, and permits rapid determination.

Hardness

A stone is only suitable for decorative purposes if it is hard enough. The greater the hardness, the longer and better will its finish last. Hardness must not be confused with toughness or firmness. The hardest stone, the diamond, is sensitive to blows and knocks. The much softer nephrite is tough and very difficult to break.

Hardness is generally understood to mean resistance to scratching, grinding, and boring. Accordingly, a distinction is made between scratch hardness, bore hardness, and grinding hardness. The various values of a given stone do not correspond to one another. If the various stones are compared, not even the sequences of the different hardness values agree.

Scratch hardness is of most practical interest; it is obtained by comparison of the stone to be determined with representatives of the Mohs Hardness Scale, as given below:

1. Talc, 2. gypsum, 3. calcite, 4. fluorite, 5. apatite,
6. feldspar, 7. quartz, 8. topaz, 9. corundum, 10. diamond.

This scale is arbitrary, and its steps are not uniform. To determine the hardness of a stone, that mineral on the scale is found which is just scratched by the stone, and the next higher one, which in turn scratches the stone. The hardness value lies between the two relevant values on the scale. In practice, the use of hardness gauges, whose tips consist of the various members of the scale, is widespread. For reference it should be noted that the hardness of a steel file is about 6. Thus stones that can be filed have a hardness of less than 6. The hardness of precious stones lies between 6 and 10 throughout, and the most valuable stones are harder than 7 on the scale. Stones of lower hardness are used for decorative purposes only if they are opaque (turquoise, malachite, azurite, microcline, as well as pearls). Some times, hardness clearly varies with the crystal face examined. Thus differences ranging from 5 to 7 occur in blue cyanite, depending on the crystal face measured. This also explains why diamond can be ground in its own dust.

The hardness of the most important precious stones

From: *Edelsteinkundliches Taschenbuch (Gemmological Pocket Book)*, Chudoba and Gübelin 1953.

$1 - 1 \cdot 5$	talc
2	gypsum
$2 - 2 \cdot 5$	amber, meerschaum
$2 - 4$	chrysocolla
$2 \cdot 5 - 3 \cdot 5$	pearls
3	calcite
$3 - 3 \cdot 5$	aragonite
$3 - 4$	serpentine
$3 \cdot 5$	jet, coral, azurite
$3 \cdot 5 - 4$	bastite, malachite
4	fluorspar, rhodochrosite
$4 - 5$	bronzite, sillemite, variscite
5	apatite, dioptas, obsidian, thomsonite, odontolite, zinc ore
$5 - 6$	anatase, chlorastolite, diopside, glass, hypersthene, washingtonite, turquoise
$5 - 6 \cdot 5$	opal

5–7	disthene (cyanite)
5·5	brazilianite, enstatite, lapis lazuli, moldavite
5·5–6	cleolite, hauyn, lazulite, sodalite
5·5–6·5	hematite, nephrite, rhodonite
5·55	titanite
6	quartz glass, orthoclase, zircon (green)
6–6·5	labradorite, marcasite, microcline, oligoclase, prehnite, rutile, zoisite
6–7	epidot
6·5	andradite, benitoite, chalcedony, precious scapolite, kornerupin, pyrite, vesuvianite, sinhalite
6·5–7	axinite, demantoid, grossularite, jade, olivine, spodumene
7	dumorierite, quartz
7–7·5	cordierite, melanite, staurolite, tourmaline, zircon (normal)
7·25	rhodolite, spessartine
7·5	almandite, andalusite, euclase, pyrope, uvarovite
7·5–8	beryl, phenakite
8	topaz, spinel, taaffenite
8·5	chrysoberyl
9	corundum
10	diamond

Streak

Some minerals leave a colored streak on a white, unglazed porcelain plate, which may contribute to their identification. Hematite (blood stone) leaves a blood-red or brown-red streak, malachite a green one, and lapis lazuli a blue one. They are all stones of a hardness of less than 6.

Cleavability and fracture

Like the differences in hardness in a given stone (cyanite), cleavability and fracture properties are based on the fact that precious stones are crystals. We encounter these crystals in the Earth's crust in a great variety of shapes and sizes from the microscopic to the rock crystal weighing a hundredweight and more. Even the layman finds it easy to accept that these clearcut geometric shapes and the symmetry of the array of the faces continue into the interior of the stone. It has been shown that mysterious directional forces arrange the molecules precipitated from the mother liquors in clearly defined geometric solids, so that even the simplest lattice unit has the same shape as the crystal visible to the naked eye. The spatial distribution of the individual building bricks of the crystal, according to certain laws of disposition, is called "crystal lattice". The basic shape of the lattice, which continues infinitely in all directions, in other words, the shape of the lattice unit, is a geometrically defined solid, in the simplest case a cube or a rectangular parallelepiped.

Most crystals can be cleaved in the direction of certain crystal planes. A well-known example is the rock salt crystal which cleaves perfectly along the direction of the cube faces; it can be split up into smaller parallelepipeds even with light blows. Euclase (the name means "well-cleaving") owes its name to its perfect cleavability. If the cleavage face is not completely smooth but extends to parallel faces, it exhibits what is called by experts "well-marked cleavability". Irregular and stepped cleavage planes are evidence of "imperfect cleavability". Great care is essential during scratch hardness experiments on diamond, and especially on topaz. Topaz cleaves vertically to the rhombic prism, diamond along the octahedral face. There is thus a danger that pieces may chip off if the material is scratched with insufficient care. Knowledge of the cleavage properties of precious stones is of course essential to the gem cutter.

Fracture surfaces occur when a stone is smashed which does not cleave, or does not do so in the direction of the blow. The kind of fracture surface, too, is characteristic of certain kinds of stone. A distinction is drawn between conchoidal, drusy, fibrous, flaky, and splintery fracture surfaces. Conchoidal fracture surfaces are particularly common.

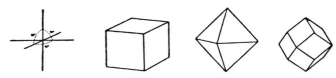

Fig. 8-1. Regular or cubic system of crystallization: 1. System of axes, 2. cube or hexahedron, 3. octahedron, 4. example: Garnet.

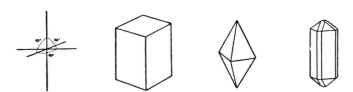

Fig. 8-2. Tetragonal or square system: 1. System of axes, 2. tetragonal or square prism, 3. tetragonal or square pyramid, 4. example: Zircon, vesuvianite.

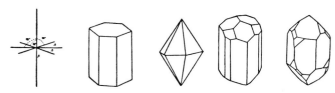

Fig. 8-3. Hexagonal system: 1. System of axes, 2. hexagonal prism, 3. hexagonal pyramid, 4. example: Tourmaline, 5. example: Quartz.

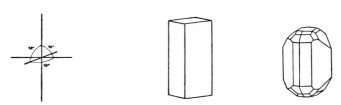

Fig. 8-4. Rhombic system: 1. System of axes, 2. rhombic prism, 3. example: Precious topaz.

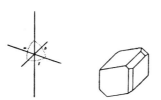

Fig. 8-5. Monoclinic system: 1. System of axes, 2. example: Orthoclase.

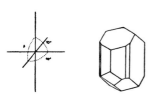

Fig. 8-6. Triclinic system: 1. System of axes, 2. example: Axinite.

Systems of Crystallization

The crystal shape is an important characteristic of a stone, and is often useful for its identification. The numerous crystal shapes have been reduced to six basic forms called systems of crystallization. Lines (axes) are drawn through the center of the crystal so that the existing crystal faces are symmetrical to this system. The lengths of these axes and the angles they include together characterize the system of crystallization to which the stone belongs. The six systems are:

Regular or cubic system: Three axes of equal length arranged vertically to one another. Examples: Diamond, garnet, spinel.

Tetragonal or square system: Three axes vertical to one another: two are identical, the third is longer or shorter. Examples: Zircon, vesuvianite.

Hexagonal system: Four axes, three of which are identical; they intersect at 60° and lie in a plane. The fourth axis is vertical to the three others and is longer or shorter than these. Examples: Quartzes, corundums, beryls.

Rhombic system: Three axes vertical to one another, but all of different length. Examples: Topaz, alexandrite.

Monoclinic system: Three axes of different lengths. Two are vertical to each other, and the third is inclined to the plane of the two others. Examples: Euclase, epidot.

Triclinic system: Three axes of different lengths, including only oblique angles. Example: Cyanite.

In nature, precious-stone crystals do not normally form with geometric precision; in fact they impede one another's growth owing to lack of space; thus cripples of all kinds, as well as mutual penetration and twinning, are found.

Optical Properties

Gems owe their beauty to their optical properties. Firstly, their colors—the green of the emerald, the red of the ruby, the blue of the sapphire—are superb. Added to this are play of light and colors: The changing luster of a cat's eye, the opalescence and opalizing of the opals, the adularizing of moonstone, the labradorizing of Labrador feldspar, and the asterism of star rubies, star sapphires, and other "star stones".

Inclusions of all kinds enliven the appearance; banded structures and striations make for lively color variations.

The effects classified under the terms of luster, brilliancy, and fire are of particular importance. Luster is the sum of the light reflected from the table; brilliancy the sum of the light that has entered the stone, is internally reflected, and emerges again through the table; fire is the dispersion of the white light, because of the different refractive properties of the various colors of the spectrum, into the colors of the rainbow. The flashing and sparkling of cut diamonds create uniquely surprising effects.

All the optical phenomena mentioned play an important part today in the identification of precious stones. Special apparatus measures the refractive index, birefringence, the so-called pleochroism of birefringent colored gems, enabling the stones to be reliably identified. The gemmological microscope still occupies a special position in the examination of stones. Although individual cases cannot be dealt with here, because this would involve discussion of the entire field of gemmological optics, it should be pointed out that perfect identification of all transparent stones is achieved by optical means. Specific gravity and hardness measurements are used mainly for the identification of opaque stones.

Synthetic Stones

The great value of some precious stones nurtured the idea of trying to discover a way to produce them synthetically in the laboratory. The first successful synthesis was that of corundums (rubies, sapphires, etc.). A mixture of powdered alumina and about $2 \cdot 5\%$ powdered chromium oxide is melted in a Verneuil furnace, which is basically a metal tube, in which a town gas/oxygen flame burns at about 2000°C. The finely distributed powder is sprinkled into the flame at a precisely calculated rate from a sieve. The molten drops fall onto the top of a sintered corundum pin, where in about four hours they grow into a boule weighing about $1 \cdot 8$ oz (50g). The synthetic rubies are cut from this boule. Likewise cornflower-blue sapphires can be obtained by the addition of a little titanium oxide and iron oxide. Spinels are synthesized from alumina and magnesium oxide according to the same principle. They, too, are marketed in all colors. It is important to note that synthetic rubies, sapphires, and spinels are not imitations, but genuine rubies, sapphires ,and spinels, with all the chemical and physical properties of the natural stones. But they are not very highly prized, because they lack the value of tradition. It is, however, wrong to describe synthetic tourmaline- or aquamarine-colored spinels as synthetic tourmalines or aquamarines, because they are, after all, spinels, and have properties that differ radically from those of tourmaline and aquamarine.

In 1935, the first successful synthesis of diamond was achieved by General Electric in their research laboratories at Schenectady, USA. In pressure chambers, perfect diamonds were produced at pressures of 100,000 atm and temperatures of 3000°C. Although production figures have since risen enormously, no stones have so far been successfully synthesized for decorative purposes. The tiny products are used exclusively for industrial purposes.

Several types of synthetic emeralds have appeared on the market. In the jewelry trade, there are Chatham emeralds, synthetic emeralds by Zerfass, Gilson, and Linde, and genuine beryls coated with synthetic emerald mass, which are known as symeralds.

Synthetic rutile (Titania night stone) and synthetic strontium titanite (fabulite) are often passed off as diamonds, because of their outstanding brilliancy and striking fire, but their softness readily distinguishes the stones from diamond.

Synthetic star rubies and star sapphires enjoy considerable popularity in the USA. Synthetic rock crystals are used as oscillator crystals in ultrasonic technology. Synthetic alexandrites, garnets, and other stones have also been developed in the laboratory.

Synthetic stones are extremely important in industry. In the jewelry trade, they are reliably identified as such, so that they will never seriously endanger the market for genuine gems.

Imitations and Doubling

Imitations are cheap substitutes for natural stones; they usually consist of certain types of glass. Glass imitations were known even to the Ancient Romans. The initial substance is generally an ordinary glass flux, colored by the addition of certain metallic oxides. Manganese produces a violet color, iron an amber one. Cobalt produces blue, uranium salts dye the glass flux green-yellow, chromium produces emerald-green. Strass creates a diamond imitation (simili); it is glass containing lead, sometimes with an addition of thallium. Such special glasses are fairly expensive. (Strass derives its name from Strasser, its inventor.)

Glass imitations are usually distinguished from precious stones by their low hardness (5). They are also often recognized by inclusions of gas bubbles and schlieren, as well as by their poor heat conductivity.

Doubling, too, is used as a substitute for more valuable stones. A doublet consists of a top and a bottom part, joined by a cementing substance. One in which the top and the bottom are diamond is called a genuine doublet; if only the top consists of diamond, but the bottom is of baser material, it is called a semigenuine doublet, a mixte. All doublets containing a glass part are designated as false. The cement usually consists of a layer of mastic (the resin of the mastic tree, found around the Mediterranean). In many doublets, the glass base is pressed onto the top without an intermediate layer. There are also doublets consisting of three parts; their intermediate layer is dyed glass. Thus the well-known Técla emeralds, considered the best emerald imitations, are composed of two bodies of poor, pale emerald or aquamarine or rock crystal enclosing a layer of green glass substance. In hollow doublets, the space between the two parts is filled with a colored liquid.

The Natural Gem Stones

Diamond

Diamond surpasses all other natural gem stones in luster, fire, and hardness. The Greek name *adamas* (untameable) indicates its extreme hardness. All diamonds used in industry for cutting, drawing, drilling, and planing are called industrial diamonds. Bort is the name given to diamonds too poor in quality to be cut. Carbonado is a granular Brazilian diamond colored black by the precipitation of carbon.

Only about a quarter of all diamonds mined are colorless. Many stones have vivid colors. Yellow, brown, gray, black, and green are the most frequent hues. Blue diamonds are rarer. Red and violet hues are hardly ever found.

Diamond consists of pure carbon, which in air burns at 850°C to become carbon dioxide. It is especially easy to cleave; blows or knocks may produce cracks or split pieces off.

Whereas in Antiquity and in the Middle Ages India was the most important supplier of diamonds, the main deposits today are found in Africa. The mines in Zaire, South Africa, and Ghana are especially important in terms of productivity. Stones of 1/32ct. are still worth mining. The largest diamond ever found, the Cullinan, weighed 3,026ct. [1ct. = $0 \cdot 007$ oz $(0 \cdot 2g)$].

Brilliant and rose are the most popular diamond cuts. Very small splinters have irregular facets and are used for wreaths set round other gems.

Inferior stones are sometimes given cover names to encourage their confusion with genuine diamonds. The simili diamond, for instance, consists of glass or strass, and the matara diamond (immature diamond) is a zircon from Ceylon. Marmoroscher, Alaska, or Alençon diamonds consist of quartz.

Ruby and sapphire

Both these stones are members of the corundum group, consisting of pure alumina (Al_3O_2). Their great hardness (9) makes them excellent abrasives and polishing materials. In addition to the red ruby and the blue sapphire, the group includes the white leucosapphire, the red-yellow padparaja, as well as aquamarine, amethyst, emerald, and topaz-colored stones.

Important ruby deposits are found in Burma, Thailand, and Sri Lanka (formerly Ceylon). The most beautiful rubies, pure red or the color of pigeon blood, come from Burma; those stones that also have a delicate, velvet sheen, as well as this rich color, are among the most highly prized of all gems. In the sapphire, a clear cornflower-blue is particularly valued; such stones are sometimes found in Thailand. Burmese sapphires are darker, and those from Sri Lanka lighter, than those from Thailand. The color of Montana sapphires (USA) is usually light- and steel-blue, while those from Australia have an olive-green tint.

Certain inclusions are the cause of forms called star rubies and star sapphires, and known by the collective term of asterias.

The corundums are ground with diamond or emery powder. Whereas asterias are polished *en cabochon*, the brilliant cut is chosen for transparent stones. Valuable stones are mounted *à jour*, less valuable ones on colored-foil bases. In the Ceylon cut, the back of the stone is without pattern to save weight.

In the case of the ruby, too, misleading covernames are used to give cheaper stones a boost. Adelaide ruby is a South African garnet; Balas ruby is red spinel. Arizona and Colorado rubies are red garnets. Rose quartz is sometimes marketed under the name of Bolivian ruby, and rose topaz as Brazilian ruby. Siberian ruby is red tourmaline, immature ruby is red zircon. Fluorspar is sometimes misleadingly called false sapphire, and Brazilian sapphire is usually blue topaz or blue tourmaline. As already mentioned, rubies and sapphires are very often made synthetically.

The beryl group

The chemical formula of the beryls is $3BeO.Al_2O_3.6SiO_2$. Like corundum, they crystallize in the hexagonal system. Precious stones such as emerald and aquamarine are members of the beryl group. Some precious beryls have special names, such as chrysoberyl and the yellowish-green heliodor. The stones are difficult to cleave, and their fracture is conchoidal. The commonest color is green in all its hues toward yellow and blue. The most highly valued hue is the pure green of the emerald. This color is heat resistant; in aquamarine and chrysoberyl, the color fades in heat. The color change of green into blue beryl is particularly important. At 400°C the stones become colorless, and turn blue during cooling. The best emeralds come from Chivor and the government mines of Muzo, Columbia. The USSR, parts of Africa, and Brazil also produce emeralds. Aquamarines are found mainly in Minas Geraes and Minas Novas, Brazil. Whereas large, flawless emeralds are among the most highly prized of all stones, heavy aquamarines are not particularly rare.

Chrysoberyl and alexandrite

Both stones consist of alumina and beryllium oxide ($BeO.Al_2O_3$). Alexandrite is really only a variety of chrysoberyl. The latter, as mined in Brazil and Sri Lanka, is golden-yellow to light-green; but the green of alexandrite from the Ural Mountains is much more intense. The change into red in artificial light is characteristic of this stone, which was called after Czar Alexander II of Russia. (Green and red were the colors of the Imperial Russian Army.) Chrysoberyl is found mostly in Brazil and Sri Lanka. The best alexandrite comes from the Sverdlovsk region of the Urals.

Spinel

This stone is single-refracting, as it crystallizes regularly (cubically). Other names for spinel are ruby spinel, almandite spinel or, misleadingly, balas ruby. Its composition is $MgO.Al_2O_3$. Only the red, and possibly the rare colorless spinels are precious. They are often found in the same deposits as rubies. Pale, reddish-yellow stones are found in Brazil.

Topaz

The precious topaz is a member of this group, which also comprises many common forms. The stone colored blue by chromium yellow or iron has the formula $Al_4SiO_2.(FOH)_2$. It crystallizes rhombically, and its ready cleavability is a typical property. The most important color is yellow, but blue and colorless stones are quite common. The yellow variety usually has a delicate reddish cast. When heated to 300–400°C, the yellow or brown topaz becomes pink, and colorless when further heated. Topaz comes from the USSR, Sri Lanka, and Brazil. The deposits at the well-known Schneckenstein mine in Saxony are worth noting. The cut is usually stepped or table.

Zircons

In addition to the common zircons, stones are found in the most varied colors, often of great beauty. Zircons consist of silicon and zirconium oxide ($SiO_2.ZrO_2$) and crystallize tetragonally. The vitreous luster of the stone resembles that of the diamond, because of its high refractive index. The colors of the precious zircons are therefore sparkling and fiery. Hyacinth is brownish-orange, but can also be green, yellow, violet, red, and brown. Blue zircons are made by fusion of gray or brown pieces. At 500°C, hyacinth becomes decolorized, acquiring a strong but somewhat somber luster. Most zircons come from Sri Lanka.

The garnet group

In the Middle Ages, garnets were the main representatives of the so-called carbuncle group. They crystallize cubically, and their crystal lattice structure is complex. The most important types are grossularite (calcium–aluminum garnet), pyrope (magnesium–aluminum garnet), spessartine (manganese–aluminum garnet), almandite (iron–aluminum garnet), and demantoid (chromium-containing calcium–iron garnet). Red stones are the most frequent. Almandite has a violet cast. Grossularite is greenish; it is also called hessonite. The very beautiful demantoid is often emerald-green, and is the softest of all garnets. Pyrope comes from the southern slope of the Bohemian Mountains, the blood-red Cape garnet is found in South Africa. The best hessonite and almandite is found in Sri Lanka, demantoid in Russia. Spessartine (deposits at Aschaffenburg and Spessart in West Germany) is gaining increasing importance in the gem trade.

The tourmaline group

The hexagonally crystallizing tourmalines have the formula $H_3Al_4(BOH)_2Si_4O_{19}$. Since their chemical composition is not uniform, the stones occur in almost every color of the spectrum, the most frequent ones being green and red. Sometimes, differently colored layers are found in a single stone, showing green, red, or colorless bands like some fancy gateau. Tourmalines with a red top are called Turks' heads, and those with a black top, Moors' heads. The most important deposits are in Brazil. The tourmalines from Swakopmund, Namibia, are famous for their beautiful color.

Peridot or chrysolite

Chrysolite is a precious form of olivine, a mineral found in many rocks. The green stones crystallize rhombically, and have the formula $(Mg,Fe)_4 SiO_2$. The olive-green color makes peridot a very popular precious stone. It is cut in step or table cut. Stones of outstanding beauty occur on the Egyptian Red Sea coast.

The opal group

Opal is not a crystallized stone, but the solidified mass of a silica gel. The stones consist of amorphous (structureless, noncrystalline) SiO_2. They also contain much water (6%). Opal is therefore very sensitive to heat. The water content is not uniform in every stone. Microscopically fine lamellae cause the well-known property of opalescence, as the light is diffracted or attenuated differentially according to wave length on the infinitely fine wafers and cracks. Such opals therefore glimmer mosaic-like in many colors, which accounts for their names of glimmering, harlequin, and flame opal. In particular it is the precious opal, inherently milky-white, gray, or yellowish, which gives an incomparable display of opalescent colors. Stones of outstanding beauty reach the value of the diamond. The most important deposits were formerly in Hungary, but today Australia and Mexico are the main sources. Some of the special varieties are gold opal, girasol, fire opal, moss opal, and wood opal.

The quartz group

The hexagonally crystallizing quartzes, consisting of pure SiO_2, comprise an outstanding number of well-known ornamental stones. According to certain differences in internal structure, the quartzes are divided into crystalline compact quartzes, chalcedonies, and types of jasper. The group of crystalline quartzes comprises rock crystal, amethyst, citrine, and smoky quartz. The colorless rock crystal was in the past often found in huge crystal vaults in the Alps. Today, Brazil is the main exporter. The clove-brown or smoke-gray smoky quartz comes from Brazil today, and also from Scotland and Madagascar. The best amethyst is found in Uruguay; its color is a beautiful violet. The dark-violet amethysts of the Auvergne are also well known. Yellow citrines are called Madeira crystal. The name of gold topaz has also become very popular, although it should be rejected. Scotland and Uruguay produce very valuable stones the color of white wine. Many citrines on the market are burnt amethysts—amethysts become brown-red at high temperatures (above 470°C), and milky, turbid, and colorless at still higher temperatures. The compact quartzes consist of a mass of tiny crystals, often visible only under the microscope. This type of quartz comprises rose quartz, amethyst prase, aventurine quartz, auriferous quartz, milky quartz, sapphire quartz, and the formations of cat's eye, tiger's eye, and hawk's eye, of which peculiarly fluctuating light phenomena are typical. The chalcedonies consist of microscopically fine quartz fibers joined together by opal matrix. The stones are diaphanous. The apple-green chrysopras, which owes its color to a content of about 1% nickel, is a chalcedony. Plasmas, sard, cornelian, and heliotrope are used as ring stones. They are the important material for the ancient art of gem carving (gems and cameos), and today are very widely used as signet stones. Banded chalcedonies, consisting of layers of several colors, are called agates. Onyx, sardonyx, and cornelionyx belong to this group. The gem cutting industry of Idar-Oberstein, West Germany, is based on deposits of agate. The fourth group of quartzes, the various jaspers, comprises a very large number of opaque varieties.

Turquoise

The triclinically crystallizing turquoise is a water-containing phosphate of composition $CuO.3Al_3O_2.2P_2O_5.9H_2O$. Its color is sky-blue to apple-green. It often contains brown veins, which consist of iron-containing portions of the surrounding rocks (turquoise matrix). The stone is sensitive to drying out. Iran supplies the best turquoises. Other deposits exist in Turkestan, Mexico, and South Africa.

Nephrite and jadeite

Both stones are known by the common name of jade, although they differ in several respects. Jadeite is harder than nephrite. Both stones are opaque to diaphanous and light-green to dark-green. They also differ in their specific gravity and in their chemical composition.

Malachite

The leek- to emerald-green malachite crystallizes monoclinically. It is a basic copper carbonate; its formula is $CuCO_3.Cu(OH)_2$. The individual layers of the stone often have different hues. This gives the surface a typical appearance with wavy lines. The largest deposits are in Zaire, and the most important ones in the Ural Mountains. The stone has always been used extensively by the jewelry trade.

Lapis lazuli

Lapis is not a precious stone, but a precious rock, which was used as a paint—ultramarine—in the past. It is a member of the so-called sodalite group, which consists of four minerals, all crystallizing cubically; $NiAlSiO_4$ occurs in their formula. In addition, lapis lazuli contains NaS_3. Crystals of the sodalite minerals are embedded in a chalky matrix. The bright-blue or dark-blue stone frequently includes sparkling golden specks of sulfur crystals. Because of their low hardness (5–5·5), cut stones must be treated with care. The main deposits are in Afghanistan, where deep-blue stones are found.

The feldspar group

Of the monoclinically or triclinically crystallizing group of feldspar, only amazonite, moonstone, labradorite, and sunstone are of any importance for decorative purposes. The surface of the turbid, translucent moonstone usually displays a beautiful bluish, fluctuating sheen called adularization. The gray, opaque labradorite, too, exhibits a wonderful play of colors (labradorizing), which shows in the alternating sparkle of various hues when the stone is turned. This is caused by small inclusions of wafers of specular iron ore or of titaniferous iron. Amazonite is colored copper-green to blue-green; it is found in the USA and in the region of Lake Ilmen in the USSR. Sunstone derives its name from tiny, luminous points of iron foil. The stone has a metallic reddish luster. It is found on Saddle Island in the White Sea, in the USA, in Siberia, and in Norway.

	Period	Subjects of metalcraft	Characteristics of design and style	Raw materials and special techniques
East Asia China and Japan	about 2500 B.C.			Beginning of the use of copper
	about 1000 B.C. up to the Birth of Christ	Ritual implements: Bells, sacrificial vessels, ewers (sacred bronzes) Dress ornaments	Austere design, linear-geometric ornaments, animal symbols, dragons, cloud patterns	Bronze in sand mold, and part molds, sometimes inlaid, engraving
	2nd–5th century A.D.	Spread of Buddhism Korea: Gold ornaments		Artistic granulation
	7th–8th century A.D.	Ritual implements: Temple bells, vessels, gongs, priests' staves, amulets, three-dimensional ornamental articles, bronze mirrors	Plant motifs, symbolic animal representations	Red and gray bronze, gilt and gold-plated, engraving, punching, silver, gold
	13th–17th century A.D.	Weapons and armor Sword blades, guards of perfect execution (Japan), mountings, oil and incense vessels, reliquaries, Buddhist ritual implements, tea-, water kettles	Naturalistic plant and animal representations	Wrought iron Forging and embossing, inlay, enamel

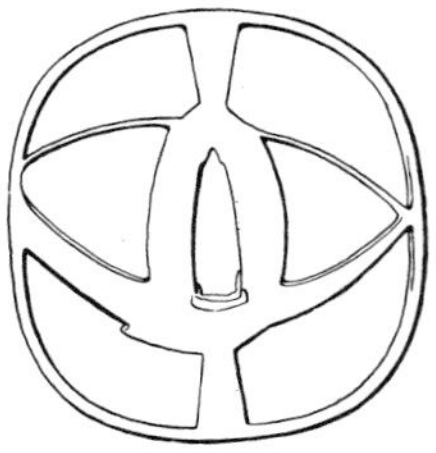

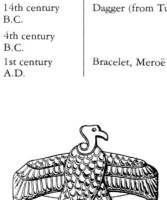

Fig. 9-1. Priest's flagon (bronze), Japan, 7–8th century

Fig. 9-2. Guard (iron), Japan, 16th century

Fig. 9-3. Cast-iron water kettle, Japan

Fig. 9-4. Guard (iron), Japan, 17th century

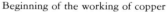

	Period	Subjects of metalcraft	Characteristics of design and style	Raw materials and special techniques
Egypt	about 5000–4000 B.C.		Neolithic period	Beginning of the working of copper
	about 3500 B.C.	Ornaments: Bracelets, anklets, headbands, etc. Metals gain importance as raw materials	Wire spirals	Gold with semiprecious stones (gold as metal of princely funeral cult)
	about 2900 B.C.	Copper implements and bracelets (tomb of Queen Hetep-heres)		Copper–tin alloy (bronze), open sandcasting
	about 2000–1500 B.C.	Pectorals, bracelets, ornamental daggers, ornate vessels, death masks, candlesticks, mountings, etc. (El-Amarna art, Tutankhamun's tomb)	Figure representations (human, animal, plant, symbols)	Gold with colored inlay (precursor of enamel): Cornelian, lapis lazuli, turquoise, etc., engraving, filigree
	14th century B.C.	Dagger (from Tutankhamun's tomb)	Affinity with Aegean art (Crete)	Granulation, chasing, opus interasile, inlay
	4th century B.C.			Transition from stone- and paste inlay to vitreous enamel
	1st century A.D.	Bracelet, Meroë	Gold filigree with colored inlay	Early occurrence of iron as a raw material which was still rare and expensive

Fig. 9-5. Gold dagger (hard gold blade) of Tutankhamun

Fig. 9-6. Egyptian bracelet, gold with colored inlay, about 1500 B.C.

Fig. 9-7. Silver vessel with gold handle, around 1250 B.C.

Fig. 9-8. Gold funerary mask of Tutankhamun, with lapis lazuli inlay

	Period	Subjects of metalcraft	Characteristics of design and style	Raw materials and special techniques
Mediterranean littoral and Western Asia	about 2700 B.C.	Gold helmet of a king of Ur (Mesopotamia), head ornaments and necklace of Queen Shubad of Ur	Fantastically rich ornaments of wire rings and naturalistic leaf work	Gold, embossed and chased
	about 2000–1600 B.C.	Flowering of Aegean metal art (Crete and Mycenae); vases, cups, daggers, jewelry, death masks (Schliemann; gold treasure of Mycenae, discovered 1878)	Linear ornaments, figure representations	Bronze, gold embossed and cast, artistic chasing, inlay
	about 1500 B.C.	Gold cups at Vaphio, nr. Sparta	Naturalistic representations: The taming of a bull	Gold
		Large monumental metalcast sculptures (votive pictures) by Greek, Hellenistic, and Roman sculptors	Archaic, classical, Hellenistic, and Roman period styles	Bronze
	about 700 B.C.	Beginning of coinage in Greece	Images of gods	Mainly silver, also gold
	about 460 B.C.	Large sculptures: Charioteer of Delphi		Bronze casting (hollow casting in lost-wax technique)
	438 B.C.	Colossal sculptures in metalwork (Phidias' Athena Parthenos) Metal utensils for daily use	Style of classical Greek art (5th–4th century B.C.)	Gold and ivory [2205 lb (1000kg) gold], height 39 ft 4 ins. (12m), presumably forged, with wooden core

Fig. 9-9. Ornament of Queen Shubad of Ur (Sumeric), about 2700 B.C.

Fig. 9-10. Greek hydra (bronze), about 460 B.C., height 21·5 ins (51·4cm)

Fig. 9-11. Gold shield decoration (Scythian), 7th–6th century B.C.

	Period	Subjects of metalcraft	Characteristics of design and style	Raw materials and special techniques
Central Europe	about 2000–800 B.C. (Bronze Age) about 900–600 B.C. (Late Bronze Age in Central Germany)	Beginning of the Metal Age Weapons: Dagger, axe, spearhead Ornaments: Clasps, bracelets	Elementary, linear ornaments, spirals, volutes Regular arrangements in rows, later plant and organic motifs, star patterns, wavy bands	Bronze casting, later hammer and embossing work, punching
	about 1000–500 B.C. (Early Iron Age in Southern Germany) (Celts and Illyrians about 450, La Tène)	Weapons: Sword, dagger, sheath, spearhead, clasps, and jewelry: Fibulas, barrel-shaped bracelets, belt buckles, ornaments, utensils (Kleinaspergle gold treasure)	Regular arrangements of linear and two-dimensional ornamental designs Fish bladder ornament	Chasing, inlay, colored paste fillings, stamping
	about 700 B.C.	Eberswalde (East Germany) gold treasure	Traced linear ornaments (rows)	Gold Hammer work and punching

Fig. 9-12. Fighting bracelet, early Bronze Age

Fig. 9-13. Neck ring, twisted (coil ring), Late Bronze Age

	Period	Subjects of metalcraft	Characteristics of design and style	Raw materials and special techniques
Italy	750–400 B.C.	Etruscan metalcraft		All the goldsmiths' techniques, climax of gold granulation
	269 B.C.	Beginning of Roman silver stamping	Miniature sculpture	Negative punch cutting

277

	Period	Subjects of metalcraft	Characteristics of design and style	Raw materials and special techniques
Britain	3rd century B.C.	Celtic champlevé (see *Fig. 9-14*) (Thames treasures: Battersea Shield, etc.)	"Trumpet" style	Bronze and iron with red melt ("blood enamel"), "furrowed enamel"

Fig. 9-14. *Bronze ornamental plate, champlevé (red in black), Late La Tène.*

Fig. 9-15. *Early Christian bronze lamp in the shape of a dove.*

Fig. 9-16. *Cantharos with masks, Roman, 1st century A.D.*

	Period	Subjects of metalcraft	Characteristics of design and style	Raw materials and special techniques
Central Europe	1–350 A.D.		Filigree style	Soldered granulated gold and silver wire Granulation
	from 350 to 550 A.D.	Ornaments (fibulas)	Early Barbarian Invasions style: With figure (raised) relief	Stone pavé, almandite inlay, colored glass pastes
	Early Roman Imperial Period	Treasure of Boscoreale (Mt. Vesuvius), Hildesheim (West Germany) Silver Treasure (tableware of a Roman nobleman): Serving table, bowls, drinking cups, mixing dishes	Showpieces Lingering effect of Hellenistic flamboyance in figure representations	Silver casting embossed and turned, hard and soft soldering, riveting, engraving, fire gilding, niello
		Silver treasure of Mildenhall, England (1944), toilet and luxury articles, silver spoons	Late Roman ornamentation: Plants and scrollwork, masks	Silver
	from 550 to 800 A.D.	Bronze mountings, dress pins, weapons, implements	Later Barbarian Invasions style: Germanic animal ornamentation and plaited ribbons	Graving-tool work, filigree, iron, gold and silver inlaid
	350–550 A.D.	Hiddensee gold treasure		
	6th century A.D.	Scandinavian gold bracteates (ornaments) Frankish-Alemannic horsemen's brooches	Early figure representations of Germanic metal art	Gold, stamping Bronze
	588–659 A.D.	St. Eligius, Bishop of Noyon and alleged goldsmith (crosses and chalices), patron of goldsmiths		
	650–700 A.D.	Gold treasure of Wittislingen on the Danube (*Fig. 5-49*)	"Colored" style and chip-carved ornamentation (a) Persian (b) Late Roman origin	Colored precious-stone pavé on punched sheet gold (almandite), colored glass pastes (purple glass on gold foil)
	5th–15th century A.D.	Byzantine Christian goldsmiths' art: St. Mark's, Venice, "Pala d'oro", staurothek in Limburg Cathedral (West Germany), silver dish, Halberstadt Cathedral (West Germany)	Further development of Early Christian themes of representation Delicate scrollwork: Two-dimensional representations	Gold-strip cloisonné, during the 12th century champlevé
	700–800 A.D.	Transition to Christian-medieval art forms in Western Europe	Influence of Byzantine and Irish metal art	Copper with nielloed silver plates
	about 777	Tassilo Chalice	Irish metal art	Stone settings of the highest perfection
	about 850	Codex Aureus (book cover), Munich Enger reliquary		
	about 870	Paliotto, San Ambrogio, Milan		Figure relief embossing, gold, gilt sheet silver, enamel, filigree
	Carolingian, about 800	Bronze casting in Germany: Door leaf and balustrade railing, Aachen Minster	Scrollwork and acanthus leaves according to antique examples ("Carolingian Renaissance")	Earliest examples of German bronze sculpture

Fig. 9-17. *Fibula, gold-silver, with almandites and green glass.*

Fig. 9-18. *Alemannic horseman's brooch, Barbarian Invasions period.*

Fig. 9-19. *Fibula in the shape of an eagle, bronze with almandites.*

	Period	Subjects of metalcraft	Characteristics of design and style	Raw materials and special techniques
Metal art of the Romanesque period	about 1000	Reichenau workshops (ritual implements)	Scrollwork, lions, birds, dragon motifs	
	about 1000	Bronze portal, Mainz Cathedral (West Germany) (Master Berengar)		
	1015	Bernward Portal, Hildesheim (West Germany)		
	1033	(Godehard-) Column of Christ	Expressive figure representations	Highly accomplished bronze castings
	about 1065	Portal, Augsburg Cathedral, West Germany	Influence of Carolingian illumination	

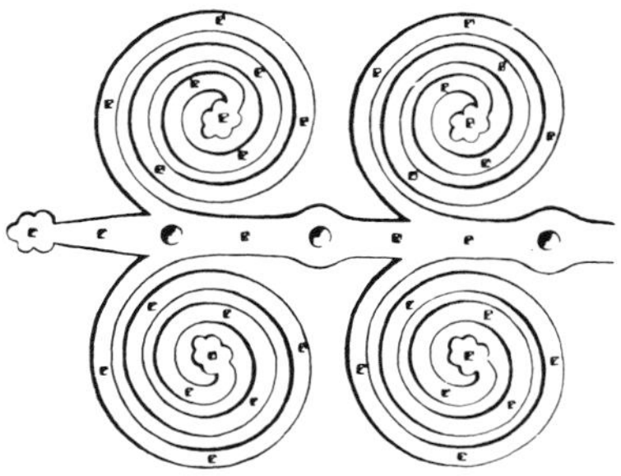

Fig. 9-20. Door mounting (iron), 13th century

Fig. 9-21. Domed reliquary of the Guelph Treasure, about 1200

Fig. 9-22. Head reliquary, 13th century

Period	Subjects of metalcraft	Characteristics of design and style	Raw materials and special techniques
about 1025	Jewels of the Empress Gisela	Eagle-shaped fibula and clasp still made	Enamel, filigree
about 1100	Theophilus Presbyter writes his "Schedula diversarum artium" (Guidebook to The Techniques of the Arts). He is probably identical with an artist known by the name of Rogerus of Hermarshausen, who influenced contemporary metalwork with important contributions		
about 1118	Portable altar by Rogerus in the Franciscan Church, Paderborn, West Germany (Fig. 5-17)	Expressive linear, graphic style	Engraved representations on gilt sheet copper, niello
	Rich field of ecclesiastical subjects: Candelabra, altars, reliquaries, liturgical implements		
1120–1140	Hildesheim processional cross (Fig. 1-9)	Scrollwork	Opus interasile
11th–13th century	Earliest wrought-metal work (door mountings Sindelfingen, Marburg, and Maulbronn, Fig. 2-2)	Securing the planks, as well as decorative	Iron—cf. iron as raw material (working)
	Red brass utensils: Cooking pots, braziers, ewers		Bronze
12th and 13th century	Workshops of the Rhine-Meuse region (large reliquaries)		
about 1150–1160	Eilbertus portable altar (Guelph Treasure)		Champlevé (figures: Gold on enamel and vice versa)
1140–1150	Antependium and chandelier of Gross Komburg (Figs. 5-18, 5-19, 5-23, 5-24)		Figures chased on gilt sheet copper. Champlevé. Opus interasile and niello
about 1155	Heribert reliquary, Deutz, by Godefroid de Clair (Meuse School)		Champlevé on copper
1181	Enamel altar by Nicholas of Verdun at Klosterneuburg		Champlevé on gilt copper plates

Fig. 9-23. Ornament, gilt bronze with champlevé, 12th century, diameter 2·5 ins. (62mm).

Fig. 9-24. Cockerel aquamanile, bronze, West German (?), dated 1155

Fig. 9-25. Lettering (illumination), enamel altar by Nicholas of Verdun

Fig. 9-26. Ewer (aquamanilè), cast bronze.

Period	Subjects of metalcraft	Characteristics of design and style	Raw materials and special techniques

Metalwork of the Gothic period

14th and 15th century

Wrought iron:
Grilles and mountings (doors, coffers), fountain niches, candlesticks, etc.

Tabernacle grille (Fig. 3-56)

Window grilles
Door mountings
Coffer mountings (Figs. 4-7, 4-15)

Grilles consisting of individual fill-in designs (quatrefoil and other tracery designs), held together by collars; Germany, Italy, Britain

Often rhombic grilles, particularly beautiful examples in South Germany
At this time mainly in France

Perhaps most beautiful in Germany

All techniques of forging: Splitting, punching, etc., forge-welding, drop forging

In connection with sheet metal

Fig. 9-27. Pewter jug, 15th century, height 15·4 ins. (37cm).

Fig. 9-28. Mounting of a wall cupboard, 14th century.

Fig. 9-29. Jug, extremely slender Gothic design.

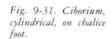

Bronze–brass casting
Monumental slabs, fonts, candlesticks, door knockers in the shape of lion masks, mortars and utensils
Gold and silver
Churchware, tableware for princely courts and city councils, jewels, and ornamental articles
Tower monstrances, pilgrims' badges

Architectural designs enter the scene: Tracery, spirelets, finials
Keen observation of nature in the use of plant motifs, change in the shape of the chalice (Figs. 2-37–2-43)

Instead of copper enamel, translucent enamel on silver

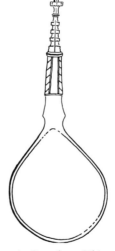

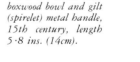

Fig. 9-31. Ciborium, cylindrical, on chalice foot.

Fig. 9-30. Tower monstrance, 14th century, with spirelets.

Fig. 9-32. Spoon with boxwood bowl and gilt (spirelet) metal handle, 15th century, length 5·8 ins. (14cm).

1404

Gold horse of Altötting

About middle of 15th century

Reproduction of drawings

End of 15th century

Reproduction of printing

"Gothic" type in Gutenberg Bible

Enamel en ronde bosse, excellent metal engraving on silver churchware

Copper engraving develops from the engraving technique as an intaglio printing method

Invention of the printing press with cast metal type

Beginning of enamel painting at Limoges

Fig. 9-33. Type specimen from the 36-line Bible, printed by Gutenberg, about 1457–1458.

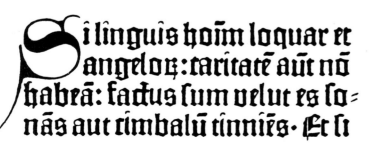

The Modern Age

Renaissance (about 1400–1620)

The "rebirth" of antique art began in Southern Europe (notably Italy) and spread gradually northwards. The German crafts tended to be swamped with decorative designs from the South; nevertheless, Gothic forms survived. In this discussion of metalcrafts showpieces have so far predominated: Centerpieces, goblets, and double goblets, often with pretentious three-dimensional figure decorations. Bronze casting was in its heyday. Goldsmiths were sculptors. Painters drew designs for jewelry. Drawing copies and ornament engravings were a rich source of affected decorative fashions: Cartouches, decorative fittings, etc. Basic techniques receded into the background, decorative possibilities were carried to extremes: See *Enameling*. Superb mastery of engraving techniques. Two famous sculptor-goldsmiths:

1500–1571 Benvenuto Cellini, working in Italy and France. Main work: Salt cellar, Kunstgewerbemuseum Vienna. Autobiography (See *Bibliography*).

1508–1585 Wenzel Jamnitzer, born in Vienna, workshop in Nuremberg (show vessels and centerpieces).

Splendid wrought-iron well-, fan-light-, and church grilles: Mainly rods, elegantly curved and scrolled. Similar line patterns (arabesques and mauresques) in panel decorations in other techniques: Engraving, inlay, filigree.

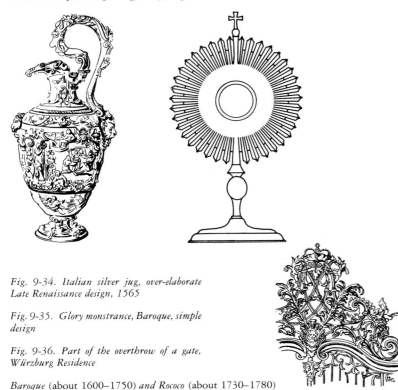

Fig. 9-34. Italian silver jug, over-elaborate Late Renaissance design, 1565

Fig. 9-35. Glory monstrance, Baroque, simple design

Fig. 9-36. Part of the overthrow of a gate, Würzburg Residence

Baroque (about 1600–1750) and Rococo (about 1730–1780)

"Splendor, pathos, exuberant opulence"—counterreformation, absolutistic princely rule as driving forces. Unbroken tradition, sensuality and creative power characteristic of the period.

Goldsmiths' craft: Jewelers' techniques spread from France.

Silversmiths: Besides sumptuous and over-elaborately decorated tableware and cutlery, many graceful designs of exemplary craftsmanship. Progressive refinement of table manners and tableware. Beginning of chinaware manufacture.

End of eighteenth century: Decay and dissolution of the guilds.

Various periods of the Baroque age in France are named after the reigning monarchs:

Louis Quatorze	1643–1715 (classical Baroque)
Régence	1715–1723
(not to be confused with English Regency)	
Louis Quinze	1723–1774 (Rococo)
Louis Seize	1774–1792 (transition to neoclassicism)

Wrought-iron: Dynamic and imaginative gates and grilles, emphasis on representation, technical refinement. Drop-forged or sheet-embossed and cut-out ornaments, as well as brilliant wrought iron work in the solid.

Neoclassicism (about 1770–1830)

Antique art was the ideal of the period. Reaction against the exuberance of the Baroque period.

Empire

Name of the neoclassical style in Napoleonic and post-Napoleonic France until about 1830, whereas the previous style of the Revolution is called Directorate.

Fig. 9-37. Silver tureen, neoclassical

Fig. 9-38. Louis Seize stove.

Biedermeier in Germany (about 1815–1848) and Regency and Early Victorian in England

End of neoclassicism in a bourgeois and petit-bourgeois environment. Forms of attractive simplicity and clarity, expressed more in the style of furniture than of metalwork. In jewelry, the accessories are romantic and sentimental.

Beginning of mechanical production and manufacturing methods on a large scale. Since 1856: Steel casting, refinement of types of steel into high-quality tool steels, permitting new machining methods for metals, in milling, planing, and turning.

Development of pressing tools and metal-plating techniques.

Since the middle of the nineteenth century: Encouragement of the crafts by the State. In schools of draftsmanship, old styles and originals were copied. Newly founded museums of arts and crafts collected mainly showpieces. But the study of historical styles led to unimaginative, slavish imitation. "Art and industry" was a much-discussed subject.

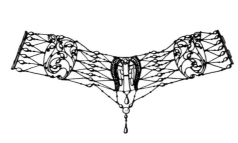

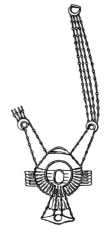

Figs 9-39 and 9-40. Forms of Art Nouveau: Necklace, designed by Karl Moser, and pendant, designed by Peter Behrens.

Art Nouveau (about turn of the century).

A group of artists (painters, sculptors, architects) attempted to lead the so-called "arts and crafts" out of the doldrums of imitation. A new "ornamentalism" was to be developed from natural forms. Lapses from the gradual rebirth of the crafts were quickly corrected, but the positive and surviving impulses of this enthusiastically supported movement are perhaps not yet sufficiently known today. The contemporary efforts to create a style of our own—contemporary in a loose sense—in the field of metalwork are described throughout this book. Any further observations are therefore superfluous.

10. Basic Terms of Heraldry

Heraldry is derived from the herald, who in medieval times was the arms bearer of kings and princes, and also acted as marshal during the medieval jousts.

Arms first developed about the middle of the twelfth century from the marks of identification of combatants, and the accoutrement of the knights. In arms, the color plays a more important part than the charge. But in most techniques of metalwork, the colors or tinctures can be represented only indirectly with the aid of hatching, adopted in the sixteenth century. Gold (or) and silver (argent) are used as "metals", red (gules), blue (azure), black (sable), and green (vert) are the original tinctures, to which were added purple (purpure) (rarely) and later brown (tenné), and natural color (proper) mainly as a flesh tone. Colors should be used in luminous, pure hues, such as vermilion and cobalt blue. An old rule is "metal on tincture or tincture on metal", for example never or on argent, never sable on vert. Originally, the arms consisted of the escutcheon and the charge. At the turn of the fourteenth century, the crest with helmet and mantle was added. That this addition is derived from the image of the galloping knight with lance couched and shield raised is obvious from the drawing on the left. Later the crest was elaborated to include insignia of rank and office (miter, tiara, hats of estate, coronets, etc.) or decorative features (wreaths of the colors, simple wreaths, and supporters).

Fig. 10-1. The complete coat of arms probably derived from the picture of the jousting knight, protecting himself with his shield, on his prancing steed. Herr Hartmann von Aue, after an illustration in the Manesse Codex.

Fig. 10-2. Complete coat of arms, from the picture of the jousting knight.

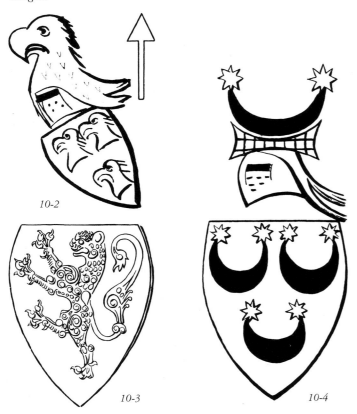

Fig. 10-3. Battle shield, thirteenth century, with heraldic animal for the identification of the knight, clearly visible from a distance.

Fig. 10-4. Shield and crest still separate in an illustration in the Manesse Codex. In this drawing, the helmet has been moved above the shield.

Fig. 10-5. Shield and crest combined, helm mantle still as real cloth. From a tombstone, 1348.

Fig. 10-6. Gothic arms: Shield as "target", close helmet, helm mantle slittered or mantled, charge repeated in crest. Slanted to the left: Arms of husband and wife.

Escutcheon and Charge

The triangular shield, still a real weapon during the twelfth and thirteenth centuries, became a heraldic design also in the seal. Anybody could bear such a seal; this was no privilege. Burghers and artisans often derived their seals from house marks and signs. City arms are sometimes derived from an older seal (image of a saint, building, town's emblem). Canting arms were a matter of fashion even in the Middle Ages. They are arms which illustrate the name with a pictorial emblem, such as the head of an ox in the Oxford coat of arms.

Charges (honorable ordinaries)

These are divisions of the escutcheon into colored areas extending to its edge. Their number is unlimited. The language of emblazonment has rules according to which charges must be blazoned. The drawings on the next page illustrate a few examples of blazonry. Other charges are called common figures.

Common figures

These were real or allegorical pictures and figures such as plants and natural forms of all kinds, animal and human figures and parts thereof, tools, etc. A distinction is drawn between "artificial" and "natural" figures. The artificial ones include everything shaped by man. Crosses can occur as charges (extending to the edge of the shield) or as common figures (not extending to the edge of the shield).

The designs of the components of the arms continuously changed under the influence of the various styles. The Early Gothic triangular shield, which could still be used for defense in battle, developed into the target of the fifteenth century, then into the curved, rent, and scrolled type of escutcheon of the Renaissance, until, in the Baroque

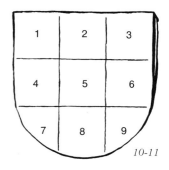

Fig. 10-11. The division of the escutcheon into "right" (dexter) and "left" (sinister) is seen not from the observer's, but from the shield bearer's aspect. Hence: 1–3 chief, 1–7 dexter, 7–9 base, 3–9 sinister. The points 1–2–3 are called chief, 7–8–9 base, 4–5–6 fesse, 2–5–8 pale. 5 is fesse, a shield in this point is called a shield fesse. A shield on its own is slanted to the right, escutcheons of a husband and wife are slanted towards each other, several shields in order of rank 3 1 2 4.

period, it was completely transformed into the cartouche. Certain ancient and widely used charges, such as the eagle, also display the influence of style so clearly that one can speak without hesitation of a Gothic or a Renaissance eagle. A further example of stylistic adaptation is the development of the mantle from the real fabric cover of the thirteenth-century kettle helmet through the Late Gothic mantled, then ornamental leaf form to the elaborate acanthus leafwork of the Renaissance, which no longer bears any resemblance to a mantle, and back again to the simply gathered cloth of neoclassicism (see *Figs. 10-3–10-10*).

The form of the crest is frequently a repetition of the charge, which, after all, was also displayed during jousts as a decoration on horse cloth and helmet. Concerning the forms of helmet, conical casque (twelfth century) and heaume (thirteenth century) did not yet appear in association with the arms (for an exception see next page, *Fig. 10-12*). Later kettle hats (fourteenth century) were used on the coats of arms of the ancient nobility, helmets with grilles or bars (fifteenth century) on those of the ordinary nobility, and close helmets (fifteenth century) for commoners' coats of arms. The most important of the other heraldic rules can be directly deduced from the drawings, or are explained in the captions.

Fig. 10-7. Coat of arms drawn by Dürer: Helmet with bars, acanthus leafwork mantle already appears in Renaissance form.

Fig. 10-8. Württemberg Coat of Arms, Baroque. The escutcheon has become an oval cartouche, the helm mantle a contemporary ornament. Symbol: "Love of Peace".

Fig. 10-9. Baroque coats of arms are often stripped of all remnants of the crest. Ornamental framework in contemporary style (e.g. "Rocailles" during the Rococo period).

Fig. 10-10. During the neoclassical period, escutcheons were rarely used, and a heraldic style of its own was not often evolved. The mantle as stage curtain.

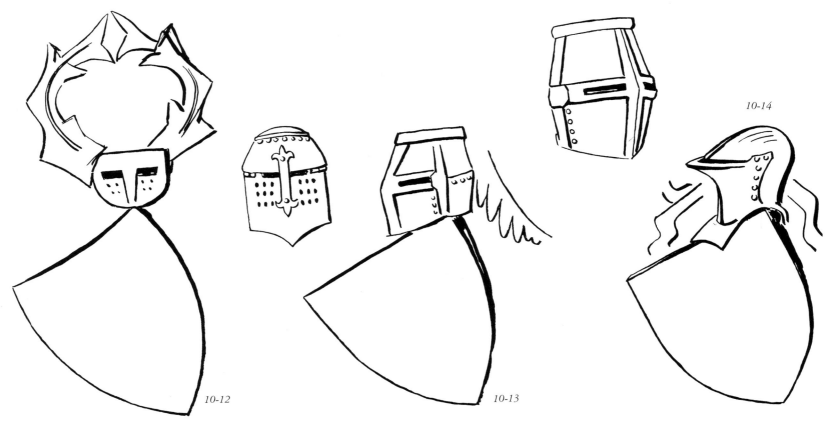

Forms of escutcheons and helmets (Figs. 10-12–10-18)

The crest consists of helmet, mantle, coronet or hat as insignia of rank, wreaths, mural crowns, wreaths of the colors.

10-14

Fig. 10-12. Early Gothic shield, heaume (flat top, thirteenth century), drawing freely modified. (Manesse Codex).

Fig. 10-13. Gothic shield (fourteenth century) with kettle hat (conical top; on the right shown obliquely from the front). On the left another form of kettle hat (fourteenth century).

Fig. 10-14. Gothic shield (fifteenth century) with close helmet (end of fourteenth to middle of fifteenth century).

10-12   *10-13*

Charges (honorable ordinaries) (Figs. 10-19–10-20)

| Shield "per pale" | "Bend" | Shield "per fesse" | Shield "base" | "Fesse" | "Tau cross" |

10-19

Common figures (Figs. 10-21–10-24)

| Eagle | Lion | Lion passant guardant | Guild arms | Goblet counterchanged |

10-21   Animals   "Artificial" figures (here artisans' symbols)   10-22

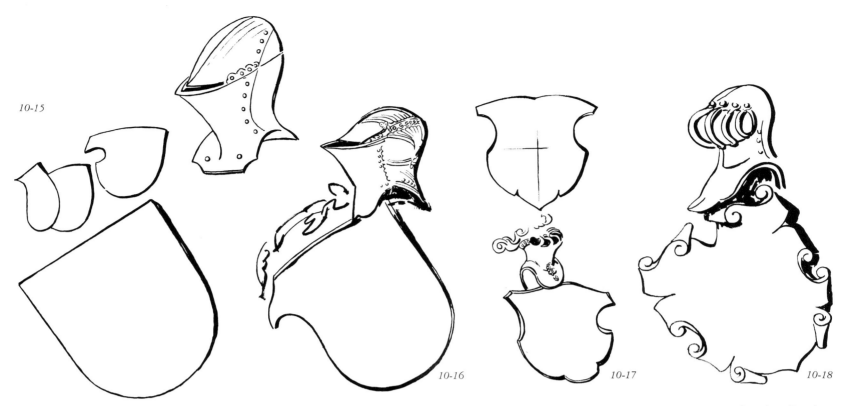

Fig. 10-15. "Target" (fifteenth century), simple form, the Late Gothic forms above: On the right with lance rest, on the left scalloped target.

Fig. 10-16. Late Gothic shield with close helmet, after a copper engraving by Dürer. Similar close helmet above (fifteenth century).

Fig. 10-17. Two sixteenth-century escutcheons: Incurved and scalloped targets. The bottom escutcheon from arms of a husband and wife.

Fig. 10-18. Renaissance shield (target with "cartouche" outline, middle of sixteenth century), helmet with bars, the form preferred during the sixteenth century.

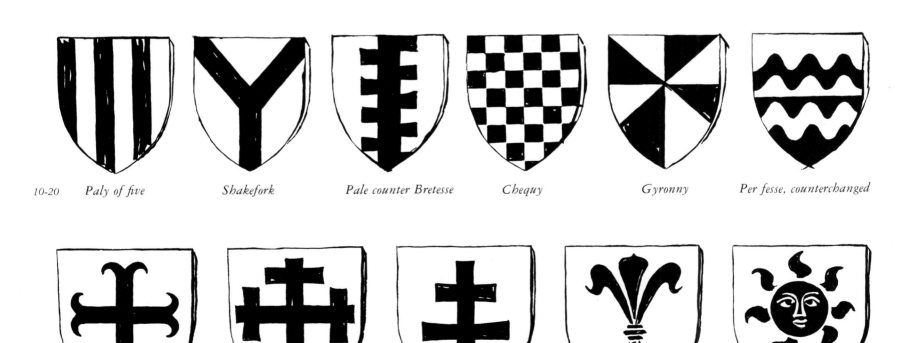

10-20 Paly of five   Shakefork   Pale counter Bretesse   Chequy   Gyronny   Per fesse, counterchanged

Cross moline   Cross crosslet   Patriarchal cross   Fleur de lys   Sun, as canting charge

10-23   Crosses   10-24   "Natural" figures

The rendering of heraldic tinctures in use since the 16th century (Figs. 10-25–10-27)

| Or | Argent | Gules (red) | Azure (blue) | Sable (black) | Vert (green) | Tenné (brown) | Purpure (purple) | Proper (natural color) |

10-25   Metals   10-26   Original heraldic tinctures   10-27   Later tinctures

Furs and damascenings (Figs. 10-28–10-29)

| Ermine | Ermines | Escaloped | Barry nebuly | Barry counternebuly | Vair | Fusil | Rose | Scroll |

10-28   Furs   10-29   Damascening

Development of styles of the mantle (Figs. 10-30–10-32)

10-31

10-32

Fig. 10-30. Crest and mantles, from Codex von den Ersten, about 1380.

Fig. 10-31. Simple mantling, Gothic, fifteenth century.
Fig. 10-32. The mantle, disintegrating into acanthus leaves, proliferates and partly obscures helmet and escutcheon of the Renaissance coat of arms; beginning of the seventeenth century.

Insignia of rank of the nobility (Fig. 10-33)

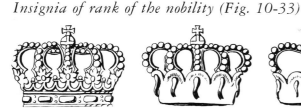

| Royal crown | Duke's coronet | Prince's coronet | Elector's coronet | Earl's coronet | Baron's coronet | Baronet's coronet |

Insignia of clerical offices (Fig. 10-34)

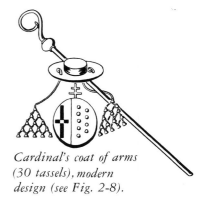

Archiepiscopal coat of arms (20 tassels) with miter, patriarchal cross and crozier.

Episcopal coat of arms (12 tassels) with miter, cross, and crozier.

Episcopal coat of arms, Renaissance (incomplete).

Cardinal's coat of arms (30 tassels), modern design (see Fig. 2-8).

Bibliography

This list of references is by no means exhaustive, and practical considerations alone have governed the selection of works; it is the creative rather than the scientifically interested reader for whom this condensed survey of the most important books on his field of activities has been compiled.

Gold and silver

Belli Barsali, Isa   *Mediaeval Goldsmith's Work*, Hamlyn, London (1969)

Boston, Mass.: Museum of Fine Arts   *Greek Gold Jewellery from the age of Alexander, etc.*, Philipp von Zabern, Mainz (1965)

Brunner, Herbert   *Old Table Silver*, Faber, London (1967)

Came, Richard   *Silver*, Weidenfeld and Nicolson, London (1961)

Dalton, O. M.   *Catalogue of the Finger Rings, early Christian, Byzantine, Teutonic, mediaeval and later, bequeathed by Sir A. W. Franks*, British Museum, London (1912)

Hughes, Graham   *Modern Silver throughout the World 1880–1967*, Studio Vista, London (1967)

Morassi, Antonio   *Art Treasures of the Medici*, Oldbourne Press, London (1964)

Oman, Charles   *English Domestic Silver*, Black, London (1968)

Story, Donald Emrys   *Greek and Roman Gold and Silver Plate*, Methuen, London (1966)

Iron and steel

Ayrton, Maxwell, and Silcock, Arnold   *Wrought Iron, and its decorative use*, Country Life, London (1929)

Gardner, J. S.   *Ironwork* (3 vols.), Victoria and Albert Museum, London (1922–30)

Gloag, J., and Bridgwater, D.   *A History of Cast Iron in Architecture*, Allen and Unwin, London (1948)

Kühn, Fritz   *Decorative work in wrought iron and other metals*, Harrap, London (1967)
   Wrought Iron, Harrap, London (1965)

Lister, Raymond   *Decorative Wrought Ironwork in Great Britain*, Bell, London (1957)
   Decorative Cast Ironwork in Great Britain, Bell, London (1960)

Schubert, H. R.   *History of the British Iron and Steel Industry from c. 450 BC to AD 1775*, Routledge and Kegan Paul, London (1957)

Umberto, Z., and Vergerio, G.   *Decorative Ironwork*, Hamlyn, London (1966)

Techniques

Cellini, Benvenuto   *The treatises of Benvenuto Cellini on goldsmithing and sculpture*, Edward Arnold, London (1898)

Coghlan, H. H.   *The Prehistoric Metallurgy of Copper and Bronze in the Old World*, University Press, Oxford (1951)

Forbes, R. J.   *Metallurgy in Antiquity*, Brill, Leiden (1950)

Littledale   *A New Process of hard soldering*, Lecture IV, The Worshipful Company of Goldsmiths, London (1935–6)

Lister, Raymond   *The Craftsman in Metal*, Bell, London (1966)

Maryon, Herbert   *Metalwork and enameling: a practical treatise on gold and silversmiths' work and their allied crafts*, Chapman and Hall, London (1959)

Theophilus Presbyter (Rugerus)   *The Various Arts (Schedula diversarum artium)*, Nelson, London (1961)

Enamel

Ball, F.   *Experimental Techniques in Enameling*, Van Nostrand Reinhold, London and New York (1973)

Belli Barsali, Isa   *European Enamels*, Hamlyn, London (1969)

Gardner, J. S.   *Catalogue of a collection of European Enamels from the earliest date to the end of the XVII century*, Burlington Fine Arts Club, London (1897)

New York: Cooper Union Museum for the Arts of Decoration   *Enamel: an historic survey to the present day*, New York (1954)

Seeler, Margaret Rosa   *The Art of Enameling*, Van Nostrand Reinhold, London and New York (1909)

Coining, steel- and punch engraving

Carson, R. A. G.   *Coins, Ancient, Medieval and Modern*, Hutchinson, London (1962)

Head, B. V.   *A Guide to the Principal Coins of the Greeks*, British Museum, London (1959)

North, J. J. *English Hammered Coinage* (2 vols.), Spink and Son, London (1960)

Seltman, C. J. *Masterpieces of Greek Coinage*, Bruno Cassirer, Oxford (1949)

Style, form and design

Dalton, O. M. *The Treasure of the Oxus. With other examples of early oriental metal work*, British Museum, London (1926)

Desroches-Noblecourt, C. *Tutankhamen*, The Connoisseur and Michael Joseph, London (1963)

Evans, Joan *A history of jewellery*, Faber, London (1970)
Pattern: a study of ornament in Western Europe 1180–1900, (2 vols.), Clarendon Press, Oxford (1931)

Ferebee, Ann *History of design from the Victorian era to the present*, Van Nostrand Reinhold, London and New York (1970)

Himsworth, J. B. *The story of cutlery from flint to stainless steel*, Benn, London (1953)

Jackson, C. J. *An illustrated history of English plate, ecclesiastical and secular*, Country Life and Batsford, London (1911)

Lindsay, J. S. *Iron and brass implements of the English house*, Medici Society, London and Boston (1964)

O'Dea, W. T. *The social history of lighting*, Routledge and Kegan Paul, London (1958)

Read, Sir Herbert *Art and Industry*, Faber, London (1956)

Scheidig, Walther *Crafts of the Weimar Bauhaus*, Studio Vista, London (1967)

Heraldry

Hope, W. H. St J. *A Grammar of Heraldry*, University Press, Cambridge (1953)

Louda, Jiři *European Civic Coats of Arms*, Hamlyn, London (1966)

von Volborth, C. A. *Heraldry of the World*, Blandford Press, London (1973)

Wagner, A. R. *Heralds and Heraldry in the Middle Ages*, Oxford University Press, London (1956)

Gemmology

Church, A. H. *Precious Stones. With a catalogue of the Townshend Collection*, Victoria and Albert Museum, London (1913)

Sinkankas, John *Gem Cutting: A Lapidary's Manual*, Van Nostrand Reinhold, London and New York (2nd edn. 1963)
Gemstones of North America, Van Nostrand Reinhold, London and New York (1959)
Van Nostrand's Standard Catalog of Gems, Van Nostrand Reinhold, London and New York (1968)

Sydal, William *A Handbook on Precious and Semi-precious stones*, Hicklenton and Sydal, London (1913)

Webster, Robert *Gems*, Butterworth, London (1962)

Index of Artists and Manufacturers

Index of Historical Examples

General Index

Objects

General Raw and Expendable Materials, Aids, and Technological Terms

Techniques and Working Methods

Source of Illustrations

The following companies, agencies, and individuals have provided photographs for reproduction in this book:

Adolphshütte Dillenburg – Arbuck, Inc. – Artaria – Balke – Bayerisches Nationalmuseum – BCoID – Braun-Feldweg – Bruckmann & Söhne – Burg Giebichenstein – Daimler-Benz AG – Dexel – Dittert – Foto Marburg – Franceschi – Fröhlich – Gnamm – Gnilka – Hajek-Halke – Hasler – Heddenhausen & Posse – Heise – Hesse – Hooker – Jensen – Koolmann – Kunstsammlungen Kassel – Landesbildstelle Baden-Württemberg – LGA-Baden-Württemberg – Lange – Lax – Lehr – O. J. Maier – Maltby Ltd. – Mataré – Maurer – Miller Co. – Moegle – Moritz – Müller-Grah – Solingen Museum – Nordiska Museet – Office of the U.S. Representative in Europe – Olivetti – Paret – Plate – Prütz – Raichle – Reidt – Rheinisches Museum – Schleebach – Schweizer – Stengele – Strelow – Treskow – Tümpel – Hüttenwerke, Wasseralfingen – Wiedamann – J. M. Wilm – WMF – Wolff – Zarges-Dürr.